JOSEPH AGRIS, D.D.S., M.D., F.A.C.S.
DIPLOMATE, AMERICAN BOARD OF PLASTIC SURGERY

COSMETIC SURGERY
PLASTIC AND RECONSTRUCTIVE SURGERY
HAND - TRAUMATIC - BURN

SCURLOCK TOWER
6560 FANNIN, SUITE 1730
HOUSTON, TEXAS 77030

17th FLOOR
(713) 797-1700

WHITE KNIGHT IN BLUE SHADES

The Authorized Biography of Marvin Zindler

By Joseph Agris, M.D.

with
Connie L. Schmidt & Ron Kaye

A-TO-Z PUBLISHING
In Cooperation With The Agris-Zindler Children's Foundation
Houston, Texas

White Knight in Blue Shades:
The Authorized Biography of Marvin Zindler
Copyright © 2002 by Joseph Agris, M.D.
A-to-Z Publishing
(In cooperation with The Agris-Zindler Children's Foundation)
Scurlock Tower
6560 Fannin, Suite 1730
Houston, Texas 77030

ISBN: 0-9712348-0-9 (cloth)
ISBN: 0-9712348-1-7 (paper)
Library of Congress Number available

Literary collaboration & graphic design services provided by

Schmidt, Kaye & Co.

Connie L. Schmidt & Ron Kaye
Houston, Texas

DEDICATION

To Marvin and the late Gertrude Kugler Zindler...
You have always made me feel like a member of the family.

To Lori Reingold and Bob Dows, my best friends...
Through the triumphs and tragedies of our work and travels, we have learned how good it is to have an angel on our shoulders.

To Laurel Ann, my daughter, and Dr. Jacob Agris, my son...
I love you very much and I am so proud of all your accomplishments.

To Mason, my first grandchild...
The future is wonderful and full of surprises. Go for it.

Life can be perplexing and uncertain at its best, but love always bears beliefs, hopes and endurance of all things — forever.

The memories of a well-spent life are eternal.

In Grateful Acknowledgment

John P. McGovern, M.D., is a quiet, unassuming,
but very remarkable man. This book pays tribute to Dr. McGovern and the
John P. McGovern Foundation. For many years, Dr. McGovern has
been quite knowledgeable of the Agris-Zindler Children's Foundation, and
supportive of its unique and productive work that must be undertaken to
provide for needy children requiring medical care.

I also personally know that he is well aware of the synergy created
by cooperative efforts between Marvin Zindler and the Children's Foundation. The John P. McGovern Foundation has generously sponsored the
publishing and printing of the initial 10,000 copies of this book.
All of the proceeds from the sale of each book will be returned to the
Agris-Zindler Children's Foundation to help provide
an ongoing source of funds for medical care to children
who, without this sponsorship, would be lost to society.

Joseph Agris, D.D.S., M.D., F.A.C.S.

C·O·N·T·E·N·T·S

 **I·N·T·R·O·D·U·C·T·I·O·N**

A photograph in an old Zindler family album shows young Marvin Harold Zindler, resplendent in a drum major outfit, baton in hand. The photographer has captured the entire marching band of Houston's Lamar High School just as they have stepped forward, all at the same time, on the right foot. Well, make that *almost* all; Marvin, snappily and very conspicuously leading the column, has stepped out with his left foot. Scrawled at the bottom of the photo, in Marvin's handwriting, is this caption, "Look, everybody is out of step but me!"

The world has always been "out of step" with Marvin Zindler, who marches, and always has marched, to the beat of his own drum.

Many photos have been taken of Marvin since that long-ago football game at Lamar High. Even if there were no photographic record, however, his white-hairpieced, blue-spectacled image has been etched indelibly into the public mind. But there are many sides to Marvin Zindler, not all of them familiar to the public that adores (or reviles) him.

There is the Marvin who broke the mold into which he was born: a well-to-do family entrenched in both business and politics. Marvin was a renegade from childhood, a young man who, according to his father's constant complaints, was a playboy and ne'er-do-well. There is the Marvin who was a prizefighter for awhile, winning almost all of his 100 bouts — with his true prize being public recognition and self-identity more than money.

There's the Marvin who was in law enforcement, as an amateur cop who loved his job, and as a deputy sheriff for more than 10 years, existing in a love-hate relationship with the department because of his unorthodox dress and independent (to put it mildly) attitude.

There is Marvin the failed haberdasher, who, to his father's everlasting dismay, was a dud at the family business. It wasn't for lack of trying, and Marvin tried many things, including some experiments with inventive (some would say deceptive) advertising. Years later, of course, he would emerge as a soldier in the war against that very type of advertising.

There is Marvin the radio star, who worked diligently and sharpened his show business instincts long before television appeared on the media landscape. There's Marvin, freelance photographer for a Houston newspaper, a stint which allowed him to combine his show business instincts, his police experience, and his penchant for action and sensationalism.

And there is, of course, Marvin Zindler the TV star, who, other than the late Ed Sullivan, has been the only performer ever to secure a lifetime contract with ABC-TV. More than a showman, he has become one of Texas' and the nation's most respected journalists. In fact, he won an Emmy in 1995 for Best Short News Series for his series entitled, "To Russia With Love" — a social, economic, and medical documentary on the fall of the Iron Curtain. Despite this, his television career got off to a rocky start, as he was fired from his first TV job for being "too ugly."

There is Marvin Zindler, master of self-reinvention, who not only changed careers several times, but changed his face with more than 30 cosmetic procedures. No longer the owner of "a great face for radio," as the saying goes, he is now quite handsome and distinguished looking. And there is Marvin Zindler, dapper dresser, whose clothing choices on his more ostentatious days might have even embarrassed Phyllis Diller.

There is Marvin Zindler the activist: the "White Knight," "the people's advocate," the inveterate altruist, whose favorite saying is, "It's hell to be poor!" There is Marvin the famous (or infamous, depending upon your point of view) muckraker, who unleashes his wrath on everything from "slime in the ice machine" to slime in the political machine. And there is Marvin the tireless world traveler, who has led medical and goodwill missions to all corners of the globe.

When it comes right down to it, there is no single way to describe Marvin Zindler. Many things are true about him: that he is fiercely aggressive when fighting for a cause, yet almost childishly shy in person…that he is forgiving, and yet almost frighteningly vengeful when he feels he or someone else has been wronged…that he is flamboyant and egotistical, and yet profoundly good-hearted. In the end, the only completely accurate description is "unique." There has never been anyone like Marvin Zindler, and there never will be again. He is truly a Texas legend, though I am not sure that even the word "legend" truly does him justice.

As Marvin's cosmetic surgeon for many years, I have sculpted his face on many occasions, and as his long-time friend, I am now attempting to paint his portrait, in words and photographs.

Like Marvin himself, this book is a little unconventional, as biographies go. Rather than being a strictly chronological presentation of the events of his life, the book is arranged more or less thematically. For example, Marvin's media career — from his early days in radio to his current gig as one of Houston television's most colorful stars — is covered in a separate section from his forays into law enforcement and politics. His brief stint in the military, and his many attempts at making it in the retailing business, are in another section. Tales of his world travels appear in another, and family matters — his late wife, Gertrude Kugler Zindler, and the Zindler brood — are covered in another section. His famous cosmetic surgeries, as well as other more serious medical issues, are in yet another section. Naturally, the Chicken Ranch saga has its own section, as does one of Marvin's most important and productive investigative pieces, the great Hermann Hospital Estate scandal of '85. During much of his early adulthood and into midlife, Marvin was pursuing multiple career avenues simultaneously, living several lives at once, as it were: he was into radio, politics, law enforcement, newspaper reporting and photography, even a little early TV news. For many years he was still putting in time at his father's shop while engaged in one or more of the above activities, and, of course, he was also being a husband to Gertrude and father to a growing family. I felt I could more easily do justice to this multi-faceted man by devoting a separate portion of the book to each facet. Nevertheless, within each section, and within the individual chapters in the section, I have made every attempt to present events in chronological order to keep the reader oriented in time.

Though I've attempted to mold the book to fit his life, I don't know if the essence of someone like Marvin Zindler can truly be captured between the covers of a book — but it is my hope that this effort will help more people better know the White Knight who lives behind the trademark blue-tinted glasses and the media hype. Of course, the thousands of people who have been the beneficiaries of his good works already have a pretty good idea. While much of the world may be out of step with Marvin, Marvin himself is very much in step with the needs of those who are least able to help themselves. As a result, he has many fans. Perhaps it is my wish that this book will help win him more, or, at the very least, that it will help a great many more people learn to truly appreciate the heart behind Houston television's most famous call to arms:

"Maaaaaaaaaaaarvin Zindler, Eyewitness News!"

Joseph "Dr. Joe" Agris, M.D.
Houston, Texas
October 2001

P•A•R•T

1

The Fresh Prince
Of Bellaire

Marvin's
Early Years

C·H·A·P·T·E·R 1

KING OF THE HILL:
ABE ZINDLER AND HIS REALM

To understand Marvin Zindler, it is necessary to know something about the man who was most influential in building his character: his father, Abe Zindler, Sr. Like Marvin, Abe was strong-willed — sometimes maddeningly so — fiercely driven, at times irascible, and yet, at his core, good-hearted and honorable. Abe Zindler came to the United States as a child from Austria. Like so many countless others in search of a better life, the Zindler family, headed by Ben Zindler, immigrated to New York City in 1888. In 1892 the family traveled by boat to Galveston, Texas, but they didn't stay there long; they moved to Houston that same year.

Houston in the early 1890s was still a frontier town, but, with a population of nearly 28,000 and growing, was rapidly developing into a modern city: a center of commerce, culture, and education. Houston's industry boasted more than 150 factories, employing over 5,000 workers. The Sweeney and Coombs Opera House, which was actually a theater, was hosting performances by the likes of Maude Adams and Sarah Bernhardt. William Marsh Rice had just donated $200,000 in a trust fund for the development of an educational institute in Houston "for the advancement of literature, science, and art" — an institute which eventually became Rice University. Houstonians enjoyed most of the accoutrements of modernity, including paved streets, electric lights, and electric streetcars — in fact, Houston was the first city in Texas to have the latter. With the turmoil of the Civil War and reconstruction firmly behind them, Houstonians, along with the rest of the nation, looked to the future with optimism.

Into this bustling city came Ben Zindler, a tailor with a strong work ethic. He set up shop on Harrisburg in east Houston, later moving to the lower end of downtown Houston, in the area now known as Market Square.

In those days, a son was expected to learn his father's trade, and as soon as young Abe was old enough to thread a needle, he went to work in his father's small shop. He never really learned to sew, but there were plenty of other things for him to do around the shop. Abe quit school in the sixth grade in order to work full time in the family business.

Times were hard for the Zindler family. There was little play or relaxation; everything centered around the tailor shop. As a result, Abe grew to be a no-nonsense young man, maturing way before his time. His self assurance and "rugged individualism" were traits that suited him well in the robust environment of late nineteenth-century Houston.

Indeed, Abe had none of the meekness one would traditionally attribute to the tailoring trade. He worked hard, displaying an honesty and energy that were to earn him the trust and acceptance of Houston's business community. As a young man, he formulated a business philosophy and developed a financial acumen that would greatly benefit him all his life.

Then when Abe was 23 years old, his father died, leaving him the tailoring business, and with it, the responsibilities of providing for the Zindler family. Fortunately, his training had been excellent, and, being old and wise beyond his 23 years, he was ready and able to handle the business.

If Ben Zindler's work ethic had been strong, Abe's was downright fierce. A perfectionist, he agonized over the tiniest mistakes. He was known to rail furiously at others and at himself for the simplest of blunders. The tailoring business grew as Houston expanded, but Abe Zindler wanted much more. Aware that "ready-made" clothing was becoming the trend, he made the decision to switch to retailing. And so, in the heart of the muddy Bayou City, on wagon-wheel-rutted Congress Avenue, Abe Zindler opened his first retail store. Zindler's would become an institution in Houston, one of the few family-owned retail chains to last through the remainder of the 20th century.

In those early years, Abe had plenty of help with the business from his brothers, Mitchell, Leo, and Jerome, and his sisters, Minnie and Rosetta. Abe helped put all three of his brothers through college. Jerome graduated from Rice University with honors, earning a law degree; he came into the business as a buyer and seller, and never did use that law degree. Mitchell handled the merchandising for the store. Leo eventually left the family business, when his wife gave him an ultimatum: choose her or the store. He chose love. It should be noted that Leo did not turn his back on retailing; he and his wife moved to Virginia, where he went into business with her father, who also had a clothing store.

In order to stock the store, Abe had to travel to New York City's garment district several times a year. Travel was an ordeal, as there were no air flights at that time, and not even any through train services. So Abe first traveled overland to New Orleans, and from there would book passage on a steamer bound for New York City.

During this time, he trusted the running of the store to his employees. One would think they'd be happy that their autocratic boss was away, but quite the contrary was true. They were terrified of managing the store in his absence, knowing that the slightest mistake would result in a verbal blistering upon his return.

The vendors in New York got a taste of Abe's forceful personality as well. Abe would thumb through goods carefully, weighing whether the latest styles would be accepted or ridiculed in the Bayou City. Houstonians were a whole different breed from New Yorkers, and Abe had an intuitive sense of what his Houston customers wanted and needed. With a sardonic smile reflecting both the seriousness of the transaction and his own amusement, he would place his orders with his New York manufacturers, accompanying the transaction with threats of returned goods and lost business. But this wasn't just a game to him; he truly had his customers' best interest in mind. His favorite saying was, "If a suit don't last a man ten years, it ain't worth five damn cents."

Abe's energy seemed endless. The doors of his haberdashery opened sharply each morning at 7:00, and there was no set closing time. The shop stayed open as long as there was a customer on Congress Avenue; many times Abe was seen in the store until midnight. Sunday was no exception.

Abe had a good reason for working on Sundays, when the rest of the retail world was shut down. In those days, barges were pulled along Brays Bayou to the point where the bayou now crosses under Main Street. Small packet ships could also reach this point. If vessels came in to port on Sunday, there would be sailors, and some of them would need supplies or clothing. Abe would rush downtown and open his haberdashery establishment, leaving it open as long as the ships stayed in port. He had a sound reason for working late nights as well. It only made sense for him to keep the store open as long as the saloons stayed open. He knew that once the ranchers and homesteaders had eaten and drunk their fill, they would be ready to head home. That was when some of the stragglers from the saloons would drop by to pick up dry goods before they returned to their ranches.

Abe's unique blend of affability, availability and affordability proved to be a true formula for success. It is a way of doing business that has all but disappeared in Houston and other large cities, despite the proliferation of 24-hour-a-day, seven-day-a-week retail establishments. Abe brought a personal touch that perhaps isn't even possible in today's high-tech, global business climate. In any case, Abe Zindler did so well in his business that within a few short years he was able to help numerous other young and determined peers start their businesses in Houston.

Sometimes his employees went off on their own too, and he wasn't always so happy about that. Two brothers by the name of Sakowitz worked in the shirt department in Abe's store, until they decided to open their own shop. The first store in what would become the big Sakowitz chain opened in a building on Preston and Main in downtown Houston. Abe got mad and bought the building, thereby becoming his former employees' landlord. The Sakowitzes then moved into the Gulf Building at Capital and Rusk, and went into competition with Zindler's. For nearly four generations, the Sakowitz chain enjoyed success as a clothier to well-heeled customers, but hard times fell in 1985, and the company declared Chapter 11 bankruptcy. The last store was closed in the summer of 1991.

Abe always appeared to be in control of himself, but he seemed to have a profound need to control other people as well. If he couldn't control a prospective project, he would not bother with it.

On the other hand, he was no whiner, and never wasted time or energy complaining if something didn't go his way.

Not even Abe Zindler could control the path of Cupid's arrows. Abe's life was to change forever when, on one of his many trips to New York City, he met his wife-to-be, Udith Meyer. The two met aboard a steamer sailing from New Orleans to New York City.

Udith, the daughter of a Civil War veteran, had been raised on plantations in Alexandria and New Iberia, Louisiana. She was very much a lady. Udith had been educated in a convent, graduating at the age of 16. In fact, this journey to New York was her graduation trip.

Abe was 11 years older than Udith, but it was love at first sight. Knowing he had to make sure he would see her again, Abe found an excuse to borrow some money from Udith, so of course he had to get her address in order to send her a check when he returned home. When he mailed back the borrowed funds, that was the beginning of a series of love letters between the two. They became engaged, and Abe was invited to Alexandria, Louisiana to meet Udith's family.

They had planned a big wedding, but Udith's father, Bernard Meyer, died, so they scaled their plans down and held a small family wedding. After the wedding, Abe brought Udith to Houston.

Abe and Udith Zindler began their life together in a modest home at 804 Westheimer. At first Abe's two unmarried sisters, Minnie and Rosetta, lived with them, but Udith wanted them out of her house. It was high time they were married, but of course they must marry well. With a little help from the *shadkhin* (the Yiddish term for a professional matchmaker), Udith's wishes came true. Minnie wed Ben Finger of the Finger Department Stores, and Rosetta married Sam Slater, owner of the Bostonian Shoe Store in the Rice Hotel.

Not only was the Zindler clothing empire growing, but so was Abe Zindler's family. The first of Marvin's brothers, Abe, Jr., was born in 1916, and two years later Sterling Zindler arrived. Marvin yelled his way into the world on August 10, 1921. A daughter died in infancy, but was shortly followed by brothers Warren in 1923 and Kenneth in 1927. The house on Westheimer was much too small for this fast-growing brood.

Fortunately, the Zindlers were prospering, due to Abe's obsessive dedication to business and some shrewd real estate investments in the rapidly growing city. So the family moved on up, or, rather, out — to "the country," a suburb known as Bellaire. Their new home, a two-story colonial at the corner of Post Oak and Bellaire Boulevard, was located on more than three acres, with a meandering drive through the tree-covered property. A barn was built out back, and a self-powered lawn care system was installed. The latter consisted of several sheep that were allowed to wander the grounds and keep the grass cropped short. And because Abe Sr. enjoyed fresh dairy products — milk, butter, and cottage cheese — which he had sorely missed in his early lean years, he took the logical step of purchasing a cow. He didn't stop there. Since his five boys were such a handful, Abe also acquired some horses to divert their energies.

Abe Zindler seemed satisfied with himself and his life. He had a good wife, and five healthy sons whom he believed would work in the store and eventually take over the family business. He had all that was worth having: prestige, power, money[1], and creature comforts beyond his dreams.

And he was more than willing to help others achieve the same success he enjoyed. It was Abe Zindler who loaned the Weingarten family $500 to get started in the grocery business, and for decades the Weingarten chain was a major player in the Houston grocery market.

With his Bellaire home and his business in order, the senior Zindler looked to politics. He entered the Bellaire mayoral race[2] in the mid-1930s, and went on to win the election. He ended up being elected for three terms, and drafted for a fourth.

Personal and family interactions aside, Abe Zindler Sr. was a generous and civic-minded man. He even refused to accept the $100-a-month salary as mayor. Instead, he requested that it be applied toward the construction of a Scout meeting house and later a larger, all-brick Bellaire community building. This community center was built off the esplanade at the corner of South Rice and Bellaire Boulevard.

Abe had a deep sense of fairness and a tendency to embrace progressive causes, and this extended to all aspects of his public life. For example, he stood firm against the activities of the local Ku Klux Klan. He also supported Franklin Delano Roosevelt. If this made him unpopular in some circles, so be it. Abe had his convictions, and he acted on them — and in that respect, too, his middle son would follow in his footsteps.

Many people felt the weight of the Great Depression, but Abe was secure, and did his level best to help his less fortunate fellows. As Mayor of Bellaire during the Depression, he pursued the Federal Government to engage in an extensive WPA public-works project in Bellaire. He was aided by long-time friend, Jesse Jones (the Jesse Jones Building in the Texas Medical Center is named in his honor), who was FDR's Chief of the Reconstruction Finance Corporation.

All in all, the senior Zindler was as successful in politics as he was in business. Certainly he was instrumental in the development of the city of Bellaire, providing very well for his constituents. Abe's word was his bond. Unlike all too many politicians then and now, he was known as a man of great integrity. It is said that as mayor of Bellaire, he

---

[1] In the 1920s, Abe took out one of the first million-dollar life insurance policies; this was so extraordinary it made the newspapers.

[2] Although it is surrounded by the city of Houston, Bellaire, Texas is an incorporated city and has its own mayor.

turned down a "sweetheart deal" to buy the land where the Bellaire City Hall now stands. Presumably, he was to purchase the land and then sell it back to the city at a profit. He would not even consider participating in such a deal. Abe Zindler Sr.'s motto was, "Make a profit on everything you sell, but do it honestly. If you don't, you are cheating your customer and you are cheating yourself."

Later on, Marvin refined this by saying, "Don't mark some items below cost as a draw because you will be cheating yourself, and you will have to mark something else up to make the difference. If you put a price on it that is more than it is worth, you will be cheating the customer."

Abe wanted his sons to live by his philosophy, and repeatedly drilled his adages about life and retailing into them. A man's character was very important to the senior Zindler, not only in politics but in business as well. Sometimes, however, he took things a little too far, erring on the side of self-righteousness and alienating those around him. In fact, he once ruined a lucrative business transaction with a stinging verbal assault on the owner's character. As the story goes, there was a downtown retailer who wanted to bail out of his failing business so badly that he practically offered to give it away to Abe Zindler. Abe knew a good business deal when he saw it.

Those present at the time remembered Abe storming into the retailer's store and saying, "I want you to know that I think you are a God-damned, no-good, lousy gambler who shouldn't be allowed to have a business on this street. I'll take it." The owner took offense and refused to sell the business to Abe.

Indeed, some of the most deeply rooted parts of Marvin Zindler's character seem to have come from his father. Growing up, Marvin was at times shy, and yet could be boisterous and overwhelmingly aggressive. Even now these contradictory traits are apparent. Like his father before him, Marvin screams and curses with incredible velocity when crossed. Within seconds after his outburst, however, what seems to be a murderous mood miraculously dissolves without the slightest trace.

Marvin explains, "I don't hold anything that bothers me inside. I may give some ulcers, but I'm not gonna get them."

The side of Abe Zindler Sr. that his business associates never did see was the tender and affectionate way that he interacted with his children when they were toddlers. This, however, was not to last, for the toddlers became preteens, and the preteens became teenagers — and Abe Zindler could not understand these young men.

As the boys grew older, the relationship between father and sons dramatically changed. Abe Sr. began to take on an increasing irascible and rigidly domineering attitude. Kenneth, the youngest of Abe's sons, vividly remembers his father as a terror. Kenneth once explained, "He was a man of his era, a dynamic and very domineering man. His primary emotion was anger."

Beyond business and politics, the senior Zindler had no other outside interests. With no hobbies or diversions, he became increasingly gruff. When not at the store, he stalked about the house, screaming at real and imagined slights and transgressions, and, of course, at the boys. And the boys, being just boys, after all, only made it worse. During their teen years, the Zindler sons demonstrated a flightiness and rebellious spirit alien to Abe's own upbringing. As a result, the Zindler homestead seemed to be in a constant turmoil of attack and counterattack between father and sons.

"In some ways," Kenneth once reflected, "Father was like the all-powerful head of the family in the play *Long Hot Summer*. Strangers could do no wrong; but his family could do no right."

Recalls Marvin, "Father used to get so mad at us, screaming and yelling and carrying on at the slightest things, that he turned red in the face. Mama would be afraid he was going to have a stroke and die. He would tell us that we were nothing but a bunch of spoiled bastards with no appreciation for anything. He would scream that our outside interests and activities were going to drive him into the poorhouse."

Perhaps the anger masked many deeper emotions. If so, one of them certainly was fear. Abe Zindler Sr. was haunted by the apprehension that his sons would turn out to be worthless playboys. And Marvin Zindler topped Abe's personal list of Least Likely to Succeed. Marvin was the most stubborn and outspoken of his offspring, and, as such, was no stranger to Abe's blistering verbal attacks.

Marvin says, "I was nineteen years old before I knew my name *wasn't* Marvin Got-Damned-Son-of-a-Bitch-Playboy. Father even pitted us against each other. If he saw two of us standing together and laughing, he would begin yelling at us, 'What are you doing? Plotting against me?'"

As soon as they were old enough, the sons were dragooned into the haberdashery stores from time to time. The Zindler clothing empire had expanded over the years, and eventually there were four stores. Abe Jr. once said, "I used to think all Dad wanted was a bunch of cheap salesmen." All of the Zindler sons worked at one time or another at the stores — but after recurrent violent skirmishes with their father, they all left.

Indeed, Abe's dreams for the Zindler empire would never be fully realized. Although his brothers and sisters had given him plenty of help over the years, his sons were, for the most part, indifferent to the business. All of the Zindler boys joined the armed forces during World War II — no doubt inspired as much by a fervent desire to escape domestic tyrannies as by a call to fight foreign tyrants. Warren Zindler, unfortunately, was killed during the Battle of the Bulge in Europe. That left four sons, but most of them were reluctant retailers at best. Abe Jr. was enthralled with ranching and the outdoor life; he grudgingly worked at the haberdashery for a while before going into the bail bond business. He did well as a bail bondsman, which allowed him time to pursue his ranching interest. Sterling Zindler did his filial duty and took the reins of the business as his father aged, but there were strong indications that he was not happy either. (He retired and later died after a long illness.) Then, of course, there was Marvin, "the playboy," who never did find the retailing business exciting enough for his temperament. Only Kenneth, the youngest, had any interest in retailing, and he eventually took over the family business.

Abe Zindler Sr. had all that was worth having, but his world was not complete, and it was not to be. For his goal above all was to have his sons continue the dynasty and the business. Instead, the palace of the king churned with revolt. The "princes" were very much determined to go their own way in life. Apart from Kenneth, the senior Zindler's goals for his sons proved maddeningly elusive.

Marvin's mother, Udith, died in 1956. She was the extreme opposite of her insufferable husband, and is remembered by her surviving sons as a "saint." Udith always had a smile on her face, and was always doing something helpful for somebody. Abe Jr. recalled, "During the Depression, Mother would take cheese, milk and butter over to people who didn't have as much as we had. If anybody ever needed anything, she was always there." Marvin's mother developed breast cancer, and underwent a relatively new operation called a radical mastectomy. Following her mastectomy, she became a hospital volunteer, comforting other women who were to undergo this traumatic procedure.

After Udith passed away, the boys were on their own to fend for themselves against their father — and vice versa. As he aged, Abe Sr.'s conviction that his sons had let him down only grew stronger. He became obsessed by the idea that if his boys were too frivolous to handle the responsibility of the store, they didn't deserve the properties and fortune he had assembled. Abe had always scorned waste, and was rock-hard in his belief that a life without extreme self-discipline was the road to ultimate ruination. Inherited wealth, he figured, was worse than a birth defect.

Marvin recalls, "My father would rant and rave that he was going to sell everything that he had and put the money into two suitcases. Then he was going to walk out to sea with one in each hand and let them be engulfed in the waters. And he damned will meant it!"

Well into his seventies, Abe Sr. still asserted his hair-trigger temper. His frequent avalanches into screaming fits continued, despite reminders of the warnings, uttered over the years by his now-deceased wife, that he would someday work himself into a "killing apoplectic fit."

Much of his ire seemed to be directed towards Marvin. Even though Marvin was married and had his own family at this time, his father still considered him frivolous and unsettled.

It became clear to Abe that despite his manipulations over the years, he would never see the name of the store changed to reflect his labor of love and the goals he set for so many years. It would never truly be, "Zindler & Sons" — and he well knew it.

In 1961, after years of threatening, the volcanic tensions between father and sons finally belched forth in one last colossal eruption. The senior Zindler, now 76 years old, prepared to cash in his properties. This time he really did mean it, so he called on his personal friend and lawyer of many decades to begin the negotiation and sale of his properties. Abe was willing to give them away at one-tenth their value rather than have his boys receive the fruits of his labor.

Marvin recalls, "I said, 'Daddy, you can't give the property away. It doesn't belong to you.'" He adds, "My brothers didn't remember what had occurred some 30 years before. The lawyers didn't remember it either. Even my father didn't remember it. But I did."

When Marvin explained as much to his father, the senior Zindler replied, "I don't give a got-damn what you remember. I am selling it."

Marvin retorted, "You are not going to sell it. Even if I have to file a lawsuit stopping the sale."

Marvin's memory served him well. During the Depression of the 1930s, Abe Sr. became concerned that his merchant empire might crumble. In those risky times, and being the good businessman that he was, he took actions to protect himself against a total financial disaster. He placed much of his accumulated real estate holdings in his wife's name. In that way, even if the stores went into bankruptcy, the real estate property could not be sold out from under him, since it belonged to his wife. Not only did this maneuver keep the property in the family, but it could also provide the means to start again should it be needed.

Abe's business acumen got him through the Depression, and over the fruitful years that followed he forgot about the transfer of the property to his wife. So did everyone else, including his lawyer — everyone but Marvin, that is. And now Abe was faced with the stark legal reality: the assets were not his to sell or give away. The point was driven home when Marvin made good on his threat and filed suit to prevent the sale.

Marvin recalls, "If I hadn't filed that lawsuit to keep Daddy from selling Mother's property, the Tax Department would have taken it and sold it for taxes. That angel was on my shoulder again." One thing you have to know about Marvin is that he sincerely believes he has a guardian angel, who not only has guided him in decision-making throughout his life, but has also kept him out of a mess of trouble.

Angel or not, Marvin won that battle, but lost — only to win bigger later. Abe Zindler Sr. lost — but won a protective control over his son's life in the end. Finally, says Marvin, "We made our peace." Apparently it was not a complete peace. The old man was urged to move in with Marvin, but refused.

In January of 1963, Abe Sr. entered the hospital. His nurse recalls that she had just sat him up in bed, made him comfortable and served him his dinner. He took several bites of the hospital food and launched one of his customary tirades over the tasteless food that he was being served. The nurse recalls that she was lowering the blind over the window when Abe began his rage. And then suddenly, the room fell silent. When she turned back to her patient, he was dead on the pillow.

The family was right: Abe Zindler Sr.'s temper finally killed him.

At the reading of the will, their father finally had the last word. The estate, amounting to approximately $4,500,000, was a small fortune in 1963. It was divided evenly amongst his sons, but in a cautious way. Kenneth, because of his interest in the store and aptitude for retailing, got his share directly. Sterling was bedridden by that time with the chronic, recurrent illness that would shortly take his life. Sterling's share of Abe's fortune was bequeathed to his wife and children.

Abe Jr., who had been married and divorced, would get nothing directly. His share was placed in trust for his children. Abe Jr. could receive the interest, but not touch the principal.

Then there was Marvin. Like Abe, he would get no part of the principal, and was allowed to draw only the interest. Looking back, Marvin says, "It was the greatest thing in the world to happen to me, really. The money is protected in an ironclad foundation. Nobody could touch it. Otherwise, if I had been sued and lost, the money would have been gone. They could have taken everything. But not the way it was set up."

Marvin continues, "The money has been invested for many, many years. My children will eventually get the principal, but in the meantime, I can take the interest and reinvest the profits. So my father still exerted control from the grave, but the way he set it up is a blessing.

"I couldn't possibly do what I am doing today without that [safety net]," he concludes. "I don't have to be afraid of anybody — advertisers, the TV station, anybody. Nobody can take the principal away from me."

Marvin was to realize no income from the store operations. But he did receive one other legacy from his father. The will directed Marvin to a safe deposit box containing nothing more than a small piece of paper with his father's handwriting. It was dated about one year before Abe Sr. died, and was written during the time of the legal grappling between father and son over the sale of Udith Zindler's property.

Marvin took the letter from the safe deposit box and slowly began to read.

Dear Marvin,
You have ruined your life up to the present date. You had a grand opportunity to make good, but you ruined it by getting money for doing nothing. Since the money you drew did not cost you anything it left you like water running out of a sieve.

How anyone with a fine wife like you have, that does not waste a penny, can waste as many thousands — yes, many thousands — of dollars as you have, has only one answer... All you wanted was money, money, more money and no work. Yes, do nothing day after day. Now you will have to learn, for the first time, how to work. I hope that it is not too late for you to learn how to work, and there is a good chance for you to make good! I hope that you will make good and surprise

everybody who thinks of you as a silly playboy with no sense in your head.
Your dear father,
Abe Zindler

This short but pointed note reflects a bittersweet resignation. In Abe's characteristic gruff manner, his letter proclaims the deep affection, love and concern that he was unable to openly express. And it contains the last piece of advice he ever gave his "playboy" son: "Make good and surprise everybody."

Marvin's life was to change after Abe's death. He can't really name the catalyst for this change; perhaps it was that oft-cited "angel on his shoulder," or maybe it was the power of the note Abe had left behind, with its final admonition to "make good," or perhaps it was Marvin's own realization that he had reached the middle of his life. Very possibly, it was a combination of these factors. By this time, Marvin was working for the Harris County Sheriff's Department and was beginning to believe that law enforcement was his life's work. After his father's death, he began working 18 to 20 hours a day, seven days a week — an exhausting pace for anyone, but Marvin was determined to do his best, and if that meant working around the clock, that was what he would do.

"That letter from Daddy," Marvin admits, in one of his rare understatements, "changed me a lot."

C·H·A·P·T·E·R 2

BECOMING MARVIN

That Abe Zindler Sr. had a powerful influence on Marvin is without question. But despite the attempts of his father to mold him in his image, Marvin has always been... Marvin.

Indeed, Marvin Harold Zindler has always showed an independence of spirit, a dedication to nonconformity, and a flare for theatrics. Today these are reflected in his silver hairpiece, blue-tinted glasses and impeccably styled, made-to-order shirts and suits. But even as a young boy, Marvin stood out. He was an incongruous mixture of Little Lord Fauntleroy and a Katzenjammer Kid. His attitude, mannerisms and mode of dress were a mystery to his peers and were disturbing, to say the least, to his family.

Marvin had every opportunity to have a typical rough-and-tumble boyhood, growing up as he did on three sprawling acres in Bellaire, with a stable of animals to boot. There was always plenty to do, and certainly there was ample room for play. As a matter of fact, the Zindler compound was a magnet for the neighborhood youngsters, who came to play football and other games. Throughout the spring and summer, the front lawn of the stately manor was host to a mob of shirtless, barefoot boys.

Football was not the type of activity Marvin cared for, however. He preferred to be a spectator or, more importantly, a performer. He would station himself on his front porch, watching the others play, and would often bring out his flute or piccolo. There he'd sit, playing one tune after another while the boisterous games went on. At other times, he would walk right into the middle of the ruckus and start twirling his baton.

Even at this young age, Marvin always dressed as if he were going to a party. Not surprisingly, the other kids periodically made fun of him. Marvin was taunted by his friends, who couldn't identify with his penchant for high-styled clothes and his dislike of dirt and pungent smells. There was nothing "sissy" about Marvin, but there was no doubt he was different, and, as such, he was a magnet for childish taunts. For the most part, however, Marvin just ignored the teasing. It was clearly his choice to be different, other people's opinions be damned. Eventually, most of the kids accepted Marvin on his own terms.

Despite the occasional jeers of his contemporaries, Marvin had plenty of brass, and liked showing off. One of his favorite stunts was sliding down the banister of the mansion's two-story staircase. The other kids, in a mischievous game of follow-the-leader, would mount the banister at the second level and take a daring ride to the foyer, at which time Marvin would do a final leap-and-roll on the floor of the main hall. The others immediately followed suit. If Marvin could do it, they could too. This stunt was repeated again and again, until finally it caught up with them. One day the jolting force of their landing brought down the massive crystal chandelier in the entrance hallway. Luckily, no one was hurt... at least not by the chandelier. Though the lord and lady of the manor did not believe in corporal punishment, Marvin's nanny, Eva Mae, was not inhibited by such high-minded beliefs. Eva took a belt to Marvin.

Once, when his older brother Abe acquired a "wild, five-dollar horse," Marvin loudly declared that he was going to break that horse. As the other youngsters stood back in awe, Marvin, with some difficulty, finally applied the bridle and reins. As he climbed aboard the skittish animal, the others shouted, "Ride 'em, cowboy!" He did break the horse, but the horse broke Marvin's leg in the process. No one could say Marvin didn't have guts.

In Houston's hot, humid summers, temperatures were in the 90s throughout June, July and August. Marvin would often join his peers at a nearby swimming hole, where he was quick to doff his fancy duds and frolic and splash with the others in the cool water.

"When he'd take off his clothes," said an old friend, Harry Dorfin, "he was the gawdawfullest thing you ever saw: a pale, spindly, though muscular young lad with the tiniest feet."

Those feet of his were the focus of more teasing from his friends. When Marvin remained aloof from the gang, they would taunt him all the more with such comments as "canary feet" and "Mr. Revolving Ankles." Marvin still wears a small super-narrow size 9 AAA shoe, though presumably the taunting about his feet has ceased.

Notwithstanding his impeccable manner of dressing, Marvin liked to ride his horse throughout Bellaire. And he continued to encounter his share of boyish mishaps. When he was eleven, his close friend Bill Tripp accidentally fired a blank pistol in his face. Marvin was blinded for almost a year. He lied to his parents, blaming the incident on a backfiring rifle — and thus scoring a real social coup with the gang. In spite of his odd ways and his occasional aloofness, when it came right down to it, Marvin would stick up for his friends.

There were times Marvin needed someone to stick up for him. For the most part he could take care of himself, but sometimes it was helpful to have reinforcements. Although anti-Semitism was not as big a problem in Houston as in other places, there was always an undercurrent. Little incidents occurred now and then to remind Marvin of one more way in which he was different from most of his fellows. During a ball game, for example, one of the other guys might shout, "Hey, Jew Boy, bring me the ball!" Occasionally the harassment was a little more serious.

So Marvin got himself a bodyguard. He paid Phil Bongio, owner of the 59 Diner, to look out for him. If anyone opened his big mouth about Marvin in Phil's presence, the bodyguard would make quick work of the harasser.

Decades before Marvin launched his one-man crusade against "slime in the ice machine," he made clear his profound dislike of dirt and pungent odors. So repulsed was Marvin by uncleanness that he refused to use the school restrooms, which he found appallingly dirty. Instead, he insisted on being taken home so he could tend to his business in a clean, safe environment.

So vehemently did he insist on having his own way at school that, more often than not, he got it. When the need arose, his theatrics would come into play. He would fall to the floor, clutching his abdomen and kicking his feet. With the class disrupted, the teacher exasperated by his actions, and the other children chiming in, the only recourse left would be to call Marvin's mother. Mrs. Udith Zindler would have no choice except to send the chauffeur to school for Marvin. He would be driven home to use the bathroom, and the chauffeur would then drive him back to school. Marvin repeated these episodes until the school authorities made concessions to cleanliness in the school's restrooms. They were perhaps fortunate that Marvin didn't have friends in the Health Department back then.

Marvin had a flair even as a child. He wanted respect, and he had his own way of getting it. Marvin had a need to control other people (shades of Abe Sr.). If he couldn't take control, then he would just abandon any project or undertakings he may have planned. On the other hand — and here again, he was just like his father — when something didn't go right, or he got hurt, you'd never hear him whine about it.

Though Marvin was indubitably the best-dressed student in school, he was consistently one of the worst students. A summer school report card dated 1934 shows he received a "U" (unsatisfactory) in conduct, and an "F" in English. Today, many people would agree that this was an early indication of lifelong patterns. There are probably many who wish he would just shut up, and his exasperated teachers, those arbiters of good conduct, surely must have wished the same on many occasions. As for English, the most charitable interpretation of his misuse of the English language is to refer to it as "down-home country," or simply to explain to his befuddled listeners that "Texans just speak differently."

Marvin attended school at Pershing, then San Jacinto and, later, Lamar High School. A class photo from 1934 shows 13-year-old Marvin positioned higher than anyone else in the row of students. Even had this not been the case, he would have stood out, because he is very snappily dressed in comparison to the rest of the students. In the photo, Marvin is resting his hand upon the shoulder of his teacher, in what looks very much like a gesture of patronizing approval of the educator's efforts. Marvin was no teacher's pet, but he wasn't about to pass up the chance to make the most of a good photo opportunity.

That class photograph, like so many others taken during his school years, reveals Marvin's constant need to be the center of attention. He found one of many outlets for this need in baton twirling. Marvin pranced his way to adolescent fame as the high-stepping, baton-spinning drum major for Lamar High School, capturing numerous awards for his expertise and showmanship as a twirler.

Marvin had innate abilities when it came to music; he played the drums in the school dance band, and played both the flute and piccolo in the school orchestra. He was also a good dancer, possessing an excellent sense of rhythm.

When it came to a strong will, Marvin more than met his match in the presence of a brilliant and talented African-American woman, Eva Mae Banks. Eva Mae was his nanny, and Marvin fell under her firm but patient guidance from infancy through young manhood. Eva Mae loved Marvin and practically adopted him as her own. She also scrutinized his playmates, and even punished them when she felt it was necessary. Marvin recalls, "Eva used to whip me, too, when I got out of line."

When the chauffeur did not appear in a timely fashion to drive Marvin to school, Eva Mae would hunker down behind the steering wheel of the family's green Pierce-Arrow and drive him herself. That old Pierce-Arrow was a tank, and when Eva Mae drove you'd better get out of her way, or you were going to be run over. There was no stopping her.

Eva kept a close watch on the boy she referred to as "my little Marvin." As he grew older, Marvin's girlfriends were also subject to Eva's approval. If Marvin took the same young lady out more than twice, Eva required him to invite his lady friend to tea or dinner, which invariably turned into an inquisition. Eva would closely question the young lady about various matters, all in the service of finding out if she was a suitable match for Eva's boy.

Eva Mae was more than a nanny; she was a surrogate parent for Marvin. His father did not spend much time with the family, directing most of his attention to the store, his political interests and a myriad of business functions. Marvin's mother was usually absent during the day, working with a volunteer group or attending a social obligation. So Eva kept Marvin close at hand. Marvin's quiet home hours consisted of practicing the piano while Eva Mae indulged in her own spare-time activity: writing adventure stories, under an assumed name, for the old *Argosy* magazine. It could be said that Eva was also Marvin's muse. Certainly she nurtured his creativity; she encouraged his piano and piccolo playing, and was often an appreciative audience of one when he practiced twirling with his baton.

His creative impulses were well tended, but meanwhile, Marvin's grades dragged at or below average. He found the discipline of the classroom confining, and homework boring. Nevertheless his list of extracurricular activities continued to grow, and it was in high school that he discovered a new passion, quite in contrast to music and baton twirling: championship boxing.

C·H·A·P·T·E·R 3

"THE BOXER"

"I go back to you, my cold father, my cold, mad, father, my cold, mad, fiery father..."
— James Joyce, *Finnegan's Wake*

As a high school student, Marvin was pale and spindly, weighing not more than 110 pounds. But it was all muscle, and Marvin was tough. He was also aggressive. Perhaps this was the result of the repetitive taunting he had received as a youngster; no doubt it also had something to do with his need to counteract the force of Abe Sr.'s domineering personality. Taking these factors into consideration, and adding Marvin's fierce need to be the center of attention, it's not so surprising that at the age of 16, he turned to boxing.

Certainly this new interest fit in with Marvin's desire to go against the grain, and to fight the establishment as well as his father. After all, the boxing ring was the last place anyone expected to see a Zindler or any other "nice Jewish boy."

In 1937 and 1938, Marvin worked with Hugh Bimbo, owner of a gym and boxing arena on Lincoln Street, which was in the vicinity of what is now Montrose Boulevard and Allen Parkway. Like everything else Marvin did, he undertook a rigorous training program before beginning his career as a boxer, and figured he had himself trained to perfection as he faced his first real fight. In March of 1938, he went up against a youngster named Tom Harris. Marvin, the 110-pound terror — who was so short he had to crawl under the ropes, not over — entered the ring wearing gold trunks with the Star of David embroidered on the left pants leg. Win or lose, he was sure to get recognition with that — and recognition was what he craved, even more than victory.

Confident of his training, Marvin was looking forward to the experience. For a little extra insurance, and some extra energy, he'd decided to drink a quart of milk before entering the ring. The bell rang, and Tom Harris immediately charged in. Harris landed the first punch to Marvin's gut, upon which Marvin spun around and began choking. And then, as if someone had flipped a switch, he followed with an episode of projectile vomiting over the first two rows of the audience — which surely must have gotten their attention, though perhaps not the kind Marvin had wanted. Harris backed off momentarily, but upon seeing his advantage quickly stepped in, landing punch after punch to Marvin's midsection. The referee stopped the fight, and Tom Harris was declared a winner by a technical knockout. Thus Marvin learned the first important lesson in boxing: You don't drink a quart of milk before you step into the ring.

Even though the first fight was a disaster, Marvin had gotten the fighting bug. He won his second fight, and went on to have more than 100 fights in Galveston, Beaumont, Port Arthur and other cities. The scrawny Jewish boy amazed everyone by winning most of them. He earned the nickname of "Bicycle Peddling" Zindler because he had a habit of running all over the ring, never staying still for a moment. Many of his opponents were Hispanic, and he got booed a lot. That Star of David on his boxing trunks surely drew some unfavorable attention, but this didn't stop him from proudly and defiantly wearing it.

Fairly early in his boxing career, Marvin decided he needed more than guts and ambition to be a fighter. He needed a manager. Marvin found his manager, adviser and instructor in a man called "Battling Sam." In the fight business, there are always those who run the show from behind the scenes, and in Marvin's case, it was not Battling Sam — it was Abe Zindler Sr. Marvin was unaware that his father was still trying to control, manipulate and maneuver him. Abe Sr. wanted Marvin to leave the boxing ring, relinquish all ambitions to the fighting profession, and turn his attention to the clothing store. So he used Battling Sam to further his cause, unbeknownst to Marvin, of course.

Even now there is a definite inflection of annoyance in Marvin's voice when he speaks of the dubious guidance he received from Battling Sam. "All Battling Sam used to tell me," he says, "was to go out there and give them the old upper cut. So I'd go out there and really try. And when I missed with the old upper cut, they would beat my brains out."

Eventually Marvin put two and two together. "Each time I would meet with Battling Sam, he had a new outfit. Sam started to dress better than I did. On closer inspection, I realized the new clothing came from my father's store."

Marvin realized that even though his father condescended to attend a few of his boxing matches, which Marvin invariably won, Abe deeply disapproved of his son's presence in the boxing ring. To Abe Sr., boxing was just another immature antic of his "prodigal son."

As Marvin became aware that his father was working with Battling Sam to get him out of the boxing profession, he stopped listening to his manager's perfunctory advice. In the end, Marvin fired him. But Marvin was not about to stop fighting. He was still driven, still searching for an identity that would set him apart. He also found enormous satisfaction in winning, and was exhilarated by the cheers of the crowd.

Of his boxing technique Marvin says, "I just watched other people. I watched other people fight and did what I thought I could get away with. I won more fights than I lost, so I continued." When he did lose, he didn't whine about it. He'd either raise hell, go into a fit over it, or he'd just walk away.

Then as now, Marvin didn't simply need attention; he commanded it. And if not by boxing, he would think up some other way to make everybody stop and look at him and listen to what he had to say.

In any case, it could be said that in boxing, as in so many other areas of his life, Marvin owed much of his success to his difficult and domineering father. The constant altercations with his "cold, mad, fiery father," as Joyce would have put it, were what kept him going, especially in his younger years. The ancient Greek philosopher Homer wrote, "Many men say he is far greater than his father when he returns from battle..." It doesn't take a psychology degree to recognize that fighting became an outlet for Marvin's aggressions towards his father, a way not only to get back at the man but to help negate any feelings of inadequacy that may have resulted from growing up in Abe Sr.'s shadow. Almost until the end of his life, the senior Zindler never let up in his efforts to cast Marvin and his other sons into his mold. But Marvin put another crack in the mold every chance he could, and his boxing career, brief though it was, and as young as he was, put a big fracture in that mold, perhaps an irreparable one.

Boxing also provided Marvin with his first public recognition, and, of course, this only fueled his yearnings for fame and yet more recognition. Surely this must have been an adrenaline high of enormous intensity, and was, perhaps, even a driving force to his future.

With this new public recognition, Marvin became more and more aware of, and self-conscious about, his features. He began blaming his large nose and his difficulty in breathing on his experiences in the boxing ring. Looking at it from a medical and scientific standpoint, and speaking as one who has performed more than two dozen individual surgical procedures — mostly cosmetic — on Marvin, I believe the cosmetic aspects are unrelated to his past as a boxer. Being of Austrian-Jewish descent, Marvin was simply genetically endowed to have a large, humped nose. However, his boxing experiences could have easily led to internal blockage, septal deviation, and airway obstruction, thus creating the breathing problems. This is a common result of recurrent facial trauma, such as Marvin endured in the boxing ring. And Marvin's boxing matches were certainly not the first fights he'd had, nor were they to be the last. At any rate, the combination of ethnic characteristics and the slings and arrows suffered in the boxing ring had given Marvin a nose that he was not proud of. In addition, he had a significantly underdeveloped chin. It would be years, however, before he would finally go under the knife in an effort improve on nature.

His face was not his fortune, but for awhile it seemed his fists might be. Marvin continued to box throughout high school and even into his college years. He fought for his alma mater, John Tarleton Agriculture College, as a Purple Glove.

Marvin has always fatalistically defined his course by saying, "God has always guided everything that has happened to me for the best." Whether one believes in divine guidance or not, there is no question that one's life is, in large part, a result of the choices one makes. Marvin's life was to be a series of unorthodox choices, some of which resulted in failure — but invariably, it was also his choice to pick himself up again after he stumbled, continuing on the bumpy path to his own destiny.

P·A·R·T

2

Matriculation, Marines & Merchandising

Marvin In Search Of Himself

C·H·A·P·T·E·R 4

MARCHING OFF TO WAR... AND BACK HOME AGAIN

T hroughout his high school years, Marvin participated not only in music, baton twirling and boxing, but also in R.O.T.C. One way of explaining this would be that he was a multitalented young man with diverse interests. That was certainly true. But it was also true that his extracurricular activities allowed him to avoid working in the family store. Marvin's many pursuits filled not just the after-school hours but also the weekends, and he had a knack for keeping his calendar full. He always had something planned.

This only made his father more determined to quash what he considered the foolish flamboyancies and extravagances of his son — a son who, in Abe Sr.'s eyes, refused to grow up. In those days, a boy in his last year of high school was expected to have a pretty clear idea about his plans for the future. And Abe wanted Marvin's future to be in retailing.

Marvin, of course, had different ideas, and often as not would simply refuse to show up for work. If he couldn't find an activity to use for an excuse, it made little difference; he just didn't show up at the store. Marvin continued to find every opportunity to frustrate his father, and the results were arguments of sonic-boom proportions. Along the way there were many short-lived truces, but little actual peace between father and son.

Marvin graduated from Houston's Lamar High School in 1939, and everybody felt things were going to change after that. At least Marvin seemed to be thinking of his future, for he had made the decision to go to college. He decided to attend a college away from home, which would provide him with a needed rest from the family, and, it must be said, vice-versa.

Marvin had chosen John Tarleton Agriculture College[1] in Stephenville, Texas, with the intention to earn a degree in music. Everyone agreed that he had a natural aptitude, having done so well on the drums, piano, piccolo and flute while in high school. Marvin chose John Tarleton because he felt it offered the best musical courses at that time.

Marvin particularly enjoyed the piccolo, which might seem an odd choice of instrument for a young man, but, as usual, Marvin has a perfectly logical explanation. "I decided to play the piccolo," he says, "because I liked the sprightly sound it produced. Also, it was the smallest instrument I could find, requiring little effort to carry around."

So off Marvin went to John Tarleton, but, after only a year away from home, he became bored with college. However, he stuck it out until 1941. His academic record at Tarleton was unremarkable; his one claim to fame in college was that within the year he had been appointed as drum major. That did not impress his father. He wanted Marvin to return to work at the store, and made him an attractive salary offer.

This was certainly tempting for Marvin, who had other reasons for coming back to Houston as well. For one thing, he had fallen in love, and his girl's family was in Houston.[2] So even if it meant he would again come under the stresses imposed by a monarchial father who was determined to mold his sons in his own image, Marvin returned to Houston and to the store in 1941. For a very short while it seemed that he might finally settle into the family business.

Fate, however, was to deal a very different set of circumstances.

In December of 1941, Japan attacked Pearl Harbor. The following day scores of enraged, eager young men, including Marvin, rushed to the military enlistment stations throughout Houston and the rest of the country. No doubt at least some of Marvin's eagerness stemmed from his desire to run away from home once again. Attractive salary notwithstanding, he was still not happy in retailing, and never would be. Unlike so many members of the following generation, who did anything and everything to avoid military service, Marvin sought the military partly as an escape from service in the family store.

With his R.O.T.C. training to boost his confidence, Marvin looked forward to joining the military; he was particularly attracted to the United States Marine Corps. The attraction, unfortunately, was not mutual. To begin with, Marvin's physique did not exactly measure up to the requirements of this elite branch of the service. With a weight of approximately 112 pounds — he had gained a couple of pounds in college — and a height of five feet, ten inches, his string bean-like appearance did not impress the Corps. He was

---

[1] Tarleton was part of the Texas A&M University System; later it become Tarleton State College, and eventually Tarleton State University, a four-year institution.

[2] Marvin's love in fact turned out to be the love of his life. See the section entitled, "Family First...and Always: Gertrude and the Zindler Children."

duly rejected. The Marines would be the first of many large organizations to underestimate Marvin's guts and ingenuity. Marvin may have been down for the moment, but it would have been a mistake to count him out.

Marvin developed his own plan to invade the Marines. The minimum weight requirement for entering the Marine Corps was 118 pounds, a goal that certainly seemed within reach for Marvin. Surrounded by a few friends, he retired to a secluded section along the Galveston beach wall and put his plan into effect. Marvin spent the entire first night and the next several days choking down bananas and filling up on water. On the day he felt he was ready, his friends helped him return to the recruiting center so he could be there when it opened first thing in the morning. He literally waddled in. He was uncomfortably full, in fact bloated, and slightly yellowish for his effort. But he succeeded, weighing in at 118 pounds, and thus was welcomed to the United States Marine Corps.

His problems were only beginning.

Marvin hastily discarded his dandy duds for GI issue, which he donned proudly. He felt exhilarated: finally, he was a man with a purpose. Alas, this was to be short-lived. Growing up, Marvin had quite forgotten the nickname he was given as a child, "Canary Feet." Even though he still wore a size 9 AAA shoe, his foot size was never an issue anymore — at least not in civilian life. The military was different. With the supply lines glutted by the demands of the war, the only boots being manufactured were in the most common sizes. If your feet were either too small or too large, you were just out of luck.

While being outfitted for basic training, Marvin was issued size 7 EE boots. The Marine Corps, it seemed, could not meet the requirements of his "canary feet." When Marvin tried to exchange the boots, he met his match. The Marine corporal he approached about the matter stared menacingly at this skinny new recruit, then flung the pair of boots back at him and snarled. Marvin was caught off guard by this abrupt response, so he tucked in his pride and left with his size 7 EE boots. He was determined to be a Marine, whatever it took.

It is not possible to put a square peg in a round hole, and it wasn't possible to put size 7 EE boots on a 9 AAA foot. Marvin did his damnedest anyway. It didn't take long before his cramped feet became blistered, and the blisters became infected. Marvin once again pleaded for new boots, this time overstepping the corporal and going to his sergeant. He was again told that they didn't have military boots in his size. Using sterling military logic, they also told him, "The extra width should make up for the lack of length."

That might be true for some articles of clothing, but it does not apply to shoes. Marvin proceeded to challenge his sergeant, and demanded he be allowed to have his father send him some specially made boots to fit his feet. The sergeant was astonished by the un-Marine-like audacity of the young recruit, and assigned Marvin to what is affectionately called "extra duty." This was designed to have him eat a little dust, the purpose being to instill some humility — something with which Marvin was not familiar. Marvin, of course, felt the sergeant and the Marine Corps were conspiring against him.

Even so, Marvin followed orders and completed his required assignments as well as the extra duty. And despite the pain and swelling, he served as drum major in the band, and was also physically fit and scrappy enough to enter — and win — the camp boxing tournament.

Throughout all of this, however, his feet became terribly infected, to the point that he could barely walk. Finally he had to hobble to the medic's quarters. A medical discharge followed, which, of course, Marvin protested vehemently. To be discharged at this time would be a personal humiliation, he felt. But his protests fell on deaf ears, and though he requested a review, it was to no avail. Marvin was separated from his beloved Marine Corps, sent home with an honorable discharge.

This did not stop him. Marvin was determined to play an active role in the war effort, just as his brothers were doing. On his arrival home, he immediately tried to enlist in the United States Navy. He offered to sign medical waivers, but the Navy refused to accept them. Whether he wanted to or not, it appeared that Marvin Zindler, who had marched bravely off to war and hobbled back home fighting mad, was destined to serve a life sentence in the family store.

C·H·A·P·T·E·R 5

THE HOPELESS HABERDASHER:
MARVIN & THE ZINDLER FAMILY BUSINESS

I t was with great reluctance that Marvin, newly home from his brief stint in the Marines, returned to the Zindler family store. Perhaps for the first time, his father understood Marvin's feelings and tried to make life at the store more bearable for him. Abe Sr. began to take on more of a tutorial role, and to capitalize on Marvin's creative inclinations.

Abe began taking Marvin on buying trips to New York City, and also gave Marvin more authority at the store, increasing his responsibilities. Even so, he was always looking over Marvin's shoulder, keeping a wary eye on what he still referred to as his son's "playboy instincts."

Marvin did enjoy the buying trips to New York. Above everything else, however, he relished one of his new duties in the store: producing "creative ads." In those days, fooling around with the ads to get customers into the store was standard operating procedure. All of the merchants did it. Marvin explains, "I didn't realize it at the time, but if you did a better job than your competition, it usually involved deceiving the public up to a point. If business was good, [that deception] was something to be proud of."

With traces of glee in his eye, but remorse in his voice, Marvin continues, "I know now [my ads] were deceptive ads." One of his most "creative" campaigns came about when Marvin was given the challenge of figuring some way to get rid of a load of scraggly rabbit-fur coats, which were to be marketed as fur coats at $29.95 per coat. He pondered the gamy looking pelts in bewilderment and then he ventured forth with his creative marketing plan.

First he found a picture of a beautiful $4,000 mink coat in a posh magazine from New York City. Never mind that it didn't even come close to the fur coats that he had on hand. He located a pair of scissors and quickly cut the picture from the slick advertise-ment. Next he lifted some creative words from Webster's Dictionary, and a few words from French class, to provide the copy for the ad. No one ever said Marvin wasn't clever.

Marvin surmised that everyone was aware that strange and wondrous animals could be found in Australia. From there it was a short leap to inventing the exotic "Australian Lapin that looks like a mink." When completed, the headline read, **_Genuine Australian Lapin: Only $29.95_**. Marvin explains, "I didn't figure many people, especially in Hous-ton, Texas, would know what 'lapin' really was." The store, by using the French name for "rabbit" — _lapin_ — was able to rid itself quickly of these scraggly coats.

∞ • ∞

Although Marvin's father had induced him back with an attractive salary, relatively speak-ing, Marvin and his brothers, who also worked at the Zindler store, fell short of executive-caliber salaries. The Zindler boys were always short of cash. As a result, they frequently raided the cash registers, always leaving behind their IOUs. Invariably, at the end of each year, Abe Sr. exploded when he added up the Zindler boys' IOUs, which he found at the bottom of the cash drawer. He handled this by declaring year-end bonuses for his sons, equal to the value of their IOUs, thereby erasing their debt. It was just another way that Abe Zindler indebted his sons to him. The Zindler boys, in particular Marvin, found it a degrading experience.

Marvin was determined to break away, one way or the other. He continued to do his work at the store in a dutiful manner, and, despite the obstacles, was able to save up quite a bit of money. But, he recalls, "I always feared my father would find out. I knew if he found out, he would cut my salary. He did not want me to get enough cash together to ever break away from him or the store." Obviously, Abe Sr. underestimated the resource-fulness and tenacity of his "playboy" son.

∞ • ∞

Throughout the 1940s and 1950s, Marvin was to pursue several career choices. At the same time, he continued to work in the store to a greater or lesser extent, never breaking away entirely until after Abe's death.

Abe tried many times to engage his son more fully in the business. At one point, as an inducement to keep Marvin in the store, his father put him in charge of the new ladies' ready-to-wear department. Abe Zindler made a very big concession in giving Marvin com-plete authority in this area. But Marvin's outside interests still took precedence, and his father grew increasingly disappointed at his son's less than total devotion to the clothing store and the new department. By this time, Marvin had begun his foray into news report-ing and radio broadcasting, and as he grew more involved with these activities, his father gradually withdrew much of the authority he'd given Marvin, and began countermanding

Marvin's running of the ready-to-wear department. As Marvin's success as a roaming reporter grew, his father, rather than being pleased for his son, only grew increasingly disappointed.

The problem with the ladies' wear department came to a head when Marvin purchased a huge stock of women's garments at an unusually good price — which was, without question, the wrong thing to do. Women's fashions, and styles in general, changed so rapidly that much of the merchandise Marvin had ordered was passé even before it was all delivered. As a result, the store was stuck with a load of out-of-date inventory.

Abe, to put it very mildly, was not pleased.

Ultimately, the new ready-to-wear department proved a financial disaster, and Abe blamed its failure on Marvin's lack of devotion to the store. Father and son continued to argue, violently and constantly.

The years passed. Styles changed, Houston was changing, the world was changing — but some things never changed. Again and again, what had been the promise of peace between father and son turned into the same old battle. Marvin would come back to the store, take on new responsibilities, and then, before long, Abe was once again heaping a torrent of complaints upon his head. Sometimes the stress from the constant stream of his father's criticism caused Marvin to break out in splotches. Marvin always wanted to be perfect, but in the eyes of his father it did not seem possible. Peace never lasted long between father and son. It always ended with Marvin drawing away and eventually seeking solace in some venture outside the store.

Besides the running conflict between Marvin and his father, the basic problem was that Marvin simply wasn't cut out for the family business. If he found the arguments with his father to be ego-bruising, he found the daily grind of the retail clothing business to be mind-numbingly dull. "I never did like merchandising," he explains. "It was too slow for me. I liked to see instant results. In merchandising, you would have to wait months, perhaps years, to know whether you made the right decision. Then, a miscalculation or a style change could bury you."

Retailing was not for Marvin, but he still had a ways to go before he found his true calling.

Despite the turmoil between Abe and his sons, and notwithstanding the fact that most of the third-generation Zindlers were so profoundly indifferent to the family business, the Zindler clothing empire continued to grow and thrive in the next several decades. The youngest of Abe's sons, Kenneth, took over the Zindler apparel operation in 1965. He made many innovative changes, including opening Houston's first exclusive Big and Tall Men's Store in the early 1970s.

At the pinnacle of the chain's growth there were four stores, and over the years, Zindler's became a Houston retailing institution, along with Sakowitz, Battelstein's, Craig's, Isabell Gerhart and others. Of these, only Zindler's was to survive through the end of the

20th century. At the time the last store closed its doors on December 23, 2000, Zindler's was the oldest independent family-owned retail business operating in Houston, and possibly in the United States. Zindler's had come a long way from Ben Zindler's modest little tailor shop on Harrisburg.

Similarly, Marvin was to travel a long road from the career purgatory that the store represented for him, to his life of fame and infamy as one of Houston's most "unforgettable characters." But he never forgot the lessons, so hard learned, that his years as a failed retailer had taught him.

White Knight in Blue Shades

3

Mean Streets & Smoke-Filled Rooms

Police Work And Politics

C·H·A·P·T·E·R 6

MARVIN ON PATROL

Of all the career choices Marvin experimented with before he found his true calling as crusader of the airwaves, law enforcement was the one he pursued with the most passion. He had been fascinated with police work from the time he was a teenager, during his father's administration as mayor of the City of Bellaire. Marvin became good friends with the Bellaire Chief of Police and occasionally got to tag along with the Chief and other officers on their rounds. Before long he was able to stretch his "just this once" agreement with the Chief into a regular affair. He particularly liked to go on night patrol.

On returning home from the Marine Corps, Marvin learned of an unpaid auxiliary police force, formed to help compensate for the manpower shortage caused by the war. Police departments in Houston and elsewhere made wide use of these forces. Marvin felt that joining the Houston auxiliary police force was the least he could do to support the war effort. Of course, he also needed some excitement and action outside the store.

So Marvin signed up for the force. He obtained his uniform, and had the store's tailor work several days until the uniform fit according to Marvin's expectations. Marvin continued to work at the store during the day, but he really lived for the evenings, when he would go on night patrol with the force. It was only a matter of time before he began stretching his volunteer police hours to the limit. He began accepting day shifts as well, returning to the store only when it could not be avoided.

Even the store provided its moments of excitement, however. There was, for example, the day Marvin nabbed the hot-check artist. It was a pleasant, balmy afternoon, one of those days when, having been obligated to work in the haberdashery, he was whiling away the hours, waiting for the moment he could escape his mundane duties and begin doing what he really loved. Patronage was minimal on this beautiful afternoon, and Marvin was enjoying the quiet, daydreaming and looking forward to his night police patrol. He didn't know it, but he was going to get the opportunity to play policeman a lot sooner that day than he expected.

It began when Marvin was asked to come to the register to verify a questionable check. The customer was growing increasingly nervous as Marvin continued to question him. Suddenly the would-be forger made a dash out the front door, with the zealous young volunteer cop in hot pursuit. The thief had no idea that Marvin was armed, and he hightailed it down the sidewalk, with Marvin on his heels. Marvin called sharply for him to stop; the man hesitated for only a moment, and then continued to scamper further along the sidewalk. Impulsively, Marvin drew his pistol and squeezed off a shot, and the bullet found its mark in the forger's wrist. This halted his escape, and Marvin made the arrest. Marvin had his man.

You would think his father would be proud — not so. Instead of hearty praise, Marvin had to endure a blasphemous barrage from Abe Sr. His father was not concerned that Marvin was packing a pistol; he was astonished and enraged that Marvin would be so brash as to fire a gun on a downtown Houston street.

Even so, Marvin was delighted with himself. His instincts heightened by the experience, he became even more tenacious as an auxiliary volunteer policeman. He worked long past his expected shifts of duty, a trait his father would have liked to have seen him display at the store. But for Marvin, the excitement was not at the store; it was on the streets.

Marvin took to law enforcement as naturally as he had to his other interests. He was friendly and outgoing, and, as a result, he made many contacts and built up a system of informants. This was to serve him well both in his law enforcement work and his media pursuits.

Although Marvin enjoyed his police patrols, he was intrigued by the more exotic side of law enforcement. He wrangled a stint on the Vice Squad — a suitable direction, you might say, for the man who would eventually gain notoriety for his role in closing down a venerable Texas whorehouse.

At that time, the role of the Vice Squad wasn't so much to crack down on vice as to maintain the status quo and keep the peace. The truth is that from the 1930s through the early 1950s, Houston was rather wide open to both gambling and prostitution. But the only form of vice that aroused the attention of the Houston police force was prostitution — and enforcement of the applicable laws consisted mostly of chasing the prostitutes from one corner of town to the other.

Gambling, on the other hand, was condoned for the most part, and the laws against it were rarely enforced. When Harris County Sheriff Buster Kern took office in 1949, he

White Knight in Blue Shades

vowed to rid Houston and Harris County of wide open gambling. But up until then, Houston was somewhat of a gamblers' paradise. It was, after all, still a young town, relatively speaking, and, 20th century notwithstanding, it was still part of the Old West. What were referred to as "sneak rooms" or "sneak bars" had in fact been common since the turn of the century. Many legitimate businesses that fronted Main Street had their back-room betting parlors and poker tables in place for many years. Late into the evenings, shouts from the betting parlors could be heard by passersby along Houston's Main Street. The poker table was always the most popular and, if you had the money to spend, there was always someone who would accommodate you. Blackjack and other games of chance were also available.

The most charitable way to describe the sneak rooms would simply be to say that they were not plush. The amenities were very minimal. But nobody went there for atmosphere; they went for the gambling, and also for the alcohol, which was available even during the height of Prohibition.

Everyone knew the sneak rooms were there, and everyone knew where they were located. Businessmen, politicians, even the sheriff stopped by. These were not just places to gamble and drink. Plans were laid, business deals were made and stories exchanged. The sneak rooms were, in a sense, the most exclusive of clubs.

Houston's sneak rooms, however, were nothing compared to what could be found on Galveston Island. If you had the time and the transportation, you could make the 35-mile trip to Galveston's then-famous Balinese Room. On occasion, even Marvin made a trip to the dice and blackjack tables of the Balinese Room.

Marvin says, "I never went gambling in Houston because it was more fun in Galveston." Today, you can still head for Galveston to go gambling, and there's no "sneaking" involved whatsoever. Though gambling isn't legal on the island or within a ten-mile radius, you can board a cruise ship which goes beyond the ten-mile limit. At that point, the casinos open and the games begin. The ships usually stay out all night and, for a minimal fee, you can have a small cabin to retire to in the wee hours of the morning. Of course, if you are doing well at the casino, you just might stay up all night at the tables.

But back in Marvin's younger days, there were no gambling cruise ships leaving from Galveston. The pleasures of the tables had to take place on the sly — which, to Marvin and many other young men, made it all the more thrilling. But Marvin's own foray into what he initially saw as the exciting world of poker, dice and blackjack came to a sudden and startling end one night. In one moment, he lost his gambling urge and his enthusiasm for trips to Galveston as well.

The awakening, as Marvin tells it, came one evening when his regular partner was off, and he was riding with somebody else in the patrol car, making all the usual stops. "At one place," Marvin says, "a man I knew to be an operator of a gambling joint came up to the patrol car and handed me an envelope through the window. He said since my partner was off, I should take the envelope this time. I opened it. It was full of money. I guess the gambling operator assumed that my partner had been splitting with me all along. He wasn't."

This was a rattling experience for Marvin, and he began to reflect on what had happened. He was starting to realize how naive he had been regarding the gambling in Houston and Galveston.

Marvin continues, "It suddenly dawned on me what was going on. The gamblers owned the police department, or a big part of it. That meant that they owned and controlled the city. They just bought it. With that kind of power, there was nothing they couldn't do if they wanted to. At that time, I began to realize that even the money I was losing in Galveston, where I had been gambling, was going to policemen and politicians to pay them off and thereby keep the betting parlors and sneak rooms safe."

Marvin quit gambling and got a new partner. He remained on the voluntary police force, but was now contemplating what role he could play in regards to the gambling and corruption in Houston and Galveston.

During this time, Marvin had begun his first ventures into both broadcast and print media. He was a part-time radio DJ, and had also been working on a little magazine published by a crusading constable from La Porte, Texas, a seaside town 20 miles east of Houston. The constable, Dale Richardson, was an ambitious soul who had set his aims for higher political office, and had launched a moral crusade against vice, particularly gambling. Marvin was given the job of prime investigator and advisor on gambling activities for Richardson.

Marvin recalls the time Richardson came into the store and said that he wanted to talk. "He was bothered by all of the gambling that was going on so openly," Marvin explains. "So was I."

Richardson lamented, "I don't know exactly what to do."

"So I told him," Marvin says simply.

One thing that I have learned over the years: never ask Marvin's advice unless you really want it, because Marvin *always* has an answer. Marvin recalls telling the constable, in no uncertain terms, "You are the one with the badge. You were elected to the office, and you're the one who needs to act."

Of course, Marvin had a plan. His broadcasting experience had taught him a thing or two about how to exploit the media, and this, along with his lifelong flare for the theatrical, provided the foundation for an audacious strategy. Richardson liked Marvin's ideas, and so the plans were laid.

Secretly, Constable Richardson gathered his posse of trusted deputies. They selected an evening when they felt the betting parlors and "sneak rooms" would be at their liveliest. If they were going to do this, it was going to be done with a splash. Marvin saw to it that all of the news media were alerted to the plan, but not until a few hours before it would take place. Marvin wanted wide news coverage, but the event had to be kept secret. Timing was everything.

On the appointed evening, at the appointed time, Richardson and his posse swept into Houston, quickly moving from one gambling den to the other. They didn't come with handcuffs and paddy wagons. They didn't come with guns drawn. They came swinging axes, a moral army as righteous and determined as any ever led by Carrie Nation. The aim was to demolish as many of the "sneak rooms" as possible. And that was how the combination of Marvin's advice and Richardson's ingenuity and tenacity virtually shut Houston down — for awhile, anyway.

The media loved it. Local media coverage continued for weeks as citizens began asking questions and demanding answers. The police and politicians, on the other hand, were not pleased. They were embarrassed, they were angry, and they were determined to get their revenge.

Ultimately, Constable Dale Richardson's bold plan backfired on him. It was rumored that he intended to use this episode to further his political aims, but, unfortunately for him, too many businessmen and politicians had been gored by his axe-swinging stampede onto Houston's Main Street. Shortly thereafter, Richardson was charged with a check swindling offense and was compelled to retire his constable position in disgrace. He maintained he was framed, and many people agreed with him. But the tables had been turned, and he had no choice but to step down. Interestingly, the charges were dropped as soon as he resigned from the constable's post. His political career was dead, and the ill-fated moral crusader returned to oblivion in La Porte, Texas. Houston was quiet again.

But Marvin... well, Marvin was just getting started.

C·H·A·P·T·E·R 7

HAVE GUN, WILL TRAVEL:
MARVIN'S LIFE AS "DEPUTY DAWG"

Marvin spent only a couple of years as a volunteer cop, but the law enforcement bug had bitten him hard. After his stint in the auxiliary police force, however, he turned his attention to other interests, chiefly in radio and newspaper work, with a brief detour into early television. Of course, he was also still trying to please his father by putting in time at the store, even though it had long since become apparent to just about everyone — particularly Marvin — that this was not where his heart lay.

Marvin did make one last-ditch attempt to make it in the retail clothing business when he bought out a Zindler's location in the Rice Village area. He acquired some backers, a car dealer and a real estate firm owner, and opened for business under the name of LeBaron Clothing Store. His brother Kenneth managed the store, and it was initially very successful. Then one day the bills all came due, and there was no money. Unfortunately, Marvin had sold a lot of clothes on credit to his friends — about $100,000 worth — and they did not pay him. Now Marvin's backers were demanding their $40,000, and Marvin had no choice except to hold a going-out-of-business sale. He made more money on that sale than he had all year.

After the failure of the LeBaron Clothing Store, Marvin decided he wanted to return to police work. How to do this was the big question.

Once again, his father was at work behind the scenes.

∾ • ∾

Clairville Vincent "Buster" Kern assumed the office of Harris County sheriff in 1949. He had served 20 years as a lawman before his election, and came into office determined to shut down gambling operations in Houston and Harris County. What Marvin's crusading constable friend, Dale Richardson, had perhaps only dreamed of, Buster Kern had the clout to do. He would leave home at two o'clock each morning to prowl the rooftops of Houston's downtown buildings, tracing miles of wiring in order to root out the bookie operations. One set of wires traversed the roof of none other than City Hall. Sheriff Kern smashed slot machines, raided big card and dice games, and, by the time he was through, closed down more than 80 bookie shops.

But putting a big dent in gambling was only the beginning of his assault on crime. Buster Kern and his men, including Texas Ranger Johnny Klevenhagen[1], used every possible means to keep organized crime out of Harris County, striking fear into the hearts of crime bosses who had their eye on the area. Many contend that Kern and Klevenhagen, known as "The Gold Dust Twins of Law Enforcement," are a major reason Harris County and Houston have been free of Mafia influences for all these years. Sheriff Kern was also known as a crime solver extraordinaire; in his first year in office, all 65 murders recorded in his jurisdiction were solved.

During his 23 years in office, Buster Kern made many other contributions to law enforcement in Harris County. He was the first Harris County sheriff to put deputies in uniform. He formed the Harris County Highway Patrol, which reduced traffic deaths by nearly 50% in its first two years. He also established a Narcotics Division and a Consumer Fraud Division, the latter of which Marvin himself was instrumental in developing.

It was the early 1960s when Marvin decided to go back into law enforcement, and he got it into his head that he wanted to be a deputy sheriff. Rather than go through a formal application process, he decided to take the direct approach and pay a personal visit to Sheriff Kern. He wasn't sure how much of a chance he had of getting the job, but, to his amazement, Sheriff Kern hired him on the spot. Marvin was overjoyed.

What he did not know at the time was that his father had arranged the whole thing.

Abe Zindler Sr. and Buster Kern had been close friends for many years, and Abe asked the sheriff to give Marvin the job. As Sheriff Kern once explained, Abe's reasoning was that the job might "help Marvin a lot." Buster Kern knew Abe's feelings all too well, since Abe told anyone and everyone his opinion that Marvin was a naïve playboy who led a flighty, purposeless life.

Never mind that Marvin had been married for 20 years, had a family, and was making a reasonable living at his various pursuits. To Abe's way of thinking, Marvin was a dilettante, and self-centered to boot. However, Abe had resigned himself to the fact that Marvin was repulsed by the merchandising business, and he reasoned that as a sheriff's deputy, Marvin might finally find ways to help other people instead of pursuing a course of self-gratification.

---

[1] Klevenhagen joined the Harris County Sheriff's Department in 1961, and later served a 10-year term as sheriff himself (1985-1995).

Marvin threw himself wholeheartedly into his new job. He soon proved he had the makings of a superman deputy, with his abundant supply of brass, his forthrightness, and, of course, his capers. Finally it seemed he had found his true calling. He was now in his early 40s, making $376.00 a month, and he was very happy. He believed he was working at the job to which he would devote the rest of his life. In fact, he spent his next ten years as Deputy Sheriff Zindler, Badge Number 108.

From the very beginning, however, Marvin was... different, displaying a sense of style that seemed incongruous in his line of work. He sported a bumbershoot — the only deputy to carry one — and his wardrobe was impeccable. Then as now, Marvin had a large wardrobe of custom-made clothing. His shirts in those days featured towering "Calvin Coolidge" collars — not what you would expect of a sheriff's deputy. He carried two pearl-handled pistols, and his coats were carefully tailored to hide these. Marvin even had a special personal calling card printed. The card was printed on glossy black stock and embossed in gold. Marvin's name appeared in Old English script — again, not quite in keeping with the stolid image of the average law enforcement officer.

Notwithstanding this outward gentility, Marvin was tough, he was resolute, and he was not someone you wanted to encounter if you were on the wrong side of the law. His integrity was as impeccable as his dress, and true to his father's wishes, the job really seemed to bring out Marvin's altruistic side. Sheriff Kern once said, "Marvin developed many programs on how to help people, and I have never regretted hiring him. Marvin also brought down a lot of heat, but he was always on the up and up."

Deputy Marvin was first assigned to the Civil Division, his job being to serve papers attaching the property of those who were lawsuit losers. As police work goes, this is considered routine and is ordinarily a humdrum task — but Marvin, indulging his personal need for recognition and using his uncommon talents, as well as his media connections, found ways to add spice to his job. He was careful to select the more interesting assignments, and he had his own criteria for what constituted "interesting." Marvin had developed an uncanny instinct for ferreting out angles of shock or irony that would titillate the public. When he was ready to serve papers on one of his potentially sensational cases he would tip off the news media, who were always willing to respond to a call from Marvin.

Marvin had a talent for creating a story and getting recognition even when serving papers in a civil case. He always had an eye for the unusual. For example, there was the case of the seaman who'd won a suit for $900 in back salary. The ship's owner and its captain refused to pay it, so, armed with a court order, Deputy Sheriff Zindler single-handedly seized an ocean-going freighter. Marvin sat himself in the captain's cabin, pistols in hand, and refused to let the freighter leave until the seaman received his $900 in back salary. The money was quickly wired by the owners to the seaman so the ship could again set sail. Only Marvin could have gotten away with this. The press loved it.

Another time Marvin was given the job of serving papers and attaching the property of a bankrupt ice cream parlor. The freezers were still full of ice cream, and they had to be emptied before they could be moved. Marvin sent runners through the neighborhood notifying all the children: "Free ice cream for everyone!"

Marvin can never forget another occasion when he showed up with a moving company to impound the stock of a funeral home that had not paid its creditors. The movers began loading the caskets into the impound van. They abruptly stopped working and suddenly and unexpectedly drove off in the moving van. Upon investigating, Marvin found that one of the caskets was occupied by a still unclaimed body. The moving people had simply freaked out. Marvin took care of things; he made sure the man in the casket had a proper burial.

By the way, Marvin got the last laugh on some of those "friends" who stiffed him at the LeBaron Clothing store. He served them papers on other business deals that they had done on "credit" but never paid. Marvin had the immense satisfaction of taking over judgments and seizing their property.

The community loved Deputy Sheriff Zindler, and the press was always on the scene with him, looking for a human interest story. Marvin thrived on it. But all was not well at headquarters. Marvin's personal attire and media-grabbing stunts did not endear him to his fellow officers. He simply would not conform, in either appearance or manner.

The deputies didn't cotton to his odd way of dressing, and it didn't help Marvin's case that his decorative pearl-handled pistols didn't always fire when he went to the practice range. And if all that weren't enough, he had the nickname of "Motormouth." He came by it honest. Typically, the other officers maintained a strong, silent image, but not Marvin. Once Marvin got an idea in his head or formed an opinion, he would stick to it, and he would share it loudly and often, overwhelming anybody who tried to tell him anything else.

More damning than his bizarre sense of style, however, was the fact that the deputy who carried Badge Number 108 was distrusted by some of the other deputies because of his relationship, past and present, with the media. There has always been a natural adversarial relationship between public authority and the media. As a result, law enforcement officers have for the most part exercised a wariness toward news reporters — but not Marvin. After all, Marvin worked for the media, off and on. And he pursued media attention with nearly the same zeal he devoted to working on his cases.

In short, Marvin's publicity-grabbing antics, his *bon vivant* wardrobe and his "Motormouth" were considered by many to be an affront to the Sheriff's Department. Conformity was *de rigueur* for law enforcement officers, but "conformity" was not even in Marvin's vocabulary. So how was Marvin able to remain on the force even for 10 years? Well, you could say he was lucky, that the angel on his shoulder was working double shifts. But luck isn't everything, and even angels can only do so much. You could also say that he was good at what he did, and in many cases it was precisely because he did it differently from everyone else.

One day Marvin and his partner were parked at the curb, listening to the police radio. A fugitive had overpowered an officer, taken his gun and escaped. Scores of deputies were participating in a manhunt in and around the downtown section of Houston, looking for this individual.

A man came up to the police car and tapped on the window. He told Marvin that he had some additional information about the man they were looking for, and added that none of the other officers seemed interested in listening to him. Marvin has always been willing to listen to anyone, after which he will make his own decision. So he listened. The man said he had recently picked up a hitchhiker and driven him to the Montrose area, a midtown Houston neighborhood, and that the hitchhiker fit the description of the man the police were looking for in the downtown area.

Following proper police procedure, Marvin radioed the dispatcher. The dispatcher abruptly reported that the suspect was located and capture was imminent. The curt reply of the dispatcher, and the tone of his voice, implied that Marvin should stay out of it and mind his own business. Instead, Marvin and his partner decided to take the witness in their patrol car so he might direct them to the area in Montrose where he had dropped off the hitchhiker. Sure enough, Marvin and his partner found the fugitive, gun still in hand, and made the capture without any problems.

Marvin arrived at the courthouse just as many very exhausted deputies were returning from their chase. They had captured a man they found running along Buffalo Bayou. Unfortunately for them, their prisoner turned out to be a local doctor who was out jogging. You can imagine how the news media played on this one. Deputy Sheriff Marvin Zindler not only got his man, but his publicity as well. This sharp-dressing, publicity-seeking, voluble nonconformist had made the rest of the department look like the Keystone Cops.

Because Marvin was so different, he made few friends among his fellow officers, but this did not keep him from doing his job. The publicity he received seemed to help his morale, and Marvin would work twice as hard after one of his cases resulted in a good story.

Marvin wasn't afraid of anything. There were times he took on some pretty bad desperadoes, trusting little more than luck, or his angel, or whatever you want to call it. He also made use of his unique talents, especially his gift of gab. "Motormouth's" m.o. was to out-think and out-talk the suspects, thus avoiding a fight. Marvin just kept talking and talking and talking, not giving them a chance to think, much less respond. It was almost as if he hypnotized them with his nonstop jabber. According to some people, the suspects would give up and come along to the jailhouse just to shut Marvin up. Others have said that Marvin tried to talk them out of fighting because he was always afraid of getting his hairpiece, which by now he had been wearing for some years, ripped off in the process.

Whatever Marvin's motives might be, there was no question that he did his job well, and within a couple of years he had wrangled a transfer to the Fugitive Division. His task was to travel the country, pick up felons and return them to Harris County authorities. Marvin brought his characteristic cleverness and pizzazz to the Fugitive Division. For example, in order to prevent his prisoners from running off, he filled two suitcases with bricks and cuffed them to the suspects' wrists. Toting that sort of load made it impossible to run very fast or very far. No one could say Marvin wasn't inventive. But Marvin also did this out of consideration for the suspects' dignity, reasoning that someone carrying two suitcases would not draw the attention that a prisoner in handcuffs or shackles would.

Marvin was especially solicitous of his female prisoners; he had a pair of mink-covered handcuffs specially made to transport them. He felt it would be less embarrassing to the ladies since the handcuff looked like a fancy muff to passersby. The mink handcuff muffs were made by his good friend and one of Houston's finest furriers, Samuel Spritzer. As usual, this tactic got Marvin the desired publicity from the media, but in Texas' heat, mink-lined handcuffs were impractical, and, if worn on a sweltering Houston summer day, would actually stand out more than regular handcuffs.

Fellow deputies in the Fugitive Squad gave Motormouth Marvin a new nickname: "Deputy Dawg," in honor of the Terrytoons ® cartoon character. The cartoon dog was an affable, easygoing sort — far from a superhero, but in any case, the nickname only added to Marvin's mystique and aura.

His talents did not go unnoticed in higher circles, and President Lyndon Johnson himself issued a special presidential warrant allowing Marvin to travel to Belgium to bring back an embezzler. The guilty party had embezzled $25,000 — a lot of money back then — from his company. Of course, the man had skipped town. He was tracked to New Orleans, where he supposedly had gone to live with his in-laws. Marvin called the in-laws and told them that he had a large check for their son-in-law. They helpfully informed Marvin that the man was presently on a ship bound for Antwerp, Belgium. The authorities there were notified, and they nabbed the man as he disembarked. He had $9,000 in cash on him. The extradition papers were signed by President Johnson, and Marvin took them to Belgium to get his man. The embezzler got four years.

Marvin's beat had expanded from the whole country to the entire world. He traveled to Montreal, Canada, to nab a child molester, enlisting the help of the Royal Canadian Mounted Police to get his man. His stint in the Fugitive Department also took him to Mexico, France and many other spots over the globe.

Marvin's flair for publicity did not go unnoticed either. He was promoted to sergeant, and put in charge of public relations for the sheriff's department. Then in 1971, Marvin was assigned by Sheriff Kern and the district attorney to establish a Consumer Fraud Division with the Harris County district attorney's office. This was a first; no other police or sheriff's department had a consumer affairs department. It brought national headlines, and would later pave the way for Marvin's introduction to television as a consumer advocate. The Consumer Affairs Division Marvin fostered is still in operation today.

Marvin and his assistant, a young deputy by the name of Adams, were given a small office from which to conduct the business of the new department. Marvin added the finishing touches to the office by hanging a sign that read, "Yea, though I walk through the valley of the shadow of death, I shall fear no evil. For I am the meanest SOB in the valley." And he was. This was where he really began to find one of his true missions as advocate for "the little people" who were preyed upon by unscrupulous business owners.

It might even be said that Marvin personified the saying, "Speak softly but carry a big stick." In Marvin's case, the big stick, or rather the sword, was publicity. (And some might argue that the "speak softly" part could not accurately be applied to Marvin.) At any rate, businessmen small and large learned to keep a wary eye out for this crusader who had seemingly came from nowhere and now appeared to be everywhere. The hucksters might be able to beat the rap, but in the end none of them could hide from Marvin's inevitable posse of newsmen who were always looking for an interesting story.

Marvin did such a good job, and the Division received such excellent publicity, that 70 to 80 people would be waiting for the Consumer Affairs office to open every day. And each day scads of businessmen would also be waiting at the sheriff's office to complain about Sergeant Marvin Zindler. Businesses counterattacked in other ways as well, but Marvin always stood his ground. Marvin, who in his young and foolish days had played around with deceptive advertising himself, was now playing on the other side. He took full advantage of the laws against deceptive advertising, using these laws more ways than you could think of making potatoes.

Things were changing again for Marvin; his fame was growing. No longer was he "Deputy Dawg," but now he was "Sergeant Zindler, The Consumer's Fastest Gun"...and "The Texas Tornado"... and "The Robin Hood of Consumerism." He was featured on local and national television, even appearing on "What's My Line" and other game shows. He was also featured in articles in *Business Week*, *Playboy*, *Newsweek*, *Time*, *The Wall Street Journal* and numerous other publications. Marvin had a knack for turning stories into more stories by using his shrewd ability to follow up leads that would rebound and multiply.

Once, a lawyer threatened to have Marvin scalped. At a news conference that followed, Marvin seized upon the opportunity and handed the lawyer one of his hairpieces. In fact, this was the first time Marvin publicly revealed that he wore a hairpiece. He told the lawyer who wanted his scalp that it was a Hanukkah present. Then Marvin turned abruptly and walked away.

Marvin managed to serve his decade with the sheriff's department without actually getting scalped. But in the end, it might be said, the businessmen and their lawyers got their wish — for awhile, anyway.

In 1972, Sheriff Buster Kern was defeated in his bid for re-election. Jack Heard was the new sheriff, and Marvin knew his days as deputy sheriff were numbered. When Sheriff Heard broke the news of his termination to Marvin, he told him he had decided not to keep Marvin in the department because the men did not like him. Furthermore, Heard added, Marvin was too flamboyant and did not portray the image the new sheriff wished to create. He told Marvin he did not fit into the new "team approach" that Heard was planning to develop within the department. What he really meant was that they simply could not afford to have Marvin around. Marvin was just too "hot."

So Marvin did what came naturally: he called a new conference announcing he had been fired. It was not Marvin's style to go out with a whimper. In fact he was angered and saddened by his ousting, for, of all the jobs he had pursued, he felt he had loved law enforcement the most and had served it above all else. Now Marvin had become a sacrifice on the political altar. He had antagonized too many businessmen, and businessmen were the financial contributors to elected officials.

But, as had happened so many other times in his life, when this door closed for Marvin, another one opened. And he was more than willing to step through and take full advantage of the opportunities that awaited him (more about that in Chapter 11). He wasn't through with the shady businessmen, the crooked lawyers, or the corruptible politicians — not by a long shot.

Regarding the latter, it must be said that Marvin has no great love for politicians or politics. Ironically, there were several times in his life when he came perilously close to becoming a politician himself.

C·H·A·P·T·E·R 8

MARVIN AND POLITICS

Over the years, rumors have periodically surfaced about Marvin's political intentions. Since his father was mayor of Bellaire, Texas for several terms, this is understandable. And, because politics is at least as much about personality as it is about policies (many would contend it's *all* about personality), his name recognition would seem to make him a natural for a political career. Everyone knows Marvin. Equally as important, Marvin knows everyone, another plus if you have political ambitions.

In fact there have been numerous attempts, by various people, to get Marvin to run for local office and even for the U.S. Congress. Many thought he could have won easily. To say the least, Marvin would have kept things stirred up. He would probably be the biggest hell-raiser they ever had on Capitol Hill, and of course, in no time at all he would be attracting national press attention. And he would work hard, doing whatever it took to get the job done. But, since he doesn't like to lose — ever — at anything he does, there'd be hell to pay if he didn't get his way.

Indeed, Marvin himself has occasionally fantasized about a job on Capitol Hill, but in the end, he always says, "I have the best job right here at KTRK, Channel 13." In many ways, he feels he has more power than a Congressman to correct what he feels are inequities, and he certainly feels he can get the job done more quickly. Most would agree with him.

In the final analysis, Marvin really doesn't have the temperament of a career politician. He is a mixed bag of characteristics, some of which suit him to politics, but many of which do not. Marvin has a tremendous will and in many ways is extremely self-centered — but these are good characteristics if you are seriously going to consider politics. However, underneath his air of what many take as overwhelming self-assurance runs a deep stream of agonizing self-doubt. This is not good for politics. Marvin is shockingly candid about personal matters, and many would say this is a plus in the political arena, particularly in these times when full disclosure is no longer a choice, but a requirement, even if one is just running for the position of assistant dogcatcher.

Marvin is clever, aware, sharp and manipulative — good for politics — but he is also firmly opinionated, and will not deviate from that opinion — which is not good in a world where compromise is part of the game. Further, he is often unwilling or unable to explain the reasoning process behind his opinion. When he is asked why he thinks the way he does, he will posture a lot, responding with growls and snarls, and will sometimes display appalling rudeness. This is immediately followed by overwhelming graciousness, as he ends his attack in an easy, soothing voice, leaving the question unanswered and the questioner bewildered. Marvin is impulsive and delights in dealing out numbingly harsh verbal abuse. However, he is quick to praise the same people he has just lambasted — which may be cold comfort in light of the abuse they have just suffered. He is also too quick to snap out exactly what he thinks on a subject, something a seasoned politician only does when he thinks the sound system is off.

Despite the impression he might sometimes give by his incessant mangling of the English language, Marvin is exceedingly bright, clever, and exceptionally "street-smart" — and this certainly is good for politics. He despises the babbling of pseudo-intellectuals — which is bad for politics if you have trouble hiding your contempt, as he does. On the other hand, he has an almost eerie ability to see the hidden character of people, which is essential for politics.

However, a successful career in politics also depends on perception, and here again Marvin runs into trouble. What some see as exuberance and zealousness in Marvin, others see as vindictiveness. In short, so great are Marvin's eccentricities, and his apparent need to display them, that he probably wouldn't make it as a career politician.

Naturally, these shortcomings didn't stop him from dabbling in politics anyway in his younger days.

The year was 1949. Marvin was only 28 years old, and was working, unhappily of course, in his father's store by day. In the evenings, he gathered stories for his radio program; he had, by now, been involved in radio broadcasting for several years (see the next section).

Marvin has usually been one to contemplate his decisions, but there have been occasions when his decisions come in a rush, somewhat like those of an impulsive buyer. In 1949 he made one such decision, taking a brief detour that offered the promise of a different form of excitement. Yes, Marvin entered the "dirty world of politics," announcing his candidacy for the job of mayor of Bellaire. This was, perhaps, not totally unexpected, given his father's background.

However, within a few days one of the local daily newspapers, *The Houston Post*, came out against him. In its statement, it labeled him a "pinhead." Marvin immediately filed suit. The newspaper promised an apology in the form of a printed retraction, which came the very next day. The newspaper had the last laugh, however, by printing their retraction under a bold italicized headline which read:

We won't call Marvin Harold Zindler a "pinhead" again.

It was at this time that the City of Bellaire changed to a city manager form of government, which, Marvin says, would have diluted the powers of the mayor. He lost interest and dropped out of the race. That might have been the end of Marvin's brief detour into politics.

Once Marvin had made up his mind, however, nothing was going to stop him. Marvin was still intrigued by the power of politics, so he took a new approach and became active in the Democratic Party. He was appointed a delegate in the Democratic Party to the Texas State Convention one year.

Marvin's temperament being as it is, his approach to politics was based on the view that the shortest distance between two points was, of course, a straight line. This was unsettling to politically astute old hardliners who preferred to walk softly, proceeding only a step at a time. In fact, many in the Party considered Marvin to be headstrong. As such, it was felt he would never be inducted into the smoke-filled back rooms of the politicos' hierarchy. Eventually, they were to be proven wrong, but Marvin had a few hard lessons ahead before he was really welcomed to those back rooms.

Marvin can produce unusual surprises in public places when the urge strikes. And strike it did at the Democratic State Convention. Marvin had taken the rostrum microphone, and decided to give the delegation a little Zindlerian advice. He began by denouncing what he considered to be the shameless lack of standards, and underhanded manipulations, by the conservative wing of the Party. All at once, Marvin was back in the news — not for his blistering denouncement, but for the fist fight that resulted. As Marvin returned to his seat on the floor, he was accosted by one of the conservative delegates who disapproved of his opinion. He launched into a verbal assault, to which Marvin, being Marvin, retorted — and the delegate landed a quick right hook to Marvin's eye. They were quickly separated. Marvin, former prizefighter that he was, remained unruffled. Instantly, he tucked in his shirt and was escorted by several delegates back to his seat.

Each of the opponents in the scuffle later filed lawsuits for defamation of character, but the suits were ultimately dismissed. One result of the incident at the Democratic Convention was that it had become clear, to Marvin and others, that he really did not have the temperament for the political arena.

But he still had a desire to be politically involved, and so, while Marvin didn't run for office himself, he was active in campaigning for others. Marvin worked diligently in the senatorial campaign for Lyndon Baines Johnson, who won. Inspired by this victory, Marvin became the campaign manager for M.L. "Fay" Wooley in the bid for the sheriff's office. Wooley lost, but it was a valuable experience for Marvin nevertheless. Through his successes and failures as a campaign worker, Marvin gained insight into how one had to "go along to get along" in politics. This was a big step from the "direct confrontation" method he had exercised at the State Democratic Convention.

It was during these years that Marvin formulated social and political philosophies which he still believes in today. He developed a strong sense of idealism, particularly in matters concerning human dignity. He favored as little government as possible, maintaining that "government ought to be more local than national." On the other hand, he felt, and still feels, that "every person has the right to medical care, and it's hell to be poor." Accordingly, Marvin preserves a warm devotion to such liberal causes as our present welfare program. This attitude is perfectly in keeping with his seemingly contradictory traits. Marvin has, over the years, developed into a strong backer of what some would consider the conservative philosophy, while others would look on it as quite liberal. Marvin would have to be diagnosed as a "conservative liberal," whatever that is! Or perhaps it would be fair to say that he was a "compassionate conservative" decades before that became a campaign catch phrase.

If you ask Marvin what he is, though, he'll say, "I can't think in terms of labels such as conservatives or liberals. I don't think anybody can really define me." In Marvin's eye, "It seems that a liberal is supposed to be someone who is not a bigot, and a conservative is someone who is a bigot. I've never been a bigot. Today there is *no difference* between 'liberals' and 'conservatives.' They just use the words to divide up the teams."

There's an old adage that no one should see how sausage or politicians are really made, because the inside knowledge would destroy one's taste for both. During Marvin's short-lived but fiery baptism in politics, he learned a lot very quickly, and certainly his taste for politics was altered radically. He entered with an adolescent and visionary naivete, and managed to escape the cannibalistic stew of the political pot without being ground up into sausage himself. Marvin would use the lesson of these experiences to form a personal view of politicians which, over time, became quite simple.

"To me," Marvin states, "The word 'politician' is really a bad name that has become a bitter pill to most people. It used to be respected. It used to be that a man would like to be in public office. It used to be a civic duty. It used to be a public trust. Today, it doesn't have a good connotation at all. When you call a man a politician nowadays, it means he's a man who is going to get into public office and take what he can and get the hell out, hopefully before he gets caught."

That's just not Marvin's style. Even with his typical "I-can-conquer-all" outlook, his oversized ego, and his endless need for attention, Marvin would rather exercise the force of his personality outside the political arena.

His native unsuitability for politics hasn't prevented Marvin from involving himself in the civic process on a local scale. After he was married he became a joiner, participating in civic clubs and various other associations, even joining the Masons. (Marvin is a 33rd Degree Scottish Rite Mason, the highest honor one can receive in Masonry.) He remained interested in politics, and has, in one way or another, been politically active at various times throughout the years.

In January of 1976 a group of influential and wealthy Houstonians invited Marvin to meet with them in one of their office suites. These businessmen had taken a political poll, the results of which showed that if Marvin were to enter politics, he could win. Based on this, the businessmen offered to pay all campaign expenses for Marvin to run for United States Congress, as a Republican candidate. In addition, they would pay him money equal to the lucrative salary that he would have to give up at Channel 13 during this time. They told Marvin they supported him because they felt he understood the free-enterprise system, and they felt the country was headed toward socialistic policies, which they wished to avert.

Marvin listened politely as each one spoke, then thanked them. In the end, he turned down the offer. He and Gertrude discussed it and decided they emphatically did not want to go to D.C., which they called "Divorce City." And Marvin would have felt more than a little uncomfortable being in the pockets of such a small and elite group. He would rather stay where he was and continue to battle for the "little people" who had neither money nor influence. To this day, Marvin has never regretted his decision.

Still, rumors persist that Marvin may run for office, but they remain only rumors. More than 50 years have passed since Marvin's foray into politics in 1949, and true to his philosophy, even though tempting offers have been made over the years, Marvin has never entered the political arena again.

Like Marvin, I have long been interested in the political process, and, like Marvin, I consider myself to be more or less a purist. I believe politicians should be more concerned about the needs of their constituents and less concerned about being re-elected. I also believe our political process has strayed too far from the intentions of our founding fathers.

From time to time I have toyed with the idea of running for office, and some years ago I even ran for Congress. I didn't win. The man who did, Congressman Tom DeLay, later told a group at the Houston Downtown Rotary Club that I was too smart, too honest, and too dedicated to the medical profession to be a Congressman. Marvin concurred.

But memory is sometimes short. I probably should have gotten my fill of politics, but, like Marvin, I began toying with the idea of political office again a few years later. Unlike

Marvin, I decided to follow through with the idea. A seat had become available on the Houston City Council, and I believed I had enough name recognition to win it. I also felt I would be an asset to the city council, and that the citizens of Houston would benefit from having a physician on the council. Accordingly I drove to City Hall and registered for the open council seat, paying the $1,500 registration fee.

The Channel 11 (CBS affiliate) television crew happened to be at City Hall at the same time, and filmed me during the registration process. Then they conducted a short interview about my entrance into the City Council race. At the time, I felt this was an unexpected coup. My triumph was to be short-lived.

The announcement of my intended campaign aired on Channel 11's 6:00 PM news that night. Marvin got wind of it and, for the life of him, couldn't fathom why his good friend Doc Joe wanted to run for a City Council seat. Marvin also wasn't happy that the announcement had aired on Channel 11 rather than Channel 13.

I was feeling pretty pleased with myself after the broadcast, particularly as I began receiving the congratulatory phone calls. And then I received Marvin's call. Marvin expressed himself as only Marvin Zindler can; the only solace was that it was over the telephone and not face to face.

When he is in the throes of righteous anger, Marvin's language abounds with colorful expletives not meant for the weak at heart. When truly excited, Marvin enters into an onslaught of curse words that he uses in the most inventive ways. And so it was during this phone call. Though the timbre of Marvin's voice was one of doom and darkness, at the same time his endless string of epithets caused me to want to go into uncontrollable fits of laughter. As the verbal barrage quickened, Marvin stuttered, stammered and raged.

By this stage of our relationship, I was quite used to these blistering attacks. At first, I admit, they used to scare the heck out of me. Later, I just worried Marvin would have a heart attack or a stroke during one of these onslaughts. Eventually I learned to take them in stride, as I did on this evening. My complete lack of response during Marvin's diatribe drove him into renewed fury, and I could visualize his posturing and gesturing on the other end of the telephone.

In the background, I could hear Lori Reingold, Marvin's producer, coming to my defense, and his cameraman, Bob Dows, seconding with his support. But Marvin was not to be denied his blurting.

"Got-damn it," Marvin screamed with each denouncement (in the interests of decorum, I am deleting some of his more colorful words). "Where the hell did you get a got-damned, stupid, damn, damn, damn, bliss sorry, damn, damn, damn, damn, idea like that? You can't do this god-damned insane thing." Finally all was quiet for a few seconds, and, to tell the truth, I was praying this verbal supernova had ended. And it had, but the catch was that I had to promise to come to the television studio and discuss it with him. I agreed, and hung up, with Marvin's voice still ringing in my ears.

Tomorrow would not do for the promised meeting; it had to be tonight. The White Knight had summoned. As I left for the television studio, I began really thinking about what Marvin had said, and, more importantly, why he'd said it. After all, he was my good and trusted friend, and if he felt strongly enough about this decision to get so worked up over it, and to request a face-to-face discussion now, maybe I'd better listen.

Knowing Marvin as well as I did, I knew that by the time I got to the studio he'd be as calm as the eye of a hurricane. Marvin would be ready to discuss the issues rationally. I also felt sure that Lori and Bob would be supportive of me. I was wrong on all counts.

I knew I was in trouble when Lori met me in the hallway at the KTRK-TV station and said, "Joe, you don't have to do this if you don't want to." I thought to myself, *Do what? I just got here!* The veil of mystery was quickly lifted as I entered the studio area.

Marvin was sitting at the dais. The cameras were mounted on their tripods and the appropriate lights were pre-positioned. I was beginning to feel distinctly uneasy, and I didn't feel much better when I was greeted by Bob Dows, who issued the same warning, "Joe, you don't have to do this if you don't want to."

Marvin, jumping to his feet, commanded, "Sit down here." He indicated a chair that had been placed directly in front of him. As soon as I sat down, the red indicator light above the camera went on. The cameras were running.

Marvin raised his hands in the manner of a gospel preacher. In his most animated voice, he screamed at me, "What possessed you? Has the Devil taken hold of you?"

I was so stunned I was unable to reply. Marvin continued, "As a doctor, you are in the noblest of professions. Only the Devil could make you enter into politics."

With an arm stretched out toward my brow and a hand on my shoulder, Marvin continued, "Promise me you will cast out the political devil within and never run for a political office again. I know you have an angel on your shoulder too. Politicians aren't blessed with this."

To tell the truth, I don't remember if I voluntarily nodded a "yes," or if Marvin's hand on my forehead forced the response. I do remember that I didn't have a chance to speak. Marvin was again talking, but slowly now and with a big grin. Marvin said, "Good, you have seen the light and will continue to practice medicine and help the needy children of Houston."

I do recall saying something to the effect that I would go to City Hall tomorrow morning and withdraw my candidacy, and that I would continue working with Marvin and caring for the needy children.

This segment ran on the 10:00 PM news. The response was awesome; the phones rang off the hook for the next several days. Comments were split almost equally about whether I should or should not run for City Council. Either way, they were very supportive of me.

In actuality, at the time I felt I could have participated with the City Council and continued to practice medicine and, of course, take care of the indigent children who wrote to Marvin and me requesting our help.

But I know now that would not have sufficed, as far as Marvin was concerned. Marvin does not consider politics an ethical or honest vocation, and now I had been knighted, as it were. It might be said that as of that night in front of the Channel 13 cameras, I too had an angel on my shoulder, and it is one I have tried to honor ever since.

P·A·R·T

4

Marvin The
Media Star

From The Night Hawk
To The White Knight

C·H·A·P·T·E·R 9

ON THE AIR

It might be stretching things a bit to say that Marvin's long career in broadcasting began with his first "public words" on the radio at the age of 12, but he has never forgotten the excitement of that first time on the air, brief though it was.

It was mostly a matter of luck; Marvin happened to win a contest held by a local store owner. In the 1930s, such contests were frequent, but less flamboyant than the ones of today. Often the contest consisted of no more than a merchant filling a glass fish bowl with jelly beans or marbles and placing it in his front window. A sign in the window would list the contest rules, which were usually simple and straightforward. The object was to guess the number of jelly beans or marbles in the jar. To do so, you would have to enter the store and fill out a small piece of paper with your name, address and the number of items you thought were in the container. The prize usually consisted of tickets to the Saturday movie show or a baseball game. In the contest Marvin entered, the prize was a personalized fountain pen and a chance to appear on a local radio station to accept it.

Marvin was not the best student, and math was surely not one of his strong suits. However, he was certainly capable of making an educated guess. After studying the jar of jelly beans for some time he came up with what seemed like a plausible number — and he won. To claim the prize, Marvin was taken to the local radio station, which was quite an experience for a young man of 12, particularly one as eager for attention as Marvin was. The announcer gave a long and flowery introduction and then presented Marvin with a personalized, engraved pen.

And what was Marvin's very first public utterance? A simple exclamation: "Golly. It's got my name on it!"

Never again was he to exercise such an economy of words on the air.

A few years later, Marvin was on the radio again, this time for real. It was the early 1940s, and Marvin was home from the war, working part time in his father's store, part time as a volunteer cop, and part time as a disc jockey for a Houston radio station. He had a one-man show which he called "The MZ Show." He opened each show with his theme song, "The Easter Bonnet." He had no particular reason for using this song other than that he liked it. And just in case anyone missed the significance of the initials, "MZ," Marvin also began each broadcast with an explanation: "That's me, Marvin Zindler." In the event that wasn't enough, Marvin continued, "It's 'M' like in the middle of the alphabet and 'Z' like at the end, *Marvin Zindler*."

During those years Marvin became more than just a disc jockey. He produced a radio news show and became Houston's first on-the-spot news reporter, referring to himself as the "Roaming Reporter."

All this time, of course, Marvin was still on the payroll of his father's haberdashery store, and his father was still lamenting, to anyone who would listen, about "My son, Marvin, the playboy."

Marvin's work as a police officer gave him a clear advantage as a news reporter. Over the years, he built up a large stable of informants. He knew how the police operated, and he had access to a police call radio. The idea of combining his police experience with his love for the radio led to his creating one of the first local "Action News" programs. This new program was carried on the now-defunct KATL radio and later on KXYZ radio, as well. Both received extremely high ratings.

Marvin equipped his car with police radios, which made it possible for him to have the latest information and often be at the crime scene before the cops. As far as Marvin was concerned, the more carnage, the better. Excitement and drama were his bywords; he was one of the pioneers of what you might call "Reality Radio."

Marvin would rush into a crime scene or fight without thought to himself, climbing through debris and wreckage to get his story. When the police arrived, they often attempted to chase him away, but Marvin would stand his ground. Encumbered with his heavy recording equipment, he would push his microphone in front of an accident victim, who might be rising in pain and soaked in his own blood.

"Hi, I'm Marvin Zindler. That's 'M' like in the middle of the alphabet and 'Z' like at the end of the alphabet. I'm the Roaming Reporter. How do you feel? It looks like you are really hurt bad. Do you think you are going to die? Can you tell us what's going through your mind at this very moment?"

In recent years, reporters using these tactics have been rightfully criticized for their intrusiveness. Undeniably, Marvin's methods were intrusive and often sensationalist. But they were also inventive, and, in his own way, he managed to produce a radio show that was exciting and kept the public's interest. He was able to take what would have been just another ordinary night of murder, mayhem, car wrecks and family disputes, and put a human face on it. In so doing, he was able to truly engage his listeners.

With his large list of informants and a car loaded with police radios, Marvin had a way of showing up when least expected. The police soon learned that Marvin was a two-edged sword. It wasn't long before rumors spread throughout the police department that it was best to stay on Marvin's good side, and the only way to do that was to cooperate with him. If Marvin liked you, he could easily overlook catching you snoozing on duty while parked behind a vacant building. Or perhaps Marvin would overlook an overly long lunch break or extended coffee stop. Marvin could even turn a blind eye to such antics as an afternoon rendezvous with a girlfriend while parked under the bridge. On the other hand, if you didn't cooperate, it was said that sooner or later the Roaming Reporter would find some way to "cut you up" on his program. So it was easier to cooperate with Marvin when he arrived on a crime scene than to attempt to chase him away.

Those who foolishly tried to extricate him from the scene would find themselves at the mercy of a verbal tyrant. Marvin would launch into a forceful and convincing tirade about his Constitutional rights as a reporter, the right to free speech, and the right to do his job. He would threaten, cajole, exasperate and even alarm the police officers to the point where they would just leave him alone unless he was truly in the way.

Some police officers actually found Marvin an asset to their duties. Since he frequently arrived at the scene before the police, he would usually already be in the middle of one of his overwhelming interviews. The police would often sit back and just wait, knowing that it wouldn't be long before those being interviewed would want to be rescued from Marvin's microphone.

One veteran officer said, "After awhile they anxiously looked forward to talking to the police and couldn't wait to get away from Marvin." Another admitted, "Marvin would liven up what would have been just another ordinary evening."

Whatever Marvin lacked in experience and taste, he certainly had guts, or what some would refer to as *chutzpah*. And though Marvin was often naive, he was devilishly clever and couldn't be misled for long by false news trails or other types of subterfuge. His accomplishments, even in those early days, seem pretty amazing when you consider that he was completely self-taught. Marvin did not have the advantage of formal classes or night courses in journalism or broadcasting. His was strictly on-the-job training, and he was an excellent student. He loved reporting, and never stopped thinking of ways to do it better. He is still learning, still thinking of ways to improve his work. Those early efforts in broadcasting turned into a lifelong quest for excellence.

The continued high ratings of his radio shows, and an ever-increasing audience, translated into a major ego trip for Marvin. Marvin was winning his battle for recognition, and as his fame grew he became more committed than ever to maintaining and expanding the

Roaming Reporter program.

The one person who emphatically did not appreciate Marvin's fame was Abe Sr. In those days, he still nurtured hopes that he would turn his playboy son into a respectable retailer. But it was not to be.

Each night and into the early hours of the morning, Marvin was seen dashing about town in his bright red Mercury, loaded down with radio equipment. He was gathering on-the-scene reports for his weekly radio program. Marvin did not consider this work. He loved what he was doing, and he worked 14 to 16 hours a day gathering the information, editing and preparing his weekly program. It was truly a one-man show and a labor of love.

The car Marvin drove was originally a pale yellow, and had been purchased as a family vehicle. This, Marvin felt, did not suit his personality as the star of "The MZ Show" or as the "Roaming Reporter." So he had the car painted a brilliant fire-engine red.

Marvin's late wife Gertrude was not a fan of that bright red car. Once, when reminiscing about those days, she confessed, "I hated it. It was too flashy." She also complained that when she was able to persuade Marvin to go out for an evening, he was often distracted by the blaring of the police radios in the car. If the chatter of the police radio announced an event that triggered his news instincts, Marvin's whole attitude would change as if a switch had been thrown. He would roar to action, turn the car in the middle of the street and head for the crime scene.

Gertrude said, "All I could do was clutch the dash for support as he careened around corners, forgetting that I was there. He would leave previously made plans for dinner and a movie in the dust." She continued, "A candlelight dinner in a quiet restaurant just isn't the same after leaving a tragic fire where the smell of burning human flesh and the screams of agony are still with you."

At least she was never bored. "Being with Marvin was one big adventure. He was very unpredictable, but he was never dull. Marvin would go anywhere. It seemed as if no authority could contain his impulse to do what he believed his broadcasting public wanted him to do or what he wanted to do on his own. He would move aside anyone who got in his way of a story. Marvin was truly the first Action News Reporter, and he spiced up the regular news coverage with his blood-and-guts approach to it."

With a twinkle in her eyes and a smile on her face, Gertrude continued. "If he was detained in any way, he would begin a verbal backlash that would usually bring an aghast police chief rushing to his rescue. Remember, Marvin had been a police officer. He knew things and he had an unlimited capacity for embarrassing people who interfered with him during a story. And the police knew it. Marvin was not one you would defy or take lightly." So, despite the interrupted dates and ruined candlelight dinners, Gertrude seemed to savor those exciting times as well. She was always very proud of Marvin.

White Knight in Blue Shades

Marvin's voice graced Houston radio for several years. Throughout this time, the Roaming Reporter always exerted himself for fun rather than profit, caring more about challenge and personal recognition than about money. When he was 28, however, he began getting restless. All of a sudden the whole thing seemed repetitious, dull and just not as much fun as it had been a few years earlier. Marvin wanted to have a daily radio program, but production demands even for the weekly "one-man show" were almost more than he could handle. He could see no way of changing this, and the weekly recognition just wasn't satisfying any more. He had outgrown this gig; it was no longer a challenge to him. As a result, his radio program became lackluster. Marvin began losing his enthusiasm for his job, and found himself sinking to an emotional low. This was highly unusual for such a flamboyant, electrifying performer.

It was then that Marvin feels the angel on his shoulder decided to call some new signals. A major event, almost an evolution in Marvin's life, was soon to present itself.

A new entity had recently established itself in Houston: KPRC-TV, Channel 2, Houston's first television station. It didn't take Marvin long to surmise that this new form of media would not only get his voice but his face before the public.

In 1949, Marvin got a call from Southwest Film Production Company to do a news shoot for KPRC. At that time, few television stations had their own news departments. News was a money-losing proposition, and to avoid the expense of an in-house news department, television stations contracted with outside firms such as Southwest Film Productions. Channel 2 wanted Marvin to do with a movie camera the same thing he was doing on radio. Marvin said he would give it a try, and in 1950 he landed a contract to provide coverage of nighttime police happenings for KPRC, at a set rate of 25 cents for every foot of film used on the air. KPRC hired two other reporters for the daytime shift, and they did it all — not just the reporting, but also the filming, splicing and cutting.

It was an instant success. Marvin's stories were spectacular, and his energetic newsgathering produced an income that rivaled that of some of the executives of the company. At 25 cents a foot for film that made it to the air, his first paycheck totaled $2,500 — not an insignificant chunk of change in the early 1950s. If you think the bosses were happy that he was doing such great work, however, think again. They told Marvin that if he was to continue at that rate, an *immediate* contract revision would be required. A new contract was in fact drawn up, providing Marvin with only $400 a month.

Marvin was not happy about this, and the contract led to the first of many run-ins he would have with Jack Harris, the station manager. He accepted the new contract anyway and, as a crew of one, continued to drag the weighty motion-picture equipment to the scene each evening. Marvin would set it up, including lights if needed, and start the camera, then mount the camera on the tripod, and focus on his subject. This completed, Marvin would set the automatic switch and race up with microphone in hand to do interviews.

This led to more run-ins. Jack Harris and the other executives at KPRC only wanted silent film. The intention was for their writers to prepare the accompanying story at the station after the appropriate cuts were made. Then the on-camera news could be read in conjunction with Marvin's footage.

Marvin, however, was still bent on getting his voice and face before the public, and he wasn't about to let any opportunity pass him by. So he continued to lug the heavy sound equipment around while he provided coverage of nighttime crime news, and he kept on conducting those live interviews.

As Marvin likes to tell it, he was ultimately fired for being "too ugly" for television.[1] In truth, however, KPRC eventually made the decision to form its own news department and produce their own programs, instead of using an outside contractor. So, for whatever reason, Marvin was out of a TV job. It would be more than 20 years before Marvin Zindler's inimitable face and voice would become etched in the consciousness of the viewing public.

But Marvin had learned a lot from this early experience. Although his first venture into TV did not have a happy ending, Marvin asserts, "Without this experience, I could not be doing what I am doing today."

[1] For the full story, see the chapter on Marvin's cosmetic surgeries.

THE NIGHT HAWK:
SHOOT FIRST, ASK QUESTIONS LATER

In the 1940s and 1950s there were three daily newspapers in Houston, Texas. Sadly, only one remains today. The oldest was *The Houston Post,* the city's morning paper, which was referred to at the time as the "old gray mare." Founded in 1880, it was super-conservative, unimaginative and lackluster. This would not always be the case, as the *Post* would undergo many transformations before finally closing its doors in April of 1995. There was even a period in the 1980s when, visually at least, it gave the tabloids a run for their money. But back in the '40s and '50s, it was a thoroughly unremarkable publication.

The giant of the newspapers, housed in a building on Texas Avenue, was the afternoon daily, the *Houston Chronicle.* Rich and powerful, the *Chronicle* exercised the restraint reflected by a well-established ownership. It had first seen the light of day in 1901, and within a year had bought out its afternoon rival, a struggling paper called the *Herald.* Now the leading daily, the *Chronicle* was, by journalistic standards, considered a good newspaper. And unlike Houston's other two dailies, it continued to expand and modernize. Today the *Chronicle* is the lone surviving daily newspaper in Houston.

Bringing up the rear, in terms of both circulation and reputation, was the Scripps Howard newspaper, the *Houston Press* (not to be confused with the free "alternative" weekly that is published today). Founded in 1911, the *Press,* also an afternoon paper, was housed in a dingy, lemon-yellow structure at the corner of Rusk and Charter streets, in a prosperous section of downtown Houston. The *Press's* headquarters was an old building that provided a suitable flavor and atmosphere for a paper that, by journalistic standards, had no standards at all. Too small to cover or carry a wide scope of news, the *Press* was not considered a good newspaper. What it lacked in size and facilities, however, the *Press* made up with editors and a staff that were totally fearless. As a result, in many ways the *Press* was a great newspaper. It specialized in shoot-the-works journalism that, to some, was reminiscent of the Old West. Others felt the *Press* was a throwback to the wide-open flapper and gun-moll era of the 1920s and '30s, in which stories of gangsters such as Machine Gun Willie and Al Capone made the headlines.

The *Press* was always struggling. To keep up its sales and remain on the streets, the *Press* primarily dealt in editorializing splash stories with what the managing editor, Vance Trimble, called "universal appeal." [1] The *Press's* feature stories, and in fact most of its stories, resembled today's tabloids. If you could combine sex, money and murder, especially if an innocent young woman was involved, you would have a front-page headline extravaganza.

Because the *Press* had such a small staff, each reporter had to be as intrepid as ten of the competitors' reporters. They all had to be as fearless as their leader, Trimble, for their constant targets were the sacred cows — in particular, politicians, corporate officials, the school board and the like. As far as the reporters were concerned, these sacred cows were soul food. As one reporter said, "Let's chew them up and spit them out so the public can really see what is going on behind the scenes." They were all looking for that one story that would clinch a front-page, eight-column banner line, which meant a feather in their cap and a bonus in their wallet.

One ex-staffer said, "It was such a fun place to work. They should have charged the employees admission when they came to work in the morning. It was like riding on a drunken trolley car."

Into this milieu came Marvin, in 1952. His stint as a reporter and cameraman doing stories for Channel 2 News had come to an end, and, although he was still on the radio, he was once again in a funk over his radio program, still longing to go to a daily format but barely able to manage the production burden of a weekly show. Things weren't getting any better at the store, either. It seemed to him that he had come to a dead end.

While Marvin was pondering his dilemmas, Vance Trimble was pondering on how he could save his newspaper.

It was probably inevitable that an audacious tabloid such as the *Press* would have an editor who would eventually think of employing Marvin. In fact, Trimble had not only heard of Marvin's antics, but was a fan of his radio program. He was greatly impressed by Marvin's sheer brass; as he once explained, "Marvin waded right into the lines, and never minded stepping on tails either. And he was lucky. He lucked into everything in the world. It must be that angel on his shoulder."

It's hard to imagine the managing editor of either the stuffy *Post* or the respectable *Chronicle* wooing a journalist who had Marvin's flamboyant tendencies. Flamboyance, however, was just what the *Press* was looking for. Accordingly, Trimble put a call into Marvin, asking him if he would consider a position as a "freelance" photographer and

---

[1] Trimble later went on to win a Pulitzer prize for an article on "Nepotism in the Government."

crime reporter.

For Marvin, the timing was perfect. Certainly he was ready for a new challenge, and, more important, he was already visualizing multiple photographs spread throughout the paper, each photo bearing a credit line with his name in large italics. This would bring Marvin the needed recognition he was not getting on a daily basis with his radio program. As a matter of fact, it would satisfy many of his goals and needs. He could still continue his investigative reporting, which he loved, but he could now add a new element: still photography. This would bring yet another dimension to Marvin's depiction of the lurid, the unusual and the grotesque. What could only be verbalized on his radio spots would once again have visuals, in a marginally more permanent form than the images he had shot for the TV news. What's more, his work would once again appear daily, with his name for all the world to see.

After receiving the phone call, Marvin set an appointment with Trimble, knowing in advance that he was going to accept the job. It wasn't that the money was that great. At that time, a staff photographer only made about $95 a week. On the other hand, his father was paying him more than $1,200 a month to keep him in the store, which wasn't small change in the early 1950s. These economic considerations didn't stop Marvin from jumping at the chance to work for the *Press*.

Just to be on the safe side, and in order not to dampen Marvin's natural enthusiasm, Trimble offered a further reward to his new photographer: an additional incentive of $5 for every one of his pictures used in his paper, with a guaranteed minimum of eight photos a day. (Even Vance Trimble didn't realize he had a bull by its tail. In a very short time it was not at all uncommon for the newspaper to carry 15 or more of Marvin's pictures in a single edition.)

One problem remained to be solved before Marvin could hop aboard the "drunken trolley car" as a freelance shutterbug for the *Press:* Marvin had never used a press camera. He had become pretty handy with a movie camera when he was doing the reports for Channel 2 news, but he didn't have the faintest idea of how to work a press camera. So, after signing the contract with the additional incentives, Marvin was given a few basic instructions on how to use the camera.

It turned out not to be a problem. Marvin was a quick study, and added one more skill to his growing repertoire. He now had everything he needed to be a top-notch tabloid photographer: basic photographic skills, of course, but also a gift of gab, the know-how of a policeman and the theatrical skills gained from his radio broadcasting. He would use these skills to produce on-the-spot photographs in unusual and intriguing angles that met the newspaper's — and, more specifically, Trimble's — need for "universal appeal."

Marvin quickly fell in step with the newspaper. He did most of his photography at night, because that's when most of the action occurred. He still worked at the store during the day, under difficult, if not strained, conditions, and he listened to the police radios and covered the stories at night. He put in eighteen hours a day, but he loved it.

Marvin suddenly found himself with new challenges, but he was happiest when challenged. He was blazing a new trail to stardom. Each day when he opened the newspaper, it was not so much the photographs that gave him a burst of pride as the bold, italicized credit line: **STAFF PHOTOGRAPHER MARVIN ZINDLER**. This did not appear on just one page, but on page after page throughout the edition. His name was prominent; he was finally in the public's eye, not on a weekly but on a daily basis. This rejuvenated him.

In his bright red automobile — still loaded with police radios and now with his press camera, which sat on the seat next to him — he sped from one investigation to the next. Marvin, now nicknamed the "Night Hawk" was unstoppable. With his flair for theatrics, he could always spot a story. When other reporters would come upon a scene and leave shortly thereafter because they'd found nothing newsworthy, Marvin would stay. In his mind's eye, he would always see what they couldn't, and he enjoyed the challenge and triumph of finding a story where no one else could. Besides, he reasoned, why waste time and a tank of gas getting there if you can't turn it into a headline? Marvin believed in creating the news, not just covering a news story. In this aspect, Marvin was way ahead of his time. He was visionary. He knew what the public wanted, and he was going to give it to them.

It was this flair that the other reporters and photographers — even most of the "Poison Pens" working for the *Press* — lacked.

A typical story would begin when Marvin, listening to the police radio in his car, would hear a routine summons to investigate a shooting. At once he was on his way, and so, of course, were other photographers from competing newspapers. When they arrived, more often than not they would learn that it was essentially a family quarrel, and no one had been shot. Family disturbances were common then as now and, unless there was a fatality, they usually did not make the news — until Marvin came along. The other photographers would leave in disgust, but not Marvin. For Marvin could see a story in the making. He would get a photo of the principals — perhaps an intoxicated, gun-wielding man comforting a disheveled woman, who was holding an infant in her arms while the police stood in the background. The headline the next day would be a grabber: "Hubby Fires at Wife and Baby." In typical tabloid fashion, the story would be written with a few details of the quarrel and a spicy description of the shooting, even though nobody had been injured.

Two photos Marvin took following a family fight truly display his gift for bringing out readers' empathy for his hapless subjects. The first photo shows a wounded man lying on a stretcher at the hospital, being comforted by his wife. Marvin's caption reads, "Bang! Bang! It's All In The Family." Not much of a story? Perhaps, but in Marvin's view, and the *Press's*, it was certainly better than nothing. Marvin's "special touch" is even more apparent in the second of the two photos. Taken in the hospital parking lot, it shows two poorly-clad little urchins leaning out a car window, patiently waiting for their mother to return.

The caption under this photo reads, "Daddy Is Shot and Uncle Tom Shot Him." An entire little drama is all there in black and white, accompanied, of course, by Marvin's name under each photo.

One quiet evening the "Night Hawk" was about to doze off when he heard the police radio begin to crackle that a woman was attempting suicide. Marvin arrived at the scene in minutes, as did other newspapermen and photographers. When they saw the woman had obviously failed in her attempt, or perhaps had simply decided not to follow through, they left. Marvin got his photo anyway. The woman was being embraced and consoled by two police officers, and though her face was turned away from the camera, it was obvious that she was crying. Marvin took full advantage of the photo opportunity, and the result was carried the next morning with the headline, "Woman Tried to Shoot Herself, Missed."

The police radio again came to life, requisitioning two officers to go to a local bar where a fight was in progress. By the time Marvin got there, it was all over. The police weren't even going to make an arrest, just issue a warning. Two slightly tipsy men, their hair a mess, shirts torn, and one with a shoe missing, were sitting quietly in a corner talking to the police officers. At the other side of the bar, sitting smugly upright, was a very attractive redhead. There wasn't enough in the story to run it in the *Chronicle* or even put it on the evening news. That didn't stop Marvin. He took a photo of the two gentlemen at such an angle as to portray the attractive redhead directly behind them at the bar. The next morning the headline read, "Two Fight To Take The Redhead Home!" Obviously that changed the whole flavor and direction of the story. It gave the readers a chance to allow their imaginations to run astray.

Marvin's creativity took all forms. In his own neighborhood, a pretty young woman had been stopped for speeding. This was hardly a newsworthy event, yet she saw herself in the paper the next day. Her mistake was sticking her tongue out at the photographer. This was all that was needed to turn a routine traffic stop into a photo opportunity, and with the right caption, it went to press the next morning. I'm sure lots of tongues were aimed in Marvin's direction by his angry subjects — not to mention a few middle fingers, fists, and probably a lot more — but the "Night Hawk" remained undaunted.

Marvin always went out with the intention of getting a story. When the elements of journalistic trash — attempted murder, the suggestion of sex, or random pathos — were not at the scene of the action, Marvin still knew how to make it appear that they were there. He was brilliant at using events to his advantage.

And the readers loved it. His was the type of brassy journalism that they ate up, because it was a diversion from the routine of their everyday lives. Marvin gave them what they wanted, not just with his photos, but with his short, catchy headlines and captions. Perception was what it was all about; Zindler's photos and captions put a "newsworthy" angle on mundane events, and they certainly sold newspapers. It was during his stint as the "Night Hawk" that Marvin learned a powerful truth: almost everything involving people can produce reader appeal if the "right" photograph is taken and it is properly packaged and merchandised. Even what Marvin called "low gossip" could result in high interest if packaged appropriately.

Victor Little, a conservative urban columnist of the day, wrote in amazement about the "Night Hawk": "We in the newspaper business are a little embarrassed about that phenomenon Zindler, the man whose mind clicks like a camera shutter. It seems as though the evolutionary process has nudged Marvin, carried him out and beyond the usual in this business."

He went on to write that the "Night Hawk" was "the hottest lensman in Houston, the hottest we have ever seen operate anywhere." The same could not be said of the *Press* staff photographers or those of other newspapers, he wrote, adding, "If they were all Zindlers, they would all get fired — probably."

What made Marvin different from the others was that news photographers were trained to think of photos in connection with the news story: their photos were taken to illustrate what the reporter was to write about. Of course, nobody had told Marvin this. His only training for the job had consisted of those ten minutes or so of instructions on how to load and shoot the camera. Beyond that, he was told to "use his instincts."

And use them he did. He would look at a situation and think of it in terms of the photo he was going to take, and only in terms of that photo. He got his photo first and asked questions, if necessary, later. The story would revolve around the photograph, rather than the photograph supporting the story — just the opposite of what had been taught all these years in photography classes and journalism schools. Marvin, however, had the clear advantage of being neither a photographer nor a journalist. He made up his own rules as he went along, and with Marvin, no one knew what to expect next; even his editor, Vance Trimble, was regularly taken by surprise.

The *Press's* circulation was mounting, due in no small part to Marvin's photo essays. But Marvin encountered the ire of the paper's ownership, and he says it's because "I did my job too well." Scripps Howard's CEO was a man named Roy Howard, who had never really approved of the blood-and-guts approach to newspapering. Howard felt newspapers should be more substantial and that the sensationalist publications had no future. Was he ever wrong. Over the past several decades, there has been less and less editorializing and more and more sensationalism. And those who have learned how to combine the two — often employing what has come to be called "infotainment" — have continued to produce greater and greater circulation and maintain their audiences.

But Roy Howard was a purist, and personally cringed at Marvin's work, which he saw as yellow journalism. Never mind that Marvin's photo essays titillated the *Press's* readership and produced greater circulation. Fortunately, at least in Marvin's eyes, Howard was at the home office in New York City. What Marvin didn't realize was that Howard's tentacles stretched all the way to Houston, and the "Night Hawk" was now under close scrutiny by his editor Vance Trimble.

So Marvin just continued doing what he did best. He was becoming more and more aggressive, and it was this aggressiveness that ultimately caused some real problems. One night Marvin was in his car when the police radio began to come to life. A crime scene had been discovered across town, and Marvin knew that he wouldn't be able to get there in time to get the type of pictures he wanted. So, snatching up the car radio, he contacted police headquarters and ordered the police dispatcher to have the officers leave everything untouched until he arrived. Today, leaving the scene untouched until it has been photographed is considered Basic Criminology 101. But that was not always the case in the 1950s. And almost certainly it has never been standard police procedure to allow a tabloid photographer to call the shots, as it were. But then, Marvin has never concerned himself with "standard procedure."

Marvin was threatened with jail on numerous occasions because police felt he had tampered with the evidence by moving it around the crime scene in order to get a better photograph. One story even intimates that Marvin, upon arriving at the scene of a stabbing, convinced the victim to lie still while he, Marvin poured a bottle of ketchup over his chest. The reason? The victim didn't seem to be hurt badly enough to warrant getting the picture in the paper.

Whether this is true or not, Marvin won't say. What is known is that managing editor Trimble called Marvin to the carpet for this. "He lied to me and told he didn't do it," Trimble once said, "but I knew he did it and he knew I knew. I don't think he ever did anything quite like it again."

The ketchup incident is not entirely implausible, given that Marvin knew the value of props, and had a gift for talking anybody into anything. Marvin would persuade crime scene subjects to reenact the drama, which, of course, gave more action and drama to his photos. Marvin was known to show up at a robbery scene where victims had been tied, their mouths taped and they had been pistol-whipped. By the time Marvin arrived, the victims had been untied and were being comforted by police and medical personnel. Others were still hysterical. Marvin would introduce himself and, speaking softly, one by one he would talk the crime victims into letting him reposition them and reenact the ordeal. Somehow he'd even talk them into letting him tie them up again, tape their mouths and put them down on the floor or wherever it happened.

Only Marvin could get away with this. What's more, the victims did it willingly and afterwards seemed less hysterical and more objective in how they envisioned the robbery. Again, Marvin was ahead of his time. He didn't know it then, but his habit of "reenacting the crime scene" was another technique that would eventually be used routinely in investigative work. Reenactment is often done today at the actual crime scene or in the courtroom. At the time, of course, Marvin didn't give a damn about the investigation. He just wanted his photo.

And so he continued with his splashy journalistic exploits, which continued to cause problems with his editor and the CEO in New York, and also with his father, who was embarrassed by Marvin's exploits. Abe was still trying to bring Marvin back into the safe and respectable environment of the clothing store, but Marvin continued to resist.

Despite its shortcomings, the *Press* was a very popular paper, and had four editions a day during the early 1950s. No newspaper could do that today. The third edition at the end of the day was referred to as the Final Home Edition; this was the one that was shipped to New York for CEO Roy Howard to review. Knowing Mr. Howard's aversion to blood-and-guts journalism, Trimble made the decision to use Marvin's pictures in the early City Edition and in the First Home Edition. The photos were then pulled for the edition that would be sent to New York for Howard's scrutiny. After that, Marvin's pictures would reappear for street sales in the evening's Night Final.

The plan seemed to work pretty well until, unbeknownst to the *Houston Press* staff, Roy Howard was on a business trip in Tokyo. On his way back from Tokyo, he had a stopover in Houston before continuing on to New York. It was only natural that he would purchase a copy of his firm's newspaper and read it while waiting. It didn't take but a few minutes of skimming the Early Edition of the newspaper — which happened to contain more than 15 photos by the "Night Hawk" — to inspire Howard to leave the airport and take a taxi for downtown Houston. He stormed unannounced into the newspaper office.

Marvin remembers that the particular edition Mr. Howard read contained a picture that filled almost half of the front page, showing an intoxicated woman sitting on a bar stool in a beer joint. She had a screaming kid in her lap, and the headline read, "Isn't This Enough To Make You Sick?" This alone was enough to make his boss, Mr. Howard, sick when he saw it in his newspaper.

Marvin laughs about it today, but the next day he was called into the editor's office, where Trimble told Marvin he would have to give up night hawking and become a full-time staff photographer. That meant taking assignments and prescribed photo coverage. "They wanted to send me out to the goddamned zoo and photograph the society crowd around the Shamrock pool," he muttered. "It told them 'pee on it.'"

The problem was that Marvin really didn't want to give up newspapering. Reluctantly he accepted the new terms, and soon found a new way to make his mark. The "Night Hawk's" wings had been clipped, but his talons were still as sharp. Now instead of the crime beat, it was Houston's café society that came under the ravages of his hungry lens. Marvin met many interesting, if not legendary, individuals during his forays into this mostly after-hours culture of the rich and famous, which he referred to as "The Sun Downers Society."

He began to focus on a brother and sister duo from the wealthy King Ranch family, Shepherd King III and his sister Pat. Marvin was out to capture their lively antics in the posh cafés and clubs about Houston, and there was plenty to capture.

Pat King aspired to be a singer. She wore low-cut dresses and leaned over much too often. No one said she was not intelligent, but she was unrestrained as she partied her way through the clubs and cafés of the Sun Downers Society.

Her brother, Shepherd, was no slouch in the swanky clubs either. It was well known that he loved wine, women and a good time, but he was eventually smitten by one Samia Gamal, the Egyptian actress and belly dancer (who also claimed to be an ex-paratrooper). Samia, whom Egypt's King Farouk had proclaimed to be "The National Dancer of Egypt," had come to the United States in 1950. American culture at the time was fascinated with the exotic, as evidenced by the endless stream of "Arabian Nights" movies that appeared in the late 1940s and early 1950s. Samia ignited this fascination, becoming truly famous in the U.S. when *Life* Magazine published a photo spread of her in full belly-dancing regalia, with a glowing light bulb in her navel.

After a short but exciting courtship with Miss Gamal, Shepherd King changed his first name to Abdullah and became a Muslim in hopes of marrying her. This was followed by anonymous threats from both families, and finally rumors that the King family would disinherit Shepherd, or, rather, Abdullah. But they married anyway. By wedding a Texas millionaire, Samia Gamal truly established her place as a media star.

The gossip columnists were having a field day with this mismatched pair. They couldn't keep up with the public antics of Samia and Abdullah, who one moment would be in each other's arms and the next would be at each other's throats. The two would also team up and tangle with passersby, just for excitement. One memorable scene occurred when some over-admiring men at a ritzy club made advances to Samia, accompanied by loud comments about her anatomy. Shepherd-Abdullah was somewhat intoxicated, but felt compelled to defend Samia through honorable combat. He was badly outnumbered, but the power of alcohol in these situations seems to defy reality, and he charged into battle: the knight in half-Scotch, half-water. Honorable though his intentions may have been, it quickly became apparent, to everyone else but him, that he was losing.

Seeing his gallant efforts on her behalf, Samia could only do what any good ex-paratrooper would. She grabbed the first weapon available, her three-inch spiked heels, and leaped into the fray. Bystanders later recalled her high-pitched and frightening war cry in Arabic. The outcome of the fray quickly changed as those spiked heels made their impression in the tops of the attackers' skulls, amidst more startling war cries. The rednecks who'd insulted her were crawling along the floor. As soon as they got out of range of the three-inch spikes, they struggled to their feet with what was left of their scalps and made a dash for the exit. This drew applause from the nightclub audience.

Due to the flimsiness of Samia's gown, it was now apparent exactly what the over-admiring men were commenting on. In fact, by this point it was difficult to tell whether the audience was applauding Mrs. King's heroic actions on behalf of her husband, or her very visible and most abundant anatomy. In short, it was not just a gossip columnist's dream, but a photographer's paradise. Marvin, naturally, was in heaven.

He began to dog the Kings, with the result that they were constantly featured in the newspaper. Their antics continued until one evening, after a rather violent public argument, it was rumored that they had split up. You can't believe everything you read, though, and Marvin was determined to either confirm or deny the rumor. He staked out their mansion; you might go so far as to say that he cased the joint. Regardless, he showed a lot of guts by sneaking into their home at night. He removed his shoes and tiptoed down the hall to the master bedroom, only to discover them entwined in each other's arms, asleep on satin sheets.

For a moment, but only a moment, Marvin had a twinge of conscience for breaking and entering. Technically speaking, though, there was really no "breaking," as people didn't lock their houses at that time. There was an invasion of privacy, but certainly it was all in the line of duty; Marvin had to prove that the rumor about their breakup was false, didn't he? A picture would do it. Marvin positioned himself directly over the bed and adjusted the camera. Granted, he was a bit fearful of what would happen when the flash bulb went off, but he couldn't let that stop him. After all, the picture was everything.

Marvin had preplanned his escape and again went over the route, making mental notes. Finally, with a slightly shaky hand, he raised the camera, hit the trigger and got his picture. When the flash went off, it seemed like fireworks in the stillness of the night... but the couple did not move.

Marvin didn't wait around; in a moment he was at the door. Glancing over his shoulder, he could still see that they were wrapped in each other's arms, completely unaware of his presence. The photo appeared in the morning's edition, pointing out that "Love Prevailed." The Kings were still together — at least for that evening. Later on they were divorced. It also came out that Shepherd King, or Abdullah, actually had only about $50,000 to his name.

It was in the opulent smoky world of the Sun Downers Society that Marvin met the legendary multimillionaire oilman "Silver Dollar" Jim West. West became one of Marvin's roaming comrades of the era. "Silver Dollar" Jim got his nickname because of his habit of flinging handfuls of freshly minted silver dollars into the street in front of crowds. He usually directed them to youngsters. A handful of silver dollars was a lot of money at the time, and his was an altruistic and philanthropic endeavor. But he also did it for entertainment; Jim West simply liked watching the antics that took place as the kids scampered for the cash.

Marvin once asked him why he threw the money into the street instead of handing it to each child. Jim West said, "Everybody ought to work a little bit for what they get."

West's financial empire was well organized. When he wasn't working, Jim spent much of his time trying to avoid boredom. Marvin's experience as an ex-cop, and his immense popularity as a photographer of the lurid, intrigued Jim West. The truth was that the two had much in common. West, like Marvin, got a thrill out of a close association with the police and the seedy life they watched over. Like Marvin with his red Mercury, Jim West had his blue Cadillac limousine, outfitted with police radios and police gear and, some said, even weaponry. Marvin rode with West numerous times, but the catch was that he had to promise not to take any pictures. In fact, he had to promise to leave his camera behind. To Marvin, it felt as if he were leaving a part of himself behind.

West was basically shy and perhaps a lonesome man in many ways. "He was a little embarrassed when he saw his photo and name in print," Marvin recalls. When West died, 50,000 silver dollars, in mint condition, were found still un-flung in the basement of his River Oaks mansion.

Marvin's father now had even more reasons to complain that his son was a playboy, squandering his time and talent in the society watering holes about Houston. To Abe, this was a definite step down. It was not distasteful work; in fact it was often humorous and it led to some interesting photos, but it was not police reporting. Worse than that, in Abe's opinion anyway, it was not the clothing business.

As it happened, Marvin himself was growing rather jaded by this point. Despite the entertainment value provided by the capers of the well-heeled, Marvin quickly tired of the "Got-damned Sun Downers and Houston's posh clubs." He put up with it awhile, but eventually, as he explains, "I said, 'pee on it' and I meant it."

With the recurrent and daily disappointments at the newspaper, and the fact that Marvin's mother was growing ill, Marvin became more amenable to his father's efforts to pull him back into the family business. When Abe Sr. made Marvin the offer he couldn't refuse — an excess of $2,000 a month if he returned to the store full time — Marvin actually thought his father might be growing mellow. But Abe was not growing as mellow as Marvin thought. The alternative he presented was for Marvin to be cut off entirely and forced to live on his *Press* salary of less than $400 a month.

So Marvin put his press camera away and went back to the retailing life. Over the next several years he made a sincere attempt to become the businessman his father wanted him to be, until he could stand it no longer, and took his great career leap into the Sheriff's Department. Scripps-Howard closed the *Press* in 1964, selling the physical assets to the *Houston Chronicle*. The heyday of "yellow journalism" in Houston was over for good.

Leaving the *Press* might have spelled the end of Marvin's media career. From World War II through the late 1950s, he had been on radio, on TV, and in print; he had, indeed, tried a little of everything. He had been successful for awhile, sometimes immensely so, but his media jobs had always ended in frustration and disappointment. Maybe it was time to turn away from all that and find his life's work elsewhere.

But remember, this is Marvin we're talking about. He did try other work, work that truly engaged him, but he never got his fill of having his face and name before the public. And along the way, particularly after he joined the sheriff's department, he found something else for which he had an insatiable hunger: helping others. Eventually he was to return to the media — specifically, television — in a big way, whereupon he would have the opportunity to indulge his appetite for both publicity and activism on an unprecedented scale.

"MAAAAAARVIN ZINDLER, EYEWITNESS NEWS!"
THE WHITE KNIGHT CHARGES BACK ONTO THE AIRWAVES

When Marvin lost his job at the Harris County Sheriff's Department in 1972, he felt for the first time in his life that the angel on his shoulder had abandoned him. He knew that his firing was a political move that bore little if any relation to the merit of his work; very simply, he had rubbed too many politicians and businessmen the wrong way, and the newly elected sheriff, Jack Heard, couldn't afford to keep him. But this did little to mollify Marvin; he was still out of a job, and it was a job he had loved.

In actuality, Marvin's angel had not deserted him at all but was setting the stage for the most exciting chapter in his life: a position that was perfectly suited to his very flamboyant personality and his more than 10 years of experience in law enforcement. Soon he would have the opportunity to do more good for his fellow human beings than any TV personality in history. Once again, whether you want to credit a guardian angel, fate or just plain good luck, Marvin Zindler ended up in the right place at the right time.

In the early 1970s, KTRK-TV (Channel 13), Houston's ABC network affiliate, was lagging behind the competition. Originally owned by Judge Roy Hofheinz and several other Houston investors, KTRK had been sold to Capital Cities Communication Corporation, a New York-based firm that owned several other TV stations.[1] Capital Cities management had felt that Houston would be a very lucrative market and they could turn a profit. But they were faced with a real challenge.

The problem was that Channel 13 was in a dismal third place in the commercial station rankings, behind NBC affiliate KPRC (Channel 2) and the CBS affiliate, KHOU (Channel 11). In addition, the two existing UHF entities, Channels 39 and 26, which were independent stations at the time, were beginning to give the big boys a run for their money. Even Channel 8, the public station, was creating additional competition.

Basically, ratings equal dollars. A multitude of programming makes up a station's "profit centers," and usually, the evening news programs — which are broadcast at 6:00 and 10:00 PM in the Houston market — are an enormous profit center. Because both of these broadcasts are widely watched, advertisers pay a premium price for commercial time. In the early 1970s, a network affiliate in Houston could make a 600% profit, or even up to double that amount, on its prime-time-news ad spots — not bad if you could get the ratings.

Channel 13 was in third place mainly because more viewers tuned into the news of Channels 2 and 11. As a result, the bottom line was that the rates Channel 13 could charge for its commercial time were significantly lower — only half the rate of the other stations. Besides the fact that Channel 13's rates were lower than those of its competitors, there were also holes in its advertising schedule during the prime-time news forecasts; spots were available but had not been purchased.

Everyone knew this could not continue for long. You can't lose money and keep broadcasting. Channel 13 needed to boost its prime-time news ratings, and it needed to do it soon. So Capital Cities brought in teams of consultants to analyze and make recommendations on how the station could change its image in order to attract larger audiences and become more profitable. The task of these TV analysts, or "news doctors," was to diagnose the problem and make suggestions to KTRK's management on how to produce a more glamorous and attractive on-screen image. One way to quickly increase the ratings, the consultants advised, was to produce a more polished prime-time news program. The New York news doctors recommended that the budget for the news department be doubled, that additional reporters be hired and the news coverage be broadened.

Channel 13's management had also been brainstorming on ways to increase the ratings. They had been considering features that might be added to the traditional news, weather and sports lineup, and one of the possibilities they considered was a consumer advocate. Consumer advocacy in the Houston media was not a new idea. Channel 2, the dominant local station at that time, had introduced a consumer expert, Roberta Hammond, into their news segment several years earlier. Additionally, the two daily newspapers had been in the consumer-watchdog game for some time; the *Houston Chronicle* had its "Action Line," and the *Houston Post* had "Watch'em."

---

[1] Capital Cities was bought out by Disney in the mid 1990s.

Channel 13's news producer, Garvin Berry, wrote a memo detailing the ways in which a consumer advocate would attract community interest and, as such, would be a valuable asset not only to Channel 13 but to Houston. Berry suggested the home office consider this idea for a possible additional feature to the usual news lineup. The news doctors from New York City thought Berry's plan was interesting, and agreed that a consumer advocate would be of great value to the Houston community. The problem was that its inception seemed more expensive than the news budget at KTRK would allow.

To save time, trouble and production costs, the New York consultants suggested the purchase of "pre-packaged" or "canned" consumer material. This was seriously considered, but the available pre-packaged material seemed bland and uninteresting. What Channel 13 really needed to make this feature work was some local color and flavor.

They soon found more than they had bargained for.

Word had leaked out that Marvin Zindler — the flamboyant ex-news photographer, sheriff's deputy and hero of the underdog — had just been fired from the sheriff's department. And suddenly everything came together to provide a shot in the arm not only for Channel 13, but for Marvin's career.

One night late in 1972, recalls long-time Channel 13 news anchor Dave Ward, "I had just finished the evening's newscast. Gene Burke[2] was sitting across from me. I was just winding down from completing the news and I looked up at Gene.

"Almost simultaneously we said something like, 'Why don't we get Marvin Zindler as a consumer reporter?' The idea, strange as it may sound, had hit Gene and me at the same time."

It was approximately 7:00 PM, and Marvin, not in a very good mood, had retired to his favorite armchair at home. Home, as it happened, was just three miles from the Channel 13 studios. Marvin had been moping about the house all day, wondering what he was going to do now that he had lost his job at the sheriff's department. He was 51 years old, and the prospect of starting all over at his age was hardly appealing. On this particular evening, he had been sitting in silence for more than an hour, somewhat glumly contemplating his future, when the silence was broken by the ring of the telephone.

Dave Ward remembers, "The telephone rang several times, then Marvin picked up the phone. I told him what Gene Burke and I were thinking about. I asked Marvin if he would consider coming over to the station as a consumer reporter."

Marvin, Dave recalls, exclaimed, "Dave, you must have been reading my mind. It must be ESP. There is nothing I would rather do than come over and discuss that very thing with you."

---

[2] Gene Burke was Channel 13's assistant news director and producer at the time.

It was agreed that Marvin would meet with several of the KTRK executives, and a time was set. As it happened, Marvin had also made an appointment earlier that same day to meet with Ray Miller at Channel 2. That appointment was never kept.

The executives at Channel 13 all had at least a passing familiarity with Marvin, as the news department had from time to time participated in stories with him while he was a deputy sheriff. They were all aware of his penchant for the theatrical, his flashy way of dressing, his outgoing manner and his instinct for unusual stories. They were also aware that Marvin was very familiar with Houston's political and business powers, as well as its social structure. Having Marvin on board could be very advantageous.

Nevertheless, because he was so different from the average TV news reporter, and because station executives are normally a conservative lot, you might think their meeting with Marvin would be the cause of some unsettlement. Not so, for it was not the flamboyant, verbose Marvin who showed up at this first meeting. In the presence of relative strangers, Marvin is extremely soft-spoken and presents an almost shy demeanor. The meeting went well, the KTRK executives were impressed, and they hired Marvin on the spot.

One of those who attended the meeting remembered Marvin declaring his loyalty by saying, "This union will be like a marriage: for better or for worse."

This impressed the KTRK executives. Just as they were ready to leave, however, a flicker of apprehension and a foreboding of things to come may have occurred when Marvin promised "to show enough shine to make the station look like a used car lot."

And so began the White Knight's longest and greatest crusade.

Marvin was hired at Channel 13 in secret, but, of course, it didn't stay a secret for long. With typical Zindler fanfare, Marvin held a press conference immediately following the signing of his contract on January 4, 1973.

There had been a lot of buzz following Marvin's ousting from the sheriff's department. Everyone anticipated that he would be extremely angry and bitter, and they were waiting to see what he would do. Rumors abounded about the circumstances of his being let go. There was talk that Jack Heard had merely encouraged Marvin to resign, but that it was to be only for a two- to three-month "cooling down" period, and then he would rehire Marvin. Other rumors circulated that Heard had fired Marvin outright but didn't want it to appear that way. In any event, no one knew exactly what Marvin planned to do, and everyone who was invited to the press conference was guessing at what Marvin was going to say. The rumors made it even more tantalizing.

Naturally, no one from Houston's news media was about to miss this press conference. Everyone expected Marvin would reveal some deep, dark secrets he had uncovered while working in the sheriff's department. They anticipated that he would give them the inside scoop on city politics and much more, presented, of course, with the Zindler dramatic flair.

When all the reporters from the newspapers, radio and TV stations were in place, Marvin quietly and undramatically informed them that he would be joining KTRK-TV 13. And this did indeed take everyone by surprise. Not even the Channel 13 reporters who were present had had any idea what his announcement would be. A ripple went through the assemblage; newspaper reporters snickered as they scribbled their notes, and television crews from Channels 2 and 11 shut their cameras down.

A new round of speculations began. Bets were made with odds of 10-to-1 that Marvin wouldn't last at his new gig. Some were betting that because Marvin had probably made as many enemies in Houston as he had friends, he would cause the station to lose advertisers — and, as a result, he would get fired. Others were betting that Marvin's directness and his aggressive "He who attacks first wins the war" approach would result in the station getting sued. In turn, Marvin would get fired. Still others felt Marvin would be cautious at first, but once he felt at ease, he would get more and more reckless — and as a result of this recklessness he would get fired. Others felt that in time, adverse viewer response in the crazy, show-business world of commercial television would result in a ratings drop, which would lead to Marvin's getting fired. There were also a few who felt that because television, as a visual medium, was "a pretty-boy business," Marvin didn't stand a chance. After all, reporters and anchors had been yanked because of the shape of their ears, the cut of their hair or their wardrobe. Marvin was considered by some to be homely (despite his cosmetic surgeries), and his dress too gaudy for a news program. As such, he would get fired. Then there were those who predicted Marvin would simply burn out: he would muster all the flair, zest and dramatics of a soap opera, and though he might be a hit for awhile, his appeal would be short-lived. Then, of course, Marvin would get fired.

So Marvin stepped into his new role at Channel 13 with most of his colleagues in the media, if not most of the rest of Houston, betting against him. Regardless of the odds, Marvin was determined to succeed, and was more convinced than ever that he had a secret weapon, an angel on his shoulder.

As it turned out, many of the naysayers' predictions came true in a very short time, but the most significant prophecy of all never came to pass — Marvin never got fired. In fact, in time Marvin was one of only two individuals to ever receive a lifetime contract with ABC-TV.

In a business which seemed to go out of its way to create uniformity in its talking heads, Marvin's differences were immediately apparent. It wasn't long before his high-percussion delivery began to rattle the executives at KTRK. At first the powers behind the scene tried to get Marvin to tone down his delivery, and Dave Ward was secretly assigned to give Marvin "a few lessons in television technique." Dave says, "Marvin was strenuously resisting these changes. But we also saw that he was getting an audience reaction to his own style of doing things. We realized we would be changing something quite unique if we made him conform to the usual format. The executives at the station decided to leave Marvin alone and see where it took him."

It wasn't just the executives who were bothered by Marvin's glaring dissimilarity to the TV-news norm; the other anchors and reporters at the station winced at his style and delivery as well. Some of the news anchors considered him undignified and found his consistent mangling of the English language embarrassing. These traits only set him further apart from the carefully cultivated flawlessness of the typical anchor. But even the perfectionists had to admit he could be entertaining, if unwittingly so; Marvin's wild semantic somersaults held the ears of his listeners, many of whom couldn't wait to hear what he would say next.

Mangled language and misplaced theatrics notwithstanding, Marvin had the courage to be radically different in a business which fostered homogeneity. And, love him or loathe him, you couldn't overlook him. Wrote *Houston Chronicle* television critic Ann Hodges in 1973: "If you put all the people on local television in a barrel and drew them out one at a time, you would see there is something the same about them. You get the feeling they all look alike, get their hair cut at the same place. They all dress alike, talk alike and act alike. Not literally, of course, but there is a *sameness*. Marvin is certainly different."

What immediately set Marvin apart more than anything else was his blunt style of delivery. Here was a man who called a spade a spade and wasn't afraid to get toe-to-toe with those in the business community who had broken faith with their customers. No soft-spoken hero with a big stick, Marvin bellowed his allegations and didn't care whose sensibilities he offended in the process. In his role as consumer's hero, he was always on the attack. Marvin rushed into battle with a figurative samurai sword in one hand and a copy of this or that regulation, ordinance or commercial code in the other. His was an honorable battle for ethical business practices, fought on behalf of "the man in the street," and Marvin seemed perfectly willing, almost eager, to kill or be killed. He stopped short of accusing some of the best-known and most respected business firms in the city of actual planned thievery. It was somewhat of a Robin Hood effect, the difference being that Marvin Zindler wasn't stealing from the rich as much as he was giving back to the poor what had been unfairly taken from them.

When asked how he developed his vociferous style, or whether it was left over from dramatics required during his radio era, Marvin said, "It's the way I am. It's just me. That's the way I see it and that's the way I do it."

In any case, the public seemed to love his style, and, more than that, they loved the results he delivered. Marvin not only uncovered the business villains but slashed them down to size with his sword. It wasn't long before a dedicated following developed. And even as the other anchors and reporters at the station, and the station managers, watched and winced, the ratings began to go up, and they kept on rising.

Says Dave Ward with a grin, "No doubt about it. We created a monster."

What does Marvin say in response to remarks about his... uniqueness? Well, as he explains it, "I raised a lot of hell but in reality I am very much a company man... [My bosses know] I raise a lot of hell, but underneath I am thinking about the station and the programming." He pauses for a minute, then continues, "If I stay on top, the station stays on top."

The ride to the top, however, was not exactly a smooth one at first, for Marvin or the station. The effect of Marvin's hiring at Channel 13 was initially felt in KTRK's sales department and the "bottom line." Several large advertisers almost immediately cancelled. One was a car dealership that Marvin, as a deputy sheriff, had stung on several occasions as the result of odometer roll-backs. Over the next several months, other advertisers would cancel as Marvin charged his way through Houston businesses at the head of his one-man crusade.

KTRK's management was upset, and no wonder. However, they were determined to honor their contract and give Marvin a chance. Their gamble paid off; Marvin's television following became so huge, and Channel 13's ratings peaked to such heights, that new advertisers were waiting in line to buy prime-time news spots. Very soon the demand exceeded the available spots, and as the demand increased, the rates did too.

Of the advertisers who had cancelled because of Marvin's presence at KTRK, Dave Ward said, "We have the viewers! If the advertiser wants to cut off his nose and cancel, then he is a foolish businessman." Although the station initially lost as much as a quarter million in advertising, that really could not be counted as lost revenue. With Marvin on the team, Channel 13 eventually doubled its ratings and more than quadrupled its advertising dollars. The sales department, and the KTRK executives, were obliged to accept a new equation: Ratings equal dollars, and Marvin equals ratings.

Though some of the big advertisers were displeased and management was uneasy at first, the viewers took to their new consumer watchdog from the beginning. From this perspective, Marvin was an instant success. Letters and calls began to cascade in, and the station had to hire additional assistants and researchers to handle the deluge.

Gene Burke, who along with Dave Ward had had the idea to recruit Marvin for Channel 13 in the first place, became one of his greatest champions. He entered some of Marvin's stories in the 1973-74 Texas Associated Press contest, and Marvin won a first-place award for news reporting. Marvin and Gene became close friends, and Marvin was a pallbearer at Gene's funeral in the late 1990s.

A few years after coming on board at Channel 13, Marvin was separated from the news department and took on an identity of his own. There was also a change in title from Eyewitness News reporter to "Action 13's Marvin Zindler." As letters continued to pour in, additional help was needed, and Marvin hired a part-time personal assistant, Mrs. Donna Gordon. She was efficient and hard-working, and many at the station thought she was very aptly placed, as she had a college degree in zoology. Even in those early years at Channel 13, someone was trying to tell Marvin something.

∾ • ∾

Marvin's knack for bringing in viewers and helping ratings soar didn't stop station management from tinkering with success over the years. There was the time, for example, when the station executives were determined to break the cardinal rule that states, *If it ain't broke, don't fix it.* They decided that Marvin's glaring sign-off should be changed. The station had run periodic public surveys, and a recent poll showed that among the 13% who didn't like him, most cited as the prime factor his trademark "Maaaaaarvin Zindler," which they perceived as arrogant.

Surprisingly, Marvin surrendered to management without firing so much as a single volley. His refusal to fight them was not only surprising, it was actually more shocking than his high-voltage fits. But Marvin felt they were wrong, and he was going to give them enough rope to hang themselves. And so, on orders of management (who claimed it was the news consultants' idea), he began to use the same low-key sign-off as other anchors.

Says Marvin, "They wanted me to do it, so I did. It was a mistake, and now they know it. I never could figure out why I should change myself to suit 13% of the audience, who didn't like me anyway."

Marvin continues, "Letters cluttered the station for a week." Overwhelmingly, the mail was against Marvin's subdued sign-off. In short order he returned to the sign-off which he still uses today: "Maaaaaarvin Zindler, EYEWITNESS NEWS!"

Once again, Marvin was correct. It was his intuition and "street sense," not backroom management brainstorming, that won the day.

∾ • ∾

Another short-lived experiment at KTRK was the "Dial M for Marvin" show. This was a fill-in show that Channel 13 aired during 13 weeks in 1974. Management planned to place the program opposite competing network heavyweights in hopes of improving the ratings and getting a larger share of the market. The show was to focus on two very basic story lines: crime and sex — a blatant attempt to capitalize on the attention Marvin and the station had received from the Chicken Ranch story. The show would be live, and, despite its name, would have two co-hosts: Marvin and Channel 13 reporter Larry Conners, who had also gained a measure of fame by working on the Chicken Ranch story.

The show featured such notables as "Miss Kitty," a working girl the Vice Squad brought over to the station to discuss the life of a prostitute. The "Dial M for Marvin" show was a rolling ball of butcher knives that could cut fast and furious, but could not endear itself to the viewers. No doubt the news analysts were scratching their heads over that one, and doubtless they spent many billable hours analyzing the situation, but, cutting to the core of the problem, the show was just plain awful. Or maybe it was just ahead of its time. Marvin feels that people simply were not ready for that type of show in the 1970s. It was too graphic, too realistic — "reality TV" a generation too early. When you look at some of the stuff that's on today — all the graphic, gory or salacious fare available at the flick of a remote — "Dial M for Marvin" seems incredibly tame.

Probably the most engaging aspect of the show was the on-air competition between Marvin and Larry Conners, who were locked in an unannounced competition for air time, that all-important badge of TV host status. Now, Larry was a fine reporter, and in fact won AP and UPI awards for a series he did on the prostitution problem in the Houston area. But he had an ego the size of Texas, and so did Marvin, and, frankly, there just wasn't room on one show for two Texas-sized egos. Co-hosting the "Dial M for Marvin" show, Conners repeatedly attempted to seize control of the mike. Whenever Marvin tried to interject a question, Conners silenced him.

Marvin quickly tired of these antics, and one evening, while on the air, he let Larry have it: "Larry, I'm going to ask this question, and if you interrupt me one more time, I'm going to hit you. I'm going to wallop you hard enough to knock your head into your pants so you'll have to open your zipper to peek out."

Wall-eyed and shaken, Conners sat in stunned silence for a few minutes.

Soon "Dial M for Marvin" was history, and not too long afterward, Larry Conners was too. When he announced he was leaving the station for another job, management, to his delight, allowed him to tape a farewell address to be broadcast on the evening news. He took full advantage of the opportunity, and at the end of his spiel he offered his unfettered opinion of what it was like to work with Marvin.

"There are a lot of people who ask, 'What is Marvin Zindler really like?' 'How is it to work with him?' Let's take the last question first. There are a lot of other employees around here who would love to voice their feelings, but I am afraid they would not use good taste.

"I know that when Marvin first came to work here I couldn't believe that a circus act, which is what I considered Zindler, would overshadow hard-working news reporters. Well, as many of you know, I soon decided I couldn't beat Marvin. So, I joined him and on his coattails I got into quite a few good stories, such as the closing of the Chicken Ranch.

"Last year when I was producing and serving as co-host on the 'Dial M for Marvin' show, I was soon demanding more money — COMBAT PAY — because handling Marvin on a live program is a real fight.

"What is Marvin really like? Well, Howard Cosell is as saccharine as Shirley Temple when compared to Zindler. Marvin is obnoxious, rude and spends most of the time trying to outshoot thunder. Marvin is a super ego, always demanding, threatening... [He is] totally impatient and thinks everybody should stop when he comes into a room.

"Well, you may gather by all of this that I don't like Marvin. On the contrary. Despite his many faults, he has become the great white wig — I mean, hope — for many people, because no one else really cares about the common people. Marvin Zindler is, in fact, a very sincere person. He at times can be a very hokey showman. But he has more honesty than many of us will ever have. I count Marvin as a very good friend and we have a very good relationship. Even though at times I was ready to kill him."

Score one for Larry Conners. Not only had he had the last word, but his farewell had run more than two minutes, making him the clear winner in the contest for more air time. Conners went on to find happiness in St. Louis, Missouri, where he moved in 1975; he has been at St. Louis' CBS affiliate, KMOV-TV Channel 4, for many years.

The public, then as now, seemed mesmerized by Marvin's zany style and demolition-like courage. Some thought he was just this side of insane; some thought he could do no wrong. The latter seemed to be in the majority; many people felt that for the first time they really had someone who not only would listen to their problems but could do something about them. It no longer mattered that they didn't know where to go or how to use the system, because Marvin Zindler knew.

No story seemed too large or too small for Marvin's attention. He had an uncanny knack for finding the "human angle" in just about any story, and he still utilized the "back-assward" method he had used back in his "Night Hawk" days. Most reporters will write their story and then formulate the title. Not Marvin. Just as he had once shot his photo first and then built a story around it, it was now his habit to first envision his promo or headline, and then sift through the ingredients of the story, forcing it to fit his preconceived opener. Backwards or not, it worked.

Even when he'd found a formula for success, Marvin was never afraid to change his style and try something different. He has always been aware that in television, as in anything else, you can't survive if you stick to one thing all the time. The public will get tired of it. Marvin, knowing this, varies his stories from the sublime to the fantastic, always looking for the human-interest factor.

He has also broadened his scope over the years. One could easily make the case that consumerism has never been Marvin's only angle; in any event, throughout his tenure at Channel 13, he has made a concentrated effort to expand his reach beyond consumer issues. In all of his stories there has always been a larger theme: in essence, Marvin is and always has been interested in inequities. There are all sorts of situations where people aren't being treated right, and that's what he's after. Marvin's best hold on his audience, as even his former rival Larry Conners admitted, is that he provides a forum for common people to vent their frustrations, and a vehicle for solving their problems.

When he first began his television reports, almost all of his stories were aggressive attack pieces. The dominant story line featured the White Knight verbally skewering a person or business, then holding them over the coals until well-done. Over the years, his style gradually changed, slowly and almost imperceptibly to his audience. Now, most of his stories have "happy endings." Today Marvin first works out the solution to the problem, and then it is reported on the air. It isn't always a skewer job; Marvin is more than willing to give full credit to erring businesses when justice is served.

For many years, Marvin Zindler has been a hornet at the capitalistic picnic. Yet he is a fervent believer in the capitalistic system. The problem, he says, is that the humanity has gone out of business, and he fears increasing socialistic controls on business if it doesn't reform.

Marvin is a man who sees all matters as black and white. There are no shades of excusable grays. For the most part, right and wrong are clear in his mind. He ignores all "yes-but" counterpoints as extraneous. And he finds it irresistible to bleat the "consumer-is-always-right" principles of his father.

Many business owners, on the other hand, have seen Marvin as having an irresponsible tendency to ignore any facts in a case that don't fit his preconceived notions. Countless businessmen over the years have claimed Marvin's stories were based on "miscommunication," and as such, were not newsworthy and had no social value. But that has never been how the man on the street saw them.

In any case, more businesses are willing to cooperate with Marvin these days. Today, businesses can't afford bad PR. They know a good public image is important, and they want the consumer to return. They want to be perceived as a friend and a trusted ally. Those who might be leaning towards complacency, however, should know that Marvin is still a giant killer. He just does it with more finesse. Time has not dulled his killer instinct, only refined it.

Naturally, in his role as consumer advocate Marvin has faced a lot of criticism, and not just from businesses. Not every viewer loves him, and some may growl in disapproval at his stories, his methods or both. But I'm willing to bet that even the most critical viewers eventually see a story that hits them where they live.

"It's that simple," says Marvin. "Then I'm a hero — for awhile."

Being a hero isn't easy when you're fighting for the truth, because people don't always like the truth. For example, when Marvin reviewed a complaint between the Internal Revenue Service and an older couple, he resolved the problem. However, Marvin found that in this case the IRS was not at fault. The audience got mad. Marvin shrugged it off. "What the hell. They'll love me the next day when I tear a yard of skin off a dishonest auto repair man."

Marvin is certainly not one to rest on his laurels. He is well aware that as a consumer advocate, he is only as good as his last successful case, and as a reporter, he is only as good as his last story. He is always cognizant of his viewers, and his ability to anticipate and respond to his audience's wants and needs is one of his great talents. Nominally he may be KTRK's "Action Reporter," but in reality, Marvin is a "Reaction Reporter."

Over the years, KTRK-TV has conducted various studies and polls to evaluate the Zindler phenomenon. A study done in the 1980s not only measured how many people recognized the name, "Marvin Zindler," but also determined if Marvin's audience felt they had developed a personal affinity with Marvin. The results showed that Marvin outranked every other television personality in the viewing area. What is referred to as "visibility," or name recognition, was 50% greater for Marvin than for the next highest-ranking news reporter or anchor person at KTRK or any of its competitors.

The study showed that 94% of the white community and more than 98% of the African American and Hispanic communities registered detailed recognition of Marvin Zindler. (A separate survey among African Americans showed Marvin is considered by a great many to be a "leader in the community.") The study revealed Marvin to be well respected by women, all lower-income groups and, of course, minority groups. Most respondents believed Marvin was honest, a straight shooter. Judging from their remarks, many felt he could virtually walk on water. A few said he was an S.O.B., but their complaints seemed to be more about his style than what he represented. Virtually everything revealed in this study still holds true today; if anything, Marvin's name recognition is even higher. If you're a Houstonian, you'd have to have been living under a rock for the past 30 years not to know who Marvin Zindler is.

To the station, Marvin's visibility means larger audiences and increased ratings. And, more importantly for the community, the affinity that minority groups feel for Marvin has helped increase racial harmony. Marvin says the station is receiving more and more calls asking him to mediate disputes between businesses or organizations and minority groups.

"They [the minority groups] know I'm going to take their side if they're right," he says, "and I'll damn well tell them if they're wrong. Like anyone else, they want you to tell them the way things are. They don't want any crap. I am straightforward and honest. I call it the way it is. That's why we get along."

Marvin said he developed an affinity for people of other races and ethnic groups as a child. "I never could understand why the black kids had to catch a bus and go all the way across town to a school instead of going to the same school I went to a few blocks away. Even as a kid I knew that things were wrong and I've always taken their side." Of course, Marvin himself has experienced something of what it is be a minority, having been faced with occasional harassment in his younger days because of being Jewish. Though his problems were mild in comparison to, say, those of a poor African-American person, his experiences helped mold him into the compassionate soul he is today.

That compassion is matched by a bull-headed determination to fight for what is right. The demographic studies and surveys, many of which have been independent reports from outside sources, all seem to prove the point that expert observers and everyday viewers alike have long known: There is only one White Knight on Houston television, and, very possibly in the country: Mr. Marvin Zindler.

Even today, despite his long track record of success and his continuing popularity, some wonder how long Marvin can ride the crest of television. They were seriously wondering this in 1973, at the very beginning of his long stint with Channel 13. 1973 was the year Marvin's investigative reports spurred the closing of the "Chicken Ranch" bordello in La Grange, Texas. There were several write-ups in newspapers about him, as well as commentaries on other TV stations. One social scientist predicted Marvin Zindler's television life span was just about over. He described Marvin as a "hot personality," slated, like a hot star, to burn out fast. According to this prognosticator, Marvin's audience would quickly be satiated by his forceful style, and then that would be it for Marvin's TV presence.

So much for predictions. Nearly three decades have passed as I write this, and here Marvin still is, armed with his lifetime contract with ABC-TV — which, it should be noted, was acquired in 1988, 15 years after that social scientist's dire prediction. Much of his fame, particularly on a nationwide basis, is due to the very incident which was supposed to spell the end of his career. Today, you can't mention Marvin Zindler without thinking "Chicken Ranch." On the flip side, when someone says, "Chicken Ranch," the only possible reply is "Marvin Zindler." [3]

Not all of the people who have wondered about Marvin's longevity at Channel 13 have put such a negative spin on their question. There are many who recognize Marvin's very special mix of talents and skills, and to these people the real question has always been whether or not Marvin would get a better offer and move on to Los Angeles, Chicago or New York City. After all, high-paying television contracts gravitate to the person with the highest profile, and there's little doubt that Marvin would be a lightening rod for a TV station in any market. His presentation and story instincts would titillate any audience, not just those in Houston, and his theatrics would be splashy no matter where he was. He would quickly develop a local following anywhere he went. Most important from a news standpoint, he would continue to build his amazing network of informants, and would make full use of their tips, funneling them to the regular news department for use in their stories as well as his. This would be an invaluable contribution to any news operation.

Other stations have expressed interest in Marvin over the years, and certainly there are those in the Houston market who would love to see him leave. If Marvin is an asset for Channel 13, it follows that he is a thorn in the side of the station's competitors. Competition between stations for market share and ratings has always been fierce, and some devious tactics have been used in the past. As a matter of fact, despite the rancor and rivalries between Marvin and his former "Dial M for Marvin" co-host Larry Conners, Conners' move to St. Louis in 1975 was not the result of anything that happened at Channel 13. Rather, it was the result of some doings at KPRC-TV Channel 2, Houston's NBC affiliate.

---

[3] Of course, you couldn't have a biography of Marvin Zindler without discussing the Chicken Ranch at length. See the section entitled, "Texas HAD a Whorehouse In It."

It was well known that Ray Miller, who at that time was the news director at Channel 2, wanted to remove his competition in the Houston market. He knew his ratings could certainly improve if Larry Conners and Marvin Zindler, Channel 13's top two reporters at the time, weren't in the picture. If he could get Conners and Zindler good offers from other cities, they might accept one of those offers and leave Houston. So Miller began a clandestine job-search campaign for Marvin and Larry; he would tape their best programs and send them to other stations far from Houston. Naturally, the subjects of these tapes were unaware of Miller's actions. Ultimately, Ray Miller was halfway successful; it was one of these clandestine audition tapes that landed Larry Conners his job in St. Louis. But Marvin stayed right where he was.

It's not that he hasn't been tempted over the years. He has received several attractive offers from other television stations, including large stations in Los Angeles and Detroit, and has seriously considered some, but has declined them all. He explains, "Nobody else but Channel 13 would put up with me and what I do. Nobody else would have the guts to go forward with the stories that I like to do. If I went somewhere else, as soon as I got started, their hair would curl and they'd need to carry an extra pair of shorts in their pocket. It wouldn't take long before they'd give me a desk in a corner somewhere and that would be the last you ever heard of Maaaaaarvin Zindler."

Nevertheless, Marvin has at times expressed his desire to fan his spark on national network news. "I could do the same thing I do here," he says, "except I could do it *nationwide*. I could set up a staff and travel. I could handle problems in New York City one week, a few days later move on to St. Louis and then over to Denver, and finish up in Los Angeles or possibly San Francisco. Anywhere. The research and preparation would be done by my staff in their respective cities. The stories would be geared to each city's particular problems. I would personalize it for each city. I would fly in and handle the story piece. I know exactly how it could be set up." He added, "I've thought about this a lot, but Houston is home and family."

It's not likely that someone so close to his children and multitude of grandchildren (and he's already become a great-grandpa too) is about to make such radical changes. We all like to dream. That said, rumors persist that Marvin will take one of those other offers, one of these days.

KTRK, for their part, is always concerned about losing Marvin, though they may sometimes play down that concern. The trend in recent years has been for stations to place less emphasis on promoting individual personalities and more on promoting the station's on-air staff as a group. For the most part, this makes sense. Anchors have a tendency to drift from market to market, striving for a more lucrative network position. The ultimate goal has always been New York City. As a result, many television stations have been gravitating away from the policy of touting any single one of their anchor persons in station promo-

White Knight in Blue Shades

tions. After all, if a station spends hundreds of thousands of dollars promoting a personality, only to have him or her lured away by a larger salary, then the station is not only out the money but will also suffer a drop in ratings. The tendency today, therefore, is to have multiple key individuals with high visibility, who are involved in community activities and philanthropic endeavors. Not only does their community involvement make them more likely to stay in that market, but if one of them does leave, the station is less likely to be seriously damaged.

Still, KTRK considers Marvin one of their top-notch people. (Dave Ward is one of their other bastions of stability in a volatile market, as are Channel 13 veterans Ed Brandon, Shara Fryer, Melanie Lawson, Bob Boudreaux, Elma Barrera, and Bob Allen.) If Channel 13 lost Marvin, they wouldn't go out of business, but I assure you, they would be lying awake at night worrying about upcoming ratings and a suitable replacement.

On the other hand, Marvin is probably correct when he says that most stations wouldn't put up with him for very long. He isn't the easiest person to work with. However, if you treat him with respect he will give you one hundred percent. What Marvin wants most, even more than attention, is respect for what he does. And, despite his oversize ego, Marvin is also right on target when he describes himself as "a company man." He is one of the most honest and sincere individuals you could have in your employment.

Marvin's ongoing frustration is that he feels his bosses refuse to give credit where credit is due. No one can deny that when Marvin joined Channel 13, they were a third-rate station, and that within a few years, they were number one, and have held that position pretty steadily ever since. Few would deny that Marvin is largely responsible for bringing Channel 13 to the foreground in the Houston market. Station management, however, sees things differently, claiming that the paramount reason for the station's surge in ratings and market share way back then was the entire new package, not just Marvin. Marvin doesn't agree, and believes management at Channel 13 hasn't always given him proper recognition for his achievements.

In his constant battles for what he thinks is right, Marvin has inevitably gone up against his own station management from time to time. More irritating to him than anything else are those situations in which he perceives management is taking pains to protect certain "sacred cows." He explains, "Too damn often the management's upper crust can come in here and con the news directors into stopping me from doing something." The result is that an important story gets swept under the rug, and, snarls Marvin, "That means I'm not being fair, and it makes me mad as hell. I get as mad as a hen trying to lay a square egg."

In those circumstances Marvin will become excited — and when he does, well, forget any comparisons to a chicken. He will begin bellowing and slinging snot like a bull in a pen, sending the boys in management for the safety of the top rail. Usually he ends his verbal onslaught by roaring, "They have no loyalty to me! I can make it cut both ways! I can just go a few blocks away where there are at least two other major television stations just waiting to hire me!"

Over the years, Marvin has learned when to fight outright and when to lie low and use guerrilla tactics. If the timing isn't right for an outright battle, he can be seen sitting at his desk, lips gently moving, voice almost inaudible, head tilted slightly down, with a devout expression on his face as his eyes gaze slightly upward. If it looks for all the world as if he is praying, that's because he is. It is said that prayer does the soul good; however, it must be said that the purpose of Marvin's whispered entreaties at these times is not to benefit his own soul, nor to give him strength for the battle ahead, but to ask a higher power to smite his enemies. It's good therapy, anyway.

Or sometimes he's not praying at all, but simply continuing to mutter about how he's going to quit Channel 13 to work at another station where his worth will be more satisfactorily recognized. Usually this surge of anger subsides after a few days, only to erupt again like a volcano — suddenly, unexpectedly and powerfully — especially if he feels he and his listeners are going to be betrayed by management. His bosses know they must go to the brink with his talent if they want to keep him. They just have to accept that Marvin will always continue to fight. I like to say to him, "Marvin, you can win all the battles if you're good enough. All of them — except the last one."

He *is* good, and he does win most of his battles. And so far, no matter how bitter the clash with his bosses has been, he has always cooled down in a few days and returned to KTRK. The paramount reason — beyond the license to be his own outrageous self that KTRK has always granted him, beyond even his lifetime contract with ABC — is that after almost three decades, a deep personal affection has developed between Marvin Zindler and Channel 13.

A 1981 cover story in the departed monthly magazine *Houston City* lamented the lack of depth in Houston TV news (a complaint which still persists today about local news, and is by no means limited to the Houston market). As an illustration of this point, writer Ronald Henkoff asserted, "The most popular television news 'personality' in town, lest we forget, is Marvin Zindler, that white-wigged showman whose trademark is a sign-off that sounds like the yelp of a forlorn canine." More than 20 years later, *Houston City* has been relegated to media history, and Marvin, "yelp" and all, is still going strong.

In fact, all evidence points to the probability that Marvin is in for the long haul. And what about retirement? "As long as I'm healthy," Marvin says, "and my good friend and cosmetic surgeon 'Doc Joe' Agris will help me out periodically, I'll keep working." So far he has. And I know I am speaking for a lot of folks when I say, "We love you, Maaaaaarvin."

C·H·A·P·T·E·R 12

A DAY IN THE LIFE:
"IT'S ONLY SHOW BIZ"

A s more than one person has been known to observe, you might not see Marvin coming, but you sure as hell hear him. I personally have experienced this on numerous occasions. One particular incident stands out. In 1994, KTRK-TV began updating and revamping their dome-shaped building at 3310 Bissonnet, in preparation for going over to digital transmission. Several trailers had been placed in the parking lot during the remodeling, and one of these was assigned to none other than Mr. Marvin Zindler. I was scheduled to meet Marvin at the television station. It was late afternoon, and Marvin was working with his very capable producer, director and writer, Lori Reingold, and his superb and energetic cameraman, Bob Dows. It was getting close to air time, and things were tense. The makeshift quarters were confining, almost claustrophobic, and adding to the frustration was the fact that due to the remodeling, the crew had only limited equipment available. Tension was mounting as the production team tried repeatedly to precisely match the story's monologue to the video. They had been at this for some time, and now time was getting short. At the time I arrived, they had made perhaps six or seven unsuccessful attempts. Now Marvin was again reading the script, and Bob Dows was trying to meld it with the video. Everything was going reasonably well.

I approached the trailer, walked up the three steps to the entrance and peered through the small window in the trailer door. I could see Lori Reingold sitting across the desk from Marvin, who appeared to be leafing through some paperwork. I knew Bob Dows had to be in there somewhere too. As I was soon to find out, Bob and his video monitor were to the right of the door, just out of my sight. In my usual cheerful and exuberant manner, I knocked, and in one swift motion threw open the door, shouting out a greeting to Marvin, Lori and Bob.

I did not receive a jubilant greeting in return. In fact, for a few seconds everything was silent. Lori's facial expression was one of sheer shock, and she sat bolt upright, frozen in her chair. Marvin, surprised by my sudden entry, was caught off guard — but only for the moment. After those few seconds of stunned silence, he came to life, shaking the script wildly and then throwing it across the desk. Almost simultaneously, a blistering wave of epithets blared forth from his mouth. You would have thought he'd been hit with the business end of a cattle prod. A torrent of curse words echoed throughout the small trailer between stammers, stutters and expressive hand gestures, which, true to Zindler form, were combined in the most inventive of ways. Finally it seemed he'd been throttled by his own onslaught, and he grew thick-tongued.

As for me, I had a broad grin on my face, and began to collapse in uncontrollable fits of laughter. It was contagious; Bob and Lori began to laugh almost simultaneously, and then finally Marvin did too. The safety valve on Marvin's boiler had blown; the tension was gone, and we all had a good laugh.

Finally Marvin picked up the script, reorganized the pages and said, "Can't you see what we are doing here?"

Bob immediately clarified the situation, and explained what was taking place in a more coherent manner. He then calmly reset the tape, Marvin picked up the script, Lori cued him in, and Marvin began reading. He went through it without a hitch. And then, with a big grin and his shoulders thrown back and his chest puffed up, he turned to me and asked, "Wasn't that great?"

I slowly turned from my seat in the corner of the trailer. With the seriousness of a judge at a grand-jury indictment I blurted out, "It stinks! It's too long. You are running sentences together. Some of the sentences aren't even sentences. You missed the point that you're trying to make."

Marvin was stunned. They had been working on this for several hours, and were now hazardously close to running out of time. It was so quiet in that trailer that if a bird had pooped on the tin roof, you probably could have heard it. Marvin was the first to break the silence, not with an outburst of temper this time, but with a calm suggestion: "Why don't you and Lori take a look at it together?"

We went over the script sentence by sentence, breaking it down into shorter segments, which, if I do say so myself, improved the clarity and gave direction to the story. Marvin and Bob contributed their suggestions, and then Lori read it aloud. Everybody clapped. Lori handed Marvin the revised script, Bob reset the tape once again, and Marvin completed it in the one minute and 35 seconds allotted to the story. It was perfect. There was now but a half hour before air time. Talk about cutting it close! Bob popped the tape out of the recorder and rushed it to the studio. Marvin made a last-minute check before leaving the trailer, then sauntered over to the studio with only minutes to spare.

This was neither the first nor the last time Marvin has murdered a script. He has learned to take it all in stride, and even good-naturedly accepts jests about his dastardly pronunciation of the English language, particularly names. (He's also a good sport about the jokes about his make-up, face-lifts and, of course, his hairpiece).

Marvin may not be the most eloquent of speakers, but he is a perfectionist in all other ways. He is demanding on the set, of himself as well as his associates, crew members, and the technicians required for each of the taping sessions. Television taping and voice-over recording techniques demand an accuracy of coordination and split-second timing between Marvin and the production technicians.

Marvin is nearly always taped, because attempts to run him on the newscast "live" have proved at times to be hysterically funny, if not disastrous. His inability to properly pronounce names and places has often caused his camera crew and director to dissolve in fits of laughter. When he makes one of his mirth-inducing gaffes, he will blush and try again, usually only compounding the *faux pas*. But generally he is a good sport about it, and he, too, will begin to laugh. Some feel his creative use of language is "Zindlerism" at its best. It's real. And if we're honest, most of us will admit that we've made a few verbal blunders ourselves.

Marvin being the perfectionist he is, however, making these blunders on the air, in the midst of a live report, is not acceptable. Therefore, he likes the option of continuing to record until he gets it perfect.[1]

Sometimes Marvin will get ahead of himself on the script. Other times, he will ad lib or make changes in the script, depending on the circumstances. He might even be distracted by his surroundings and lose his train of thought momentarily. And, of course, it wouldn't be Marvin if he didn't mispronounce someone's name or muff the words during a take. Regardless, he will want to shoot it again. Even if his reading of the script goes well, he will demand a retake if he blinks his eyes, declaring that this takes away from his glaring authority. On an off day he will ruin take after laborious take, and when this happens, nerves can wear thin and voices are often raised.

I recall a particularly irritating set of circumstances requiring 11 retakes. After struggling several times to get through what have been a straightforward taping, Marvin blew it in the last few seconds. One of the highly irritated technicians then switched on the studio speaker system which allowed general announcements to be made throughout the station. From a safe distance in the upstairs control room, the now frustrated and exhausted technician boomed out to the whole station: "Marvin Zindler spent $20,000 to get his got-damned face fixed last year, and now his mouth don't work. He needs to go back and get his tongue oiled!"

And, amazingly, Marvin, who had been just about to blow up in anticipation of the re-taping, laughed as hard as the rest of the crew. The next taping went quickly and was a complete success.

---

[1] The other advantage of being on tape is to allow for time limitations and changes due to the spread between the two nightly forecasts at 6:00 and 10:00 PM. In many cases, it would be impractical to go "live" with these rigid time limitations, particularly in light of the unconventional format of Marvin's stories.

Filming of Marvin's segment for the 6:00 PM newscast is usually scheduled between 3:00 and 4:00 in the afternoon. If everything goes well — and, despite the legendary gaffes, it usually does — Marvin may have an hour or more to himself. He usually works at his desk, making phone calls to his contacts to check out the validity of future stories.

Periodically, however, Marvin gets saddle itch and starts moseying around the station, alternating between being helpful and being a pest. Occasionally he wanders into the sales department to see what he can stir up. In particular, he looks for new faces. When he spots one, that's when the fun begins. Perhaps he'll gleefully inform the rookie that he plans to do an exposé on one of his or her big accounts. This declaration creates varying degrees of wide-eyed alarm, but Marvin usually doesn't stay around to set things straight; instead he just skedaddles out of there with a big grin, chuckling to himself. He knows he probably shouldn't do things like that, but, as he says, "It is fun. And it keeps the sales department on their toes." Fair's fair, after all. If they can have an occasional laugh at his expense, he can have one at theirs.

Now that he has finished stirring up a ruckus in sales, he usually meanders back to his office, where he can lovingly torture his own staff. He can almost always find something to exasperate them with; if all else fails, he will throw a hissy fit over some minor mistake he himself made. Of course, it has to be someone else's fault, the result of some carelessness or lack of insight on their part, but never on his. He will holler his usual string of profanities, which seasoned staff members have learned to ignore, but which has caused more than one of his newer assistants to break into tears. At that point, he will make a clumsy effort to apologize, but when you are always right, and everybody else is always wrong, it is difficult to verbalize remorse.

Not that Marvin has never received a taste of his own vitriol. Often as not, his tirades spur a loud and sometimes simultaneous counter-chewing-out by his help — at which point Marvin flees, only to return a few minutes later a much humbler individual. Those who have worked with Marvin for many years consider it all in a day's work. They acknowledge that he has his idiosyncrasies, but he will go all out for his staff. They will laugh with him, yell at him, and, certainly, get yelled at by him, but wouldn't even consider working for anyone else at the station.

Marvin's explosive and domineering personality disrupts the station's operation in other ways as well. Even in a business noted for its vainglorious and temperamental employees, he stands out. This does not make it easy for the news editors, who not only have to deal with the egos of the station's talking heads, but are also riddled with the daily pressures of deciding which stories to select, and how much time to give each one. Naturally, when they don't make the "right" decision regarding one of Marvin's stories, there's hell to pay. More than once Marvin has been known to back a hapless news editor into a corner and give him what-for because he cut Marvin's time slot for the sake of another story. On one occasion, Marvin was so outraged at the editor for "weakening" the story and leaving it (in Marvin's view) anti-climactic that he cornered the poor man, and could be heard throughout the station screaming, "You don't know what to make of me, you don't know what to make of me, gosh-dammit. You want me to tone down. But, got-dammit, I am not going to." And then, in a burst of pure and righteous rage, he declared, "I know why. You don't like me!"

And as quickly as it had begun, the tantrum was over. Walking away from the incident with a wide grin of pleasure, Marvin conceded, "I probably shouldn't have done that. The poor son-of-a-bitch didn't know how to respond. I had him, I had him good."

It is this type of incident that makes Dave Ward shake his head and say, with a helpless grin, what he has said so many times before: "No doubt about it. We created a monster."

Marvin looks at it differently, insisting that when he raises hell over something, he is thinking about the station. Marvin has to be allowed to be Marvin, and do what he knows how to do best; otherwise the ratings will drop. That's just the way it is in this business, and the right to throw a tantrum is considered one of the perks of stardom. Others may look upon him as an egomaniac or a snorting exhibitionist. They may describe him as undignified and, on many occasions, downright embarrassing. But Marvin pleads artistic license. After all, he is not a newsman. He is an entity unto himself; he is, in every sense of the word, show business.

More detached or charitable observers feel that while Marvin Zindler is sincere and well-meaning, he will always be unable to separate himself from the overwhelming vanity that drives him. But isn't that true of all stars?

In his early days at Channel 13, Marvin and his staff were relegated to a tiny office wedged between the two studios at the television station. There was one door, and there were no outside windows. When the KTRK-TV headquarters were renovated, Marvin was given a spacious suite of offices on an outside corner with a patio, directly across from the swimming pool. (Yes, Channel 13 has a swimming pool. It also has a workout room; this is not typical for a television station. Many of the employees avail themselves of these luxuries, but not Marvin. God forbid that Marvin would do anything resembling exercise — well, except for those exhausting rounds of golf.) Marvin's office suite is only a few steps away from the coffee bar, where he likes to make fresh coffee himself, several times a day.

Marvin's office has been equipped with all the latest high-tech devices, including sophisticated telephone messaging systems to help ward off the avalanche of callers who want to talk personally to Marvin Zindler. The voice-mail system informs callers how and where to write for help, and it also logs the calls; it has logged as many as 1,500 calls in a day. When time permits, however, Marvin still likes to answer his own telephone — much to the surprise of the caller.

Then there are the letters; Marvin's assistants handle more than 100,000 of them a year. Each day the letters are opened, read, sorted, placed in manila folders and centered atop Marvin's desk for his perusal.

The office Marvin calls home during his hours at the station is bright and cheery, with a private bathroom (excuse me, *the star's dressing room*) where he can primp himself prior to going on the air. On the wall to the left of the entrance is a large, eye-catching show poster depicting Marvin, Burt Reynolds and Dolly Parton, advertising the movie of *The Best Little Whorehouse in Texas.* Along the same wall are some file cabinets and bookshelves, upon which there are a myriad of photos I have taken of Marvin, Lori Reingold and Bob Dows on our many international medical mission trips.

In the center of the large workroom adjacent to his office is a small conference table, which I don't think has ever been used for its intended purpose. The table is always cluttered with scripts, tapes, snack food and assorted electronic equipment used for filming and recording. God forbid someone from the cleaning crew should attempt to put some organization to this clutter. Everyone knows exactly what is there and where to locate it — most of the time, that is. Guests are welcome to sit in the chairs that surround the conference table, but unless someone offers to make room on the table, you are to keep your hands off.

Marvin does not believe in the intercom, or perhaps has not mastered the multitude of buttons on the state-of-the-art communication system. From his partitioned-off private office area, he repeatedly bellows maddening requests for all sorts of information, research material and telephone numbers. Later in the afternoon, as he reviews scripts, there are more repeated requests, this time for someone to give him proper pronunciations of names and places — as if it would make any difference. In short order this is followed by curse-ridden demands for judgements on how the script sounds as he reads it aloud. And all this takes place amidst the din of telephones, electronic equipment, and personnel trafficking to and from the suite. It is a chaotic and cacophonous scene, to be sure. But somehow, time after time, from all this chaos and cacophony there rises order in the form of a story or a series of special reports — the kinds of stories and reports that help keep the viewers tuning in night after night to Channel 13 news.

How does Marvin choose his stories? Normally, he will select several prospective stories from the mound of letters or multitude of phone calls he receives, and he and his staff will then begin investigating them thoroughly. The actual filming usually takes place several days prior to the air-date for the story. That's for the everyday, run-of-the-mill consumer-issue stories.

Sometimes, however, there is some local, national or international event that is earthshaking or of significant human interest. These stories usually go far beyond his consumer-advocate beat, but have become part of the overall Zindler phenomenon. Once

Marvin makes up his mind to do a story in some far-flung place, he springs into action. With fingers racing across the telephone keyboard, he makes travel arrangements in minutes. Visas are cleared by foreign consulates and State Department personnel. And almost before you can say "Eyewitness News!", Marvin and his staff are on their way to the airport — again.

Marvin's staff must keep one suitcase always packed and at the ready, because they never know what's coming next. The adventures really began in the late 1980s, and haven't stopped since. Marvin and staff were in Germany when the Berlin Wall came down. They trekked into the heartland of Mother Russia so Marvin could report on the dissolution of the USSR. They were knee-deep in sand when Kuwait was under attack and Desert Storm was imminent. When Nicaragua elected a woman president, the big questions were, *Is the Sandinista-Contra conflict really at an end? Are national, democratic elections possible in Nicaragua?* — and Marvin and his faithful entourage were right there in the thick of things.

And then there was Cuba, a destination forbidden to most US citizens. But Marvin, as may be abundantly clear by now, is not your average citizen. "Who said we can't go to Cuba? Give me that got-damn telephone. What's the number for the State Department? *We are going!* We'll get our story and send it back via satellite if we have to." Naturally, he did go to Cuba, and, as usual, he got his story (see the chapter entitled, "A Country Embargoed" in the "Man on a Mission" section).

Whether he's off on a humanitarian mission to Central America or a fact-finding trip to the Middle East, it never ends. Most reporters half his age could not keep up this pace.

His impulses don't always take him so far from home, and he puts just as much passion and energy into his stateside treks as he does his global journeys. Drop by the station at Easter time, for example, and you're likely to hear Marvin barking out questions and commands as if he's about to do the hottest story of the year. "Do we have reservations on Continental Airlines for Washington, D.C.? I want to do a shoot on the White House lawn during the Easter egg hunt — TOMORROW MORNING. It's our once-a-year national tradition!" No, it's not a global crisis or a burning consumer issue, but it does have that human-interest element, and, as Marvin says, it *is* tradition. So his staff had better be prepared to hop on that plane for Washington.

At best, Marvin is impetuous, perhaps even a little self-righteous. But his stories are almost always compelling, and he keeps the viewers on their toes; they never know what, or from where, he will be broadcasting next.

A story Marvin did a few years ago illustrates how a typical story shoot goes. Just before the Christmas holidays, Marvin received a letter from a nine-year-old girl. She had a tumor growing out of the side of her face, and it was getting larger. She had been told she needed an operation, but her family could not afford the surgery. And so, with the help of her teacher, she printed a letter to Mr. Zindler, describing her problem. She added that the children at school had started to tease her because of this problem, and she was not going to go back to school after the Christmas holiday. She went on to say that she was not expecting many presents, but had everything that she needed. She ended the letter by declaring she loved her family, and the only thing she wanted for Christmas was to have her surgery. "It would be the best Christmas present."

This prompted Marvin to call me, asking if I would be willing to do the surgery gratis. I agreed, so Marvin said he would come over to my office in the Texas Medical Center late Monday afternoon to talk to me about it.

Meanwhile, Marvin called the mother and arranged to visit with her and the child at their home. He planned to shoot the story in front of their Christmas tree in their living room. He did not want to do a story of this nature in the sterile atmosphere of the TV studio. "No formal interviews," he ordered. "We will do the story in their home." The only person he forgot to tell about this in advance was yours truly.

When Marvin arrived at my office with Lori Reingold and Bob Dows, the first thing he said to me was, "Are you ready to go?"

"Go? Go where?" I responded, stunned.

Marvin was at his most charming, with a broad grin and eyes sparkling. "It's Christmas! We're going to do a Christmas story at this child's home. You know, with all the decorations and the Christmas tree in the background. It won't take long. It's only a few minutes away."

I knew him well enough by now to recognize Zindlerisms when I heard them. "It won't take long" meant it would take at least two hours. And "It's only a few minutes away" meant it was at least a 30-minute drive in each direction — *if* we were lucky enough to be going against traffic on Houston's infamous freeways.

In order to be around Marvin and keep your sanity, and your temper, you have to learn to decode those Zindlerisms and go with the flow. I learned long ago, for example, that "I'm on my way right over" can mean just about anything *except* that he will be there shortly. And "I'll be there about noon" means you might see him sometime between 1:00 and 3:00 PM. Once you get used to being on "Marvin time," you can plan your schedule accordingly.

But sometimes there's no chance to plan, because he'll just pop up with a plan of his own. Fortunately, this particular day was one of my cosmetic-surgery-only days; the cases had been completed and I had already made rounds at the hospital. The day's mail and chart dictation could wait until tonight. However, there was a hospital staff meeting at 5:30 that evening, and I needed to be there. Of course Marvin was very reassuring: "I'll get you back on time, don't worry about it." And of course, everyone else was thinking to themselves, *Houston traffic...5:30 PM — not a chance!*

Since there was no avoiding it, I figured we'd best get started on this adventure, so I said, "Let's get out of here before the traffic starts leaving the city." We took the Scurlock Tower elevator down to the parking area where the Action News 13 van waited. Bob was to drive, with Lori riding shotgun and giving him directions. This suited Marvin fine, as he does not like to sit up front. He usually positions himself behind the driver, where he can be of most help. I climbed in alongside Marvin, and we were off.

Marvin, it must be noted, is no back-seat driver. It's just that he always knows the shortest, quickest route to go anywhere, anyplace, any time, in and around Houston. If you don't believe it, just ask him! Unfortunately, his route planning never allows for trivial details such as roadwork or traffic conditions. To him, it is of little consequence that the elevated portion of I-45 has been completely closed because it's being rebuilt...that Interstate 59 has multiple lanes closed in various areas for widening...that the junction of Loop 610 and the Galleria area is almost impossible to get through after 4:30 PM...or that there are bypasses such as the new 288 and outer Loop that may be a few miles out of the way, but will often save hours. None of this matters. Marvin knows the best way, and that's that. Having Marvin on board is somewhat like having one of those GPS navigational systems, except somewhat less accurate and infinitely more annoying. And Marvin's driving instructions are only the tip of the iceberg. He is like the little Eveready ® bunny that just goes and goes and goes, and everyone in the van wishes they knew where the "off" switch was.

Fortunately, Bob is a good driver, and knows the Houston roads, back streets and traffic patterns. He is equally adept at dealing with Houston traffic and Marvin's mouth, having had many years of experience with both.

On this particular afternoon, Marvin's "It's just a few minutes" took us about an hour of driving. The child's home was further outside the city than anticipated. School was already out by the time we arrived, and children were playing on the lawns in front of their homes in small groups. Bob parked the Channel 13 van in front of the home, opened the back of the van and hoisted the 50 pounds of camera and battery packs to his right shoulder. With the press of a button, it was ready to go.

Bob knew the routine well; all of Marvin's stories are filmed according to a formula that has been tested and perfected over the years. First Bob filmed the van with the Channel 13 logo, then he filmed Marvin and me getting out of the van. He then ran to the porch and filmed Marvin coming up the sidewalk towards the house, and he repeated this several times from several different angles. The goal was to produce a shot of Marvin getting out of the van gracefully, and moving quickly but forcefully towards the house.

This, of course, attracted the attention of the children who were playing nearby. The kids came running, shouting, "Maaaaaarvin Zindler, Eyewitness News." Soon others were gathering as if the Pied Piper had just arrived. Echoing one of Marvin's trademark phrases, they shouted, "Slime in the Ice Machine!"[2] Meanwhile, Bob was catching all the action on

[2] Expanding on his role as consumer watchdog, Marvin has become famous in Houston for his restaurant reports, in which he exposes eating establishments that have been cited for various violations of public health codes. No restaurant, from the most swanky to the most humble, is immune, and Marvin's graphic descriptions of rodent droppings, food storage violations, and, of course, "slime in the ice machine" have been regular Friday-night fare for many years now.

tape. Marvin took time to shake hands with everyone, signed some autographs and passed out his popular Zindler-Mickey Mouse cards.

I guess I should take a moment to explain those cards, for the benefit of those who aren't familiar with them. Disney bought out Channel 13's parent company, Capital Cities, in the mid-1990s, and, as we all know, Mickey Mouse is Disney's most significant cartoon character. When Disney acquired Marvin's contract, he started telling people, "I work for the mouse now."

Marvin was visiting me in my office one afternoon shortly after he began "working for the mouse." I have one examining room that's specially decorated for kids, and in it are several large stuffed Disney characters, including a four-foot Mickey Mouse. Marvin picked the mouse up, put one of Mickey's arms over his shoulder, and asked me to get my camera, which is never very far away from me. I ended up using my entire roll of film on Marvin and Mickey.

A few days later, I got the pictures back, and Marvin and I selected our favorites. We got into his car, drove over to the printer's, and Marvin ordered a few thousand business cards with the picture of him and the mouse. When I visited the Channel 13 studios a couple of weeks later, Marvin proudly showed me his new business cards, which featured a full-color photo of Marvin and Mickey. (I protested that I should have been given photographic credit on the bottom of the card. Marvin wasn't sure if I was kidding or not.) Later Marvin had an even larger card made. It was postcard-size and showed Marvin with a real person in a Mickey Mouse costume. The photo was taken at a Disney function. That's the card he uses for his handouts; youngsters and people of all ages are crazy about them, particularly if he signs them. By the way, I need to get one for myself...

Anyway, needless to say, those Mickey and Marvin cards were a big hit with the children who now congregated in front of the little girl's house. Marvin's patience with his fans, particularly children, is one of the most endearing things about him. He will patiently answer questions and sign autographs, and will never walk away until they all have one.

Bob was now back on the sidewalk, and he took a wide-angle shot of the entire home as Marvin, Lori and I walked up to the home and across the porch to the entrance way. Bob, now running, lowered the camera to almost ground level as he got a close-up of Marvin's feet. This emphasized purpose and determination as Marvin stepped lively across the porch to the front door. Bob then returned the camera to his right shoulder and took a close-up of Marvin ringing the doorbell with great purposefulness. He positioned himself so he could get a shot of both Marvin and the expression on the face of the person who opened the door. Bob is very, very good at his job, which is, essentially, making Marvin look good for his television audiences.

In a few moments, the child's mother opened the door. She stood there wide-eyed and open-mouthed, but nothing audible came forth for a few seconds. This is a not uncommon response. Even though Marvin always calls ahead, people almost always seem surprised to see Marvin and his news crew show up at their front door. It is as if they just can't believe that the famous Marvin Zindler could actually be at their home.

Once the initial shock passed, the mother greeted Marvin warmly and invited everyone in. Bob took this opportunity to set the heavy camera and light equipment on the floor for a few minutes, as Marvin talked to the mother, the young lady who wrote the letter, and some very excited siblings who had come into the living room on the run.

The room, as expected, was decorated for Christmas. There was a fireplace at the far wall, and stockings were hung over the hearth. Just to the left of this, in the corner of the room, was a small tree, which was also decorated and had a few strings of lights around it. One of the children threw the switch to enhance its beauty, and the multicolored lights began to twinkle. There were a few small packages at the base of the tree, but nothing elaborate. It was not quite the picture of a "hard-candy Christmas," but it was obvious the family did not have much money to spare.

Marvin introduced Lori, Bob and me to the family, and this gave everyone a chance to get over the initial excitement and to prepare for the story. First, Marvin wanted to do a shot of everyone coming down the hall and entering the living room. Lori set the stage, and Marvin and I again stepped outside. Mom was instructed to open the door and greet us.

On cue, Marvin stepped through the door once again, with a big smile exuding endless energy, whereupon he was greeted warmly by the mother. I was introduced again, and then we continued down the hallway, the cameraman documenting our progression by walking backward slowly in front of us. There's a real trick to moving backward with 50 pounds of camera equipment, trying to capture the poignancy of the moment while avoiding tripping over furniture. Bob has it down to an art form. He filmed us as we entered the living room, and then the whole scenario was repeated several times, at different angles.

Then came the interview. Because it was Christmas, this was a Christmas story, so naturally the interview had to be done in front of the Christmas tree. This meant a quick interior decorating job as furniture was shuffled so everyone could be filmed in front of The Tree. However, all the children gleefully participated, so it only took a few minutes to prepare.

Bob turned the camera on Marvin first. He asked the young lady to read the letter she wrote him.

Immediately Bob shouted, "No! No! Marvin, you have to turn your mike on first."

Marvin pushed his coat back and looked for the control box, which was clipped to his belt. He pushed the switch forward and the red "ready" light went on.

Then Bob checked the sound levels and did some more tinkering and, finally, we were ready to shoot.

Marvin positioned himself with the young lady in front of the Christmas tree, and she read her letter. Bob got a wide shot of both of them together with the Christmas tree, then a close-up of the young lady's face as she was reading. This clearly showed the tumor growing on the side of her face. Bob now moved behind her in order to get a close-up of the letter itself as she was reading it.

At that point Marvin motioned for the mother to join the group in front of the Christmas tree, and Bob immediately pulled back for another wide shot. Lori then signaled me to join the group. I examined the child's face and, using a surgical marking pen, circumscribed the facial tumor while commenting on the planned surgery. Bob zoomed in to get a close-up of the tumor, taking it from several different angles.

The camera was rolling again as Bob focused on Marvin's face. This was going to be a close-up. Marvin, with a broad grin, said, "Dr. Agris, you're going to put the incision behind the ear so there will be no scar, like you did with my face lift, when you take out this young lady's tumor." It wasn't a question so much as a demand.

I explained I was planning a similar approach to the one I had used on him, so that there would be no visible scar on her face when the surgery was completed.

Marvin then stated, "Dr. Agris, you're going to do this FREE of charge since this family does not have the funds for medical care."

The mother began crying, rushing in to give Marvin a hug. Her daughter began to cry as well, as she threw her arms around her mother's waist.

Bob went to a wide shot as I replied, "Of course, this is her special Christmas present."

This concluded the interview, and Bob silently moved across the living room, getting close-ups of this highly emotional scene.

Mom disappeared into the kitchen then, declaring she had some doughnuts and iced tea for everyone. Meanwhile, Marvin signed some autographs for the children, and I whipped out my 35-mm camera and began taking some candid photographs. These were to become part of my collection of more than 40,000 photographs of children from Houston and around the world.

After I had shot a few photos, Bob graciously offered to take a group picture of me with Marvin and the children. Each child also wanted his or her own picture with Marvin, and Marvin patiently complied. Meanwhile Mom was good as her word, serving us doughnuts and iced tea. Lori made last-minute notes and got everyone's names spelled correctly. Bob packed the camera gear as he sipped on his iced tea. And as we left, there was a small crowd of neighbors and children waving and shouting, "Maaaaaarvin, Maaaaaarvin!"

It was almost 5:00 PM as we headed at back into the city at last. This time around, we faced an open road; most of the traffic was outbound.

Back at the station, the reason for all the action around the Christmas tree became apparent. Marvin had a preconceived notion of some Christmas music he wanted to use with the story. He'd even made a cassette recording of some holiday theme songs, and insisted we listen to the music. It was a bit of overkill, but why not? After all, 'twas the season...

I asked Bob to drop me off back at the hospital so I could pick up my car. Lori went over to the computer to begin preparation and review of the evening's story, and Marvin went to his desk to begin his own preparations. I took the roll of film from my camera so I could drop it off for developing on the way home that evening. The best photos would then be selected and duplicated; Marvin would sign one set of these photos, and they would be mailed as a Christmas gift to the family. A second set would be put in my own personal collection, and a third would go into an album I prepared for Marvin and his late wife Gertrude every year, to give to them on Christmas Day.

After depositing me back at the hospital, Bob rushed back to the television studio to work with Marvin and Lori, putting the finishing touches on the evening's story.

And so ended another one of Marvin's famous success stories. Though each of his stories is unique, most follow the same format. They all begin with Marvin bursting upon the scene, like a gunfighter entering an Old-West saloon. Then there is the face-off that we all know will follow. Marvin will again be the main focal point as he stands there, surrounded by those who need his help. As the story ends, Marvin will be seen in the summation — figuratively blowing smoke from his pistol, returning it slowly to his holster, and smartly stepping through the swinging saloon doors. When possible, that summation will contain a shocking or otherwise emotionally charged one-liner.

It is almost show time. Marvin is getting a little anxious, finding more and more to complain about. But he is primed and ready, having psyched himself by reading and rereading the script. And by the time he heads for the studio, he is in a playful mood, the frazzled nerves, temper tantrums and random harassment of the past few hours all but forgotten. He jousts with the other anchors and personnel as he makes his way towards the studio. No one needs to look up from their keyboards or away from the monitor to know that Marvin has arrived. After all, you can hear him coming.

He takes a seat beside Dave Ward, the teleprompters swing into place, the signal is given, the bright red neon sign outside the studio flashes "ON THE AIR." And Marvin now is truly in his element.

C·H·A·P·T·E·R 13

IT'S ALL IN THE PACKAGING:
CLOTHES (AND HAIRPIECES) MAKE THE MAN

Two of the character traits for which Marvin is best known, his egocentricity and his perfectionism, are displayed to the extreme in his clothes and his hair style (or, more accurately, his hairpiece style). It might be argued that these traits are also reflected in his many cosmetic surgery procedures...but those are worthy of a chapter unto themselves.[1]

Marvin has always dressed colorfully, and isn't about to stop now. He wears specially made extra-wide ties, and has monograms of assorted styles and colors added to his shirts and jackets. Then, of course, there is his shimmering silver hairpiece and distinctive blue glasses. All this and more add to his pizzazz.

At this point I should mention that those blue glasses are more than mere theatrics. They're actually a medical necessity (which I'll discuss in a later chapter). Even so, they've become part of the overall "package."

Nowhere is the evidence of Marvin's lifelong passion for clothes more apparent than in his closet — or, rather, *closets*. Marvin has two very large closets in the dressing area adjacent to his bath, and he has the clothes to fill them. The closet walls are lined with row after row of neatly pressed suits, all precisely hung so there's no danger that they will touch one another and risk wrinkling. There are at least 200 suits, as well as a plethora of sport jackets and formal attire.

Next, there's a row of slacks, neatly arranged by color and meticulously hung to avoid creasing or wrinkling. There are the usual black, gray and navy, but also a multitude of bright reds, vibrant greens and whites. White is a popular color in the South, and

---

[1] See the section titled, "Marvin: Under the Knife, and Up On the Soapbox."

Marvin feels that it can be worn in any month in any season. This, as much as his muck-raking, has led to the affectionate name, "The White Knight." (Others who are not so enamored of Marvin refer to him somewhat sarcastically as "Mr. Clean.")

Centered below each of the suits are 50 to 60 pairs of scrupulously polished shoes. Again, the basic colors are well-represented, but there are many two-tone pairs, as well. Most of these are white and black or white and brown. Since Marvin is an avid golfer, there's a myriad of golf shoes. And no Texan is worth his salt without at least one pair of cowboy boots. But Marvin has rarely been known to stop at one of anything, and several pairs of boots line the wall in the rear of the closet. Particularly striking is a pair of all-white boots, beautifully tooled in a classic southwest design. The white boots were given to Marvin more than 30 years ago, but they look like they just came off the shelf. Then again, he only wears them once or twice a year.

Marvin says, "I wear those damn white boots only once each year when I board the float as the master of ceremonies for the Houston Livestock Show and Rodeo." On occasion, he has also worn them when he has been the honorary drum major with the Texas A&M band during the annual rodeo parade in downtown Houston.

Indeed, those boots were made for marching. Marvin was 78 years old in February 2000 when he took off in front of the Texas A&M band, in near-freezing weather, clad all in white and twirling his baton. He out-marched and out-twirled the 20-year-olds. They were fascinated and amazed with what he could do with that baton. During a pause in the festivities, the other twirlers attempted to emulate him — but to no avail. Marvin graciously and patiently worked with them, teaching them the tricks of the trade. Marvin's persistence, his experience, and, of course, his innate ability to twirl that baton, brought cheers from the A&M band — not to mention from the jubilant crowd, which stood eight to ten deep along Louisiana Avenue, chanting loudly, "Mar-vin! Mar-vin! Mar-vin!"

Marvin's accessories include hundreds of pairs of socks, which he buys by the dozen as the whim, not the need, arises. His ties are too numerous to count, and he has neckwear in every color of the rainbow, as well as the more subdued blacks, whites and browns. These extra wide, custom-made ties are considered by many to be a Marvin Zindler trademark. Each tie is cut so that when it is properly positioned and knotted, the visible portion is an almost diamond-shaped configuration that fills most of the exposed area between the coat lapels, and then tapers sharply at its base. All in all, not your usual tie. But then, when has Marvin ever done anything the way everyone else does?

Draped over a walnut valet in Marvin's closet are some 20 belts, but these are seldom worn. Marvin prefers suspenders. He feels the suspenders are more comfortable and allow the trousers to hang more evenly.

The remaining space in the closet is filled with shirts: everyday shirts, sports shirts, golfing shirts, formal shirts... and more and more and more shirts. He keeps a minimum of 300 to 400 shirts, and as styles change and his moods vacillate, he purchases them a dozen at a time and in every color.

Where clothes are concerned, Marvin may seem the very picture of excess, but many others (besides the clothing merchants) benefit from his penchant for new threads. For example, because Marvin purchases suits almost as impulsively as he does his shirts, he is constantly giving the older ones away to make room for more. Expensive suits usually go to family and other close relatives. He gives others to the Salvation Army, or to the county jail for prisoners to dress up for courtroom appearances. Nothing goes to waste.

I plead guilty for introducing Marvin to the collarless Stubbs Davis shirts he is so fond of wearing. I made the mistake of telling Marvin he looked younger in this style of shirt. And he does, but let's face it; Marvin doesn't need any extra encouragement when it comes to purchasing clothes. He manages quite well on his own.

It began in 1996 when, shortly after one of his many cosmetic surgical procedures, Marvin and I were dining out at Pino's, one of Houston's finest Italian restaurants. I had started wearing a new style of shirt made by Stubbs Davis of Dallas, Texas, a designer known for the quality and originality of his men's shirts. This particular style of shirt is referred to as a collarless or banded-collar shirt that can be worn open for casual occasions, and closed with a collar button when more formal attire is required. Though I am a cosmetic surgeon, I am also conscious of nonsurgical methods of enhancing one's appearance, and I found this style produces a younger, sleeker, more streamlined look.

While having dinner with Marvin and Pino, I suggested we might go out and purchase a Stubbs Davis shirt for Marvin. It's not as if Marvin didn't have enough shirts already, but he was apparently inspired by my suggestion, and off we went to Harold's in the Heights, one of the most highly regarded men's stores in Houston. It is in fact one of the finest specialty clothing stores anywhere, and the service is impeccable. Owner Harold Wiesenthal has been in business for more than 50 years, and has dressed many celebrities and high-profile people, including both Presidents George H.W. Bush and George W. Bush. In January 2001, George the Younger was sworn in as the leader of the free world while wearing an outfit purchased at Harold's.

Harold counts Marvin Zindler among his long-time customers, and Marvin considers Harold a good and trusted friend. His friend was pleased to supply him with a number of different colors and styles of Stubbs Davis shirts. The Old Turk of television couldn't resist adding his own touches to this new style; he had colorful button covers made, and an elegant single button cover was placed where the collar joined. And thus a new style was born.

Two nights later, when I was watching Channel 13 news, I saw Marvin wearing one of his new shirts; this one had a stunning onyx and diamond button cover at the center of the collar. Marvin also had on a new hairpiece. It was not as full as those he had previously worn, and it was cropped short in the front and along the sides, giving a more youthful, clean-cut appearance. I have to admit, the overall effect was very flattering.

As soon as the program ended I called Marvin at the studio and told him, "I was watching the news with some friends, and we were commenting on the new you. Everybody thought you looked great in the new style shirt and that you had become a real trendsetter."

At the very least, Marvin was setting a trend for himself. Night after night, he appeared in a different colored Stubbs shirt with a multiplicity of dazzling and interesting collar buttons. I noticed that these shirts also had his initials emblazoned on both cuffs. The body of the shirts were one color, with the cuffs and collar a contrasting color.

When I spoke to the people at Harold's about Marvin's latest infatuation, Ken Patteson, one of Harold's long-time sales personnel, told me, "Marvin buys everything in every color we have, if we have a size and style that fits him."

That's certainly consistent with Marvin's clothes purchasing habits. In any event, his new style seemed to be here to stay, and it was a far cry from the tie-and-blue-blazer combo that has long been the standard apparel of prime-time news personnel. Even after nearly 25 years on television, Marvin was setting a new mode of dress.

For his part, Marvin insisted that this new way of dressing had nothing to do with television theatrics. He was simply carrying on his tradition of dressing colorfully, and he felt that this new style became him. His television audience apparently agreed, if the many letters of approval he received were any indication.

Any man who has ever laughed or complained about all the time and energy women devote to their appearance should know that this trait is not the exclusive province of women. When it comes to attention to detail, Marvin could probably put the vainest woman to shame.

His late wife Gertrude once said, "I would put Marvin up against anybody for being vain. He is a very, very vain person."

If you mention the word "vanity" in front of Marvin, however, he will bellow, "Vanity, vanity. What is vanity?"

And then, more than likely, he will continue: "Being vain is caring about how you look and how you smell. It's not just how you dress but your hair color, your teeth, the shoes you wear, and the way you conduct yourself."

So it's not that he denies being vain, just that in his view, vanity is not at all a bad thing.

More than once, Gertrude said that Marvin was both extremely easy and excruciatingly difficult to live with. This paradox was, and is, certainly reflected in Marvin's attitude towards his wardrobe. His suits are always pressed to a razor's edge, and he has always insisted on doing all of his own pressing, as well as most of his other clothes-maintenance tasks. "He does everything but wash his shirts and underwear," Gertrude told me. "I believe a lot of wives would appreciate that in a man."

In all honesty, however, Marvin's insistence on taking care of his clothes stemmed less from a desire to be helpful than a belief that if you want something done right, you have to do it yourself. As a matter of fact, Gertrude did iron Marvin's shirts in the very early weeks of their marriage. But, as she explained, "Marvin's too persnickety. He didn't like the way I ironed them, so I told him to do it himself. He tried the local laundry, but that never satisfied him."

She added, "When the permanent-press fabrics came out, I got back to washing them at least. But Marvin has his own ironing board set up in the dressing area, and he irons them himself every morning before he puts them on."

Marvin's persnickety qualities go even further. He maintains a collection of cleaning solvents in his closet, as well. You'd think he had a small dry-cleaning operation set up in his home. Using his own mixture of cleaning solutions, he carefully and lovingly removes any blemishes that may appear on his suits.

Gertrude told me, "Marvin doesn't hold back on personal opinions when things don't go the way he likes. He loses his temper all the time and usually at the slightest things. I mean, constantly. It starts in the morning almost as soon as he gets up. He'll be rummaging around in one of his two large closets looking for a particular shirt and yelling at himself, 'Got-dammit, got-dammit. It's just like playing hide-and-seek in here, dammit, dammit.'"

She laughed and continued, "I'll tell him the shirt he's looking for is dirty and hasn't been washed yet, and it just sets him off again. It isn't like he doesn't have any other shirts to wear. There are at least 200 others hanging in the closet. He'll finally select another shirt, and it will start all over again, 'got-dammit, got-dammit.' It's never anything earth-shaking. Marvin just can't find his cufflinks fast enough to suit him.

"Or he'll be looking for a pair of shoes and start yelling, 'All my shoes are in boxes.' So I have to tell him all over again, for the ten-thousandth time, that I keep his shoes in boxes to keep them neat because he has so many and all he has to do is look on the boxes where I've written things like 'black and white loafers with gold trim,' or 'black and white golf shoes,' or whatever. And his language is just terrible, but that's Marvin."

Outsiders may think that Marvin was an intolerable husband, but the relationship between him and Gertrude was, in its own unique way, especially loving and tender.

When they were young, Marvin tried to instill his some of his own dressing habits in his children, with little success. According to Gertrude, "When our children were small, Marvin wanted to make sure they were dressed properly. He took little Marvin Jr. down to the store and bought him everything. Marvin bought him velvet pants and all that silly stuff. When Marvin Jr. went to school, he was dressed in Sunday-go-to-meeting clothes. Marvin Jr. didn't know any better for the first few days at school. Then one day, he came home and took off all his clothes in the middle of the room. He threw them on the floor and said he wasn't going to school anymore if he had to dress like that.

"I immediately took him downtown and got some ordinary, everyday children's play clothes for him. When his father came home that evening and saw Marvin Jr., he thought it was just terrible. From then on, I had to dress the children for school. Marvin wouldn't do it anymore."

For the children, this was no doubt an immense relief.

Although he never could mold his kids to his tastes, that never stopped Marvin from going his own way, fashion-wise. According to Gertrude, "Marvin used to coach a Little League team when the children were small. He would wear a coat and tie. Can you imagine that! Marvin even took the family fishing wearing a coat and tie."

Conceding that her husband is a lifelong perfectionist, she added, "The older he has gotten, the worse it gets."

I can't argue with Gertrude's assessment of Marvin's sartorial perfectionism. The days of coaching Little League in a suit and tie are long gone, but Marvin is still always impeccably dressed, regardless of the activity — and the location.

Even in the jungles and rainforests of South and Central America, Marvin had on a tie and a three-piece suit. I remember one medical mission in Central America, where Marvin had joined me and the medical team in a hospital that was not much more than a MASH unit. Temperatures reached 110 degrees, and with the lights from the television cameras, it probably exceeded that. In minutes everyone had soaked through their lightweight cotton operating room attire. At the completion of the surgical procedure, you could take your shirt off and wring it out. It was as wet as if it had just gone through the wash.

Marvin was there the entire time, consummately dressed in a white suit, white shirt and tie. But he never seemed to even break a sweat, remaining cool, calm and collected while everyone else wilted in the heat and humidity.

As for the natives, they just couldn't seem to take their eyes off the White Knight. No one in those parts had ever seen anyone like this silver-haired, blue-spectacled gentleman who dared to wear a full dress suit in this heat. On subsequent days when Marvin and the medical team returned to the hospital, fingers would point and we would hear, in muffled tones, *"El Jefe, El Jefe"* (the boss man).

On this occasion, as well as during our many other trips, I enjoyed watching the facial expressions of the people — both children and adults — when they encountered Marvin. What was going through their minds? What was behind their stares, their smiles, their nervous laughter and, it must be said, their occasional smirks? It surprises me that Marvin can hear people poking fun at him, and he just laughs about it. The truth is, Marvin doesn't seem to care what anybody thinks of him, or whether they agree or disagree with him, as long as he makes a good appearance.

It all comes back to Marvin's belief that he owes it to his audience to make the best appearance he can. Marvin's audience is not just those who watch and listen to him on television, but those with whom he interacts wherever he may be at any time of the day or the night. And in his own way he is a commanding presence; once the initial shock or surprise dissipates, his dress, carriage, and mannerisms bring respect if not fear.

It has often been said that "Clothes make the man." I don't know if that is completely true, but the way you dress definitely sends a message — even if the people around you don't always understand that message.

∽ • ∽

Marvin, as you must surely know by now, is very opinionated. He feels he is a fashion connoisseur and, at times, a fashion consultant. Many who are on the receiving end of these largely unsolicited consultations no doubt think he is more akin to a fashion cop. At any rate, Marvin will tell you exactly what he thinks about how you are dressed and what you should wear.

Needless to say, I have been the recipient of some of Marvin's fashion advice, having attended hundreds of events with him over the years. When I arrive to pick him up at the Zindler homestead, or meet him at a designated hotel or restaurant, I never know what to expect. More than once, I have been greeted with "Got-damn," and "That awful tie" (or vest, or shirt, or other article of clothing), followed by, "Your mother wouldn't let you out of the house looking like that."

Marvin will stammer and stutter for a minute and then continue, "Take that got-damn thing off! We'll get you something else." Accordingly I have learned to keep a few extra ties in the trunk of my car. In other words, I usually succumb to the dictates of the man whom Gertrude and I winkingly used to call, "Mr. Fashion, Himself."

∽ • ∽

Marvin's obsessive and compulsive habits regarding his clothes seem like normal behavior compared to his attitudes about his hair, or lack thereof. It all started in the 1950s, when Marvin was put in charge of the ladies' ready-to-wear section of the family store. As part of his job, Marvin made several trips a year to purchase new merchandise in New York City's Garment District.

Marvin said, "I was in New York in 1954. I hadn't lost my hair yet but I decided I was going to go get me a hairpiece. Someone told me about a guy who did hairpieces for people like Frank Sinatra. So, I went into an office with this guy and he said, 'What do you need a hairpiece for? Is it for somebody else?'

"I said, 'No, my dad is bald, my uncle is bald, and I know I'm going to be bald, too. I'm going to shave my head and I want you to fix me up with a hairpiece so nobody knows I've got one.' So, he shaved my head right then and there and put a hairpiece on me and then made me a spare one. I never told anybody about it. I came home from New York City and my kids never knew I had a hairpiece. Then I began to play around with it and I got a bigger one, and then a bigger one than that. The first thing I knew, I was starting to get gray, so I decided to have a gray hairpiece made to match my natural shade."

Today Marvin possesses many hairpieces. He has one hairpiece for golf, a hairpiece for sleeping, a hairpiece for casual wear and another for more formal appearances. The styles have changed over the years, of course.

Marvin has had straight hair and even a flipped curly pompadour. The pompadour hairpieces of the 1970s — a style that was lampooned in some of the stage productions of *The Best Little Whorehouse in Texas* — were an accident. Marvin keeps his hairpieces in boxes rather than on forms, feeling that this keeps them from getting dusty. One of his hairpieces happened to have been placed in its box crooked, resulting in its being re-shaped into a pompadour. When Marvin put it on, however, he liked it, and had other hairpieces similarly styled.

Though the hairpieces had long been one of Marvin's trademarks, everything almost changed in 1975, when Marvin learned he may not have needed a hairpiece after all. Because of travel and time commitments, he was unable to shave his head and replace his hairpiece for several days. Finally, when time allowed, he walked into the bathroom and peeled back the hairpiece, only to behold a fine growth of new hair.

Marvin said it surprised him, and for an instant, just an instant, he thought, *I may let it grow out under the hairpiece. Wouldn't it be funny to just whip the hairpiece off someday and show that I had my own hair?* However, it wasn't to be. He decided to continue shaving and not bother with trying to grow his hair.

At one time, Marvin had a series of hairpieces, each a different length. He would start at the beginning of the month and progressively change the hairpieces to make it look as if his hair was growing. After four to six weeks, Marvin would repeat the cycle again. It was a clever ruse, but very expensive. Each of these hairpieces cost several thousand dollars, not including maintenance and regular trips to Tom Magliaro's Hair Additions in the uptown section of Houston.

His hairpieces became fuller throughout the 1980s. In the 1990s, there were more radical changes that gave Tom Magliaro fits at times. All at once Marvin decided that he wanted a short, conservative, clean businessman cut, feeling this made him look younger. This new hairpiece style, in conjunction with his Stubbs Davis shirts, resulted in the "new Marvin" that was so favorably received by his friends and his public.

It might be said that Marvin's hairpiece was one of his worst-kept secrets. His daughter Helen remembers how her cousins and friends taunted her about her father's vanity. She says she defended him and stoutly denied the hairpiece allegations until she was finally told the truth. To most others, however, the hairpiece revelations were anticlimactic.

Marvin didn't mind people *knowing* he wore a hairpiece, but he was damned if he'd let anyone *see* him without it. Even during the multiple cosmetic surgery procedures that I performed on him, neither Gertrude nor any shospital personnel apart from me ever saw Marvin without his hairpiece. Marvin was fanatical about this.

Gertrude said she thought he must have driven me crazy. Sometimes he came close, but I knew that complying with Marvin's wishes, no matter how unconventional, was the path of least resistance. As one of the many concessions to Marvin's orders, I had to write a special note on his chart to allow him to wear his hairpiece to the operating room. Marvin made me promise that I would keep it in place until he was asleep. I was instructed to replace the hairpiece after the surgery was completed and before he left the O.R. The night before the procedure, Marvin gave me a briefing, and I also called Tom Magliaro to learn more about the care and feeding of the hairpiece.

Furthermore, Marvin insisted that I alone was to change his bandages, and wasn't even allowed to have a nurse in the room to assist. He actually talked me into helping him wash the hairpiece, replace it, and comb it to his satisfaction. Gertrude once said that I had to have been a saint to work with Marvin. I make no claims in that direction either; it's simply that where Marvin is concerned, it's easier just to go along.

For a long time, then, Marvin could claim, with reasonable accuracy, "Nobody — and I mean not even my wife — has ever seen me without my hairpiece." Towards the end of her life, however, Gertrude was finally allowed to see Marvin sans rug. In 1996, Marvin had his second open-heart surgery. Recovering at home, he was still quite ill, and was sleeping in a bedroom adjacent to his and Gertrude's. He only wore a cap at night, and because Gertrude had to check on him several times a night, she finally saw him without his "hair addition." From all indications, this did nothing to compromise her love for him.

Through the details Gertrude revealed, and from my own travels with Marvin, I learned how much planning and preparation is required for Marvin to be ready face the world. Again, any man who has ever complained that women take a long time getting ready to go out should consider Marvin, and then thank his lucky stars. Marvin has his own routine, and whether he's on the road or at home, that routine is unvarying.

Not wishing to leave anything to chance or a last-minute time crunch, he plans his outfit for the next day the night before. Making a choice is no small task, there being so much to choose from. He selects one of the carefully tailored suits that has been made to his specifications. The coat collars, for instance, are narrowed so more of the shirt will show. Sleeves are a little shorter than most so that the cuffs will show. If the jacket has even one or two vents in the back, they are sewed shut so it will hang straight and not flare. Marvin inspects the suit and removes even the tiniest speck from his clothing. He then selects a shirt.

Marvin immediately begins to iron the clothes he will wear the next day. With his travel iron or the larger steam iron he has at home, he first begins with the lapels, ironing them to perfection. The sleeves of his coat, like his trousers, are sharply creased rather than having a gentle roll. "If you iron them without a crease, they rumple," he will tell you. "And you will look disheveled in an hour."

With equal care, a tie is selected and inspected, and then the clothing is meticulously hung. In a similar fashion, a pair of shoes is selected, polished and set aside.

To ensure that he awakens on time, Marvin uses a buzzer-type alarm. He says he cannot stand music or singing that early in the morning, and he particularly objects to those "got-damn farmer boys trying to sell me manure at that time of the morning."

The first thing Marvin does is head for the bathroom to begin the morning ritual. He first removes his hairpiece, the one worn only for sleeping. Originally, it was an all-purpose hairpiece and quite expensive. After trying to restyle it himself, Marvin decided he had cut it too short. Rather than discard it, he simply designated it for sleeping only.

To Marvin, the bathroom is a think tank as well as a place for performing his morning ablutions, and it is here that he first contemplates the day's schedule. He often formulates his most striking story ideas during these early morning think-sessions.

"That's where I really do the whole thing," he says. "I decide how we're going to shoot the story, what kind of special lighting I might need, what questions I'm going to ask and what answers I want. Even such details as to how I am going to have the film cut for the broadcast. I don't start with a story idea, I start with a deadline, and then practically write the whole thing out in my mind."

During this solitary planning session, he may also consider the vocal intonations and gestures he's going to use. He considers how factors such as his stance or camera positioning might make the story more interesting for the audience. And he contemplates possible rebuttals to any smart-aleck comments that might be made by persons he plans to confront that day. Once these matters are firmly settled in his mind, he hops into the shower. Pleased with himself and looking forward to the day's activities, he will break into loud and robust song.

After toweling, he shaves his face. He also shaves his head if necessary, to ensure a skin-tight fit of a fresh hairpiece. He precisely positions the hairpiece and spends what seems like an inordinate amount of time melding it with natural growth, while spraying and brushing, until he gets it just the way he desires. This is followed by a combination of several after-shave lotions or colognes.

Then comes the makeup, because Marvin never goes anywhere without makeup. He does not like the heavy pancake variety of makeup used in most television studios. Instead, he uses a very light tan commercial brand that produces "just the right tone under the television lights."

Finally, Marvin is ready to get dressed. He is excruciatingly careful not to get any of the makeup on his collar or clothing. Slowly, painstakingly, he dons his attire, and finally steps into his shoes.

And then at last, Marvin is ready to face his public... but is the world ready for Marvin?

C·H·A·P·T·E·R 14

Ringside:
Zindler Versus Donaldson

Two titans of the same television network slug it out over the airwaves. It's the broadcast brouhaha of the decade, and Round One is about to take place in Houston, Texas.

"Pretty Boy" Marvin Zindler is the one in the white trunks. As a former welterweight champion and lifelong muckraker, Zindler has more than a passing familiarity not only with the boxing ring, but with controversy and conflict of all sorts. Both in the ring and out, he has long been known for his hard-hitting and direct approach. It is, to be sure, an approach that has left him with a few literal as well as figurative bloody noses in the past, but in most of his fights he has come out the winner.

Savage Sam Donaldson, the one in the black trunks, is a comparative newcomer. Savage Sam hails from New York City. His friends say he tends to prance around the ring and is not as direct as Zindler. Donaldson tends to throw a rapid series of punches, putting up a good smokescreen, but retreats quickly to the safety of his corner when threatened. He will then re-enter, taking a few jabs before he backs off again.

All in all, two very different approaches.

It is Donaldson who has brought the fight to Houston, Texas, a long way from his home turf. But the fight will be broadcast over the national airwaves, and the nation will be anxiously awaiting its outcome.

There goes the bell...

Both "Savage Sam" and "Pretty Boy" Zindler worked for the same boss, ABC-TV. So what got these two titans into each other's faces? Why were they squaring off on national television?

It started on September 30, 1993, when, on a segment of *Prime Time Live*, Donaldson jabbed and jabbed again at Houston's internationally recognized Medical Center. In a scathing report on the one of the Center's most well-known institutions, The Methodist Hospital, Donaldson insinuated that the hospital catered to wealthy patients and had a tight-fisted attitude toward the less fortunate regarding medical care.

Marvin said, "It hit me in the gut like a punch." After catching his breath, he didn't back off, but came out swinging. In his flashy white trunks, Pretty Boy Zindler fought an unprecedented three-night (Monday through Wednesday) series to take on Sam Donaldson and the *Prime Time Live* piece. In so doing, of course, Marvin was actually taking a swing at his own bosses in the Big Apple. This did not daunt our White Knight, who led with a strong right to the heart of the matter.

"Donaldson's report was a hatchet job filled with lies and half truths," Marvin said. "That wasn't journalism, that was Sam doing the ol' show-biz routine, making it seem a lot worse than it was." Perhaps because this is exactly the type of thing Marvin has been accused of doing in the past, he qualified his statement. "I'm show biz, too, but I wouldn't twist the facts and take things out of context like Donaldson did."

> *Savage Sam is stunned by this frontal attack, but Pretty Boy lets the punches fly again....*

"I objected to Donaldson making The Methodist Hospital seem like an exclusive country club for the rich and famous," asserted Marvin. "Forty-eight percent of their patients are on Medicare."

> *Zindler has landed a stunning series of blows. He backs off and does a little soft shoe. He is way ahead in points, and it is only Round One...*

"I have no problem with the basic premise [of Donaldson's piece]," Marvin went on to explain. "Methodist hasn't been doing its fair share of charity work." What Marvin took exception to was the overall tone of *Prime Time Live's* broadcast, and Donaldson's attitude. The issue that really riled him was the handling of each of the segments. He felt many of the details were taken out of context, then reassembled to present Donaldson's viewpoint on the subject. According to Marvin, "Donaldson's report was a hatchet job, filled with lies and half truths. It struck below the belt, and was just not consistent with good journalism."

With his opponent down for the count, Marvin freely admitted that he has a "soft spot" for The Methodist Hospital, one of several area hospitals which regularly provides assistance, free of charge, for the needy. He has featured this hospital several times on his television show.

Besides that, Marvin himself has been a patient there on numerous occasions, with his multitude of cosmetic surgery procedures as well as two coronary bypass procedures. "Yes, I paid my way," he said. His wife Gertrude was also successfully treated at The Methodist Hospital in the 1950s, for colon cancer.

Savage Sam Donaldson is obviously staggering under Pretty Boy Zindler's flurry of punches, but don't count Sam out just yet. The bell rings, and the two return to their respective corners. The verbal rhetoric has caught them short of breath, and they need to plan their strategies for Round Two.

During this short intermission, Richard Kaplan, Executive Producer of *Prime Time Live,* grabbed the mike at ringside in support of his fighter. Kaplan fired off a verbal retort, "Okay, Marvin Zindler is hot stuff in Houston, but it is irresponsible for a news department to let him run loose like that. He shouldn't be allowed to masquerade as a newsman. Donaldson's credentials are impeccable, and what are Zindler's? An embarrassment."

Donaldson, recovering from the first round, added, "Obviously ABC believed the report was accurate and fair, or it wouldn't have been on the air. But [to have] another arm of the same company — Channel 13-KTRK in Houston, which is also owned and operated by ABC television — calling it a hatchet job...is appalling."

In his corner Pretty Boy Zindler just smiles, raises his shoulders, arches his back and yawns. He is way ahead. He has staggered Savage Sam in the first round. His opponents are just blowing steam. They brought this fight to Marvin's turf — their mistake.

In Marvin's corner at ringside was Channel 13's news director, Richard Longoria. Longoria was sitting back, relaxed, with a smile on his face. Longoria knew he had the home-turf advantage, and all of Houston was betting on Zindler to win the day. When asked for his opinion about Richard Kaplan's remarks, Longoria had no comment. Why should he? Marvin was saying it all, and he wasn't finished yet.

The press was persistent, however, and continued to pester Longoria for a statement. Finally, with a wild twinkle in his eyes and a smirk on his face, he acquiesced. "Even though we are an ABC affiliate, we call our own shots here. Zindler's pieces were, I believe, labeled as commentary. That means opinions, and everybody knows Marvin has a lot of those."

The crowd began to laugh. Others stamped their feet and clapped. They were anxiously awaiting Round Two, as was Pretty Boy Zindler himself. He wasn't going to let his opponent get away so easily.

Locking horns with his own television network did not seem to phase Marvin. With the microphone only inches away from him, he turned quickly to his right before the ringside commentator moved off, and at the top of his voice said, "When I took this job 21 years ago I said there would be no sacred cows, and I still believe it."

Donaldson, behind in points in the first round, felt that he needed reinforcements. "I am writing letters to 13's General Manager, the news director and Marvin, telling them in the strongest terms possible I do not appreciate this," he asserted. "No one questions my integrity like that without a response. Credibility is my most important asset. I can't rely on a pretty face." (Memo to Sam: That's why God made cosmetic surgeons.)

Is the Savage Sam versus Pretty Boy Zindler bout over? Not by a long shot. The Houston crowd is up on their feet, cheering on their hometown hero. The bell rings loudly, echoing across the nation, as Round Two begins.

Zindler, cheered on by the crowd, adrenaline pumping, virtually leaps from his corner. Donaldson is taken by surprise as the "good guy" in the white trunks lashes out again at the man from the Big Apple. Maybe Donaldson never heard, "Don't mess with Texas" and, more important, "Nobody lays a glove on Marvin Harold Zindler."

Marvin was once again on the attack. "If you saw the Donaldson report, you probably got the idea that The Methodist Hospital is an exclusive country club for the rich and famous."

Marvin then began to take Donaldson down one punch at a time, striking out at each of the points Donaldson portrayed in his *Prime Time Live* program. Chief Executive Officer of The Methodist Hospital, Larry Mathis, was in Marvin's corner tonight. Taking the mike, he agreed, "Donaldson certainly did us a disservice. We answered his questions fully and with the truth, but he was not interested in the full truth."

What about those deluxe hospital suites Donaldson talked about? What about those claims of wet bars and king-sized four poster beds? Marvin landed a resounding second-round punch with, "What about those wet bars? There aren't any. Just a small refrigerator, and that is NOT A WET BAR."

The big question was this: Was Donaldson's report an exaggeration or an outright lie?

Trying to hold his ground, Donaldson declared, "If you have insurance, you can get some of the best care available in surroundings that are nothing short of luxurious, beginning with an opulent lobby, valet parking and polished marble floors."

Pretty Boy Zindler backed off a few steps and let Savage Same prowl aimlessly about. It was, after all, just part of his show business cover-up.

But finally Marvin could take it no more, and let go. "Is it immoral to have a beautiful hospital with some of the best doctors in the world and excellent nursing and patient care? It certainly sounds like it the way Sam Donaldson describes it."

Again they were in each other's faces, and the blows begin to fall fast and heavy.

In response to Savage Sam's snide remarks about the luxurious lobby of the hospital,

Marvin explained that the lobby, fountain and sitting area were all paid for with private donations from a physician, Dr. L. Crain, and his friends, in memory of Dr. Crain's wife. Dr. Crain wanted a place of beauty in the hospital. He thought the entrance should be lovely, peaceful and inviting — more like a five-star hotel than the stark, cold, intimidating entrances of most hospitals.

There is also a chapel — a place to pray, contemplate, rest and recover. All were donated. All were gifts to the hospital.

> *Pretty Boy Zindler is scoring points and the hometown crowd is cheering him on...*

Marvin was all the more determined. He wasn't about to back off now. "What about that chamber music [reported by Donaldson] in the lobby of the hospital? The clarinetist...just happens to be a 'charity patient.' A cancer patient at that. He was enjoying himself by entertaining fellow patients. He wasn't getting paid for it."

Then Marvin let go with another right to the point. "What about the valet parking? This service is not exclusive to The Methodist Hospital. What about M. D. Anderson Hospital, St. Luke's Hospital, Texas Children's Hospital, the Texas Heart Institute, the Hermann Hospital and hospitals outside of the Medical Center such as Southwest Memorial Hospital? All have valet parking. Why, Sam, even Randall's supermarket offers valet parking to its customers. It is not just a luxury. It is to make things easier for sick people, the elderly and the handicapped."

> *Can Savage Sam stand up to this pounding much longer? Will he retreat to his corner? Not on your life.*

Donaldson insisted the hospital is "set in surroundings nothing short of opulent." However, he obviously wasn't scoring many points with this one, so he tried again. The best he could come up with was, "Not everyone can get to be a patient here."

But Marvin continued to hammer back, and he was relentless. "Donaldson in *Prime Time Live* makes it look like Methodist is only for the rich and famous, and no one else."

> *Once again, Savage Sam is saved by the bell. It resounds loudly, and he and Pretty Boy Zindler return to their corners. Zindler appears to be ready to put his opponent away...*

Marvin took this opportunity to ask Methodist Hospital CEO Larry Mathis a few questions. "How many Medicare patients come to your hospital?" he asked, and Mr. Mathis verified Marvin's earlier statement, "Forty-eight percent of our patients are on Medicare."

Said Marvin, "I can assure you most of the forty-eight percent of Medicare patients are not rich and not famous, and most are in the lower fixed-income brackets. Flashing

White Knight in Blue Shades

his famous broad smile, he added, "Sam Donaldson makes it seem like it is a disgrace to have a clean, beautiful hospital and to have the services that Methodist provides."

Larry Mathis concurred. "It *is* good to have a clean, beautiful hospital for people who are sick. They need some nice surroundings. There is nothing wrong with that."

He continued, "We have only one source of income, and that is patients who can pay their bills, and if we don't attract them here, there is no money for anything — for education, for research and for charity care."

In an unprecedented third round, Marvin again came out swinging on Wednesday night, with Channel 13 continuing to provide coverage. By now, everyone's money was on Pretty Boy Zindler. He continued to counter effectively and landed some well-placed criticisms of the Donaldson story.

Awaiting the knockout punch that would send Savage Sam back to the Big Apple, the crowd was on their feet. Savage Sam turned in his corner, leaning through the ropes to make a comment. As all of his other approaches had failed, he had decided to give the audience a historical and religious perspective of medical care. Accordingly, Donaldson opened Round Three by saying, "This matter should be handled in a manner consistent with the hospital's religious heritage. The hospital was established in 1922 by the Methodist Church. Although the church does not direct hospital policy, the Book of Resolutions talks about church founder John Wesley's attitude toward health care in this way."

Reading from the Book of Resolutions, Donaldson concluded, "John Wesley was always deeply concerned with health care and with providing medical services at no cost to the poor."

Which, of course, could only raise the question: *Where is the money to come from?*

In a classic example of real TV showmanship, Sam Donaldson stood in front of a Methodist church and asked Larry Mathis about that statement from the Methodist Book of Resolutions.

Larry replied, "Sam, The Methodist Hospital is not the Methodist church. Why don't you ask that question to the bishop of the Methodist church?"

Meanwhile, Marvin continued to hammer away. "Sure, both Sam and I work for the same company, but we don't have to agree on everything. We certainly didn't here. The folks at *Prime Time Live* do a great job. But you know me. I have to speak out when I think something is unfair.

"Methodist's president says nineteen million dollars has been set aside this year for charity health care. This is eleven million more than last year. I hope all tax-exempt hospitals will give more to the poor. I would like to see more dollars go to our charity hospitals and clinics."

In the end, you might say, Pretty Boy Zindler won the match. At the very least Savage Sam learned that nobody gets the last word on Marvin. The White Knight, all but holding his arms above his head and making the victory sign, concluded, "It is hell to be poor, especially when you need health care."

And the crowd went wild.

P·A·R·T

5

Family First...
And Always

Gertrude And
The Zindler Children

C·H·A·P·T·E·R 15

Two Silver Hearts:
The Love Story of
Marvin & Gertrude Zindler

They were married for 56 years. Their nearly six decades together were filled with successes and failures, dreams and adventures, disappointment and happiness. Like most long marriages, their union survived countless ups and downs — professional challenges, surgeries and more surgeries, children and grandchildren. Romantics might declare them soul mates, fated to be together. That may be, but the marriage between Marvin Zindler and Gertrude Kugler began with numerous factors working against it, including the disapproval of the Zindler family patriarch.

Marvin and Gertrude also began married life with a big secret. When they exchanged their wedding vows in April of 1942 at an elegant hotel in Houston, it was not the first marriage — for either one of them. This was a secret they kept for decades.

It was inevitable that Marvin Zindler and Gertrude Kugler would eventually meet, as they were moving in the same circle of friends. Their first meeting was in the summer of 1939, and it was definitely not love at first sight on either side.

At that time, Gertrude was casually dating one of Marvin's good friends, Harry Dawson. One hot summer afternoon, Marvin and Harry were returning to Houston from a day at the beach on Galveston Island. Gertrude and some of her friends had also spent the day at Galveston.

Harry Dawson had seen Gertrude and her friends at the beach earlier that day, but hadn't approached her, and had said nothing to Marvin. An idea was brewing in Harry's head. He and Gertrude were just good friends, no real chemistry there. But Marvin and Gertrude... well, now, that had possibilities.

From experience, Dawson knew that the girls would be hungry and thirsty, and would most likely make a stop at Prince's Drive-In over on Harrisburg Avenue when they left the beach. Prince's was a popular teenage hangout, and Gertrude's brother had been dating a young lady who was both a niece and employee of owner Doug Prince.

As the young men arrived at the drive-in, Harry spied a convertible full of sunburned, wind-swept young ladies — Gertrude and the other girls, just as he had expected. The girls' long hair hung in tangled ropes after a day of saltwater spray and wind. They were sticky and hot and spotted with sand, and their faces were red and puffy, their eyes bloodshot from the saltwater.

Harry pulled in, placed his order and then walked Marvin over to the car where Gertrude and her friends sat. Casually he introduced Marvin to Gertrude and the other young ladies.

Marvin was not impressed. Rumor has it that he thought Gertrude looked like a real beast. What would you expect after a wind-swept day at the beach?

Gertrude was, in fact, an exceptionally pretty young woman who was blessed with a petite, graceful figure. Besides that, she was smart, had a cheerful personality, and was sensitive to others. Under the circumstances, however, Marvin quickly dismissed this girl from Philadelphia — and her friends — as unkempt, untidy, and, frankly, unsightly.

Summer vacation over, Marvin returned to his studies at John Tarleton and forgot about Gertrude. Then in the winter of 1939 he returned to Houston for the holidays. Marvin recalls, "I had a date one night, and Harry Dawson had a date with Gertrude, but my date stood me up. Harry said, 'Come on and go with us.'"

So Marvin, Harry and Gertrude went to the High Hat, a non-drinking teenage dance club on South Main Street. This time around, Marvin was entranced when he saw Gertrude. He would not believe that this very feminine, petite, lovely young lady was the same Gertrude he had met last summer. At one point, Marvin excused himself and dragged Harry over to the men's room for a quick conference. Marvin told Harry that this absolutely could not be the Gertrude that Dawson had introduced him to last summer after the day at the beach. As he tactfully put it, "That one was so ugly, the tide wouldn't take her out."

Harry assured Marvin that this was the same young lady he had met last summer at Prince's. Marvin just stood there pondering this for a minute, scratching his jaw, and then he blurted out, "This Gertrude is rather cute." Marvin says, "I asked her out on a date the next night, and on our first date, I asked her out for another date."

And that's how it began.

For her part, Gertrude found Marvin unusual, perhaps even a bit unsettling — but interesting nonetheless. Marvin was hardly your average garden-variety young gentleman of the 1940s.

"He beat anything I ever saw," Gertrude once told me. In fact, by the second date she had formed a rather strong opinion of Marvin. "I thought he was *nuts.*"

It was on the second date that Marvin dramatically showed some of his unsettling tendencies. They were again at the High Hat Club, dancing and having a good time. It was hot, crowded and noisy. Marvin convinced Gertrude that he needed to get some fresh air and just wanted to sit for awhile in the car. Of course, this is the same line that guys have been using on girls ever since the automobile was invented. Some things never change.

"I still recall the expression on Marvin's face," Gertrude said. "It was if the cat were inviting the mouse to dinner." So Gertrude had her guard up as she stepped out into the night with Marvin. But what was to happen could have knocked her over with a hummingbird feather.

With the din of the High Hat Club behind them, they walked to Marvin's car, and got in. They hadn't been there very long when Marvin dropped the bomb. Decades later, Gertrude still recalled Marvin's words with clarity.

"Guess what?" he began, ever so nonchalantly. "You may think this is silly, but I had a dream last night that I asked you to marry me."

What followed was a seemingly interminable pause. Gertrude appeared to be searching high and low for the right words, but they didn't come. So Marvin, as usual, filled in the slack. He turned his head to look out the window and then, looking back at Gertrude, he took in a deep breath. With eyes wide and a big grin, he said, "That's not a bad idea! Let's get married!"

Gertrude thought he was crazy, and told him as much. "I told him that he had a screw loose in his thinker assembly — either that or he had eaten locoweed with his Wheaties for breakfast that morning." Then, she told me, she laughed and took Marvin by the hand to pull him from the car, and they returned to the dance.

After that they continued to date, but it was not easy for Gertrude, who certainly was accustomed to more conventional guys. Sometimes Marvin would break off a date early. In the middle of the event, he would simply take Gertrude home — and then spend the rest of the night riding around with his buddies or the Bellaire police.

It was a strange relationship, but one thing wasn't in doubt: Marvin was a "take-charge person." He always made all the decisions about when and where they went, and Gertrude never had to worry about a thing. As they continued to date, Marvin periodically would bring up the subject of marriage. He was quite insistent. In response, Gertrude would usually laugh or make a funny comment. This, at least, was one area in their relationship in which Marvin was definitely not calling the shots.

As the months went by, however, Marvin's unique qualities began to work their magic on Gertrude. She was coming to the conclusion that Marvin was the most manly man she had ever met. Further, she thought that he would make a marvelous husband. Without a doubt, he would always be able to walk right in and take charge of everything. This was a characteristic she liked about him very much.

In June of 1940, he dropped a rope on her and insisted that they go steady. She said yes; really, what choice did she have, if she wanted to keep on seeing him? After that, with each date, Marvin became more and more insistent about getting double-ringed. Finally Gertrude said yes to that too, and in July of 1941, Marvin and Gertrude went to the Fort Bend County Courthouse in Richmond, Texas, and were married by the Justice of the Peace.

After the wedding, they went back home, vowing to keep their marriage a secret from family and friends. And for more than 50 years, almost no one knew Marvin and Gertrude had been married twice, both times to each other. It may have been the best-kept secret in Texas.

In December of 1941 the United States entered into World War II, and Marvin went off to be a Marine. In short order he was back home, and not too long after his return, Marvin made up his mind that he wanted to do the wedding thing right. Accordingly he asked Mr. Kugler, Gertrude's father, if he could marry her — even though, of course, they were already married. Mr. Kugler gave his blessing. That part was easy.

The real challenges lay within the walls of the Zindler compound. The most difficult obstacle, required of all of Marvin's girlfriends, was for Gertrude to pass inspection by Eva Mae, Marvin's nanny. To Gertrude, that seemed particularly absurd since they were already married.

But Marvin said it was the way it had to be. "Eva wanted to see if I was right for him," Gertrude explained, still amazed about it more than 50 years later. "I'd never heard of anything like that in my life!" Gertrude was invited to a formal dinner at the Zindlers. Eva first served dinner, then sat down for a gentle inquisition with Gertrude.

Fortunately, Gertrude passed Eva's inspection.

That obstacle cleared, there was still opposition from within the Zindler family. Everybody liked Gertrude, but there was one problem: she wasn't Jewish. They didn't want Marvin to marry a Gentile. Abe Zindler in particular disapproved, being afraid such a union would eventually come to divorce. He and Marvin argued back and forth over the matter, and Marvin, on numerous occasions, was tempted to tell his father that they were already married — but he bit his tongue, stood his ground and kept the secret.

Gertrude was dumbstruck by the force of the Zindler family, by their strongly expressed views and the fiery arguments that often resulted. She had been brought up in a quiet family where people talked out their disagreements calmly. That certainly wasn't the case in the Zindler house. The prevailing attitude here seemed to be shoot or give up the gun (figuratively, thank goodness, not literally). To a sweet young lady such as Gertrude, the screaming and verbal lather that took place in this house was a terrible thing to behold.

Gertrude said, "I had never seen such abuse. Words just leaped out of Abe's mouth." But after awhile, she came to accept the family, quirks and all. It was "just the way they were."

However, there were more obstacles. According to Marvin, "The rabbi refused to marry us in the Jewish temple unless Gertrude converted to Judaism." Marvin, however, did not feel this was necessary, and adamantly refused. He was determined that somehow he would work it out.

And so, despite the obstacles, they began planning a second wedding, a big one. Eschewing the synagogue, they booked the Plaza Hotel for their wedding venue. This was an elegant hotel located on Montrose Boulevard; it was, in those days, the site of some of the town's most fancy parties. In April of 1942, even though they had secretly been married for nearly a year, Gertrude and Marvin exchanged marriage vows before God, Abe and all the world.

The second ceremony being the "official" wedding, Marvin and Gertrude elected to celebrate their anniversary in April. This was not so simple in the beginning, for as their children grew older and wanted to help celebrate their parents' anniversary, they sometimes received conflicting stories about just when the anniversary was. One child might go to Gertrude and, without thinking, she would give the July 1941 date; another would ask Marvin, and he would give the April 1942 date.

With each new addition to the Zindler family, the confusion as to when Mom and Dad got married seemed to escalate. When they caught Marvin and Gertrude together, the couple always could agree on the April '42 date, but next year it might start all over again.

Finally Marvin told Gertrude that he was going to set the story straight — on their 50th anniversary. Gertrude was worried what the kids would think of them. She told me, "Even though it was 50 years after the fact, I was shaking like a leaf when he called all the children and grandchildren together in the living room and began to tell them the story."

As usual, Marvin was very direct and didn't spend a lot of time with details. After the kids were seated, and the grandchildren were all in place on their parents' laps or cross-legged on the floor, Marvin just said, "We got married twice: Once secretly in 1941, and the second time in April of 1942.

"That's why you were always confused. Occasionally, there was a slip of the tongue, and you would hear 1941 from Mother or me. Then one of you would ask a few years later, and we'd tell you it was 1942."

Gertrude needn't have worried, for the news did not seem to come as a shock to them at all. As a matter of fact, they began to laugh. Afterward, one of the granddaughters came up to Gertrude and said, "Oh, Nana, I think that's so romantic."

After the matter had been settled at home, it was time to tell the world.

Marvin believes in the sanctity of marriage and of the family. He also has an abiding respect for the elderly and for longevity. Some time ago, as part of his nightly TV broadcast, he began to announce birthdays for those 100 and older, and wedding anniversaries of 50 or more years. In order to qualify, the person or a family member would simply write to the station with the details — the event, the name(s), and the date — accompanied by a photograph.

And now tonight it was Marvin's turn. That evening, in front of seven million viewers, Marvin told their 50-year-old secret.

If he and Gertrude had had any reservations whatsoever about revealing their secret to the world, the audience response must surely have dispelled their fears. The letters that poured into the station were very similar to what their granddaughter had expressed that evening, and could be summed up in two words: "How romantic!"

Indeed it was.

C·H·A·P·T·E·R 16

THE ZINDLER BROOD

Although Marvin would be well into mid-life before he found a career that would suit him, he was a family man from the beginning. Despite his father's criticisms, Marvin did have a sense of responsibility even at a young age. Settling into married life in the early 1940s, he realized he needed a job, and at that point felt he had no choice but to return to the clothing store. It was a choice he accepted reluctantly, of course, but his responsibility to Gertrude came before anything else.

It was at this time that Marvin also first became active in various civic organizations and clubs. His professional life seemed too quiet, so he joined the local Shrine, which offered him a chance to put on a flashy outfit and show off his baton twirling abilities as a drum major in their parades. It was also at this time that he first became active in the local Democratic party and the American Legion. These activities were really a form of networking, though nobody called it that back then. People got to know him, and this was good for business. Being a sociable sort, he also enjoyed the participation.

He may have thought his life at home was "too quiet" as well, but that quiet was broken before very long. Helen Faye Zindler, firstborn of Marvin and Gertrude, arrived in January of 1943. Two years later, Marvin Jr., joined them. Life would never be the same for the young couple.

Although they began married life in a small rent house, Marvin and Gertrude found that with the new arrivals, they needed more space. A new home was built for them on the back of the Zindler compound in Bellaire, and they settled in.

Marvin was now in charge of the family store's fledgling ladies' department. He was given autonomy over the department, which proved to be a financial disaster. As always, he and his father argued violently and constantly, until finally Marvin had had enough. He had an uncle who ran a haberdashery in Virginia, so he called and asked if he could work for him. His uncle was agreeable.

Marvin had made the phone call from Abe's store, and after hanging up with his uncle he picked up the telephone again and called Gertrude. He simply said, "Gertrude, we're moving to Virginia." Gertrude was aghast, but she knew Marvin wanted to be as far away from his father as possible. And so, before very long, Marvin went to work for his uncle in the Virginia store.

Gertrude tried to adapt, but she had never been away from home before, and she was disconsolate. She missed her parents and all that was familiar to her in Houston. Virginia was just not the same as Texas. So intense was her homesickness that, on a visit to Houston to see the family, Gertrude told Marvin that she wouldn't return to Virginia with him.

Of course, that wouldn't do. They had been in Virginia six months, but his marriage was more important to Marvin than any job. However, he did feel an obligation to his uncle, and thought they should go back and tell him in person that Marvin needed to quit his job and return to Houston. From a job perspective, it all worked out anyway, because Abe wanted him back in the Houston store. Father and son struck a quick but uneasy peace, and Marvin and Gertrude moved back to Houston. And Marvin went back to the same old grind.

Meanwhile, the Zindler family continued to grow. Donny Zindler arrived a few years later, then Mark, and finally, Danny. That made five, with poor Helen being outnumbered by her four brothers.

As the children grew older, Marvin developed a good balance between authority and love. He was determined not to repeat some of the mistakes of his father. There would be no iron rule, no verbal abuse, and certainly no physical abuse.

In fact, with severe misconduct the exception, Marvin generally refused to physically punish the children. He also played the role of comforter very well. When the children were scared or sick, he'd take them to bed with him and Gertrude.

Marvin had no qualms about helping out, even bathing the children. Sometimes he would get into the tub with them when they were small, and would splash about as if he were a kid himself.

According to Gertrude, "He never paid any attention when they [were babies and] wet on him or anything else, which is saying an awful lot when you know how fastidious Marvin is. He was a marvelous father."

He certainly enjoyed playing with the children when they were little, but as they grew older this wasn't always the case. Gertrude said, "I used to get after him when the children were older, because he wasn't too good about taking the boys fishing and things like that. I once told Marvin that he wasn't being a buddy to his children. Marvin retorted that he wasn't their buddy, he was their father, and they had lots of buddies their own age."

She continued, "But Marvin did go to all their school plays and their ball games at school. By the way, the children have always been enormously proud of their father and his accomplishments, in spite of periodic episodes of embarrassment resulting from some of his more flamboyant actions."

"He does some pretty corny things," daughter Helen concurred. "But he does like to know what we're thinking, and if he asks us what we think about [something he's done], we'll tell him. He might get mad, or he might tell us what was behind his actions. He knows we love him, and we're proud of what he does."

Helen continued, "Dad has always insisted on a certain amount of self-reliance among us. He has insisted that we all work for our own spending money either at home or away. The spending money was only for frills. He has always encouraged us to live at home and has provided all the home amenities."

Marvin is a person his children feel they can truly count on. "If you ever have anything drastic happen — any emergency — he's right there," Helen said. "He can make monumental decisions at the drop of a hat. He can take care of major problems very well. But don't ask him about little nitpicking things. He simply won't hear about it. He won't do them."

This is all quite in keeping with Marvin's way of doing things. Even a White Knight has to choose his battles, and Marvin would rather save his strength for the big ones.

In good time, the Zindler children grew up and acquired lives and families of their own. Helen Faye is married to Mike Rodgers and they have three children, Shay, Kelli and Courtney.

The Zindlers' eldest son, Marvin Harold, Jr. is the senior vice president of Commonwealth Land Title Company of Houston. He is married to Linda, and they have two beautiful daughters, Lauren and Leslie.

Don Gregory, who was born in August of 1950, is married to Charlie, a very beautiful and talented lady. Charlie's daughter Ashley was warmly welcomed into the family.

Mark Steven, born in April of 1954, is the only one who followed in his father's footsteps and works at (dare I mention it) the Channel 2 television station in Houston. He is married to June, and they have provided three more additions to the Zindler family: Austin, Seth and Adam.

Dan Jerome (Danny), the youngest of the Zindler boys, was born in July of 1955. He has added another Zindler to the clan, grandson Aaron.[1]

Gertrude told me, "I am very fortunate to have them all in the Houston area. That way I get to see everyone quite often. I wouldn't have it any other way." Having come from a very small family — "There was only my brother and I," she explained — Gertrude delighted in being the matriarch of such a sizeable brood.

"My mother came to Houston as a bride," she mused. "Her family always lived in Philadelphia. When she was expecting my brother and later me, she made Daddy move back to Philadelphia; then it would get cold in Philadelphia, and my daddy would pack us all up and move us back to Texas. My mother thought Texas was the Wild, Wild West."

But Texas suited Gertrude just fine, and having her family around her always brought her joy.

From the beginning of their life together, the holidays were a particularly pleasant time at the Zindler homestead. After Marvin and I became friends, our families joined in holiday celebrations together. For example, Marvin and Gertrude were guests at my home for the Passover holidays. The Zindlers reciprocated for many years, and my family and I joined Marvin, Gertrude, their children and grandchildren on Christmas Day.

On each of these occasions, and on countless others, it always struck me anew how very important family is to Marvin Zindler. He may have an outsized ego and more personality quirks than the law should allow for one human being, but he definitely has his values in order.

[1] And the generations continue: in April of 2001, Marvin welcomed his first great-grandson, Aiden Rodgers Wernig (grandchild of Marvin's daughter, Helen).

White Knight in Blue Shades

C·H·A·P·T·E·R 17

"NOT JUST MY BETTER HALF...MY EVERYTHING"

In *The Many Faces of Marvin Zindler*, Ken Demaret noted that while Marvin and Gertrude Zindler may have seemed to be an unlikely couple, they made an ideal match in many ways. In areas where Marvin seemed indolent and uncaring, Gertrude was conscientious and diligent. If Marvin grew too emotionally intense, Gertrude laughingly put matters into intellectual perspective. Marvin was "numbingly" rude at times; Gertrude was lavishly gracious.

Gertrude was infinitely patient. She did not get irritated easily, and it took a lot before her fangs were flashing and her nails twitching. She told me she believed that was one reason she and Marvin get along so well. Of course, there were times when Gertrude's purr would turn to a growl. It would definitely not be in public — she was too much of a lady for that — but at home, well, that was a different setting.

Gertrude seemed always to know when to veer Marvin from the most devastatingly impulsive courses of action. Still, she respected his overall judgment, allowing him to persevere in matters where there may have been doubts as to what he should do. She had an uncanny knack for ignoring his momentary tantrums without losing any self-identity or respect.

She openly supported him, enjoying his triumphs and, it must be admitted, also enjoying it when he "got what he deserved."

"Being married to Marvin," Gertrude said to me, shortly after their 50th wedding anniversary, "has been one big adventure. No two days are exactly alike, and life is never dull. He's very unpredictable. You can't tell what's going to happen... Only fools and newcomers predict the weather in Texas or what Marvin might do next.

"Sometimes," she added in wide-eyed wonderment, "I think he's loco." (Which, if you recall, was the conclusion she'd come to very early in their relationship.)

The one thing that was always a bit of a sore spot with Gertrude was Marvin's impulsiveness. Marvin might be thinking about something for weeks, and then suddenly he'd look up from behind the newspaper he was reading, or he'd leap up from his chair in the middle of a television program, and announce his intentions to act on whatever it was he'd been mulling over. Usually it was something big — like the purchase of an automobile.

Gertrude recalled one such incident in the early 1970s, when he just stood up and announced, "We're going to buy a new car." He promptly got into his two-door Lincoln Continental Mark IV, which only had a few thousand miles on it, and headed for the dealer. In a period of only a few minutes, he traded in his Mark IV and purchased a brand new four-door Lincoln Town Car, fully equipped.

"When I asked him why he'd decided to do this," Gertrude added, "he said, 'The old car looked like a Mafia vehicle.' He also wanted a car with four doors. He thought it was embarrassing to go somewhere with family or friends and have them climb all over the seats to get in the back of the car."

The color of the car was another matter, however. Marvin's philosophy was, "A car this expensive ought to be either black or white. If people want a car with bright colors, they should get a Chevrolet."

But Gertrude was to have the last say, for awhile, anyway. With a stern face and only the slightest trace of amusement, she told Marvin that his black luxury sedan was a "funeralizing car." A few weeks later he decided he agreed with her and gave her the black sedan, then went out and bought himself a lavishly equipped black Chrysler Cordoba. He tired of the Cordoba quickly, however, and, knowing Gertrude did not like the large black car, he traded it in, gave her the Cordoba and bought himself a new white Mark IV. Throwing her hands up, Gertrude exclaimed, "I've never been able to know what was going to happen and when. Now he trades his cars in every two years whether he needs to or not."

Though she never really won the car wars, Gertrude still knew how to handle Marvin in all the important matters.

"After 50 years, I learned a few tricks myself," she said. Though normally a quiet and gentle woman, she confided that sometimes, "I've had to get really mad in order for him to pay attention to me. I might even slam a door or throw a shoe. [On those occasions] he will look so surprised, and then he'll ask me, 'What is wrong, Dear?'

"I learned to raise my voice and answer him back. I have my own opinions. I also discovered that being ignored hurts his feelings more than anything. When you ignore him, he gets quiet and comes as near to sulking as a person can. He will get himself wound tight as an eight-day clock. Then he will try to start the conversation up again, usually with a little teasing and poking fun, and everybody starts laughing. If he doesn't come around he knows that I am going to stay mad and I am going to stay that way until he makes up."

Early in their married life, Gertrude learned to be self-sufficient. It was a trait she nurtured over the decades, and even after the children were grown she had a great deal of responsibility. With Marvin often working 14 hours a day and traveling as much as he did, Gertrude had to run the house. She once said to me, "What every woman needs is a wife. My mother never had to do anything like this. In fact, she never even drove a car. Mother would walk to the grocery store. She would select the merchandise and leave the groceries with the checker, then call my father, and on his way home he would pick up the groceries. He was everything to her, but she was the boss of the family.

"But things changed during my generation. With the husband and, in many cases, the wife, working, both needed to be able to drive. I had to take the kids to school, to baseball and football games, and other school activities as well. There were also the routine household chores as well as getting things fixed if they broke. Every day there was something new and different. It was on-the-job training. You just kind of got the hang of it, and as a result, learned to be very independent."

∾ • ∾

After the children were grown and had their own families, Marvin and Gertrude had more time to be together. They spent it well. They would eat out several times a week, visit with friends, occasionally see a movie. And then there were all those functions where Marvin was a featured guest.

It was always interesting to see the two of them together. I recall one particular evening when we were all dining together, along with some other friends, at Pino's Italian restaurant. The conversation was lively; politics was the subject. Marvin and I, along with well-known Houston attorney John O'Quinn and Pino's brother, Adriano, were in a heated discussion. The ladies were occasionally commenting, but mostly talking amongst themselves. At one point Marvin expressed an opinion as if he were speaking for the group. Gertrude was quick to pipe in, telling Marvin he should speak for himself. To me this was a metaphor for the way that Gertrude always stood her ground. She was a petite, gentle woman, but she could be feisty, and had plenty of spunk when it came to expressing her own opinions.

Marvin caused Gertrude, on more than one occasion, to cringe when they were out in public, particularly if they were at a restaurant. You might expect the originator of the infamous "Rat & Roach Report" to be at his most demanding when in restaurants, and he was. As Gertrude once put it, "He has made me more embarrassed than a preacher with a broken zipper. More than once I have wanted to crawl under the table and not come out until he left."

With a chuckle, she continued, "Once he told a waitress that he only wanted half-a-cup of coffee. As long as I have known him, he always orders half-a-cup. He likes to add his own fixings to this and he is so fastidious he doesn't want any of it to spill over and get on his clothes. Well, the waitress brought him a full cup. He had a hissy fit, just pitching and squealing at that waitress. She just stood there quietly looking at him. He again reminded her that she had been told to bring only half-a-cup of coffee.

"She waited until he was finished, smiled sweetly, looked at him right in the eye, and then said, 'Mr. Zindler, your half is on the top, *Sir*.' She turned and walked away.

"I thought that was a real knee slapper. And he thought it was hilarious, too. You couldn't help but laugh."

Despite the occasional embarrassing moment, Gertrude mostly learned to simply ignore Marvin's quirks, or to respond with, "Oh, Marvin, you are just so silly sometimes." That would usually bring an end to any awkward public moment. Outsiders may think that Marvin is intolerant, but it is really his own unique way of expressing himself. We all have our idiosyncrasies, and few people understood Marvin's better than Gertrude.

Although they moved around a few times in the beginning, Marvin and Gertrude spent most of their life together at the home where Marvin still lives. After the last of the whippersnappers, Danny, arrived in July of 1955, Marvin moved his brood from the Zindler compound to a new home near the Meyerland section of Houston. It was a traditional English-style home with antique brick, and over the years, it was modified and updated several times to meet the needs of a growing family.

Even after that family had grown and scattered to other homes, the Meyerland abode remained a site for family gatherings.

To tour this home is to get a fascinating glimpse into the soul of Marvin Zindler. The formal dining room and living room are seldom used, except for those occasions when Marvin plays the electric organ. Marvin has had several electric organs over the years, upgrading as new and more sophisticated electronic wizardry has become available. He is, however, shy when it comes to playing the organ, and unless coaxed into it he usually does not play for a group. He plays to relax, often when home alone in the company of his cats, Sweetie and Sugar, who sit and purr to the music.

The hub of the home is the den, which connects to a screened-in porch on one side and the kitchen on the other side. Towards the end of her life, Gertrude had the den redecorated and painted white, making it bright and cheery. There is a large comfortable couch, and it sits directly across from a wide-screen television set that is capable of acquiring some 250 stations via a satellite dish. There are more controls on it than in a 747, and everybody thinks he is an expert. Push the wrong button, and you won't forget it. It will take 30 minutes to reprogram the monster. Gertrude seemed to have conquered it, but professed that she could turn it on and off and select stations, and never touched any of the other buttons. I know that she was just being modest.

A comfortable reclining chair is strategically placed in juxtaposition to the sofa, directly in front of the large-screen TV. This is the King's throne, and God forbid some unknowing soul should sit in it. Next to the throne is a small end table, which holds the telephone and a note pad, should His Highness get an urgent call.

The TV's remote controls tend to move by themselves at times. Nothing will throw Marvin into rooster mode more quickly than to hunker down in his favorite chair, put his feet up, and find the remote control has walked away. When this happens, Marvin will bellow. When Gertrude was alive, she knew how to deal with this. Having long since learned how to ignore his noise, she would just look up at him, smile sweetly and wait until he finished. And then, quickly scanning the room, she would spot the remote control sitting on the coffee table, or perhaps just across from Marvin on the couch, but outside of his reach. Grinning, she'd ask him if he would like her to get it for him.

Upon which Marvin would snarl, "I can't very damn well reach it from here, can I?"

Gertrude would stop whatever she was doing to go get the remote and hand it to him. Then she would walk around behind his chair, stopping to gently massage his shoulders for a few minutes.

No matter what the situation, she always knew just how to handle him.

Marvin's inner sanctum holds more surprises for those who know only the flamboyant, outspoken showman. From the den, one passes through two very large French doors to the pleasant screened-in porch. Often a visitor is startled by a sudden squawking and the fluttering of wings, as if geese were on a new feeding ground. The squawking and fluttering emanate from Marvin's private flock of birds, of which there sometimes are hundreds. Depending upon the season, you can see cardinals, blue jays, sparrows, doves, and, of course, pigeons.

Like weevils in cornmeal, squirrels of all ages and sizes skirt in and out along the flower beds and dart down the tree trunks to steal a peanut before the next blue jay swoops in. Once the thieving rodent is up the tree, the birds settle in again, blanketing the lawn, and the scenario replays itself throughout the day. It is so much fun to watch. Marvin's porch is a great place to sit a spell, and let the rest of the world go its own way.

This is a side of Marvin that few people get to see. Gertrude knew it well, of course. He has literally and figuratively taken his flock under his wing. Regardless of the weather, Marvin periodically heads out to one of Houston's oldest family-owned garden shops and feed stores, Southwest Fertilizer on Bissonnet. Marvin purchases a variety of bird seeds and peanuts, some in 40-pound and some in 80-pound sacks. Marvin's cars can always be found parked in the driveway, because half of the garage is filled with large sacks of bird food and peanuts (the other half being littered with hundreds of discarded golf clubs). Marvin sees to it that each of the bird feeders is kept full, and, in addition, he will scatter five to ten pounds of select bird seed and peanuts over the back lawn. Next to Gertrude, who definitely had her brand on his heart, his little friends have always taken priority.

In an age when some people change marriage partners almost as often as they change clothes, and even those who make a genuine effort to remain married often fail, a 56-year marriage is something to behold. Certainly there are not too many couples anymore who keep the vow, "Till death do us part." Death did part Marvin and Gertrude Zindler on Friday, November 28, 1997, when a heart attack claimed Gertrude's life.

It was the day after Thanksgiving. The following Monday, December 1, family and friends gathered at St. Philip's Methodist Church in Houston to celebrate the life of this lovely lady.

Among those mourning were Anh and Dung Nguyen[1] and their parents and grand-mother. Anh and Dung were just children when, in 1988, Marvin traveled to Vietnam and got permission to bring them to Houston to join their father. They are now U.S. citizens, and Dung, though now living in Virginia, drove all the way to Houston to attend the funeral. For the Nguyens, as well as for everyone else who gathered there that day, it was, as the *Houston Chronicle's* Ann Hodges put it, "a service of remembrance and thanksgiving, indeed."

When the service was over, it was time to begin the somber journey to the Beth Israel Cemetery a few miles away. This marked the only time that Houston's famous 610 Loop was ever closed. Although it was a high-traffic time on the freeways, the police and sheriff's departments closed all exits and entrances for the funeral procession. Marvin said to me, "Gertrude is up there looking down on this and thinking, 'What foolishness — closing off an entire freeway for me.' She must be smiling, maybe laughing at us. She was such a modest person."

For Marvin, it was a public farewell to the woman who had been, as he said, "not just my better half, my everything."

[1] The Nguyens' story is in the chapter entitled, "A Right to Be Free" in the "Man on a Mission" section.

Marvin...

Under The Knife, And Up On The Soapbox

A WORK IN PROGRESS:
MARVIN AND COSMETIC SURGERY

To many people, nothing illustrates Marvin's vanity, egocentricity and utter perfectionism more acutely than his penchant for cosmetic surgery. He has undergone more than 30 separate cosmetic surgical procedures, most of which I have performed. (On more than one occasion Marvin has referred to *me* as an egocentric perfectionist. I might argue with the "egocentric" part, but for a plastic surgeon "perfectionist" is actually a wonderful compliment.)

Marvin's decades-long experiment with cosmetic surgery began back in the 1950s, when he was shocked into seeing himself as others saw him — or at least as one other person saw him. At the time, he was producing news reports for KPRC-TV, Channel 2 in Houston. The way he likes to tell it now is that he was let go by the KPRC powers-that-be for being "too ugly."

Marvin relates the story this way: "I had the opportunity to interview Humphrey Bogart. The station manager, Jack Harris, saw the interview I had done and left orders I wasn't to appear on camera again," he laughs. "Jack Harris said I was too ugly!" Marvin can laugh about it now, but initially he was quite upset.

Harris went on to say that the station was planning to form its own news department and produce its own programs. Therefore, the plan was to cut off all outside contracts. That meant Marvin, who was actually employed by one of KPRC's contractors, Southwest Film Productions, would have to go. In reality, then, even if he'd been a dead ringer for Gregory Peck or Cary Grant, he probably would have been given his walking papers.

In any case, the wheels began turning in Marvin's head. More than losing the television job, Jack Harris' comment, "You're too damned ugly," really did bother him.

"I went back to the store," says Marvin, "and took a long, hard look at myself in one of our large three-way mirrors used to help in fitting clothes. I could see myself from all angles at once. And I decided that Jack Harris was right. I *was* an ugly son-of-a-bitch."

He explains, "My nose stuck out. It was too long. It had a big hump on it. I had no chin. I looked like Andy Gump. My ears, though normal in size, looked too large because I had no jaw. My mouth didn't look right either."

Marvin, however, never did know the word "defeat." He had eaten dust, but ultimately would triumph again... this time with the help of a little plastic and reconstructive surgery.

Given his enormous self-interest and his lifelong vanity, some might find it surprising that Marvin had not considered cosmetic surgery earlier than he did. But in the 1950s, very few men underwent aesthetic surgical procedures, and those who did really didn't wish to elaborate upon their surgeries. Even the ladies were more discreet when electing this type of surgery. Besides, even in 1950s' dollars, plastic surgery was expensive and was considered quite a luxury. Marvin's first surgical procedure cost $736, which wasn't chump change in the 1950s. By today's standards, of course, that would be a real bargain; nowadays, $736 wouldn't even pay for the anesthetic.

Even so, almost anyone who desires cosmetic surgery can afford most procedures today. Furthermore, plastic surgery is openly discussed and, in some circles, actually flaunted. The topic is discussed on the radio, vividly portrayed on television, and commented upon in the newspapers, magazines, and on the Internet. Attitudes have changed a lot in the last 50 years, as have plastic surgery procedures.

Not a few people have commented on the inherent irony of Marvin Zindler's plastic surgery habit. Here, after all, is a man who has spent half his life attacking false advertising, and yet is living proof that, contrary to the line in the old commercial, it *can* be "nice to fool Mother Nature." But Marvin believes there is nothing wrong with wanting to look better, and cosmetic surgery is one way to accomplish this. And there is really no irony here; one might have been able to accuse him of "false advertising" if he had been less than forthright about the fact that he's had so much cosmetic work done — but, as you probably know, Marvin will talk openly to anyone and everyone about the subject.

Whether or not Marvin was actually fired from his news gig at KPRC because he wasn't handsome enough, his reaction to Harris' comment about his looks was the starting point for a series of cosmetic surgery operations that strikingly changed his face. Over the nearly 50 years since then, he has periodically undergone additional aesthetic surgical procedures, revisions, and touch-ups.

The first procedure took place in 1954, when Marvin was 33 years old. He decided to have his nose made smaller and his chin enlarged. First he went for a consultation with Dr. William K. Wright, now deceased, who was practicing in the Texas Medical Center.

Marvin says, "Plans for facial cosmetic changes had taken shape in the back of my mind since I was first told I was ugly. But at first, I said nothing about them — not even to Gertrude."

In fact, the first Gertrude knew about Marvin's plans was when he called home from Dr. Wright's office. He told her he was going into the hospital for plastic surgery, to have his nose fixed. Gertrude was flabbergasted when he told her this. Her first response was that there was nothing wrong with his nose, and she didn't understand. But Marvin was adamant. It was something he had thought about for some time now, and he was finally going to do it.

Perhaps in part to convince Gertrude that this was not a frivolous move, Marvin rationalized his reasons for the changes. He explained to her, "The poundings I took as a boxer years ago altered my nose, and have made it hard for me to breathe." In addition to his breathing difficulty, he had recurring headaches and hoped that surgery would reduce or cure this problem as well. Marvin also said that the plastic and reconstructive surgery procedure on his nose was recommended as a cure for his allergies.

In the beginning, Marvin cited the various medical considerations when explaining his surgery to friends and family. Privately, however, he was very realistic about the whole thing. The main purpose for having the surgery was that, very simply, he didn't like the way he looked, and he wanted to do something about it.

Psychologically, in fact, Marvin was an excellent candidate for plastic surgery. One of the best reasons to have cosmetic surgery is to change something you don't like about your looks — provided your expectations are realistic regarding the outcome, and you are not depending on the results of the surgery to make other changes in your life or lifestyle. Marvin didn't want to change what he was (as if that were even possible); he just wanted to be happier with his looks. He wasn't searching for miracles, and certainly didn't expect his situation in life to change as a result of the surgery. In other words, he wanted some cosmetic changes for good, healthy reasons.

Cosmetically, the major problem with Marvin's nose was that it was large, with a central hump. This was due to an overabundance of cartilage and bone on the bridge of the nose. Such a condition is often the result of injuries to the nose, and certainly Marvin had sustained his share of these during his more than 100 bouts in the boxing ring. But of course, the size and the shape of the nose is also influenced by such factors as heredity and ethnic background, and these factors entered into Marvin's equation as well.

However, Marvin's claim about medical problems was not a fabrication. Dr. Wright's examination revealed that he had a deviated septum, which could have been developmental, or could indeed have resulted from his boxing a few years earlier. Regardless, Marvin had difficulty breathing, and as such, was a good candidate for a submucous resection and septoplasty. This is an operation that straightens the curvature of the bone and cartilage dividing the nose into its two compartments. This usually improves breathing. And so the decision was made to perform a cosmetic nose job as well as internal reconstruction to improve breathing.

But his nose was only one aspect of what Marvin wished to improve upon. He asked the doctor if there was anything that could be done to accentuate his chin. Marvin had been born with a receding chin, producing the infamous "Andy Gump profile." He wanted very much to change this, and also hoped that the chin enlargement would reduce the pucker or pout effect at the corner of his mouth.

On a woman, a little recession can actually be attractive unless, of course, it is very extreme. On a man's face, however, a receding chin is not considered masculine. Regardless of the man's body physique and stature, it gives the impression of a "wimp." In most cultures, strong facial features and a prominent jaw line on a man are considered attractive, virile and sexy.

How do cosmetic surgeons determine an ideal profile? Technically, looking at the profile, if you drop a line from the base of the nose and over the upper and lower lip, the chin should fall along that line or very close to it. Calculations can then be made as to the advisability of reducing or enhancing the chin.

Accordingly, photographs were taken of Marvin's profile, and his surgeon plotted the changes to his nose and chin. Usually both of these operations are done at the same time, and Marvin was agreeable to having both procedures done simultaneously.

Today, these procedures are done safely on an outpatient basis, with either general or local anesthesia. In the 1950s, however, most "nose jobs" were done with only local anesthesia. But general anesthetic was available, and was used on patients who were particularly anxious or otherwise difficult. Marvin's doctor offered him this option. Dr. Wright sensed that Marvin would be easier to treat if he were fast asleep, and he was right. Marvin is anxious, controlling, and, contrary to what he has always liked to claim, intolerant of pain.

But Marvin refused the general anesthetic, feeling that if he stayed awake, he could direct the surgical procedure the way he did everything else in his life.

He also refused to remove his hairpiece.

Having done so many cosmetic surgeries on Marvin, I can empathize with the late great Dr. Wright for having to do this procedure with only local anesthesia. I also have more than a passing familiarity with the hairpiece battle. At least the good doctor was able to convince Marvin to accept some tranquilizers prior to receiving the local.

After preliminary preparations were completed, the local anesthetic was injected around Marvin's nose. The injections contained novocaine, the anesthetic used by dentists. They are not pleasant, but not particularly uncomfortable either. Then some cotton was placed in the nostrils; the cotton contained a medication to shrink the nasal membranes and reduce bleeding. After several minutes, and with Marvin fully conscious, the doctor inserted a scalpel into each nostril and made a small incision. Then he separated the skin from the bone and cartilage of the nose. Wearing a headlight and using a small speculum to expand and visualize the area, he removed a portion of bone and cartilage with surgical clippers. A stainless steel rasp (similar to a small file) was used to smooth and round the nose.

Marvin, being Marvin, fired off a continuous barrage of muffled and garbled suggestions between each of the stages in the procedure. Despite this the procedure continued, and with the help of small delicate scalpels, and the experience of a surgeon (and the talents of an artist), the cartilages were carved to produce the desired result. Additional delicate scalpel work separated the mucous membrane from underneath, until the base of the nose was reached. This was necessary in order to straighten the deviated septum and correct the breathing problems. A channel was then created at the base of the nose and to either side. This would be used later for placement of a very fine, specially-angled chisel to produce a cut in the bone that would allow the surgeon to narrow the nose.

With this procedure, now as then, there is no pain during the operation. What most people object to is the sound of the instruments while the plastic surgeon is working. Today, these unsettling noises can be muffled by wearing earphones and listening to your favorite music. Or you can elect for a general anesthetic.

The procedure and its attendant noises did not seem to phase Marvin, however, and he continued his barrage of questions and suggestions as the doctor proceeded. Finally, the scalpel work was completed, the obstruction corrected and the nose shortened and narrowed. Small dissolving sutures were placed in the nose to close the wounds and realign the structures in their new position. The skin was made smooth and taped to ensure accuracy and reduce swelling.

The result: a new nose, and no cuts or marks on the outside. Mission accomplished!

Well, almost.

Marvin's chin still needed to be done. This could be accomplished in one of two ways: by making an incision in the mouth and leaving no external scar, or through a small incision in the natural crease just under the chin. Marvin's vanity being what it is, you can guess which option he chose. For perhaps the umpteenth time, he reminded his surgeon, "No cuts outside."

The doctor gently opened his mouth and pulled the lower lip forward so he could make a small cut between the lip and the gum line. The incision was extended and deepened until the bone which formed Marvin's small chin was exposed.

There are many materials today that can be used to enhance the chin, including a range of plastics. Back then, however, the first choice would be to use the patient's own bone or cartilage. If that wasn't feasible, cartilage and bone which had been irradiated and stored in a medical bone bank could be selected as well.

With Marvin's approval, the doctor chose irradiated cartilage from the bone bank. This was carved in a half-moon or a horseshoe-like fashion to produce the desired shape, and was then fitted over the bone of the lower jaw, after the skin had been stretched and expanded several times to accommodate the addition of the new material. It was then meticulously sutured in position, extending and projecting Marvin's chin and lower jaw so that it would harmonize with his other facial features. The tissues inside the mouth were then placed over the implant and sutured. Through this portion of the procedure, the doctor had some advantage. Marvin's mouth had to be open, and cotton had to be placed in the cheek area, thus restricting Marvin's verbal barrage and limiting him to only a few occasional muffled words.

And then... *Voila!* It was over!

Almost.

The bandages and cast still had to be applied. But Marvin couldn't wait, and he demanded a mirror. In due time, however, his chin and nose were taped, and a plaster cast carefully applied to the nose until it was hard. Marvin's nose was encased in plaster for several days.

After all that trouble, however, Marvin didn't like his first nose job. He wanted his nose to be shorter, and he wanted more tilt to the tip. Actually, these revisions are minor and they are easily performed, but it is advisable to wait until all the swelling and discoloration disappear before doing any revisions.

When Marvin makes up his mind to do something, he is not very patient, and he was knocking on the doctor's door several weeks later. Marvin remembers the doctor telling him, "I'm not going to take any chances getting into trouble with you. Frankly, it makes me a little nervous to operate on someone with a reputation like yours." Even back in the 1950s, Marvin's reputation preceded him, and not a few people were intimidated by the force of his personality.

Doubtless, every doctor who has ever treated Marvin has had to deal with the fact that Marvin is ... well, pushy. Of course, Marvin doesn't see it that way as he goes round and round with this or that physician. In his eyes, most doctors are simply too conservative. I've sometimes found it a challenge to keep Marvin from going too far. With cosmetic surgery, as with most other medical procedures, it is better to be conservative. You can always make a revision. You can always do small touch-ups or take a little more later. But if you take too much, it is very difficult to correct, and in fact may be impossible. I think I've finally convinced Marvin of the virtues of conservatism, because he now seems more willing to admit that I've kept him from getting into trouble by having too much surgery.

Once he was back in the OR for correction of that first procedure, Marvin got his way. His nose was shortened and a little more tilt was added to the tip. In my opinion, although I think Marvin is a very nice-looking man, his nose is a little bit *too* short and the tilt exaggerated. Men usually have larger noses than he has — but that is the way he wanted it, and that's what he got.

Marvin is very forthright about his reasons for cosmetic surgery. He explains, "When I did it, I did it for myself. Now, if I didn't have the face I have, I wouldn't have had the television job all these years. Television just ain't going to have you around if you are ugly. I know that from experience. It's just a fact of life."

Once, when Marvin was asked about the pain and discomfort associated with his cosmetic surgery, he puffed out his chest, threw back his shoulders and declared, "There's no pain in surgery for me because I know it is necessary. Period. To me, pain is something that hurts when it doesn't have to."

What gets to Marvin is the noise, he says. "That got-damned scraping noise drives me crazy," he shudders. Having proven his machismo by undergoing several surgeries with local anesthesia, these days Marvin has himself put to sleep when he's having plastic surgery. In fact, he even requests intravenous sedation and general anesthesia for dental work. After snoozing under the influence of an intravenous hypodermic during extraction of a wisdom tooth, he claimed, "I didn't elect to go to sleep because it hurts. I do it because I can't stand all those scraping and crunching sounds. That is the only thing that bothered me about my nose job. The only thing." Whatever you say, Marvin!

As soon as his first surgeries healed, Marvin revealed himself to his public. Even back then, Marvin was surprisingly forthright about some of the most personal and intimate things. His attitude has long been that if you are hiding something, you are going to give people something to gossip about. If you tell them what you've done, there's no mystery. Nothing is left for them to question, wonder about or talk about. It was in a full-page newspaper story, written by a local gossip columnist, that Marvin revealed his secret — complete with before-and-after photographs.

When Gertrude saw the newspaper article, it amazed her, and that's really saying something, since by that time she had thought nothing Marvin did could surprise her anymore. Admittedly, she had been taken aback by his decision to have the cosmetic surgery in the first place, but once she learned how determined he was to go through with it, she had accepted it as just another of her husband's quirks. But to tell the world about it? She thought *that* was strange, to say the least. She asked him, "How in the world could you let anybody know that you are that vain?"

But Marvin was undaunted. After all, he believed, if there is nothing wrong with wanting to make yourself better looking, there's nothing wrong with letting everyone know how you did it.

Not everyone agreed with him. As Gertrude explained, "His parents and mine almost had a fit. They thought it was terribly strange and far-out — something only movie stars did, and at least stars were smart enough to keep quiet about it."

She continued, "Remember, though, this was the 1950s. Cosmetic surgery was something for only the rich and famous. It was a hush-hush subject and definitely not something a man would do." She conceded, however, that "he was proud of it and it made him feel better. He could breathe better. The surgery helped his headaches. And some of the benefits were psychological."

Despite the flak he got from a few folks back then, Marvin says he would do it all over again. "I wouldn't hesitate a minute."

Knowing how upset Marvin was at being told he was "too ugly for television," it's easy to understand why he underwent that first procedure back in 1954. What many find more difficult to comprehend is why Marvin has continued to undergo so many cosmetic surgical procedures since then. The truth is that he is quite wrapped up in the fact that his appearance makes a great deal of difference in his career. In addition, he seems driven by a desire for constant improvement. Marvin sums it up by explaining, "It's like a woman who gets started on improving her house and just won't quit."

For example, in 1974 he spent, by his estimate, his entire ABC television salary on clothes, hairpieces and surgical touch-ups. That was the year Marvin had a complete facelift. In addition, fat was removed from his neck and jowl area, and the neck skin was tightened. At the same time, he had his ears pinned back.

More improvements were effected that year. In fact, cosmetic surgery has always been only one part of an overall self-improvement program for Marvin. In the 1970s, Marvin became a tennis freak, often playing four to six hours at a stretch. He remembers looking down one day at his skinny legs sticking out of his tennis shorts, over which a pot belly then protruded. "I looked funny as hell," he says, "and I knew I had to do something about it." This led him into a weight-loss program. He set a goal and approached this, as everything else he did in life, with determination, and was able to meet his goal.

With a new face, an impeccable wardrobe, several new hairpieces, and a newly slender body, Marvin Zindler at 53 was content with his life. He was healthy, and had a wonderful wife and family. He felt good about himself and what he was doing. He harbored no delusions that the cosmetic surgery was the cause of his happiness; it was simply an embellishment.

You might be curious about how Marvin and I first got hooked up. I have to confess that our first real encounter did not take place under the most favorable of circumstances. There was a time when, if someone had told me that Marvin Zindler and I would one day be the closest of friends, I would have thought that person was off his or her rocker.

Some years ago I was working on a difficult and dramatic case. A young girl had been born without a nose, a very rare congenital anomaly. (I have only seen two such cases in over 30 years of medical practice.) As the child's parents could not afford the expenses of reconstructive surgery, a team of doctors and I were going to perform the surgery free of charge. We began the long preparation — the special studies, X-rays, CAT scans, MRIs, blood tests, facial measurements and models, etc. — all the steps necessary before undertaking this delicate and complex procedure. I even sent photos and X-rays to a physician in Paris, Dr. Paul Tessier, the world's leading expert in craniofacial surgery. Dr. Tessier was interested enough to offer to come to Houston and do the surgery, without charging for either the trip or the surgery. All was in readiness, when Marvin Zindler received a letter, accompanied by a photo of the unfortunate girl. The letter had been sent by a well-meaning teacher, who obviously had no idea of the surgery plans that were already in progress.

Without further investigation, Marvin made arrangements for Continental Airlines to fly the girl to the Craniofacial Institution in Dallas. I found out about this only by chance. Since this child's case became a subject of one of Marvin's stories, it was on TV. There I was, watching the news, when what did I see but footage of my patient, boarding a Continental aircraft for Dallas. And Marvin was the hero who'd made it all possible.

I was livid. I had spent four months on this case — well over 80 hours of consultation. Then there were those $30,000.00 worth of X-rays, MRIs and lab tests, and the free services from our French surgeon, Dr. Tessier. I gathered all of the X-rays, lab work, and consultation reports, as well as the letters from Dr. Tessier, and I bundled them up and headed for the Channel 13 studios, unannounced.

Marvin was at his desk, and to say that I caught him by surprise is an understatement. In fact, he was downright shocked when I dumped nearly 20 pounds of X-rays and paperwork on his desk. They hit the desk with such force that they bounced.

I proceeded to attack with a verbal barrage, not dissimilar to Marvin's approach when doing one of his more passionate consumer-advocacy stories. This is one of the few times I've seen Marvin with his mouth open and no sound coming forth. He was completely unable to utter a word while I was talking.

Then I turned and left, without waiting for a Zindler retort.

I made my point, and he has not forgotten it. In fact, I don't think anyone has ever been so brazen with him. Later that day, after Marvin had had time to recover, I received a very nice telephone call from him. We have been the best of friends — no, *family* — ever since.

And, oh, yes, I became his cosmetic surgeon as well.

Marvin was pleased with the results of his cosmetic surgeries, but, because facelifts only last a few years, he elected to have the facelift redone in 1982 and again in 1988. It was in 1988 that he "went public" with his cosmetic surgery on a whole new level.

He had several other procedures besides a facelift done that year, but not all were cosmetic. For many years, Marvin has been bothered by tiny spasms on his eyelids. This problem usually originates from some type of irritating lesion on the seventh nerve, somewhere in its course from the brain to its peripheral location on and around the eyes. This neural irritation results in what is often referred to as a "tic," in this case, a fluttering of the eyelids. Bright lights, such as those used in television studios, or lights mounted on television cameras, will exacerbate the spasms. Although the condition is sometimes referred to as a "nervous tic," it has nothing to do with being nervous. It is light-stimulated. As a result, Marvin started wearing those famous blue-tinted glasses. Many consider the blue glasses one of his trademarks and part of his theatrics but, in truth, the blue glasses were medically indicated because of this condition.

In addition to the glasses, these spasms can be controlled by a series of injections. They are, however, more than just a little uncomfortable; they are downright painful. Marvin has periodically required this type of treatment, but in 1988 he was seeking other answers to his eye problems. Besides the fluttering, there was some asymmetry (his eyelids were more prominent on the right side than the left) and right upper-lid ptosis (a droopy brow). These conditions possibly made his "tic" more pronounced. Some patients have realized benefit from the removal of select muscle groups in and around the eye and forehead area to control this problem. Marvin elected to have this done, and the drooping eyelid, or "lid lag," would be corrected at the same time.

Again, it seemed logical to have multiple procedures done at once. Marvin reasoned that since he was going to be asleep anyway, it wouldn't hurt any more if he had a few nips and tucks when I performed the operation on the muscle to control the twitching.

More cosmetic work was in the offing as well. Over the years, some of the bone and cartilage that was originally placed over Marvin's receding chin had gradually resorbed. In addition, Marvin decided he wanted a John Wayne dimple in his chin. He also thought his neck was fuller, and that fat tissue had been collecting under his chin again. The solution this time was liposuction. Since I am very experienced in this procedure (and, in fact, am the author of the first book on liposuction), it seemed only fitting for Marvin to request that I remove the fat from under his chin, and tighten the skin of the neck.

I knew that if all these procedures were done at the same time, it would take five to six hours. The question was whether or not Marvin was a good candidate for such extensive surgery. He was, after all, 67 years old. Fortunately, Marvin was in good health, and all of his blood tests were normal. After an examination with his cardiologist and internist, Dr. Robert Fulweber, the surgery was scheduled for March 1988, at The Methodist Hospital in the Texas Medical Center.

Because of the complicated and extensive procedure, I decided that Marvin was to remain in the hospital for a week. Of course, Marvin had different ideas. "I can't be off the air that long!" he insisted. "Got-damn it, I should be able to go home in two or three days."

Knowing how insistent I can be, however, he was already working on a Plan B. To interviewer Ken Hoffman, who at that time was with *The Houston Post*, Marvin declared, "If I'm there more than three days, I'm going to do my television show from my hospital bedroom, even if the bandages are still on. I don't have anything to hide. My viewing public and fans know I've had some nips and tucks before. Now they're going to see me as soon as Dr. Agris takes the bandages off."

Marvin being Marvin, everyone knew he meant it. Several days before going to the hospital, Marvin did a television promo telling everybody exactly what he was going to have done, and adding that he would be coming to them again in a few days from his room at The Methodist Hospital.

On March 3, 1988, I met Marvin at the hospital. Before the surgery, I made some crucial measurements and markings for the reconstructive and cosmetic portions of the procedure. Making these marks is a routine process and should have gone smoothly... but remember, this is Marvin we're talking about. There was the usual hassle about the hairpiece, of course. Things would have been a lot simpler if Marvin would let me take his hairpiece off, but we all knew that was not going to happen. When I hinted at it, Marvin laid down the ground rules very quickly.

"Dr. Joe," Marvin said, "There is no got-damn way this hairpiece is coming off. You are going to have to find some way of working around it, under it, through it, but it is staying where it is."

So, as usual, we compromised. It was agreed that the marks and measurements would be completed with the hairpiece on, and Marvin would wear it to the operating room. The hairpiece would stay in place until he was asleep. It would only be removed as a last resort, and only when the skin of the forehead and the area over the eye would be operated on. It was agreed that the hairpiece would then be replaced, and bandages applied, before leaving the OR.

Just as we started to take Marvin back to the OR, Marvin's cameraman Bob Dows and producer Lori Reingold arrived on the scene. Marvin had indeed meant what he said about going on television. They began filming as Marvin lay on the gurney and moved through the hallways to the OR. As they reached the sterile area, the camera crew and Gertrude were told that this was as far as they could go. Gertrude gave Marvin a big hug and a kiss as the automatic electric doors began to open.

But Marvin was going to have the last word.

He raised himself until he was resting on his elbows, and looked directly at me. With a broad grin and a chuckle he said, "Agris, if you screw this one up, the whole world is going to see it! When the bandages come off in two days, everybody is going to get to see the new Maaaaaarvin Zindler. Perhaps seven million people will be watching." The cameras were still rolling, and that big, broad grin was still on Marvin's face.

Gertrude gently chided, "How could you say that to Dr. Agris? You're going to make him nervous — and he's the one that's going to be holding the knife to your throat."

I chimed in, "I've been doing this too long, and even the FAMOUS Mr. Marvin Zindler is not going to intimidate me or make me nervous." I hoped that this segment of video would end up on the cutting-room floor with the "bloopers." Fortunately, it did.

As anticipated, the surgery lasted approximately six hours. Other than the open-heart procedures Marvin has undergone, this was probably the most complex. The majority of the operation — and the most delicate part of the surgery — was devoted to correcting functional problems and improving vision.

First an incision was made across the top of the scalp from ear to ear, and the scalp was carefully raised from the skull and separated all the way down to the eyebrows. Nerves were painstakingly located and isolated so that they would not be injured.

Then I selectively removed portions of muscle, which would not only benefit Marvin's "tic" but would also decrease the frown lines and leave him with a smoother, more relaxed forehead. Excess skin was removed, and the eyebrows were elevated. This would give the eyes a fuller, more youthful appearance. It would also improve his ability to open his right eye, and thus make it possible for him to continue functioning as a television newsman. Once I had sutured the scalp, this portion of the operation was completed.

A second incision was made in the right upper lid to correct the sagging and further improve Marvin's ability to open his right eye fully. This went well and was also sutured

The nips and tucks were yet to begin. The first step was to compensate for the resorption of bone and cartilage around the chin and jaw line. An incision was made in the mouth, and more material was added to reestablish the desired chin and jaw line. In addition, Then it was time to create that John-Wayne-type dimple Marvin wanted. First, the fat was removed from just under the skin in the area of the planned dimple. Sutures were then used to fix the top layer of the skin to the chin muscle, creating a permanent depression, or dimple, in the mid-portion of the chin. Once the dimple was created, I sutured the wound. Since the surgery was done through the mouth, this would never be seen, and there would be no scar.

Next it was time to remove some of the extra fat that had collected under Marvin's chin and in the neck area. Through a small incision in the natural crease just under Marvin's chin, I suctioned out the fat. This part of the procedure actually took only a few minutes.

The final procedure, and another one of the more delicate parts of the surgery, consisted of Marvin's third facelift. This incorporated a muscle plication or neck sling, a technique used to tighten the muscles of the neck and lower face. This is accomplished by placing a row of permanent (non-absorbable) sutures along the edge of the neck muscles on each side of the neck. Then these are sutured to the fibrous tissue over the bone behind the ears. It is similar to raising the ropes on the end of a hammock to elevate and tighten the hammock. The human neck muscle is actually a hammock-like configuration that drops with gravity, and, like the hammock, needs occasional tightening to reduce the "sling" effect. This tightening procedure gives a better, and longer lasting, result to a facelift.

With each facelift there is a distortion of the anatomy and additional scarring. One result is that the important facial nerves are distorted, to a greater or lesser degree, with each operation. Particular care must be taken to avoid nerve injury; otherwise the patient may never be able to smile again. With an experienced surgeon this is rarely a problem, but a facelift is definitely not an undertaking for a novice.

The extensive cosmetic and reconstructive procedure went well, and, as Marvin had intimated prior to surgery, a camera crew was in his hospital room when I entered to remove his dressings on the second day. He had made good on his promise to let the public see the unveiling of his new face.

This, from my point of view, made it particularly important that the procedure prove to be a success. And it did; Marvin looked great. Furthermore, the eyelid spasms had improved. There was almost a total lack of spasms on the right side of the face, and improved visual function. So Marvin not only looked better, he could see better. As soon as the bandages came off, the blue-tinted glasses went on. Even though the eye problem had been partially corrected, it just wouldn't be Marvin without those blue-tinted glasses.

What drew the most comments, however, was not Marvin's eyes but that new chin dimple. Everybody immediately noticed this. The delicate eyelid surgery went almost unnoted, but then, that was to be expected.

Marvin's television show was transmitted from his hospital room that night at 6:00 and 10:00, and he continued to broadcast from there until he went home several days later.

The extensive surgery had taken some of the fight out of Marvin; you might say his mainspring had run down. But this didn't stop him from being very demanding during his recovery. He would call any time, day or night, and request that I come and see him for the slightest thing. Most of the requests dealt with the management of his hairpiece. At that time, no one, not even Gertrude, was allowed to see him without it, except for me. That meant I had to start my work day early, at 5:00 AM. This would allow me time to make my rounds with my other patients, and then tend to Marvin, before heading to the surgical suite for my first case at 7:00. Every morning before I went to surgery, I visited Marvin and changed the dressings — of course, only after Marvin had instructed Gertrude and all hospital and nursing personnel to leave the room. After everyone had gone, I had the honor of washing and blowing dry Marvin's hairpiece as well as combing it into place. (Maybe that's where they got the term "barber surgeons." Could it be there was another Marvin Zindler type around at the turn of the century?) Although I accepted my duties as guardian of the hairpiece with good humor and a sense of fun, make no mistake about it: Marvin was damn serious about this matter.

After his recovery, Marvin continued to wear his blue sunglasses for many years. Eventually he would try using clear glasses on the air, because they let in more light, enabling him to see the teleprompter more easily. He wore the clear lenses, off and on, for three or four weeks, and actually got a lot of fan mail about it. But those blue glasses had become such a part of his persona that he returned to wearing them. Although they still play a small medical role, their purpose is more to enhance his image than to improve his eyesight. As I said, it just wouldn't be Marvin without those blue shades.

For the next several years Marvin satisfied himself by coming to my office for minor surgical procedures. He also had periodic collagen injections in the folds around his mouth to "plump them out." Overall, Marvin was pretty content with his looks, but in 1990 things began to change again. Marvin felt he had too much fullness in the cheeks and jowl area, and felt he needed a re-tread, as he called it, or a little "mini-lift."

I agreed that there was some fullness in the cheek and jowl area, but was not going to be stampeded into another major operation. I did, however, discuss a new technique called "buckle extraction." This is a form of liposuction that is done through the mouth and leaves no external scars.

Buckle extraction is a very delicate and precise procedure that removes part or all of the cheek and jowl fat pad that lies between the facial skin and the muscle. It cannot be done from the outside because there is danger of damaging the facial nerve and the muscle; therefore, the suction procedure must essentially be done in reverse, from inside the mouth. This removes the "pudgy" look from the face and highlights or enhances the cheek bones, giving a more youthful appearance to the face.

Marvin insisted that if we were going to do this, he wanted a mini-lift at the same time. As usual, I was cautious. Although he seemed healthy, I asked Marvin to have a complete physical and cardiac examination with his internist Dr. Fulweber. Even though Marvin was in good shape for his age, the truth is that nobody was anxious for Marvin to have more surgery — except Marvin.

In fact he was downright giddy about the whole thing. Returning to my office after his examination by Dr. Fulweber, he was grinning from ear to ear as he said to me, "Let's do it. It's a spit-and-baling-wire job for you. If I live long enough, you'll be able to give me an entire head transplant."

I said, "I'll call Dr. Fulweber and discuss it with him."

Marvin wasn't going to take "No" for an answer. He retorted, "You know you don't have to call Dr. Fulweber. He's going to tell you I'm as fit as a fiddle, but there's an increased risk at my age. I know it! But you and him are going to get me through this in good shape." With a chuckle, he continued, "If not, I'm going to be the got-damnedest, best-looking corpse at the buryin'. Everyone will be saying, 'Doesn't he look just wonderful!'"

We both laughed, but I knew Marvin was serious. I also knew he was going into this operation with both eyes open. This was, of course, far from the first time we'd had this conversation, but I still felt it was my job to keep Marvin safe, and to keep him from going too far. Finally I reached an agreement with Marvin: If Dr. Fulweber gave medical clearance for the procedure, I would do the liposuction and mini-lift. Nothing else!

I discussed the procedure with Dr. Fulweber and said, "You know Zindler is going to get this done, one way or the other; it's up to us to see that it's done properly and safely."

Dr. Fulweber, who had been through almost identical arguments with Marvin, said, "Let me know when you schedule it. I'll be there to look after him." I agreed, vowing that after this procedure, there would be no others until and unless medical science did indeed perfect the full head transplant.

Later I sat down with Marvin to once again discuss the procedure and its complications and his expectations. I wanted him to understand what a delicate operation this was. But Marvin was determined, so he selected a date and said, "Y'all can tattoo it on your calendar."

Thus it was that on October 12, 1990, Marvin was admitted to The Methodist Hospital for another nip and tuck. Again, the cameras were rolling.

This time, Gertrude looked a little anxious as she walked alongside of the gurney on the way to the operating room. As for me, well, I was listening to a song I had heard many times before. The refrain was: "Agris, keep your got-damn hands off the hairpiece. It stays on during the surgery."

I retorted with a smile, "Would you like to do it with just local anesthesia and direct the procedure? You can tell everybody how to do the operation. Of course, when we do the liposuction through your mouth, you might find that a little difficult. Give your wife a kiss, and let's go in there and get this done."

Marvin looked up at Gertrude and said, "Don't worry, Dear. I told all the doctors to be sure to finish the operation because I want to be the got-damnedest best looking corpse in the funeral parlor." Which did nothing for poor Gertrude's nerves. But she took a deep breath, smiled, gave him a kiss and wished him good luck. I put my arm around Gertrude and gave her a reassuring hug. I then walked her back to the waiting area where there were several other family members.

The surgery lasted only a few hours. It consisted of facial sculpting — liposuction of the face and neck with a buckle extraction of the fat pad through the mouth. This was all accomplished with two small incisions that were less than a quarter of an inch in size. A mini-tuck followed to tighten the skin of the face and neck area.

Most patients would go home the same day, but Marvin wanted to linger awhile on Fondren Twelve, the secure, private top-floor retreat at The Methodist Hospital. It looks more like a private suite in a super-deluxe hotel than a hospital. Marvin preferred the larger corner room.

Even with all of Fondren Twelve's amenities, Marvin still had special requirements. He says that he could never get comfortable in the standard hospital bed, so he requires a king-size bed. With each of his operations, a four-poster, king-size bed is ordered and placed in this room. But it doesn't end there. Marvin requires a firm mattress to go along with that big bed. By now, however, the staff was well aware of Marvin's desires and eccentricities, so both the large room and the special bed were awaiting His Highness.

Marvin emerged from surgery in playful good spirits, and after seeing to him I went to sit awhile with Gertrude and other members of the Zindler clan, who had been waiting with some anxiety. I told them, "Marvin is fine, and the surgery went well. Anyway, Marvin ain't ready yet to check into Heaven. He'd insist on seeing the kitchen first and checking the upstairs for a four-poster bed."

At this, everyone seemed to relax a little. When we all walked into Marvin's room, it was apparent he was well on his way to recovery. He had the phone in his hands, and was making up for the couple of hours that he was unable to talk while under anesthesia. You would have thought that one of the steps in the operation was to have that tongue of his retread.

Marvin was making arrangements for tonight's television program, much to the astonishment of Lori Reingold, to whom he was talking on the phone. Although newly out of surgery, Marvin was ready to give it to 'em with both barrels, and he wanted to do it from his hospital bed tonight.

He certainly seemed to be ready to show his face in public. I heard him exclaim to Lori, "I thought I was going to look like I was sitting inside the outhouse when lightning struck. But I ain't even black and blue. I look good enough to give a sermon, like a picture out of a wish book. I'm going to do the television show from my room here in the hospital. You and Bob come on down here about 3:00, ya hear? Have Bob bring the camera."

Lori asked him if he was in any pain. "No," said Marvin, "I'm snug as a bug in a deep-pile rug, which is what I think the doctor's got wrapped around my face. Y'all be here at 3:00," he added again.

Given that bandages were wrapped completely around his head and his mouth was full of stitches, we figured his audience would have difficulty understanding him. But Marvin came through like a champ: he did the television show and he did it well. As before, he insisted on doing his television program from the hospital for the next several days. The TV ratings went up.

Of course, this all meant that I would have to play barber surgeon again, because Marvin was still not going to allow anyone else in the room during dressing changes. No way was he going to let anyone see him without his hairpiece and makeup.

Marvin is probably going to be pushing for more cosmetic procedures for the rest of his life, and I, of course, will play my part: trying to talk him out of it, doing my damdnest to keep him from stepping over the line, and then, finally, doing my very best to see him safely through the latest surgery. It's a dance we've done many times before, and for me, sitting it out is never an option.

Very few of Marvin's undertakings are completely self-serving. Though some might think his decades-long experiment with cosmetic surgery is the ultimate in vanity, something quite wonderful has grown from it. Perhaps because he was often taunted as a child, and even as an adult had problems gaining acceptance due to his unconventional looks, Marvin is acutely aware of the pain of being "different" in a society with little tolerance for aberration of any type.

Even as long ago as his first cosmetic procedure, Marvin was saying, "An ugly or deformed person can grow up feeling like they are not much good in the world." He has always been particularly concerned about children, and has often said, "A child has the right to look normal. No single act is as important to the future development of a child as [doing something for] his health and well-being, for this child is our future."

I also feel Marvin's sympathy and concern, particularly for children born with cleft lip and other facial deformities. Marvin has worked very closely with me, The Methodist Hospital, St. Luke's Episcopal Hospital, and the Texas Children's Hospital to help deliver needed medical attention to children suffering from these devastating deformities. To better achieve these goals, Marvin and I founded **THE AGRIS-ZINDLER CHILDREN'S FOUNDATION** in 1981. At the end of this book you'll find more information about this organization, including how and where to send donations.

I have also traveled to numerous third-world countries to inspire, teach, and perform plastic and reconstructive surgical procedures for children, and Marvin has been right there with me on many of these journeys. Since the late 1980s, we have traveled the world together on medical mission trips.[1] When the Berlin Wall fell and the Soviet Union collapsed, we were there. When China opened its doors in 1991, we were there. When the ORBIS eye plane went to Bulgaria, Marvin participated. There have been multiple trips to Central and South America and even to the far reaches of the rain forests, as well as to the Middle East.

But our priority has always been to take care of the children at home first. *Charity always begins at home,* and anyone writing to Marvin or me gets our immediate attention and help if it is at all possible.

No doubt, many people scoff at Marvin's seeming obsession over his looks. Like everything else about Marvin, however, there is far more to this story. If Marvin spares no expense or energy in sculpting his own face, he also spares nothing in helping countless children all over the world, for whom cosmetic surgery is not a luxury, but a ticket to a normal, happy life.

After decades of tinkering with what nature chose to give him, Marvin may have a perfect nose, chin, jaw line, or whatever... but if you ask me, the most perfect thing about Marvin is his heart.

---

[1] For details on some of these trips, see the section entitled, "Man on a Mission."

C·H·A·P·T·E·R 19

THE HEART OF THE MATTER

One autumn afternoon in the mid-1990s, Marvin came to see me in my office. He periodically was in the Medical Center for a checkup or blood test, and would usually stop by to talk or have lunch with me. But on this day it soon became apparent that Marvin had much more on his mind than lunch.

Marvin told me Dr. George Noon, his heart surgeon, was going to do bypass surgery again. Marvin had had a triple bypass in December of 1979, and it had served him well for all these years. A recent examination by Dr. Fulweber, however, showed that changes had taken place, and four or five bypasses would be needed. Other studies showed that there was an obstruction in Marvin's carotid artery in the neck, resulting in 80% closure.

Marvin told me that he had actually been made aware of this the previous year, but had put off doing anything about it. Finally, however, he had decided to have the surgery. It was scheduled for October 30, and I was invited. Specifically, Marvin wanted me to be there to close the incisions.

As he explained it, "I'm confident that Dr. Noon knows what he's doing on the inside. I want a plastic surgeon so I won't have any scars."

I told Marvin, "Well, you'll always have a scar, but there are techniques to close the wound that will minimize the scarring and make it look better."

"Yeah, that's what I mean. I want you to do it. Can you be there on October 30?"

"You know I'll be there. You've already had ten jillion cosmetic procedures. I just can't believe there isn't something else you want done at the same time. Perhaps I could just assist Dr. Noon and show him how to tidy things up with those nice little sutures that plastic surgeons use."

Smiling at me, Marvin said, "You do your job, and let George Noon do his. Remember, I have that lifetime contract with KTRK Channel 13 to outlive."

"I'm not worried about you outliving your lifetime contract. You're just mean enough to do it."

I could tell Marvin was worried, and that he was having the expected thoughts about his own mortality, but I, for one, was determined to put a more cheerful spin on the matter. I said to him, "I don't know where you're going to hold your 100th birthday party, perhaps Disneyland, perhaps the Palladium in London — but I intend to be there." And I intended to do my part to see that he reached that landmark birthday.

On October 30, as scheduled, Dr. Noon did a quadruple-and-a-half bypass and the carotid artery procedure. I did the cosmetic wound closure, as Marvin had requested. Afterward Marvin said, "Agris knows me inside and out. He can testify to the fact that I have a *big heart.*"

Gertrude and the rest of Marvin's family were at his bedside throughout the hospital stay. Later Gertrude said to me, "Marvin is always very positive, but in the hospital he was, you know, a little down. I reminded him that he had to get well because I'm going first, and I'd let him know when I was ready." Sadly, her prediction about being the first to go would come true.

The day after the surgery, Marvin was sitting up in a chair, various tubes and intravenous lines in place. Not surprisingly, Marvin was insisting on doing his television program from the hospital again. He continued to improve rapidly and had an uneventful recovery.

No doubt, Marvin's penchant for publicity served the public well once again, this time by raising people's awareness of heart disease. In 1997 he was in the hospital again, and it was then that he probably saved more lives than at any time in his career.

A POSITIVE PSA...
AND A LIFESAVING P.S.A.:
MARVIN'S BATTLE WITH PROSTATE CANCER

I n 1997, Marvin once again used his public forum to save lives, when he openly shared the details of his fight with prostate cancer. It began when Marvin went for his yearly medical examination and blood tests. One of the blood tests included in his annual checkup was to monitor for prostate cancer. This is the *prostate-specific antigen* (PSA) blood test. Most doctors recommend that men have this test every year after age 50, and that men who are at high risk for prostate cancer have it annually after 40. Elevated levels of prostate antigens are a clear sign that something is wrong with the prostate.

Unfortunately, men tend to be remiss in getting annual physical examinations, refusing to get even the simplest of tests. Perhaps it's that macho attitude that gets in the way, or it's an attitude that serious illness is something that happens only to other people. It's ludicrous, when you think about it: guys will tell the dirtiest jokes, but when it comes to talking about a rectal exam or prostate cancer, they clam up and refuse to deal with it. That's sheer foolishness.

In Marvin's case, the PSA test proved to be positive, and the White Knight was faced with another major battle — this time for his life. Instead of hunkering down for the fight and temporarily removing himself from the public eye, however, Marvin once again used his nightly television program as a one-man public awareness project. He brought prostate cancer, one of the leading causes of cancer in men, into everyone's living room.

And he's mighty glad he did. Even today, men approach him all the time and tell him that his series saved their lives. At fundraisers, parties and just on the street, men come up to Marvin to shake his hand thank him for that program. Women are equally grateful. He can't count the times he's heard a woman tell him, "That program saved my husband's life. I've been trying to get him to have a test and examination for years, but you finally convinced him to do it."

As you probably know, Marvin has always been truthful with his audience, even about the most personal aspects of his life. However, he did have some doubts about this one at first. After he found out he had prostate cancer he was unsure, for the first time in his life, about how he was going to deal with this. He thought about it for several days. Finally he called Lori Reingold and Bob Dows into his office and told them he was going to go public with it.

He was determined to bring prostate cancer out of the closet, because he felt it would save lives. After all, you couldn't pick up a newspaper or magazine without reading something about the need for breast examinations, frequent mammograms, new surgical procedures, medications and plastic and reconstructive breast surgery. But prostate cancer received very little media attention.

This, of course, was all to change.

There were a few sensitive logistical details to be worked out, however. With his characteristic broad grin and his head cocked to one side like a shy little boy, Marvin said to Bob, "You're a damn good cameraman, Bob, but how the hell are you going to portray the rectal examination on television? You know the producers are going to cut it. They'll never let something like that go on the air. But it's an important part of the examination. I want it in the story."

Bob recalls that they all had a good laugh. Then he turned to Marvin and said, "If you want to do the story, we'll work it out." Bob was clever and creative, and he agreed with Marvin: they needed to emphasize the importance of a yearly physical examination — including the rectal exam — if they were going to be truthful and have continuity in the story.

The plan was to produce a series of stories to show the need for appropriate blood tests and regular examinations, and to discuss the treatments that were available, should they be needed. Marvin wanted to take his viewing audience through each step of his ordeal. Even though other patients with prostate cancer were to be interviewed, Marvin was going to be the focus of the series.

Lori Reingold set to work planning a powerful, enlightening and informative series. Interviews with doctors specializing in prostate surgery, chemotherapy, radiation and even some new experimental treatments were scheduled to be aired. Permission to televise the world-famous M.D. Anderson Cancer Treatment Center was procured. At the television station, computer graphics were being prepared to explain the more complicated procedures of prostate cancer treatment. Everything was falling into place.

Well, almost everything. Bob Dows was still in a quandary over how to show the rectal examination to the public.

But it was full speed ahead anyway, and Marvin went public with the announcement of his condition. Following his announcement, which aired on his 10:00 PM broadcast, everyone thought Marvin was very forthright and brave. And his viewing audience was surprised when Marvin announced the series on prostate cancer that was to follow — especially when he said he would be the patient.

Things continued as planned, but there was still that one little problem. Bob had yet to shoot the rectal examination, and was still mulling over how to handle this part of the show.

Inevitably, the day of reckoning finally came.

There stood Marvin behind the curtain in the examining room, ready to get undressed. And there stood Bob, with his customary 50 pounds of television camera equipment mounted on his shoulder, complete with a 200-watt light. The exam room was aglow.

The doctor was aware that he was going to be interviewed about Marvin's prostate cancer, and he understood that he would also be asked to discuss the need for regular blood tests and examinations. But he seemed bewildered at Bob's insistence on being in the examining room with the television camera. This was not the type of interview the doctor had in mind. The possibility struck him that Marvin just might be carrying one of his most striking story ideas a little too far.

No doubt the doctor was expecting Bob to leave, any moment now... but no, Bob remained in the room, camera poised on his shoulder. He turned to the doctor and said, "Doc, put your gloves on — slowly." Bob could hardly keep from laughing when he saw the man's face.

The doctor stood frozen for a few moments, until Bob spoke again. "You can't steal second base and keep one foot on first. Let's get those gloves on, please. Thinking about it ain't doing it, Doc. We need to take the bull by the tail, and face the situation." Perhaps it was a questionable choice of words, given the circumstances, but it got the message across.

Bob says, "That poor doctor, he had such a somber expression on his face you would have thought he was going to be the examinee rather than the examiner." But the doctor complied with his request, slowly slipping one glove on and then the other as Bob zoomed in with the camera. You could hear the latex glove snap as it was pulled over the doctor's wrist — an ominous sound at best. Then Bob pulled back on the lens to get a wide shot as the doctor turned and stepped behind the curtain.

Sometimes, of course, less is more, and Bob sensed this was one of those times. The video, he knew, was sufficient to make the viewers aware of what was going to happen next; a verbal explanation would not be required. And after the doctor disappeared behind the curtain, nothing else need be shown.

But Bob, whose sense of humor is legendary, wasn't willing to let a good opportunity slip by. There was one more shot he wanted to take, even if it ultimately wasn't used. When it was all over and the patient had dressed, Bob made his request. He had Marvin hunker down in front of the examining table, elbows on the table, chin resting on his palms. Bob placed the camera inches away from Marvin's face, then asked him to raise his eyebrows as if suddenly surprised, and look wide-eyed straight into the camera.

That close-up, with the raised eyebrows and sudden expression of shock, was worth a thousand words. It was clever, and certainly told the story, perhaps a little too well. This shot was used on Marvin's TV show, followed by the shot of the doctor, coming out of the examining room and loudly snapping his gloves. If a picture is worth a thousand words, a sound can be worth several thousand.

At any rate, the biggest hurdle had been cleared at last. Bob later said, "I was fishing with an empty hook for a while, but once I figured out how we were going to shoot the rectal exam, the series could proceed."

Proceed it did, and it was absolutely phenomenal. It told the story that indeed needed to be told. It was also the front runner to newspaper and magazine articles on prostate cancer. Others saw the need to jump on the Zindler bandwagon, and they did. I can't give Marvin enough credit for being brave enough to go public and for tackling a subject that many would have considered taboo.

Marvin is now doing fine. He continues to be an early riser, so he can get in a round of golf, if the weather is nice, before going to the television station. Marvin's fit as a fiddle and more feisty than ever. It must be that angel on his shoulder. Or maybe it's sheer stubbornness. In any case, Marvin is still bound and determined to "outlive his lifetime contract," and believe me, if anyone can accomplish that feat, he can. He will avail himself of any surgery, medication or anything else medical science has to offer, just so we can continue to see him every evening at 6:00 and 10:00 on KTRK-Channel 13's Eyewitness News.

God bless you, Maaaaaarvin.

P·A·R·T

7

Texas HAD A Whorehouse In It

~∞ • ∞~

The Saga Of The Chicken Ranch

"WHY THE CHICKEN RANCH?"
MARVIN'S MOTIVES

It was a stage show. It was a movie. It was a ratings-grabbing television news series, a magazine article or two, and several books. It was the "Chicken Ranch." As real as life itself, it was a legend that became a scandal that became yet another legend, and, for good or bad, it will haunt Marvin Zindler for the rest of his life. At the time of this writing, nearly 30 years have passed since the Chicken Ranch story first broke. But people are still talking about it, and nearly everyone who talks about it has an opinion about Marvin's role in the shuttering of Texas' (and, possibly the nation's) oldest continually operating whorehouse.

No doubt, much of that opinion has been shaped by the media. In virtually all of the popular literature about the Chicken Ranch, and certainly in the Hollywood version, Marvin, or the character based on Marvin, is the bad guy — a self-righteous muckraker, an egocentric publicity hound, and more than a bit of a buffoon. True, the hypocritical politicians — or, as *Best Little Whorehouse in Texas* author Larry L. King would have it, the "candy-assed politicians" — and other public officials are portrayed as bad guys as well, but since Marvin is remembered as the one who started all the fuss, he's the one who gets most of the blame for breaking up Miss Edna's happy home in Fayette County, Texas.

Like most stories, however, the reality is more complex. Apart from the fact that the stage show and movie romanticized this little country whorehouse and its inhabitants to the extreme — the facts behind the workings of this or any other brothel are neither very glamorous nor all that erotic — the popular literature has never done Marvin justice. Painting him as the bad guy in this tale makes for a good story, perhaps, but not a true one. The true story about the Chicken Ranch has never really been told, and there are still a lot of questions that haven't been answered. What Marvin did and didn't do, and why, is still largely unknown.

Regarding Marvin, the first question that needs to be addressed is, *Why the Chicken Ranch?* Everyone who knows him pretty much agrees on a few facts about Marvin. Even those who don't care for him concede that he is smart. Most would also agree that although he is sometimes impulsive on small matters, he's generally a lot more careful about the big ones. It is not his habit to rush into things, but rather to scrupulously weigh people and events, seeking the opinions of others before taking action. He gathers the facts and carefully considers the outcome before making any major decisions.

So, again: Why the Chicken Ranch? Why did Marvin choose to get involved in something that was bound to bring so much trouble raining down on his head?

Naturally, most of his detractors say he did it for the publicity and ratings. Jan Hutson, in her 1980 book, *The Chicken Ranch: The True Story of the Best Little Whorehouse in Texas,* summed up a lot of folks' opinions when she wrote that Marvin "was not seeking salvation through good deeds; Marvin was seeking publicity through any deeds, whether good, rotten or indifferent." Even among those who gave him the benefit of the doubt where his motivations were concerned, a good many thought his outrage would have been better vented in the real cesspool, Houston.

Others have a different view of Marvin's motives. It's true that he craves publicity and that he sometimes comes across as self-righteous. Even his closest pals won't argue with that. But when it comes to the big battles, Marvin's main motivation is "what is right." Once he makes that decision, he is capable of fighting with the voracity of a kick-boxer: first, fast and hard. Once the determination of "good or evil" is made, he jumps headfirst into the fray. The Chicken Ranch was no exception.

True, the Chicken Ranch was a Texas legend, a name familiar to every schoolboy and politician in Texas — and, as such, it had some fiercely loyal friends in high places. Jokes were made about it on the floor of the Texas State Legislature. When the main highway near the Chicken Ranch was widened, a paved spur was built running to the first cattle guard that marked the entrance of the dirt road leading directly to Miss Edna's. There was no outcry from citizens complaining about this use of their tax dollars.

Even today, few whorehouses are regarded with the nostalgic affection reserved for the Chicken Ranch. And there's no doubt that Houston had, and has, many times the number of prostitutes that Fayette County had.

Marvin, however, never set out to battle prostitution. As he so adamantly stated, "I'm no moralist" — at least not when it came to the world's oldest profession. As for the legal aspect of the matter, it's not up to "the badge" to decide whether prostitution is legal or illegal, Marvin says. That's something for the courts to decide. The job of law enforcement is only to uphold the law, and clearly, the law was not being upheld if the local sheriff's department was allowing the Chicken Ranch to remain open. Marvin and others were also convinced that the Chicken Ranch was connected to political corruption and organized crime.

There are many who will argue with that notion, of course. But Marvin still believes he was right, and if he had to do it all over again, he'd handle it exactly the same way.

At any rate, although Marvin wasn't the sole player, he was the front man in the event that would, for better or worse, be instrumental in bringing an end to a 130-year-old tradition. No doubt there are some folks who will never forgive him.

C·H·A·P·T·E·R 22

FROM MRS. SWINE TO MISS EDNA:

A BRIEF HISTORY OF THE CHICKEN RANCH

Before getting into the story of how and why the Chicken Ranch was closed down, it's only fair to take a look at the history of this legendary Texas institution.[1] Given polite society's attitude towards sex for hire — not to mention the longstanding laws against prostitution — some might think it truly amazing that the Chicken Ranch remained open for business for nearly 130 years. Indeed, the good citizens of La Grange, Texas could have demanded that it be shut down long before it was. With the Chicken Ranch, however, there were always other factors at work besides the law and the attitudes of the society at large.

One of the most important factors was that in La Grange and Fayette County, a certain frontier tolerance still prevailed, the operating philosophy being, "Work hard, play hard, and just get along." Few citizens saw the brothel as a threat to the moral fabric of the community, and a good many, even those who did not avail themselves of the Chicken Ranch's services, acknowledged that this small country cathouse was an economic boon for the county. It was a major tourist attraction, for one thing. Furthermore, the working girls of the Chicken Ranch shopped at the local stores, and commodities and supplies for the Ranch were bought strictly from local merchants. And the brothel's most famous madams, Miss Jessie and, later, Miss Edna, contributed generously to local civic causes.

Beyond being a tourist attraction, the Chicken Ranch was an object of veneration, and this is another factor that worked in its favor for so long. The Chicken Ranch was,

---

[1] A much more detailed account can be found in Jan Hutson's book, *The Chicken Ranch: The True Story of the Best Little Whorehouse in Texas* (currently available in a paperback edition from Authors Choice Press, a division of iUniverse.com).

after all, not just another brothel — it was an institution; it wouldn't be much of an exaggeration to call it a shrine. In any case, the Chicken Ranch could not have survived to a ripe old age of 130 in and of itself. It had loyal, and powerful, supporters and friends not only in Fayette County, but throughout Texas.

Despite its legions of supporters, there was no lack of effort to close the Chicken Ranch down long before Marvin Zindler came onto the scene; apparently, not everybody loves a legend. In the enemy camp were the Texas Rangers (at various times), a few fundamentalist Baptists, and more than one irate wife. Nevertheless, the Chicken Ranch stayed in operation, through good times and bad, until that fateful summer of '73.

Most people agree that institutionalized prostitution in La Grange can be traced back to 1844, only five years after the city was established. The woman who brought the first ladies of pleasure to La Grange was hardly a paragon of sex appeal. Nicknamed "Mrs. Swine" as much for her appalling personal habits as her stunningly porcine appearance, La Grange's first madam came from New Orleans with three homely young women in her wake. They settled in a small pine-board hotel near the saloon, and, despite their deficiencies in the looks and hygiene department, a lucrative business was born. Men had needs, after all.

One of the smartest things Mrs. Swine did was to begin a tradition of interaction with the community and local law enforcement officers. In 1844, laws were few and enforcement rare, but Mrs. Swine clearly understood the advantage of having lawmen in one's corner. This alliance between madam and lawmen would continue, from election to election, for nearly 130 years.

Mrs. Swine and her girls used the hotel lobby for entertaining and the upstairs room for services, and this continued pretty much to everyone's satisfaction until the Civil War, when Mrs. Swine and a faithful prostitute named Tillie were run out of town — not for being purveyors of flesh, but for being suspected Yankees and traitors.

Nevertheless, prostitution continued to flourish in La Grange, particularly after the war, but by the end of the 19th century, the working girls and their madams had moved out of the hotels and into a red-light district on the banks of the Colorado River. It was there that one Miss Jessie Williams, newly arrived from Waco, bought a small house in 1905.[2] She had run a small but profitable house in Waco, and proved equally successful in her new location.

---

[2] Purists might point out that 1905, rather than 1844, is the true year of origin of the Chicken Ranch, since 1905 is the year the first madam of the house that would become known as the Chicken Ranch settled in Fayette County. Even so, most everyone agrees that prostitution existed more or less openly in La Grange and surrounding areas for over a century — and whether you hold that the Chicken Ranch itself was in business for nearly 130 years or merely 68 years, its place in Texas folklore is secure.

Miss Jessie ran the only "respectable" house on the banks of the Colorado; she admitted politicians and lawmen, but turned away drunkards. Wisely, she continued Mrs. Swine's tradition of maintaining good relations with the law — in this case, the Loessin brothers. August Loessin was sheriff of Fayette County, and his younger brother Will was chief deputy and marshall of La Grange. The Loessin brothers were widely known and respected as law officers.

Not surprisingly, Miss Jessie acquired a lot of friends among the influential class, and it was through some of these connections that she learned of an impending crusade against the red-light district. She sold her remaining real-estate holdings in Waco, and bought two houses on eleven acres just outside the city limits of La Grange, two blocks from the Houston-Galveston Highway. This would become the location of the Chicken Ranch.

As Miss Jessie's business grew, so did her house. Rooms were built onto the main house in a haphazard way as needed. There was nothing fancy or even remotely elegant about Miss Jessie's house, but nevertheless it had legions of loyal clients.

Miss Jessie remained on good terms with the law, namely with Will Loessin, who had succeeded his brother August as sheriff of Fayette County. Sheriff Loessin visited every night to catch up on gossip and gather information on criminals who might have paid a visit to the brothel and made the mistake of bragging about their exploits. As a matter of fact, many crimes in La Grange were solved in just this way.

Miss Jessie ruled her house, which was still known simply as "Miss Jessie's House," with a firm hand and an iron rod — literally. No exotic sex play was allowed, and any customer who gave one of her girls a hard time was chased out of the house by Jessie, wielding her rod. If his infraction was serious enough, the errant customer was never admitted again.

When the Great Depression hit the country and the economy went south, Miss Jessie was obliged to lower her prices. At first things weren't so bad, for customers were still plentiful, but as times grew harder, the customers grew scarcer, and the girls grew hungrier. Something had to be done. It was at this time that Miss Jessie enacted the famous "poultry standard," charging one chicken for one roll in the hay. Before long, there were chickens everywhere on the property, and the house became known as the Chicken Ranch.

The poultry payment plan was a win-win situation. The customers got what they wanted, and Miss Jessie's girls never again went hungry. Further, Miss Jessie was able to supplement her income by selling the surplus chickens and eggs.

The economy in those parts began to turn around as the Civilian Conservation Corps began construction of Camp Swift, near La Grange. Before too long, the shortage of men and money eased, and once again Miss Jessie's girls were paid in good old American currency. The hard times had come and gone, but the moniker "Chicken Ranch" stuck.

When World War II began, the girls of the Chicken Ranch sent packages and letters to the local boys fighting in the war, just as they'd done during the first World War. Although Miss Jessie was getting on in years and was confined to a wheelchair by war's end, she still ruled the house, literally, with her iron rod. In the 1950s, however, she was confined to her bed, and died in 1961 at the age of 80.

She left the Chicken Ranch in good hands. Edna Milton had come to the establishment from Oklahoma back in 1952. She soon took over for Miss Jessie, and showed that she was just as capable a businesswoman as her mentor. By the time of Miss Jessie's death, Edna had established herself as a more than competent madam. She bought the Ranch from Miss Jessie's heirs for $30,000, which was actually much more than the property value.

Edna had long since established a good relationship with the sheriff, T.J. "Jim" Flournoy, who had been elected in 1946. One of the first things Sheriff Jim had done upon assuming office was to put in a direct phone line from his office to the Chicken Ranch, so he could replace his predecessor's nightly visits with nightly phone calls. Not only did this eliminate the trips every night, but it made communication instantaneous should the madam or one of her girls require it. They could make one call to Sheriff Jim and within minutes, have an obnoxious customer removed.

Like her predecessor, Edna also maintained good relations with the community at large, mainly by keeping a low profile and pumping money into the local economy. Social contact between the working girls and the citizens of La Grange was strictly forbidden, but the girls and Edna patronized local merchants.

The Chicken Ranch flourished all through the 1950s and 1960s. On some weekends there was a long line at the door, comprised of soldiers and college students. There were at least 12 military bases — Army, Navy and Air Force — within a hundred-mile radius of the Chicken Ranch. One base was even thoughtful enough to supply its men with helicopter transport to the brothel. Another rich source of income was college students, specifically, those from Texas A&M in College Station, and The University of Texas in Austin. A visit to the Chicken Ranch became part of freshman initiation at Texas A&M.

At some point in the 1960s, Edna decided she needed to add some more exotic sexual thrills to her repertoire in order to keep the college boys and soldiers coming in. After all, there was a sexual revolution afoot in the outside world, and more and more of the "girls next door" were giving away what was for sale at the Chicken Ranch: straight sex. Oral sex and group sex were still considered somewhat exotic to the mainstream, however, so Miss Edna added these to her list of available services. These additions would have been considered very risqué by Miss Jessie's standards, but they did wonders for Edna's bottom line.

Edna maintained high standards of cleanliness and health at her house. The girls were seen by a doctor weekly. All new employees of the Ranch were fingerprinted and photographed by Sheriff Jim Flournoy before they could begin work. They also underwent a background check, and a criminal record of any type disqualified them from employment with Miss Edna. As a matter of fact, these background checks enabled Flournoy to catch a few women wanted on warrants. Conscious of the Mann Act, Edna refused to hire any girl from outside the state of Texas. Nor would she accept any girl who had a pimp. Once they were at the Ranch, the women had to abide by strict rules written by

Miss Edna. All in all, the Chicken Ranch was, as Sheriff Jim was once quoted as saying, "a clean place to go to... Ain't got no pimps, no narcotics, no alcohol, and no trouble."

If Edna had standards for her girls, she also had standards for her clientele. Customers had to look presentable and not be visibly intoxicated, and no cursing or drinking were allowed on the premises. There was one other restriction that, benign as Edna's intentions might have been, was undeniably racist: customers had to be white.

Visitors to the Ranch were generally greeted by an attendant, who usually doubled as a maid and sometimes a cook. Although she herself was invariably black, she turned away any potential clients who were black or Hispanic, explaining that those were "Miss Edna's rules." This points out just one more way in which the Chicken Ranch was romanticized by Hollywood. In the film, *The Best Little Whorehouse in Texas*, a scene in which the Aggie boys and their chosen ladies of the night are merrily dancing and singing shows at least one African-American pair. In Miss Edna's house, however, there were no black "boarders" and no black customers.

So what could a well-mannered, presentable, reasonably sober white boy get for his hard-earned money? Well, for a base price he could get fifteen minutes of straight sex (at the time of Channel 13's famous exposé, the going price for the no-frills service was $15.00, or a dollar a minute). The more exotic options would cost him more. He could also expect to be grievously overcharged for extras such as cigarettes (75 cents), soda pop (one dollar), and a chance to listen to old country songs on the jukebox (a quarter a song). Those were steep prices for the times. In fact, the only real bargain at the Chicken Ranch was sex. Everything else was overpriced in order to discourage loitering.

There was no doubt that Miss Edna was doing all right for herself. With an average of 14 young ladies in residence at any given time, each attending to eight to 20 gentlemen a day (an average of 12 visitors each), the gross income more than likely exceeded $500,000 a year. And this wasn't counting the profits from the Cokes, cigarettes and jukebox. The prostitutes themselves weren't doing too badly either. Even after giving an estimated 75 % to Edna, they still averaged $300 a week — not bad wages in those days — and they had no expenses. Edna paid all taxes, insurance, utilities, laundry bills, food bills (two meals a day), and medical expenses, including the weekly doctor visits for each of the girls. She took good care of her employees.

In return, the girls who worked at the Chicken Ranch were much more loyal and devoted to Miss Edna than the average hooker was to her madam. Most of the young ladies stayed for many years at the Chicken Ranch, and employee turnover was almost nil.

Though Edna devoted all her efforts to running the Chicken Ranch, she also became La Grange's number one patron. Through her support the Little League Baseball team was kept well equipped with bats, balls and gloves. She also put up the money needed for a new community swimming pool, and was the largest contributor to the new county hospital. Miss Edna's philanthropic commitments endeared her and the Chicken Ranch to La Grange and its citizens.

Even so, Edna maintained the lowest of profiles. Life at the Chicken Ranch carried on as it had for many decades. Money kept rolling in.

It was too good to last.

Edna had always placed top priority on maintaining a good relationship with Sheriff Flournoy and his deputies, but it was this relationship that, ultimately, led to her downfall. Some people believed that the sheriff had an interest in the business, and actually had a role in running the bordello. Some even suggested that the Chicken Ranch was connected to organized crime.

And it was the rumors of political corruption and organized crime that attracted Marvin Zindler's attention — or, more accurately, the attention of someone who put a bug in Marvin's ear. These rumors spelled the beginning of the end for Miss Edna and her girls.

C·H·A·P·T·E·R 23

WHITE KNIGHT VS. YELLOW JOURNALISM:
HOW THE CHICKEN RANCH BECAME A (TOO)-COLORFUL STORY

I n the summer of 1973, Marvin had been working at KTRK-TV Channel 13 for only half a year. At that time, most of his stories were attack pieces. He could thoroughly squash individuals and businesses accused of wrongdoing, giving him the reputation of a "giant killer" in those early years. What was poison for the giants, however, was meat for the television ratings. His fans were happy, the executives at KTRK were ecstatic, and Marvin was delighted. After decades of searching, he had finally found his calling.

Then came the Chicken Ranch. The unexpected backlash from Marvin's news coverage, which spurred the closing of the legendary whorehouse, put both Marvin and Channel 13 into a headspin.

Even so, the Chicken Ranch was hardly the biggest story of 1973, not even in Texas. In comparison to, say, the cease-fire in Vietnam, or Roe v. Wade, the landmark Supreme Court ruling on abortion, the closing down of a little country whorehouse was pretty small stuff. Indeed, throughout the long, hot summer of '73, the television viewing audience had plenty of bigger issues to occupy their time. You couldn't turn your TV on without hearing something about the Watergate scandal. Gasoline shortages and inflation weighed on everyone's mind. And in the Houston area, a gruesome story was unfolding around the same time as the Chicken Ranch incident. It started with the shooting death of a 33-year-old electrician named Dean Corll, by an 18-year-old man named Elmer Wayne Henley. It turned out that Corll, Henley, and another accomplice, David Owen Brooks, had sexually assaulted, tortured and murdered numerous boys and young men. Ultimately, 27 bodies would be discovered — the largest serial murder in U.S. history at that time — and the unspeakable acts of Corll and company would be revealed to a horrified public.

With all of this going on, you could almost say the Chicken Ranch was comic relief — except for the fact that a lot of people didn't find it funny at all.

Despite popular perception, the Chicken Ranch story did not begin with Marvin Zindler. Although many may find it difficult to believe, Marvin didn't just wake up one morning and decide he wanted to do a sensational, sexy story to increase his ratings. Nor did he fabricate the notion that the Chicken Ranch was associated with political corruption and organized crime. He didn't seek out the Chicken Ranch story; it would be far more accurate to say it sought *him* out.

It is fair to say that this story really began at the Texas Department of Public Safety (DPS). For several years both the DPS and the Texas attorney general's office had been investigating the Chicken Ranch, on suspicion that the house was involved in organized crime. Late in 1972, the intelligence division of the DPS conducted a surveillance on the place. In November of 1972, from early afternoon until early the next morning on two consecutive weekend days, two units from the DPS surveillance team stationed themselves on the highway right-of-way to either side of the Chicken Ranch. The DPS agents counted the vehicles entering the Chicken Ranch, recording the number of occupants in each vehicle, and making note of how long they stayed at the Ranch.

Sheriff Jim Flournoy made clear his displeasure at what he perceived as interference from the DPS. At one point, Flournoy confronted the DPS teams and wanted to know what they were doing. He informed them that he had been in charge of the county for 25 years, and would call the DPS if he needed their assistance enforcing laws in his county. He added that he was going to advise Austin and the attorney general's office of what was taking place, and he would personally go to the capital and visit with the governor.

According to the DPS report, Sheriff Flournoy and his deputy were very hostile towards the DPS officers; the deputy with Sheriff Flournoy had a shotgun that was pointed at DPS personnel.

Not that Sheriff Jim's fierce loyalty did any good at all for the Chicken Ranch, in the long run. If anything, it served to cast even more of a suspicious light on the Chicken Ranch's operations.

Also targeted in the DPS investigation was another small bordello that was only a few miles away, just outside of Sealy, Texas. Although almost everybody was familiar with the Chicken Ranch, fewer people knew there was a second similar operation near Sealy. It was located in a rundown building that had once been the Wagon Wheel Motel. By 1973, the former hotel had been in operation as a bawdy house, off and on, for at least fifteen years. The Sealy house, according to the DPS report, was run by a woman named Linda Bartholomew, who went by the name of Connie. The DPS estimated that the Wagon Wheel took in between $6,000 and $8,000 each weekend, and that approximately $1.5 million went through the house in a year.

By DPS estimates, the Chicken Ranch and the Wagon Wheel together were grossing in excess of $3 million a year. It was suspected that money was being laundered through bank accounts in Mexico. Supposedly, some of the money was also going to local and state officials as a pay-off, allowing the Chicken Ranch and the Wagon Wheel to remain open. DPS intelligence sources believed that the money was going to political allies whose power reached all the way to the state Capitol in Austin.

In the DPS report, Agent George Reed of the department's Intelligence Division noted that both the Chicken Ranch and the Wagon Wheel had become part of their respective communities, with most of the citizens of these communities overlooking or simply accepting the bawdy houses. There was no pressure from the citizenry to close down the locations; to the contrary, the general feeling seemed to be that the presence of prostitutes kept "nice" women from getting raped on the streets. Nevertheless, the law was the law, and, Reed pointed out, allowing the whorehouses to continue to operate in La Grange and Sealy would be a mockery to the laws regarding prostitution not only in the Houston and Galveston area but throughout the state of Texas.

"It is our duty and responsibility," he wrote, "regardless of the amount of pressure that might occur, to first be right and to enforce the laws of the state... It is my opinion that these operations should be closed down and permanently put out of business in the following manner: that each location should be raided on at least two occasions and conjunctive proceedings be instituted in the district court."

Political corruption is one thing, but was the Chicken Ranch really involved in organized crime, or were Marvin and Channel 13 overreacting to the implications of the DPS reports? Jan Hutson wrote in *The Chicken Ranch*, "The mention of organized crime usually brings to mind the Mafia, but Marvin uses the term loosely. Two eight-year-olds planning a cookie-jar heist could qualify."

The Chicken Ranch fell somewhere on that vast middle ground between a cookie-jar conspiracy and a Mafia operation. As a matter of fact, the DPS investigation failed to uncover any clear evidence of a connection with organized crime. But there was enough evidence to convince Marvin, and many others, that some type of organized crime was involved.

Organized crime or not, the Chicken Ranch and the Wagon Wheel were doomed. Although many had long known of these bawdy houses, and most had dismissed them as being of little significance, times were changing. Maybe Watergate had made everyone a tad over-sensitive about anything that even resembled corruption. In any event, the issue was no longer whether or not there were, in fact, whorehouses in La Grange and Sealy. The issue, or one of them, anyway, was whether or not public officials were taking payoffs to allow these houses to stay open for so many decades.

To many, of course, the main issue was that prostitution is illegal in Texas, and these houses were — for whatever reason — still open for business.

∞ • ∞

The DPS report was filed at the end of 1972. Months later, however, no action had yet been taken. In fact, it seemed that some state officials somewhere, somehow had managed to hide or squash the DPS report. Naturally, this made the continuing existence of the Chicken Ranch all the more suspect.

Though there was some fear that pressure would come from high state officials, including state representatives and senators, a growing faction of law enforcement officers still wanted the Chicken Ranch and the Wagon Wheel brothels closed. Trouble was, they couldn't find a way to get it done. The intelligence division of the DPS couldn't do it; their role was merely to gather information. The power to take action was in the hands of another DPS division, the famous Texas Rangers, who had done nothing so far. (In fairness to the Rangers, they had, at various times, attempted to close the place in the past, without success.)

Marvin got wind of the matter in April or May of 1973, but he really had nothing to go on so he couldn't do anything. He only became involved when he was invited to do so — not by the DPS, but rather by the Texas attorney general's office.

Why Marvin? The short answer is that the Texas attorney general, John Hill, was told by one of the undercover investigators that he should get Marvin involved. The longer answer is that it was, and is, widely accepted that when someone in law enforcement has been prevented from doing what he or she knows to be right and lawful, turning to the media is the only recourse. It was felt that Marvin had the experience and background for the job, having been in the sheriff's department for more than 10 years.

There was another reason too, of course — there usually is — and it had to do with political expediency. To put it bluntly, using Marvin as the catalyst in the matter would protect those in power. Marvin could do the dirty work of publicizing the illegal doings in La Grange and Sealy, and then the elected officials could either blame Marvin or make him a hero. Whichever way it went, they would be politically clear.

At any rate, John Hill nudged his assistant attorney general, Herbert Hancock, and in June of 1973, Hancock called Marvin and requested a meeting with him. Although Hill talked to Marvin about the matter too, it was Hancock who really threw his weight behind it and supported Marvin (up to a point). On July 4, 1973, Hancock and Marvin met in the coffee shop of the Rice Hotel in downtown Houston. At that time, Marvin was given a copy of the official state intelligence department file on the Chicken Ranch and the Wagon Wheel Motel. The report contained, among other things, the DPS surveillance information. Marvin was told that the attorney general had tried to conduct an investigation of the Chicken Ranch, but had been "warned off."

Obviously there were some pretty powerful forces behind the Chicken Ranch, and Marvin, even as he was being asked to help out, was given fair warning that if he took this on it would create a lot of heat for him. He might even lose his job as a result. Marvin wasn't too worried about losing his job. His worries came later, when, as he put it, "I got my ass whipped by the sheriff in La Grange." Then, he says, the officials who had initially contacted him got scared and couldn't stand the heat.

But that was all to come later.[1]

After the meeting with Herb Hancock, Marvin had a decision to make. Even though the matter interested him greatly, he was a little reluctant to take it on. There could be serious repercussions; was he really prepared to deal with them? But Hancock seemed very intent on getting Marvin involved, as did several other officials who subsequently called him. Their persuasiveness, and Marvin's own sense of right and wrong, led him to the conclusion that pursuing the matter was the right thing to do. He took the intelligence report back to the news director at Channel 13. This was too big for one man — even Marvin! — to take on alone. Conferences were held with the television station's executives and other news reporters to discuss the multi-faceted problems, and opportunities, inherent in a story such as this one.

The first task for the station executives was to confirm what most already knew about the Chicken Ranch. Even though it was common knowledge that the place was a whorehouse, one has to be careful with a story like this; verification of the facts is essential. So, on an expense account of $20.00 each — remember, this was 1973 — several brave Channel 13 personnel were assigned the exhausting and rigorous chore of verifying that carnal pleasures were indeed for sale at the Chicken Ranch and the Wagon Wheel.

Only single men at the television station were allowed to volunteer for the undercover work. Marvin, being married, was not as lucky as his intrepid colleagues. He would only get to report what those on the front line found out.

The hardy volunteers began by renting a small van and putting up curtains so they could conceal Eyewitness News photographer Frank Ambrose. Then Eyewitness News reporter Larry Conners, cameraman Ambrose and a third reporter paid a visit to the Sealy operation. At first glance, it looked to be nothing more than a rundown, abandoned motel. The grass was not cut, the shrubbery and trees were overgrown, and the building itself, a one-story, wooden framed structure sitting back from the road, was in disrepair. The old sign on the roof near the front entrance was still legible, though the paint was chipped and peeling, and the tubular neon bulbs shattered.

It was still daytime, and there was no apparent activity in the place at all. The few windows that were not completely hidden by the overgrown shrubs were heavily curtained or shuttered. There really wasn't much to report. So Conners and his group left, and returned at midnight in the unmarked van. Conners and Frank Ambrose dutifully carried out their investigative mission, sparing no effort to find out if whoring was in fact

---

[1] See the chapter entitled, "Marvin Goes to Fist City: The Chicken Ranch Revisited."

White Knight in Blue Shades

going on within the walls of the old motel. Conners later went on television and said, "I can state as a fact that prostitutes are working here."

Tough job, Larry and Frank!

You would have thought that our brave investigators would have been tired out, but there was still research to be conducted. Next they visited the Chicken Ranch in La Grange, and cameraman Ambrose stayed in the unmarked van filming while Conners and another reporter went inside. Conners carried a small still camera in his coat pocket, and took pictures as he went. Ambrose was filming customers as they arrived and left; nearly three dozen came and went in a little over an hour.

Perhaps it was inevitable that one of the investigators would get busted. "At one point," Conners reported, "one of the girls spied my pocket camera. I was sent outside but was told I could return without the camera. All the while I kept asking if I could take or purchase pictures of the girls. My request was denied."

That's when Conners and the others returned to the unmarked van and left the Chicken Ranch.

The next day Conners again returned to the La Grange site, this time in a van marked with the Channel 13 news logo. Photographer Rick Armstrong joined him on this fact-finding expedition. They began filming, and within minutes, a woman who identified herself as Edna Milton came out of the house.

Larry Conners introduced himself, and Miss Edna let it be known that she wanted the television crew to leave. Rick Armstrong remained in the van with the camera running as Conners began interviewing Edna. She was not the most cooperative of interviewees. He ended the interview by asking, "What kind of business are you running here?"

To which she replied, "I don't think that's any of your business!"

That night Conners used a portion of this interview on his nightly newscast. It was a teaser, calculated to get the viewers' attention and bring them back the next night for more. "You'll be seeing much more of this interview, and the La Grange and Sealy bawdy houses, on future stories," he said. "Marvin and I have positive proof both are houses of prostitution, and we have reason to believe that big money is involved."

Although Marvin received the highest visibility during the Chicken Ranch series, he actually did little of the directing, and, of course, none of the "undercover" work. At the very beginning, he was merely the contact person, by virtue of having received a copy of the long-suppressed DPS report. For the story itself, Marvin's role was confined mainly to that of anchorman. He sorted through reports submitted to him from the other staff reporters who had jumped on the Chicken Ranch assignment. He also helped prepare some of the scripts, in collaboration with Larry Conners, Dave Ward, and Garvin Berry.

On his own and in conjunction with fellow reporter Conners, however, Marvin also conducted an extensive round of interviews with the principals in the story. Besides interviews with Edna Milton, there were numerous interviews with high-ranking local and state officials. Among these were Colonel Wilson E. Speir, head of the Department of Public Safety; Fayette and Austin Counties' District Attorney, Oliver Kitzman; Austin County Sheriff T.A. Mattox; and Texas State Attorney General John Hill. There were several meetings with members of the intelligence division of the Texas Department of Public Safety. And, without knowing the exact purpose or intentions of their visit, Sheriff T.J. Flournoy welcomed Marvin and Larry, and gave them an interview he would immediately regret.

There were hundreds of phone calls to other individuals, including the Texas Rangers and other agents who had been investigating the whorehouses for more than two years. And, not wanting to leave any stone unturned, the White Knight got into his black Continental Mark IV and drove to the state capital to have a friendly little chat with Governor Dolph Briscoe himself.

The interviews in this chapter are taken from Channel 13 transcripts. Although portions of these interviews were aired during the famous "Chicken Ranch" series on Channel 13, some of them were never used. Much of the material below was filed away and never seen until now.

∞ • ∞

Marvin made his first appointment with Colonel Wilson Speir of the Texas Department of Public Safety. Speir did not know at that time that the state's assistant attorney general Herb Hancock had been in touch with Marvin, nor did he know that Marvin had a copy of the DPS report on the bawdy house operations in Sealy and La Grange.

After the usual introduction, Marvin asked, "Colonel, are you aware of prostitution that is going on both in La Grange and Sealy?"

Colonel Speir replied, "We're aware that these places have been in operation for a certain period of time." That was such an understatement that it provoked laughter from everyone in the room — Marvin, his cameraman and Speir.

Regaining his serious demeanor, the Colonel continued, "Certainly we don't approve of this type of activity. Prostitution itself is only a misdemeanor. We have sought the aid of some local authorities in these areas to close them down, and we're also conducting, and will continue to conduct, investigations to see if the activities here have reached further."

There was a slight pause. Marvin wasn't going to let it end there. Because he suspected syndicated crime was involved, he wanted to know more.

Marvin fired back, "Define 'reaches further' for me, Colonel."

The Colonel was an experienced law enforcement man and a good politician, and he remained unshaken. Without raising his voice, he continued in a flat monotone, "We're particularly interested in any organized crime aspect, to see if indeed it does have any connection, and if so how much more and where. We've been conducting an investigation not only of these areas but several other areas for a long time — several months. Of course we have to take what information we can get, evaluate it and see where we go from there." No doubt about it, Speir was good. He'd given Marvin nothing. But if he thought Marvin was going to give up, he had another think coming.

"Colonel, do you think there are any political payoffs in any [of the] operations — both at La Grange and Sealy?"

"Not to my knowledge at this time. I'd not be in a position to speak on that. I do not have any information, myself."

This was beginning to sound a lot like the Watergate hearings....

Marvin pushed on. "What about the fact that two of your intelligence officers were intimidated by the sheriff in La Grange several months ago?"

Speir replied, "Of course it's been the policy of the DPS all the while to cooperate with local officers, and that's what we have tried to do in this instance, and of course were disappointed when we did not receive the cooperation from local officers that we felt should be extended to us."

Marvin went for the jugular then. "Do you think that the Department of Public Safety will move in on these operations very soon? Do you think you'll close them down?"

"Well, of course. Actually we're seeking to go much further. As I just said, prostitution within itself is only a misdemeanor of which we do not approve, [but] we're seeking to see if there are indeed tentacles that stretch out into other areas, into organized crime. I'm not in the position to say just when, but certainly we do have these aspects as part of our concern and our interest. We'll do what we can just as soon as we can."

Yes, the Colonel was very good indeed, thought Marvin — he was an expert in saying much and divulging nothing. It was obvious Speir was not committing himself to a course of action, certainly not to closing down the Chicken Ranch and the Wagon Wheel. He certainly had not provided any information on political payoffs or money laundering. So Marvin decided to ask the same questions again, but with a different slant.

"Colonel, have you ever instructed anyone not to raid these places in Sealy and in La Grange?"

For the first time Colonel Speir began to flush. His eyes seemed to dilate, and his voice was a little higher pitched.

"Definitely not! I have never instructed my people not to raid any place, if they thought the time was appropriate and the need was there to raid the place. I think that all of our people are interested in making the most effective case that we can."

Marvin asked the same question a third time, from yet another perspective.

"Don't you think that the rank and file of the DPS would like to see these places closed down? That it is really embarrassing to them that these places are allowed to remain open? Other places in the state — in the big cities — are closed down."

The Colonel seemed to be getting a bit annoyed at Marvin's line of questioning, but maintained his drawling monotone, and continued to meet Marvin's insistent questions with the most wishy-washy statements.

"I think all of our people always are pleased when they see the law enforced to be the best that they can. I certainly agree with them on this, and I hope that they can maintain this philosophy."

Speir took a slow, deep breath, turning up the corner of his mouth on one side and then the other, trying to project a pleasing smile. He added, "In fact, I hope all law officers entertain this philosophy."

Marvin tried for a fourth time to get a straight answer. By now, he was more than annoyed at these noncommittal replies. He demanded, "But do you think they are embarrassed because these two places are allowed to stay open?"

"Well, actually, we are not receiving any great number of complaints at this time from the citizenship."

Marvin, outraged, snapped back, "We are talking about law enforcement officers themselves, *your* law enforcement officers."

The Colonel remained calm, and began to rise, pushing his chair back. It scraped annoyingly across the floor. Then he stood, arms to either side, hands palm down on the top of his desk. He was maintaining his composure, but obviously he had had enough of Marvin's questions, and was letting it be known that this interview was over.

He concluded, "I haven't had any of them express [embarrassment] to me, but there could well be some instances when they were embarrassed because they thought the whorehouses were still in operation." His voice trailed off at this point, and that was it. The interview was concluded.

Marvin returned to the Channel 13 studio, and reviewed Colonel Speir's interview with Garvin Barry, Larry Conners and Dave Ward. It was clear that the Colonel had provided nothing of substance, which only reinforced the doubts and suspicions. Why had Wilson Speir not acted on the information his own law enforcement department had provided? Had he gotten the word from higher-ups to stay out of it? Had he been intimidated by local law enforcement agencies?

More importantly, was he involved? On that point, at least, Marvin felt the Colonel was in the clear. He felt that although Speir knew exactly what was going on, he wasn't involved in any payoffs or other shady deals. And, after all, Speir had been the one to send the undercover agents to the Chicken Ranch. He felt he had the backing of Attorney General Hill and Governor Briscoe.

Portions of Marvin's interview with Colonel Speir were used on Channel 13 news. The transcript of the report was filed away and all but forgotten for nearly 30 years.

After his rather unsatisfactory interview with Colonel Speir, Marvin headed for the capital in Austin to meet with the Texas attorney general, John Hill. Hill had spoken to Marvin briefly about the matter, but it was Herb Hancock who had taken the ball and run with it. And Hancock, as would soon become apparent, hadn't kept his boss fully informed about his communications with Marvin.

"General, did you talk to the governor about the operations of the bawdy houses, both in La Grange and in Sealy?" Marvin began.

"Yes, I did, Marvin."

"What was the conversation about?"

"The governor relayed to me that he had this complaint concerning the operation of these facilities and requesting that our office conduct a full investigation along with the Department of Public Safety, and I assured him that we would do so."

Marvin went for a slam dunk. "Are you aware that your men have *already* conducted a full investigation of this?"

There was a long pause, and finally the attorney general said, "Uh." After another pause, he said one of his office assistants had informed him of Marvin's claim that there had been an investigation. "But I am not aware that it is so," he said. "And I don't believe [it] to be so. You know that I have a group of lawyers who are investigators that are in my organized crime strike force, and they work with the DPS. I believe the facts to be that they have learned enough [in] discussion with the DPS that there has been an investigation underway for something, in the neighborhood of several months, into the possibility of organized crime activity."

Attorney General Hill seemed nervous in Marvin's presence, and his answers were, to say the least, somewhat rambling. They also indicated that he, too, had been unaware that Marvin had a copy of the DPS investigation report.

Marvin continued, "Are you able to file injunction suits against these two bawdy houses at all?"

"We have that legal authority."

"If the governor was to ask you to do it, would you do it?"

"Yes, we could!"

"Could you do it without the governor's say-so?"

"Yes! We could."

"Well, are you going to file these charges, or these injunctives?" Marvin demanded.

"My plan, Marvin, is that I am going to see Colonel Speir on Friday. I talked with him, and told him that I would like to come out and review with him what information he had compiled with regard to the entire investigation that he is making. I want to fulfill the request that the governor has given to the office to complete, and to assist in that investigation so that we can see if there are any broader ramifications. When the investigation is completed, I will report back to the governor. I told him that I would. Then we will take such action as the investigation indicates."

There was one law enforcement officer who had been around longer and knew more than anyone else. It was the legendary Sheriff T.J. Flournoy, boss man in La Grange and Fayette County. Nothing went down without his knowing about it.

Virtually everyone who knew about the Chicken Ranch knew about Sheriff Jim's dedicated phone line between his office and Miss Edna's house. They knew that every time the madam took on a new young lady, the sheriff obliged her by having the new girl fingerprinted, and mug shots taken. These were then circulated through local, state and FBI files to be sure that there were no outstanding warrants. (No doubt some were outraged that their tax money paid for this, but for the most part, nobody complained.) Some even say that Sheriff Flournoy picked up some extra cases on busy weekend evenings by parking cars and directing traffic at the brothel. And Marvin, having read the DPS report, knew about the hostility Flournoy and his deputy had displayed to the DPS surveillance team.

The big question was, would Sheriff Jim consent to an interview with Marvin? Flournoy might not like the idea of being an item on Marvin's agenda. Flournoy, and, for that matter, virtually all of the residents of La Grange, had been following Marvin's recent television episodes. To put it mildly, the exposé had not endeared Marvin to the sheriff or his constituents.

There was no doubt, however, that without the old sheriff's interview, the story would not be complete. So Marvin did what he has always done in the past — picked up the telephone, and went directly to the source.

Sheriff Flournoy did not seem surprised at the phone call, and invited Marvin to visit with him in La Grange. Was the sheriff naive, crazy or simply left with no other choices? In retrospect, it doesn't much matter. The fate of the Chicken Ranch was already sealed.

On a steamy July day, Marvin, Larry Conners and a Channel 13 television crew that included cameraman Frank Ambrose set off for La Grange. Marvin looked forward to this interview, and formulated his questions and the sequence of their presentation on the drive to Fayette County. Driving through downtown La Grange to the nearly 80-year-old courthouse in the center of town, Marvin noticed that the streets were empty. The heat was keeping everyone inside. It had been a very hot month and hadn't rained in weeks. There wasn't even the slightest breeze. Even walking the few feet from the parking lot beside the courthouse to the sheriff's small office complex within this building was stifling.

Sheriff Flournoy met Marvin and Larry Conners at the door, introducing himself. "The name is Flournoy, but in these here parts they call me Sheriff Jim."

He stood six feet four inches, and weighed at least 250 pounds, but he was in good shape. He was a proud man, obviously comfortable in his surroundings, and, though he couldn't have been very happy about this meeting, at the beginning he was quite cordial to Marvin, Larry and the crew. Before the interview started, they sat down and had a little conversation about the terrible heat wave, the town, the local people — and then finally they got around to talking about the Chicken Ranch.

"Sheriff, how long have you been in law enforcement?" Marvin asked.

"All my adult life."

"Well, you are 70 years old, so about, over 40 years?"

"Close to 50 years."

"How long have you been sheriff here in Fayette County?"

"I have been sheriff, this will be 27 years."

"Sheriff, we had a little conversation, and we talked about the house called the Chicken Ranch. A house of prostitution, or whatever you want to call it. How long has that been in operation?"

"It was there before I was born. It was there when I was a little boy. It was there when I was a deputy sheriff, and it is still there. It don't give nobody any trouble."

With the DPS investigative report in hand, Marvin asked Sheriff Flournoy, "Well, tell me, is the estimated figure that the whorehouse is supposed to be taking in — a million and a half dollars — is that true?"

"It is absolutely not true. It isn't even possible. To take in that much money out there? The lady that runs it is in debt." The sheriff paused for a minute, deep in thought, and then continued. "She bought a little place in town not long ago. She owes for it. She has a mortgage with the bank. They financed it for her."

Marvin thought to himself that the sheriff knew an awful lot about the madam and her personal business, finances and bank obligations. This is something that is usually very private. Marvin decided to continue in the same vein, and asked, "I understand that she (the madam) makes quite a bit of contributions to the community here?"

The sheriff flashed a big smile as he replied, "That is right. Ten years ago when they built the new hospital and asked for donations and pledges, she pledged to give $1,000 a year for 10 years. She just paid another $10,000 toward the new hospital."

"What about the churches here in La Grange?"

"She donates to the churches. She donates to the Little League every year, and she donates heavily to the private swimming pool here in town which she, of course, never gets to use, and never did."

Larry Conners, who was sitting across from the sheriff, asked, "Does all of her money then go back into town? Is that what you are saying?"

The sheriff turned toward Larry, flashed him a jaw-busting grin and said, "I believe all the money that she makes out there is spent right here in town."

In a quiet monotone, Conners asked, "Sheriff, you don't believe that [the Chicken Ranch] is linked to any organized crime, here or anywhere else?"

Well, it was pretty apparent that the sheriff didn't cotton to this kind of questioning. Suddenly he sat bolt upright in his chair, as if a wasp had stung his private parts. He slapped his palm against the top of his desk, and raising his voice sharply, declared, "I know damn well there is no organized crime connected in any way whatsoever."

Larry didn't give the old sheriff the chance to catch his breath.

"Has your office, or you or any of your deputies ever accepted any money from [Edna] or in any way like that?"

"Not a thing. There was no payoff anywhere in the world to anybody."

The sheriff was obviously not happy being in the hot seat. Just as obviously, he was not a man to be trifled with. It wasn't just his size and imposing demeanor; there was also that deadly-looking collection of knives, pistols and rifles that hung on the wall behind him. All had been confiscated during the course of one case or another over the years by Sheriff Flournoy and his deputies. There were some pretty scary rumors about Flournoy and his dealings with people (usually, but not always, criminals) who crossed him.

Larry Conners had heard all of these stories, and sitting across from the old sheriff now, was in no position to judge which tales were true and which ones weren't. But this was hardly the time to dwell on that. Marvin and Larry were now playing good cop / bad cop with the sheriff, and they were deep into the game. Conners, who approached this type of newsgathering with a feisty zeal, continued, "You don't have a deputy that goes out there at 3:00 AM Monday, and makes a pickup of any money?"

Sheriff Flournoy's face reddened, but without the slightest hesitation, he growled, "Absolutely not. It is pure horse-shit. None of my deputies ever picked up a nickel out there." His blue eyes were flashing with anger, but Larry Conners was relentless, and continued his line of questioning.

"You don't consider that you are giving [Edna] any protection at all?"

"I give her the same protection that I give other citizens here in town."

"Well, do you think that you *should* give her the same protection, since we are talking about a violation of state law?"

"Yes! She is entitled to protection."

Marvin sat there quietly taking it all in, and waiting for Larry Conners to complete his questions. When Larry was done, Marvin politely asked, "Sheriff, not long ago, well, say back in November, two DPS officers came out here and were making a surveillance. One of your deputies detained them, and then they called you and got you out there. I think you were investigating a double murder at that time."

The sheriff, readjusting himself in his chair so he could face Marvin, said, "That is right."

Marvin continued, "The officers who were parked across from the Chicken Ranch, who were on an undercover assignment and were photographing the cars entering and leaving the property, claim that your deputy held a shotgun on them while you questioned them, and you told them — I understand according to the DPS report that you told them that you had been handling this county for quite some time and you didn't need their help. Is this correct?"

The sheriff puffed rapidly on a cigarette butt that had almost burned down to his fingertips, and then stomped it out on the desk. "The part about holding a shotgun on them is a got-damn lie. But, uh, we didn't know who it was out there. I had the deputy stand by while I got there. He didn't hold no shotgun on them. Didn't even get out of his car. When I got out there, well, I saw who it was. I introduced myself, and they introduced themselves. I asked them what they were doing. They said that they were taking pictures of the cars that drove in and out of the Chicken Ranch.

"I said, 'Well, who sent you down here?' They said, 'The boss did.' I said, 'Who is your boss?' They said, 'He is out of Houston.' I said, 'You with intelligence?' They said, 'Yeah.' I said, 'It doesn't take very much intelligence to know what is going on up here.' I said that every little farm boy knows what is going on up here."

Larry Conners jumped in again, apparently not satisfied with the information Flournoy had given them earlier about Miss Edna's income. "Sheriff, when you speak about these figures, does this money go out of here into bigger organized crime? Who is right, you or the state investigating team?"

The sheriff extracted another cigarette from his pack. With some effort, he lit up and took several quick puffs. The hand holding the cigarette trembled slightly, but it was impossible to tell if this was from agitation or just from the periodic trembling that he suffered.

"The state is a got-damm liar, if that is what they say."

"Well, let me ask you this. If the state comes down here and tries to close the Chicken Ranch down, and tries to find out where the money is going, what are you going to be doing?"

The sheriff raised both hands, stretching his arms to full length in the classic gesture of helplessness. "What can I do?"

"That is what I am asking."

The old sheriff spat into the trash can. It was a bulls-eye.

"If they can find out where that money goes, let them close it down. If they think that it is that kind of money. There is no such money as that spent out here. They are not taking in that kind of money out there."

Marvin asked, "If you received orders... let me reword that... not orders, but [if you] heard that state officials were going to make a move, would you assist them?"

The sheriff took a long puff on his cigarette and then, with a broad smile, looked at Marvin and replied, "The only move it would take is just for me to pick the telephone up and tell them to shut it down."

Marvin's gestures and voice revealed his growing excitement. He jumped on this one. "You mean you can close down the Chicken Ranch by just making a telephone call?"

"That is right, yesssss sireeeee!"

Marvin, almost jumping out of his chair, demanded, "Why *haven't* you, Sheriff?"

The sheriff took several more quick puffs on his cigarette and let one hand drop down over the top of his gun butt. "You hard of hearing, boy? Because, as I said, it has been there since when I was a little boy. It gives nobody any trouble. The majority of my constituents want it. I haven't..."

He paused for several seconds with his blue eyes fixed on Marvin. Then he continued, "Inasmuch as there has been no trouble, out there, I haven't shut it down. I would rather have them out there than in the back alleys over in nigger town and spreading venereal disease. We don't have no venereal disease at the Chicken Ranch. Those girls are examined once a week by a local doctor in downtown La Grange."

"You mug and print them girls, too, don't you?" Marvin asked.

"Every girl out there is photographed and fingerprinted."

"By your office?"

"By my office."

"Sheriff, let me ask you this. Last year I understand that the Texas Rangers did give you a call, and asked you to close it down. Did you close down?"

"When they came down and told me I said, 'Well, I am going to talk to Colonel Speir.' I did. I said, 'Colonel, it is just before the election.' He told me to tone them down awhile at the Chicken Ranch, and take a little vacation, and I did."

"Sheriff, I still don't understand. Why are you allowing them to operate?"

The sheriff placed both hands on the armrest of his chair, and, raising himself up to his full height, said, "Well, that is something that you probably won't ever understand."

Larry Conners asked, "And you get no money for letting them operate? You are getting nothing in return for it?"

"No money, whatsoever! It isn't there. I worked for the old sheriff here for thirteen years, and I was chief deputy, and I never found out any money that he got, and I haven't got any payoff either."

Between Larry Conners and Marvin Zindler, the sheriff had not one but two polecats by the tail, and he knew it. Marvin now took another turn at the man. "Sheriff, have you taken the heat over this type of operation for some time?"

"Well..."

"When I say the heat, I mean a lot of people have maybe said something about it to you?"

"No. Not the local people here."

"The local people are pretty well established to the fact that it is here, and they haven't put any pressure on you to close it down?"

"Well, if there was heat on and if it was such a bad violation, we have a grand jury here, two or three times a year, and we have never had a grand jury investigation about it."

"I wonder why?"

"Wonder why?"

"Yes," Marvin prompted.

"People just want it. That is the reason."

"Do you think that the people may have changed their mind now, and may be ready for a grand jury investigation?"

The old sheriff took another long slow puff on the cigarette, held it for a minute and then breathed out. Through the cloud of vapor and smoke that now enveloped him, the sheriff responded, "I don't know about that. There would be a few of them. Most have been hearing about this whole business on television. They don't like it."

Marvin snapped back sharply, "You mean they don't like the coverage, right?"

"We have got a good, peaceful town here, and a good county. Good, peaceful, law-abiding citizens, and they don't want somebody trying to ruin it...to make a big show and just to ruin our town here. I ain't answering no more questions." The sheriff had clearly had enough of Marvin, Larry and company. He didn't just show them to the door; he picked the smallest one of the bunch, which so happened to be Frank Ambrose, and threw the cameraman out the door. That definitely got the message across: the interview was over.

This was not Sheriff Jim's finest moment. In *The Chicken Ranch*, Jan Hutson wrote, "As an honest man, he gave honest answers, something a real politician would never dream of doing." Later he would say he hadn't realized the microphone was live.

∽ ● ∽

Marvin was not going to let it end there, of course; he was just getting warmed up. He made an appointment to speak with Oliver Kitzman, who was district attorney of both Fayette County, location of the Chicken Ranch, and Austin County, where the Wagon Wheel Motel was located.

Once in Kitzman's office, Marvin began with a rather benign question, much as if he were administering a polygraph test. "Mr. Kitzman, are you D.A. of both Austin and Fayette Counties?"

"Yes sir, I have both counties in my district. I have been in office since September of 1967."

Well, enough of that; it was time to step up the pace. "Are you aware of two bawdy houses that are operating in both Sealy and La Grange, Texas?" Marvin continued.

"I think most knowledgeable people in this community have heard about those places." Well, *there* was an honest answer.

"As D.A.," Marvin went on, "have you ever tried to close these places down, either with a civil injunction or by a criminal raid of any kind?"

"No! Frankly we have never had indication by anyone that these places are a problem, to law enforcement or otherwise."

"They are against the state laws of Texas, are they not?"

"If they exist, as everyone assumes they do, they are against the law."

It was time to cut to the chase. Marvin lashed out, "Have you ever received any protection payoffs to allow these places to operate?"

There was a long silence, and small beads of perspiration begin to appear on Kitzman's broad forehead. His face assumed a reddish hue, and his eyes seemed to dilate. He had suddenly become fidgety, tapping his fingers lightly against the desktop. He swallowed hard, and in a voice a little higher than before, the district attorney replied, "I have not and have never been approached. I am somewhat indignant [about] such a question."

Far be it from Marvin to lose an opportunity, or to let D.A. Kitzman off the hook. So, just as he'd done with Colonel Speir, he approached the same question from another angle. "Do you think any protection payoff is existing in these counties to allow these places to operate?"

The D.A. continued to drum lightly on the edge of the desk. "I have no evidence to lead me to believe that any public official receives any payoff from anything in this county."

Marvin still believed that organized crime played a role, particularly in the Wagon Wheel Motel in Sealy. It was hard to believe that it could remain open most of two decades without some type of payoffs. Although the same was true for the Chicken Ranch, in operation for many more decades than the Wagon Wheel, the general feeling was that the Chicken Ranch probably operated more on a local level. Of course, there were others who insisted that the Chicken Ranch operation went all the way to the state capital and beyond.

With all of this in mind, Marvin asked, "Do you think organized crime is involved in these two places, outside of La Grange and Sealy, that has something to do with these places of operation?"

"I have no knowledge of organized crime being involved in prostitution in this county at all or anywhere else in the district."

"What about the law enforcement agencies in this situation? Why don't they enforce these laws?" continued Marvin. It was a fair question, and he got a somewhat honest answer.

"I presume, Marvin, it is a matter of selective law enforcement, for everyone. Particularly in large communities. You know, you have to apply the law where you feel your time is best spent."

But Marvin wasn't satisfied. Marvin sees things differently than many people; to Marvin, the law is the law — for everyone.

"Are you aware that elected officials could be removed from office if they knew the laws were being violated, but yet they did nothing about it?"

The drumming on the edge of the table became more rapid and a little louder. Marvin glanced downward, and D.A. Kitzman all of a sudden became aware of his nervous gesture and stopped. He then looked over at Marvin, and from his expression you'd have thought Marvin had unloaded some buckshot in the seat of his pants. Clearly agitated and annoyed, the D.A. responded, "Well, certainly. We have this problem in every precinct in the state of Texas. It is impossible for us to enforce all of the laws, but we try to enforce the laws in a manner consistent with the best interest of the community as it may be."

That still wasn't good enough for Marvin, who slid to the edge of his chair, leaning forward to close the gap between himself and Kitzman. He suddenly raised his hand, and pointing his finger at Kitzman he demanded, "Would you cooperate and assist the Texas attorney general in obtaining injunction suits against these establishments to close them down, personally?"

Kitzman seemed a bit nervous, evidenced by the fact that he had resumed the drumming with his fingertips. He was going to have to commit himself on this one. Suddenly, with a broad smile, the district attorney leaned across the desk, and replied, "Certainly, Marvin. My office and the peace officers in this district are consistently and earnestly interested in sound law enforcement and safety in this district."

That was not a strong enough commitment to satisfy Marvin. It was a bit vague — of

White Knight in Blue Shades

course, the D.A. wanted to keep it that way — but Marvin wouldn't let it rest.

"Now that I have called your attention to these two places, will you still allow them to operate?"

There was a long pause. The fingertip drumming stopped again. Then Kitzman began to laugh. "I, uh, go back to the idea that I don't know for certain. I assume that they do operate. But if it's to the best interest of the community that some action needs to be taken in this area, certainly the appropriate action will be taken."

Now Marvin was laughing too — not only at the vagueness of the response, but also at its believability, or lack thereof. Kitzman claimed he didn't know for certain that the bawdy houses existed and were in operation. Who was he trying to kid? They had been there long before he was elected to his position as D.A., and had continued to remain in operation during his appointment.

Obviously, Marvin wasn't going to get any satisfaction from Oliver Kitzman, though certainly not from lack of effort.

Marvin wasted no time returning to his office at Channel 13. He called T.A. Maddox, sheriff of Austin County, home of the Wagon Wheel Motel. Maddox invited Marvin to visit with him — but then again, what choice did Maddox have? Either he could meet with Marvin on the battlefield of words and wits, where at least he would be given the opportunity to explain his position as sheriff of Austin county to his constituents — or he could say "no," and Marvin would voice his own assumptions during his television commentary.

Marvin and the crew headed out to Austin County in a Channel 13 van. It was a hot, steamy July afternoon — hot enough to fry an egg on top of the van. The heat radiated from the pavement, and the humidity was stifling, making it difficult for some to even breathe. Marvin, as usual, was in a three-piece suit, and, as usual, there wasn't even a drop of perspiration on his brow.

The interview began with Marvin asking Sheriff Maddox, "How long have you been sheriff here in Austin County?"

"Almost 21 years, Marvin."

"Before that?"

"I was Chief Deputy and Senior Deputy in Sealy for four years prior to that."

"Are you aware that there is a house of prostitution operating on Interstate 10 about two miles outside of Sealy?"

"Well, Marvin, it is common knowledge of most of the people that there have been some girls out there. As far as knowing that there is actually a house of prostitution, I wouldn't be able to swear to it myself."

"Now tell me, how long has it been in operation?"

"I have heard of it, off and on, for 15 to 18 years."

"Have you ever closed down the Wagon Wheel operation?"

With a big grin Sheriff Maddox said, "Oh, yes. We have closed it a few times."

Marvin, nodding in agreement, continued, "Do local people ever put pressure on you to keep it closed down?"

"No! I do not have any pressure from the local people."

As was the case with the other interviewees, Maddox had no idea that Marvin was in possession of the DPS' investigative report. Nor did he know, at the time, that Channel 13's undercover reporters had visited both whorehouses and were well aware that sex was for sale. And he almost certainly wasn't aware that Marvin had photos of the sheriff's own deputies going in and out of the Wagon Wheel Motel.

Marvin continued the grilling. "There has been an estimated figure of about one million or a million and a half supposedly that this place is taking in. Do you suppose this is true?"

"Well, Marvin, I have no idea about the dollars that change hands in a place like that because, see, I am not associated with it, and I have no idea about the money that has changed hands."

"Sheriff, I am going to ask you this question. Have you ever taken any money for protection as far as that place is concerned?"

Sheriff Maddox snapped back, "I certainly have not."

Marvin waited a few seconds for the sheriff to relax and compose himself, then asked, "Do you think that there is any organized crime connected with this establishment?"

"No! I don't think that there is any organized crime or any of that. We have checked, along with the state and other agencies, to possibly see if there is, and we haven't found any indication whatsoever that there is any type of any organized crime."

Well, this was interesting. Just a few minutes ago, the sheriff had denied knowing anything. Now he admitted to investigating the place. Why the sudden change?

Marvin prepared Sheriff Maddox for what was coming next by saying, "I am going to ask you another question." He paused a moment, and then continued, "Do you think that any of your deputies get any money out there?"

A bit more relaxed this time, the sheriff responded, "No. I am sure that they don't."

Marvin wanted to ask if Maddox or his deputies got any other benefits out there, but he felt that was better left alone. Instead he asked, "Have the Texas Rangers ever asked you to close down your operation?"

Now, with some of the things that come out of Marvin's mouth, you can't tell if he's made a slip of the tongue or has just bluntly stated what he's really thinking. It is, perhaps, significant that in his question to the sheriff, Marvin referred to the Wagon Wheel as "your" operation.

However, the sheriff chose to overlook it, replying, "Yes, I have had talks with them a few times, and we did close it down."

"Did they ask you very often?"

"No, it was only once or twice as far as I know."

"Has Colonel Speir ever called you?"

"Colonel Speir has talked to me one time, and the place was closed at that time."

"Sheriff, do you think that if the state wanted to close it down, would you close it down, if they called you?"

"I would do my best to keep it that way if I thought there were complaints from the local people, and they don't want it there. Yes, I would close it."

Marvin, perhaps showing off some of the knowledge of civil and criminal law gained in his years at the Harris County sheriff's department, next asked the sheriff, "Would you do it by civil injunction, or by criminal law?"

Surprisingly enough, Marvin got the honest answer he had been wanting but hadn't expected.

With a big grin, the sheriff replied, "I don't think that I would have to do either one. I think that I could just call them up. Tell them to close it down. Keep a watch on them pretty good. I believe that it would stay closed."

"Just call them up on a telephone, and close it down? An interesting approach."

To think that the sheriff had that kind of power, and that was all it would take. Which just brought up the same question: Why was the Wagon Wheel still open? After all, prostitution is against the law.

"Sheriff, I just have one more question for you, please. Do you protect these people at all in any way?"

The sheriff remained calm and unflustered, but his facial expression clearly showed he was annoyed with Marvin. After a short pause to organize his thoughts he responded.

"The only way that I protect these people at all is the way that I protect other people in this county. If we get a complaint, and there is a violation, we try to check it out. If we get a violation, we try to take care of it. Other than that, well, there is no protection as far as their part at all."

In the end, it was the same old refrain: the diligent lawman who was just doing his duty to protect the citizenry, and would be more than willing to cooperate with the authorities if there ever was a demand to shut down the whorehouses — assuming, in fact, that there really *were* whorehouses in these little Texas towns. These officials, sworn to uphold the laws of the great state of Texas, were all dancing (as the song in the musical would one day put it) the same old "little sidestep." And Marvin, for one, was getting pretty fed up.[2]

The one individual who had really started the ball rolling — you could call him the "Deep Throat" of the Chicken Ranch story — did not permit an interview during the ongoing

---

[2] In the end, after it was all over and the Wagon Wheel was shut down, Marvin and Maddox actually became good friends. Marvin even got to be Parade Marshall in Sealy, riding with Maddox in the Rodeo Parade.

investigation by Channel 13. This individual was Texas Assistant Attorney General Herbert Hancock. Though Hancock spoke to Marvin on many occasions, he chose to keep a low profile when the heat was on. In fact, he had made Marvin promise not to reveal his name.

Many years later Hancock, by then a former state attorney general, did permit Marvin to interview him regarding the Chicken Ranch, the Wagon Wheel, and the people involved in the matter.[3] But it sure would have been a nice touch if he'd been willing to go public at the time the story was unfolding.

In retrospect, however, Herbert Hancock's lack of participation probably didn't make much difference to the final product, the story that aired on television. Unfortunately, much of the material gained from the exhaustive interviews and research was never used on Marvin's or Larry's broadcasts. Even though these were the areas where the "real story" was, the powers-that-be at Channel 13 decided to exploit the sensational aspects of the story.

It didn't start out this way. Garvin Berry, who at that time was responsible for producing much of the 6:00 and 10:00 news programs for Channel 13, was considered the seasoned journalist on staff. Berry recalls that during one of the early news huddles, the decision was made that the Chicken Ranch story would be investigative journalism, not sensationalism. The staff acknowledged that the mere closing of a house of prostitution was not a real story, just a "cheap shot." The real story — the story that Marvin and Larry subsequently strove to uncover in the interviews just cited — involved who was actually running the Chicken Ranch, other than its well-known madam, Edna Milton. Was money changing hands? If so, between whom? What was the relationship between Sheriff Flournoy and various local and state officials, and this house of prostitution? Why were the DPS investigative reports buried or "lost?" Why were reports coming in constantly and steadily and no action being taken? Was there any truth to the allegation that state officials would contact local authorities and have them close the Chicken Ranch just prior to a local or state election, or any time when "the heat was on" — and then, a few weeks later, allow the Chicken Ranch to reopen? Supposedly, this could all be done with a simple telephone call.

If investigative reporting could answer these questions, then it would be a great story, not just a report on the closing down of a whorehouse. As the story progressed, however, it seemed to lose sight of the important questions that were originally raised, veering more towards tabloid journalism. Even Garvin Berry seemed to get caught up in the notion that this was, in fact, a sexy story. After the series began to air, he submitted a two-page outline entitled "Boarding House Suggestions." This was a general outline for parts two and three of Marvin's and Conner's stories on the whorehouses, with suggestions for follow-up programs. It contained remarks such as, "Use a sexy title."

---

[3] See the chapter in this section, "'Deep Throat' Speaks: The Missing Piece of the Chicken Ranch Story."

The mutation of the story wasn't just Berry's doing, however. The piece had taken on a life of its own. After all, this *was* show-biz.

Berry's involvement in the Chicken Ranch story became less and less significant as Marvin and Larry Conner began taking more control over the story. Eventually Berry was completely out of the loop; he concerned himself with other duties at the station and had no further involvement with the Chicken Ranch episodes. Because this was potentially such a hot story, however, other staff reporters wriggled their way in.

The station and those left on the story lost sight of their original high ideals in taking on this project, and they ended up doing everything that everyone had originally agreed *not* to do. Most of the reporters who stayed with the story were immature in their approach and limited in their depth. Marvin said, "They were not investigative reporters; as such, they didn't know what they were doing and left out most of the story."

Due to Marvin's visibility, the Chicken Ranch saga became, instead of a complex tale involving many players, a simple one-on-one: the White Knight, Marvin Zindler, versus the purveyors of illicit sex, and those who protected them. The dramatic elements of the story began to take precedent, and the original goals were forgotten. The story simply got away from everyone concerned, and sensationalism, rather than investigative reporting, became the focus.

As a consequence, the segments that aired contained little of the information that Marvin, Conners and Berry, as well as other Channel 13 reporters, had spent months gathering. Most of that information was relegated to a pile of manila envelopes that collected dust and yellowed with age, all but forgotten until recently.

To make matters worse, once the Chicken Ranch series began to air on Channel 13, the DPS quickly crawled into its shell. The apprehensive state intelligence team wouldn't support Marvin or Channel 13. They were not under any obligation to do so; Marvin had promised them he would not divulge where Channel 13 got the information about the bawdy houses, and he had sworn not to disclose the DPS report. And, of course, the folks at the attorney general's office, Herb Hancock included, were silent on the matter. Because of the promise he had made, Marvin was not at liberty to reveal their names either. Since the station didn't have the official backing of the state agencies, the chances of the Chicken Ranch story being a serious piece of investigative journalism were compromised that much further.

All in all, the Chicken Ranch story was a premiere piece in which the station was restricted by hasty promises to authorities, a lack of investigative reporting, immature, unprofessional reportage, and the overwhelming lust for the dramatic impact of the story. Ultimately, Channel 13 was embarrassed by the series, to say the least. Furthermore, because the station took the cheap shot, and because the state officials involved in the matter refused to speak, the full story of the Chicken Ranch has never been told — not in the slightest.

Marvin always says that if you want to get the job done, you need to go to the top. After his interviews with Colonel Speir at the DPS, Attorney General John Hill, District Attorney Kitzman of Austin and Fayette Counties, and the respective local sheriffs, Maddox and Flournoy, it was apparent to Marvin that this bunch was not about to take action. To the contrary; they all seemed perfectly happy to preserve the status quo. So Marvin headed to Austin to talk to the governor himself, Dolph Briscoe.

While he was waiting outside the governor's office, Marvin met a young newspaper reporter who was looking for a story. Marvin told him why he was waiting to see the governor, and that must have given this cub reporter what he was looking for, because in short order the Chicken Ranch story appeared in the *Austin-American Statesman*. It was picked up by the wire services and after that, there was no stopping it; it ran all over the country — resulting in overnight fame for the town of La Grange. That's about when writer Larry L. King got wind of it and decided to mosey on down to La Grange to get some material for an article that would eventually appear in *Playboy*.

Meanwhile, back at the governor's office, Marvin was primed and ready for this most important meeting. He had brought with him a copy of the original DPS intelligence report, as well as copies of all of his and Conner's previous interviews. With all of this information in hand, he knew he could foil any of the governor's attempts to sidestep the whorehouse issue. He had more than enough ammunition to get Governor Briscoe to close down the Chicken Ranch and the Wagon Wheel Motel.

In the end, it wasn't such a hard sell. The governor had been briefed by his staff, and as soon as Marvin made his presentation, Governor Briscoe agreed that he had no choice. He would close the whorehouses down.

As one can well imagine, while all of this intrigue was going on in Houston and Austin, the citizens of La Grange were not thrilled. It wasn't just that they were angry about Marvin horning in on their affairs; they were also embarrassed because their town had become a national joke. Even Johnny Carson was joking about it on the *Tonight* show. It could scarcely be beneficial to the town to be known solely as the location of the most famous bordello in Texas (and now in the country).

Despite the embarrassment, many supported the Chicken Ranch, and Sheriff Jim circulated a petition asking that the house be allowed to remain open. He was able to collect several thousand signatures — not just from men, but from women as well — and planned to take the petition to Governor Briscoe, with whom he was scheduled to meet on Thursday, August 2.

That meeting would never take place.

∾ • ∾

What were Miss Edna's feelings during these final days, while the fate of her business was being decided? In an interview with Larry Conners, part of which was aired on Channel 13, she shared some of her thoughts.

Her eyes downcast and her voice raspy, Edna said, "I honestly hope that they don't decide against us. At least they could give everybody a chance to find a job if they see the handwriting on the wall for January." She was referring to the fact that the Texas Constitutional Convention was scheduled to meet in January and overhaul the state constitution. Prostitution was, in fact, one of the issues to be decided — should it be a crime or merely considered a "sin?" It was certainly Edna's preference to let the framers of the new constitution decide this matter. She said, "If they want to make it a crime, okay. Or, if they just want to leave it as sin. But they should wait."

She acknowledged that the Chicken Ranch might have withstood this latest onslaught, as it had other crackdowns in the past, except for one major factor: it was not a local story anymore. It had become a national event, and it seemed the entire country was looking at Texas, and its attorney general and governor, as well as their law enforcement agencies, including the famous Texas Rangers. There was more pressure to "do the right thing" than there ever had been before.

Edna continued, "The law should be written to allow local communities to decide what the social norm will be, because that is what I thought the law was for. For the people, by the people. I didn't go too far in school, but I did learn that much."

When asked why the community had tolerated the Chicken Ranch for so many years, Edna explained, "We run a clean and open operation. There are no drinks served here. No white slavery. No narcotics and no children involved. No one is forced to do something that would be different."

Referring to claims that the Chicken Ranch took in one to two million dollars a year, Edna said, "Anyone that saw my home would say that anyone making that much money wouldn't have my furniture. When you are trying to buy a home, and so forth, that is not much profit, and I don't get a new car except every five to six years."

She denied allegations that her operation was in any way connected with organized crime. She also scoffed at the charges that payoffs were made to local law enforcement officers, calling the notion a "pack of lies." (Years later, however, a friend of Edna's said Edna told her, "How the hell do you think Sheriff Flournoy could afford that Cadillac and the ranch that he had?")

Edna was proud of La Grange and of her gifts to charitable causes. "The Ranch has been here for decades, and they haven't run me off yet!" she declared. "The community approves of my home."

In this case, community support just wasn't enough.

Joseph Agris, M.D.　　　　　　　201

The day following Marvin's meeting with Governor Briscoe, a meeting called by Governor Briscoe brought together Attorney General John Hill and Department of Public Safety Director Colonel Wilson Speir, "the Big Three." The upshot of the meeting was that they agreed the long-established houses of prostitution should be put out of business.

Attorney General Hill announced to reporters that there would be a meeting the following Thursday, August 2, with the three state officers and Sheriff T.J. Flournoy. "The approach we, as a state, need to take is not to focus attention on one situation, but to convey that we feel the laws of the state cannot be selectively enforced," Hill explained. "You've got a situation where the law is not being enforced on a local level. We're going to say to the local people, "We want the law enforced and we want it enforced now.""

Hill went on to say no evidence had been presented linking the Chicken Ranch and the Wagon Wheel Motel with organized crime or outside criminal elements. He admitted it was "recent publicity" that caused them to look into the matter — said publicity, of course, being the Channel 13 series.

When asked why the Chicken Ranch should be closed when it apparently had local support, and there was no proof that it was linked to organized crime, Governor Briscoe echoed the Big Three mantra, "The laws of the State of Texas must be equally and fairly enforced." He continued, "We decided to inform local officials that we now know that there is a prostitution problem, and have asked them to clean it up. If nothing is done on a local level, then we will clean it up."

Added Wilson Speir, "With the rapid growth of our state and increased potential for organized crime activity, we believe a more vigorous course of action against prostitution is needed. We are seeking the cooperation of appropriate local officials in the effort."

When Flournoy received his summons to appear before the governor Thursday, he realized he had run out of time and choices. Either he would close down the Chicken Ranch, with a simple phone call to his old friend Edna, or the Texas Rangers (or some other branch of the law) would do it, with all the attending media fanfare.

On Tuesday night, July 31, 1973, Edna Milton received the phone call from Sheriff Jim that she had always feared, but had never really expected would come. By the next day, the Ranch was closed, and Miss Edna's girls had headed on out to Houston, Austin, Dallas and parts unknown. Only Edna and a few maids were left at the Ranch.

Flournoy, however, had not given up hope entirely. He still had that lengthy petition containing thousands of signatures in favor of the Chicken Ranch. Perhaps the governor would let the will of the people prevail, and the Chicken Ranch would be allowed to re-open. So Flournoy left for his meeting with Governor Briscoe Thursday, petition in hand.

When he got to Austin, however, he was met with the news that the governor, on hearing the Chicken Ranch was closed down, had cancelled the meeting. Briscoe had also announced to the press that the house had been closed down "permanently."

Of course, a hell of a lot of people were mad at the news about the Chicken Ranch. The consensus in the corridors of the State Capitol was that the credit — or the blame, depending upon one's point of view — for closing down the whorehouses should fall squarely on the shoulders of Marvin Zindler.

"Good work, Marvin!" a few were saying — but these, it must be acknowledged, were in the minority. After all, many of the power players in Austin had availed themselves of the Chicken Ranch's services at one time or another. Marvin, many claimed, was only out for higher television ratings by insinuating that organized crime elements were involved in the Chicken Ranch.

This seemed to be the general consensus of the public, especially many of the citizens of La Grange. Indeed, Marvin's supporters were few and far between. He was being called a cheap-shot headline grabber, and worse. Naturally, there was no shortage of indignant questions about why Marvin didn't go after home-grown talent in Houston.

At the time of the Chicken Ranch's closing, the Wagon Wheel in Sealy was shut down as well, with a phone call from Sheriff Maddox. There were no raids. No one was arrested.

Other smaller, less well-known houses of prostitution were closed throughout Austin and Fayette counties at the same time. These, however, were raided, girls were arrested, and madams and pimps taken into custody. What was different about the Chicken Ranch and the Wagon Wheel? Kind of makes you wonder, even now...

How long the Chicken Ranch would remain closed was the big question by the end of that first week in August. The word from both local and state officials was still the same: "permanently." But quite a few diehards were pushing for a re-opening.

Throughout the week of the closing, the rumors flew. It was said that the La Grange Chamber of Commerce would be circulating a petition, but the Chamber of Commerce President and several members emphatically denied this, claiming it was "a county matter."

Sparked by rumors and reports of this and other petitions, as well as letters and phone calls from housewives, teachers and businessmen in support of the Chicken Ranch, a new influx of TV crews and news reporters swarmed into La Grange seeking interviews with anyone who would comply. They got less than they came for, or at least a different reaction from what they apparently expected. There was a growing tendency among the citizenry to disclaim any part of the petitions. Besides, the locals were fed up with Marvin Zindler and the press in general, and had just about had it with the jokes and negative publicity.

Before the closing, Lester H. "Buddy" Zapalac, publisher of the La Grange *Journal*, took a personal, if not an official editorial, stand on the Chicken Ranch. "I think that it is all right," he said. "There is no organized crime attached to it, and it is beneficial to the community. The girls from the Chicken Ranch buy all of their clothes from here. Their eats. It brings in business for the community." He continued, "The people are all for it. They say that it has done no harm, and a lot of good. I don't know anybody who is against it."

What a difference a day (or two, or three) makes! By the end of the week, after the Chicken Ranch had closed, opponents of the Ranch began crawling out of the woodwork. When radio station KVLG allowed people to call in their opinions without giving their names, there was plenty of anti-Ranch sentiment. The final count was 59 callers opposed to the whorehouse, 43 in favor.

Of those in favor, perhaps the one that received the most response from listeners was that from a woman who called in and said, "I feel that it ought to be reopened, but only if a second such establishment was open for us women."

Some of those opposed to the Chicken Ranch's reopening applauded Marvin, but that didn't mean that Marvin was the new town hero — far from it. For the most part, he was seen as an "outsider" meddling in local affairs.

With the announcement of the closing of the Chicken Ranch, Marvin and Channel 13 were flooded with letters. Marvin said, "We got thousands and thousands of letters. Even little old ladies wrote us." The flood of letters was not unexpected, of course, but to the surprise of the Channel 13 staff, most of the letters supported the Chicken Ranch and attacked Marvin Zindler for its closing.

The letters echoed many of the opinions already stated in the previous weeks. Supporters of the Chicken Ranch declared that it had never done any harm and was, in fact, an asset to the community. It was good for the economy, and kept down rape and venereal disease. Few seemed to believe there was organized crime attached to the Ranch, and more than one person declared that Marvin should spend his considerable energy cleaning up Houston. Many expressed the sentiment that Marvin Zindler was no longer welcome in La Grange.

There were, however, a few letters in support of the action taken. One writer declared, "People in the community feel that enough is enough and we don't want them here any more." Overall, though, the letters — from women as well as men — supported the Chicken Ranch and found fault with Marvin.

Texas, as Jan Hutson pointed out in *The Chicken Ranch*, still has plenty of sex for sale. It is available at sleazy massage parlors and "modeling studios," from high-priced call girls in major cities, and, of course, from streetwalkers. Old-fashioned brothels such as the Chicken Ranch, however, are probably gone forever. Not that there ever was a brothel exactly like the Chicken Ranch; it was one of a kind.

And when this one-of-a-kind institution closed its doors for the last time, that might have been the end of the story. Might have been, if it hadn't become such a media event, and if it hadn't raised such an outcry from its supporters and detractors alike (as well as from Marvin's supporters and detractors). And then there was that brouhaha a year and a half later, when Marvin ventured to La Grange for a follow-up story. But even with that, the Chicken Ranch saga might have eventually faded away, had it not captured the attention of another Texas journalist: a hell-raiser by the name of Larry L. King, who milked the story in more creative and flamboyant ways than Marvin would ever have dreamed of. King would write an article that would eventually lead to a play, and then a movie, *The Best Little Whorehouse in Texas.*[4]

The closing of the Chicken Ranch was certainly not the end of the story for Marvin. In the months and years to follow he would not only bear the brunt of Sheriff Jim Flournoy's wrath, but he would also have the dubious distinction of being immortalized on stage and screen as a self-righteous, egocentric moralist who almost single-handedly destroyed a beloved Texas institution.

The press would never let him off the hook. In fact, the closing of the Chicken Ranch is still referred to by many as "Marvin's Massacre," as if he were the only player in the entire saga. That moniker is partly a result of journalists' love for alliteration, but mostly it's a result of Marvin being perceived, by the press and the common folk alike, as the one person responsible for bringing 130 years of proud tradition to an unceremonious end.

The Chicken Ranch — in both its factual and fictionalized versions — was the story that, for better or worse, Marvin Zindler would never live down. In many ways, the end of this tale was just the beginning.

[4] See the chapter entitled, "The Biggest Little Story in Texas."

MARVIN GOES TO FIST CITY:
THE CHICKEN RANCH REVISITED

The year 1974 was drawing to an end. Although nearly a year and a half had passed since the closing of the Chicken Ranch, many folks were still angry about it, and Marvin Zindler was still something less than a hero in Fayette and surrounding counties. For example, after the Brenham (Washington County) Jaycees invited Marvin to speak at their annual Law Enforcement Day fish fry, popular outcry forced the Jaycees to rescind the invitation.

But never mind that; the news must go on. In December 1974, Marvin's boss Walter Hawver, who was then the news director at Channel 13, decided to do a follow up of the La Grange-Sealy story. Hawver felt a postscript on the Chicken Ranch would interest the viewing audience. His plan was to send Marvin back to La Grange to show that the Chicken Ranch was really padlocked, and had been for the last 18 months. He also wanted Marvin to show that the closing of the Chicken Ranch did not have the deleterious effect on the La Grange economy that many thought it would. The story was scheduled to run on New Year's Eve, 1974.

Sending Marvin to La Grange was, to put it mildly, probably not the best idea, particularly since Sheriff Flournoy had made it clear he never wanted to see Marvin in those parts again. And since Sheriff Jim's constituents were calling Marvin everything from "the Benedict Arnold of Texas" to far worse epithets, it might have been wiser to send someone else on this assignment. Marvin himself had a gut feeling that if he set foot in La Grange, there might be an ambush. But he made preparations to go anyway. Marvin has never been one to back away from an assignment just because it might be a little risky.

An outline for the story was prepared, and Marvin wrote a script. The intention was to begin the piece with Marvin standing in front of the Chicken Ranch, saying, "Many folks have asked the question, 'Is the Chicken Ranch really closed?'

206   *White Knight in Blue Shades*

"The answer, of course is, 'yes,' but to dispel rumors that it [has reopened], camera-man Frank Ambrose and I went to La Grange."

Then the camera was to zoom in on the Chicken Ranch, with its padlocked gates, at which point Marvin would confirm, "Well there it is: closed down a year and a half ago, it has never reopened. An establishment that has stood for over 129 years, where, possibly, Texas governors and many other VIPs received nocturnal pleasures. Where beautiful women plied their trade of prostitution, charging roasting hens (chickens) during the 1930 de-pression and as much as $150 [in the brothel's latter days]... Where local public officials allowed this million-and-a-half-dollar illegal operation to exist..."

The second part of the story was to be devoted to showing that downtown La Grange was still prospering despite the demise of its most famous business. In the first shot, Marvin was supposed to appear in the town square across from the courthouse, saying, "Many citizens, mostly public officials, said that the city of La Grange could possibly go bankrupt when their local house of ill repute was closed. But you can see for yourself that a city does thrive, and much better, without a foundation of organized crime.

"The Fayette county folks are fine churchgoing, law-abiding people, who don't have to be embarrassed any longer. The local hospital is still operational without any further donations from the Chicken Ranch madam — money that came from selling the flesh of young ladies like so much meat in the market place."

Then there would be music, accompanied by the promo: **Yes, the Chicken Ranch is closed.**

Following this, Marvin, sitting at his anchor desk, would conclude, "I have nothing against sex. I think it is beautiful, but sex can become awful ugly when public officials commercialize it for their own personal monetary gain." And then, finally, Marvin would give his characteristic sign-off: "Marrrrrvin Zindler, Action 13 News!"

This was the script, never before made available to the public, that was to be used on December 31, 1974. But it was not meant to be; circumstances beyond even Marvin's imaginings were to create a story that received significant local news coverage, and cap-tured the attention of the national media as well. The unwilling star of this drama would appear on television, radio and newspapers, and the story would escalate for several months, sparking the national fancy. Ultimately a Broadway show, and later a movie star-ring Burt Reynolds and Dolly Parton, would be produced from the ashes of the Chicken Ranch and Marvin's return to La Grange, Texas.

But that would come later. Having accepted the assignment from his boss, Marvin needed a cameraman to accompany him to La Grange. Frank Ambrose was the natural choice to assist in this assignment, especially since he had been along for the ride during the initial Channel 13 investigation the previous year.

Accepting a tough assignment was one thing, but there was no sense in being fool-hardy. Given the general ill feelings surrounding the Chicken Ranch matter — not to mention the threats against his person — Marvin decided he needed some protection. He couldn't help remembering last year, when someone had told him he had better wear a bullet-proof vest if he was going to continue his series on the Chicken Ranch and the Wagon Wheel. The remark had been made in jest, but given the heated feelings about the matter, Marvin knew he couldn't be too careful. Perhaps his pals at the Department of Public Safety would help out and loan him a Texas Ranger for the day. So he called Ranger Pete Rogers, explaining he had an assignment to return to La Grange and needed an escort. "I heard rumors in the past that I would be jailed or beaten by Sheriff Jim Flournoy if I return," he said.

Rogers said he would have to call his bosses in Austin first, and would get back to Marvin. When he returned the call, however, he told Marvin there was no one available to go with him.

Marvin is as stubborn as he is well-connected, but even he has his limits. He knows when to push for something and when not to. In this case, the message was clear to Marvin: no amount of string-pulling could get a Texas Ranger to go with him to La Grange.

Well, at least it would be a good idea for him to take someone who had a legal background. Besides the threat to his physical safety, Marvin feared he might be framed by authorities in La Grange who were eager for revenge. He invited Neil Duval, a former district attorney and assistant attorney general of Texas, and now a member of the Organized Crime Division of the Texas attorney general's office. Duval agreed to go, and they planned to leave on Friday, December 27. But Marvin was still uncomfortable about the threats, of jail or worse, that he had received, so he called his good friend Mark Vela, a former assistant D.A. of Harris County. Vela now has his own private law practice on Westheimer Street in Houston.

In order to accommodate everyone's schedule, the trip to La Grange was moved from Friday to Monday, December 30. Then things began to change, as if it just weren't meant to be. One morning at approximately 9:00, the telephone rang at Marvin's home. Neil Duval was on the other end. He said he wouldn't be able to accompany Marvin because his mother-in-law had had a stroke, and he and his wife had to leave immediately for Austin.

A less determined person might have taken Duval's dropping out as a sign that the trip should be cancelled. But not Marvin. Even though Duval would be unable to go, and even though there would be no Texas Ranger along for protection, Marvin decided to proceed with the trip. At least Mark Vela would be with him. Vela, Marvin and cameraman Frank Ambrose met at the Channel 13 television studios on Monday morning. Their first stop was the Harris county courthouse, where they sat in on a civil hearing involving a story that Marvin had done on prior date. Then it was on to La Grange and the Chicken Ranch.

The little group left Houston at approximately 11:00 in the morning. It was a rather cool December day. Although there was a bit of chill in the air, the sun was playing peek-a-boo with occasional clouds; it would be a pleasant drive. All things considered, they felt comfortable with their assignment.

As the group ate lunch in Columbus, a small town west of Houston, Marvin's apprehensions faded. After all, he was with friends. Vela was a man he knew to be honest, someone he had worked with on criminal cases in the past. He was also comfortable in the knowledge that the only others who knew about his return trip to La Grange, apart from Vela and Neil Duval, were his assignment editor and the cameraman who was with him.

This wasn't technically true, of course. For one thing, the Texas Rangers had almost certainly gotten wind of it, since Marvin had originally requested, but been denied, their assistance. In retrospect, maybe this is something Marvin should have taken into consideration.

After lunch, they got into Marvin's gleaming new black Continental Mark IV, and continued their journey to La Grange. If deciding to go to La Grange in the first place was Marvin's first mistake, perhaps the second blunder was his choice of vehicles. When you plan an expedition into enemy territory, one of the basic tenets is to blend in — in other words, look like the natives, dress like the natives, and *drive a vehicle that doesn't stand out*. In a land of pick-up trucks and second-hand cars, a brand-new Continental would be a pretty clear announcement that strangers were in town.

Apparently, however, someone was watching them even before they reached La Grange. Marvin later learned that his car had been spotted on its way from Columbus to La Grange, and, even though neither Marvin nor the vehicle was in violation of any law, the La Grange sheriff's office asked for a license check through the Department of Public Safety in Houston. The request was transmitted by police radio. The license number came back within minutes, confirming that the Continental Mark IV en route to La Grange belonged to none other than Marvin Zindler. Sheriff Flournoy and his deputies knew Marvin was on his way.

At the time, of course, Marvin was unaware of this. Later it became very obvious that Flournoy was forewarned about Marvin's arrival, so the sheriff's actions were almost certainly premeditated. This makes me believe there was a conspiracy, perhaps one that went beyond Flournoy and his deputies. In any event, it seems clear that Sheriff Jim and his boys were just waiting for an incident to act upon. If that incident did not occur, the sheriff was in such a mind that he was going to manufacture it.

Still following Marvin's prepared script, the threesome turned onto State Highway #71. Their first stop was at the Chicken Ranch, so Marvin could be filmed announcing that the place was padlocked. Approaching the front gates, Marvin motioned to Mark Vela to join him. There they both laid hands on the heavy chains that were wrapped around the gates, and gave a good tug while Frank Ambrose filmed the scene.

Just because the front gate was securely locked didn't mean that there wasn't a back entrance. Even a little rabbit has the sense to always have a front door and a back door, since you never can tell when you might need to make a quick escape. Marvin was determined to show that there wasn't any activity at the front or the back. So the little group walked back to the car and climbed back in, with Ambrose carefully balancing the camera on his lap in the front seat next to Marvin. Mark Vela sat in back. Just beyond the fence, Marvin spied a gravel road, so he took a sharp left and bounced along the road for several hundred yards as Ambrose struggled to steady the camera in his lap. Marvin spied an open gate which had no sign on it but seemed to lead onto the grounds where the main house was located.

He drove through the gate and made his way around to the front again, where he parked the car. He and Mark Vela ambled to the small front porch, reminiscing about what had taken place some 18 months ago. Meanwhile, Ambrose was shooting film that would later be aired on Action 13 News. They came to the edge of the porch, and like so many before them, took those several steps toward the door. Now, however, the door was pad-locked.

Ambrose walked around to the back of the boarding house, where he took a shot of a "Closed" sign. There was obviously no activity in back either. The threesome then made their way back to Marvin's car, and just as they were about to leave, a man came up to the car and introduced himself as a caretaker for the premises. Marvin and the group also identified themselves.

Marvin noticed the man had a pistol in his belt, which was not uncommon in rural Texas; it didn't make anyone particularly nervous. The caretaker asked them to leave, but that wasn't a problem, seeing as how they were preparing to do just that. Marvin reached down and gently turned the key in the ignition, waving to the caretaker as they left the establishment. Ambrose continued to keep the camera rolling, showing that there was no traffic and no business there.

They returned to Highway #71, passing the "Bad Curve" sign as they headed in a north-westerly direction toward La Grange. It was while driving through downtown La Grange, towards the city hospital, that Marvin noticed the sheriff's car. It appeared about a block away to his right, making a turn just in front of them.

Ambrose wanted to take a picture of Marvin in front of the hospital, as this institution had been started with an initial $10,000 gift from Miss Jessie when she was madam of the Chicken Ranch. Marvin wanted to show that the hospital was still up and running and doing well, even without the patronage of the ladies at the Chicken Ranch. They finished the shoot in front of the hospital, then motored along slowly through downtown while Ambrose continued to take pictures. In the center of town, they parked on the west side of the courthouse in an area designated for public parking. Ambrose continued to take more pictures.

Then Marvin spied Sheriff Flournoy again. Flournoy, accompanied by a man in a white shirt, was driving into the county courthouse parking lot.

They had to stop photographing at this point, because the film magazine they were using had run out of film. Film magazines used at that time contained 400 feet of magnetic strip film, which meant that photographs and sound were being recorded simultaneously. After Ambrose applied a new magazine to the camera, they took a few more pictures and returned to the car.

None of the locals took particular notice of Marvin or the film crew. It was approaching two o'clock in the afternoon on a cool winter day, and there weren't many people on the street. The sun was already low on the horizon, and in a few hours it would be dark. Marvin wanted to get some additional film footage of the downtown area and the courthouse, so they drove around and pulled in front of the Sears Catalog Store, which was directly across from the courthouse.

Everything had gone well so far, but Marvin didn't want to take any chances, especially since he'd already spotted the sheriff a couple of times. Marvin did not wish to attract unnecessary attention, so he stayed in the car and chatted with Mark Vela while Frank Ambrose got out of the car and began taking pictures. Presently, Frank returned to the car and got back in, positioning the camera in his lap.

He turned to Marvin and asked, "Did you see the sheriff? He just turned around and he is coming toward your car."

Marvin did not hesitate a second. He started the car and, looking over his shoulder to make sure there were no other cars or pedestrians, he backed out and slowly began to accelerate. He had an interview at two o'clock with the editor of the La Grange newspaper, the offices of which were just one block away.

He would not make it to that interview.

Suddenly Sheriff Flournoy jumped out in front of the car, wildly waving his hands and yelling for Marvin to stop.

Marvin hit the brake. The tires grabbed the dry, dusty pavement, and with a loud screech, the Continental came to an abrupt stop. Marvin could not maneuver, since the sheriff was now blocking his car. Flournoy approached the driver's side of the car, cursing as he reached into the open window and grabbed Marvin by his vest — which particularly upset Marvin, since this was a brand-new suit. It was clear that the sheriff intended to have a one-on-one with Marvin. He had a firm grip on Marvin's beautiful tailored vest, and was trying his damdnest to drag him out of the car via the driver's side window.

Marvin, Ambrose and Vela had broken no laws by driving in La Grange. Sheriff Flournoy had no reason to obstruct their leaving, much less to attack Marvin in the manner that he did. The sheriff had come looking for trouble, his only purpose being to embarrass Marvin with a good bashing. At no time did he make any direct statement or request; he only continued to curse Marvin over and over again as he repeatedly slammed him up and back against the door in his attempt to extricate him from the vehicle.

Though rattled, Marvin tried to calm Sheriff Jim. Very quietly but firmly, he repeatedly told the sheriff, "Please quit grabbing me. I was only on an assignment to do a story." This was interspersed with, "You're hurting me!" and "This is not necessary!" But nothing he said would stop the furious sheriff.

With his left hand, Marvin instinctively triggered the electric door locks on the Continental, but of course, this did not stop Sheriff Jim. The husky Flournoy retained his grip on Marvin and repeatedly slammed him up and back, up and back against the driver's door, still trying to pull him through the window. All the while, the sheriff was cussing Marvin.

Marvin maintained his composure as well as he could and continued to speak softly, trying to calm Flournoy down, but to no avail. The sheriff, cussing and screaming the whole time, was still trying to pull Marvin through that window.

Meanwhile, Ambrose, who was sitting next to Marvin with camera in hand, did the logical thing. No, he didn't get out of the car and bop Sheriff Jim over the head with the camera. He did something far more useful: he started taking pictures of what was taking place.

At one point Sheriff Jim's coat flew open. This was the only time Marvin became truly concerned. Being a former law enforcement officer himself, Marvin thought the sheriff was going for his gun. Marvin later said, "I made up my mind that the sheriff was going to have to kill me to get me out of the car."

By now, a crowd was gathering; the locals were taking in the entertainment, so to speak. What happened next left everyone gasping and probably saved Marvin from father harm, though not from humiliation. Sheriff Jim, perhaps inspired by the crowd's presence, reached in with his other hand and grabbed Marvin's head in a stepped-up attempt to pull him through the window. In so doing he "scalped" Marvin — he came away with Marvin's hairpiece.

When he saw what he'd done, Sheriff Flournoy retreated from the car at last, waving his prize jubilantly over his head. He then proceeded to do an Indian war dance, whooping it up and yelling, "Maaaaarrrrrvin Zindlerrrrrrrr" again and again, in imitation of Marvin's trademark sign-off, all the while brandishing the hairpiece.[1] This continued for several minutes.

At last Sheriff Flournoy tossed the hairpiece into the gutter, where it landed in some water. You might have thought this little coup would have dissipated his anger — not so. Instead he was now in a full-blown rage, and he ran around to the other side of the car and grabbed the camera out of Ambrose's hand, and the tape recorder from the seat. These he set on the sidewalk.

Still cursing at the top of his voice, the sheriff returned to the passenger's side of the car, reaching through the open window. He grabbed cameraman Ambrose and began shaking him violently. The cursing continued unabated. All the time, attorney Mark Vela was sitting in the back seat, observing the whole incident.

Finally the exhausted sheriff retreated from the car.

Marvin turned and looked over his shoulder, saying, "Mark, would you please retrieve my hairpiece?" Like his suit, this hairpiece was brand-new, and it was expensive. It

---

[1] It should be noted, however, that it was a less than perfect imitation, as he left out the "Eyewitness News!" portion of the sign-off.

White Knight in Blue Shades

had cost Marvin over $400, a fairly steep price for the early 1970s.

Mark Vela got out of the car. The sheriff said nothing to him as Vela picked up the hairpiece, quickly returned to the car and climbed in the back seat. Vela handed the hairpiece to Marvin, who wiped it off with a handkerchief and placed it back on his head. After all, he couldn't be seen without his hairpiece, no matter what condition it was in.

Meanwhile, Sheriff Flournoy had apparently gotten a second wind, and he resumed cussing. Finally he made a request, or, rather, a demand. "I want you," he growled, "to get your ass out of La Grange — and the next time it's going to be a lot worse than it was this time."

Marvin slowly started to drive away. Over his shoulder he could see Sheriff Jim picking up the television camera in one hand and the tape recorder in the other, after which the sheriff began walking down the sidewalk toward his patrol car.

Marvin could not leave very quickly because of the crowd. As they parted, allowing the Continental to continue its slow progress out of town, Marvin saw the sheriff's car turn off the main road into a filling station about a block away. As Marvin drove by, he saw the sheriff standing by the side of his patrol car, watching as they drove slowly out of town.

Marvin, Ambrose and Vela were shaken and immediately headed back for Columbus. They stopped off at the Holiday Inn, where Marvin rushed to the phone to contact his boss, Walt Hawver. Hawver was not in, so Marvin talked to assistant news director Gene Burke, describing the incident.

It was only then that Marvin began feeling pains in his chest and face, results of the altercation that had just taken place. Marvin remembers turning to Vela and saying that he was not feeling well. Marvin said, "My chest is hurting real bad." In addition, the left side of his face was beginning to swell and feel uncomfortable.

The three men were shook up from the experience, and decided to sit a spell in the coffee shop to regain their composure. Meanwhile, Walt Hawver returned Marvin's call. Marvin recounted the experience he'd just had, and told Hawver they were leaving for Houston now. They left the Holiday Inn and returned to the Channel 13 Studios at about 6:00 in the evening — just in time for Marvin to make the first telecast of the incident.

Marvin began to feel ill later that evening. He called his doctor, J. E. Liepman, M.D., and was advised to have a chest x-ray and an EKG. As was typical of Marvin, however, he told his doctor that he would have it done later that evening — but nothing was going to make him miss his 10:00 evening newscast. You have to understand that Marvin was really hurting by now; there was the possibility that he had broken ribs, and worse. But this story was just too, too hot to wait.

Marvin was in pain, but more than that, he was incensed by what had taken place. Although the beating the sheriff had given him had hurt him physically, it was the "scalping" that annoyed Marvin the most. After all, as you may recall, Marvin did not even permit his own family to view him without his hairpiece. The snatching of Marvin's hairpiece, and the Indian war dance that followed in La Grange's city square, had been a truly mortifying experience for him. To many individuals in La Grange, of course, it seemed only fitting that such humiliating circumstances would befall a man of Marvin's mystique. But the citizens of La Grange, and their belligerent sheriff, were not going to have the last laugh on Marvin.

Unfortunately, because of the football game that night, the evening news program did not take place until 11:00 that evening, which gave Marvin an extra hour to stew. But he waited patiently until the game ended so he could air his story.

Once on the air, Marvin explained to his television audience that he had been on assignment in La Grange to photograph the Chicken Ranch and to establish the fact that the city of La Grange remained prosperous even though the whorehouse had been closed for nearly eighteen months. Marvin explained he'd had no intention of speaking with Sheriff Flournoy, nor did he plan to accost the sheriff with cameras, microphones or embarrassing questions. The only person Marvin had planned to interview was the editor of the La Grange newspaper. This interview, of course, didn't take place. Marvin recounted what had happened instead. It was clear that he was mad as a bull in a red-dye factory. But at least the world now knew what had happened.

And by now, the old sheriff surely must have been aware of what a big mistake he'd made by accosting Marvin Zindler and confiscating Channel 13's camera and tape recorder.

Events following Marvin's Eyewitness News program progressed rapidly. Immediately after the newscast, Marvin was driven to the Memorial Downtown Hospital for a medical exam, including x-rays and a cardiogram. He did indeed have two fractured ribs. The doctors wrapped Marvin with surgical tape and applied an elastic support bandage, and ordered him to see Dr. Liepman in his office the next morning. Then Marvin was taken home.

The next day Dr. Liepman examined Marvin, confirming he had two fractured ribs, the seventh and the ninth. After the examination he re-wrapped Marvin with the elastic support bandage and gave him a prescription for his pain. "It's going to take about six weeks for your ribs to heal," he told Marvin.

Marvin, already thinking ahead, asked the doctor for a letter certifying his findings. Marvin planned to turn it over to the FBI and, later, to the Justice Department in Washington, to support his account of what had taken place.

KTRK contacted federal authorities to bring action under civil rights and freedom of information statutes. Marvin made a formal statement to FBI Special Agent Boone and Agent Johnston. He also filed a three-million-dollar assault-and-battery lawsuit against

Sheriff Flournoy and Fayette County.

On December 31, the film was returned to the Channel 13 studios, packaged in a brown manila envelope that was tightly wrapped with tape. The tape recorder was also returned, but the tape inside seemed to have been lost. The missing property was brought to the television station by an official with whom Marvin had conducted one of his futile interviews the previous year when the Chicken Ranch story was being developed. Oliver Kitzman, district attorney of Fayette and Austin counties, was the bearer of the package, and he stayed in the developing room at the KTRK studios while the film was processed. The film was then placed on a projector in the presence of the district attorney as well as an attorney from the firm representing Marvin and Channel 13.

The plaintiffs, of course, were thinking that the film would prove to be valuable evidence, since it contained proof of the assault. Unfortunately, the film did not have any images on it. Would anyone have expected less? It was obvious that almost as soon as the sheriff got his hands on the film he'd exposed it.

But Flournoy failed to cover his tracks completely. Not being familiar with magnetic tape, the sheriff was unaware that the film was not only designed to produce images, but also to simultaneously record sound. Exposing the film to light destroyed the images but not the recording track. Surprise, surprise! The sheriff's verbal assaults, and Marvin's pleadings, had been accurately recorded and retained.

Sheriff Jim had stepped over the bounds just once too often — and now it was all on tape.

Now Flournoy was faced with one of the biggest obstacles he had ever encountered in all his years as sheriff, though perhaps he didn't know it at first. He couldn't have been too thrilled to have a three-million-dollar lawsuit looming over him, but at the very beginning, when he was still blissfully ignorant about the surviving audio portion of the film, he must have felt fairly secure that he would emerge from this latest battle unscathed.

Reached at his home in La Grange on New Year's Day, 1975, Flournoy denied laying hands on Marvin at all. "I didn't hit him or strike him and didn't hurt him," he said. Of course, at that point he was still unaware that an incriminating sound track existed. The sheriff did concede that he had opened the camera carried by Marvin's cameraman "to take a look at the film" — and, gee, he must have accidentally exposed the film. He also, by his account, accidentally pulled the tape out of the cassette recorder.

His take on the matter was that Marvin had returned to La Grange after 18 months to rehash an old story and to smear him. Sheriff Jim really seemed to believe that Marvin was out to get him personally. Marvin, he claimed, had ruined his reputation.

Despite his denials that he had accosted Marvin, however, Sheriff Jim hinted that if Marvin was at all concerned about his own welfare, he shouldn't be in a hurry to visit Fayette County in the next thousand years or so.

When Sheriff Flournoy was informed that there was a sound recording of his attack on Marvin, he was shocked and obviously shaken. The first thing he asked when he regained his composure was, "What did the tape contain?"

Soon not only Flournoy, but the whole nation, would know what that tape contained. A copy had been made by Walter Hawver, and the original was given to the FBI for their investigation of Marvin's civil rights complaint against Flournoy and Fayette County. The tape was released to the national news media and on January 1, 1975, the 28-second audio portion of the film made its national debut on ABC-TV's 6:00 PM newscast. The expletives were bleeped out, but the gist of the confrontation remained. It was all quite dramatic. Once again the nation's attention turned to La Grange and Houston. The saga of the Chicken Ranch had been rekindled, and it was hotter than ever.

About the first thing Sheriff Flournoy did, upon learning that he might be in more trouble than he'd originally figured, was to retain one of Houston's most famous criminal attorneys, Richard "Racehorse" Haynes. The battle between Marvin Harold Zindler and T.J. Flournoy began in earnest.

For his part, Marvin was saying that more than his civil rights that were violated. Leave it to Marvin to find the bigger story, the larger issue. He felt that the freedom of the press guaranteed by the First Amendment to the U. S. Constitution had been threatened. And who knows; he may have been right. Journalists have been under assault for a long time now, although usually that happens in more repressed societies. At any rate, the U. S. Justice Department in Washington would decide the course of action on the matter.

In support of his sheriff, Lester Zapalac, editor of the *La Grange Journal,* said, "All the people here are behind the sheriff 110%. He has served them well." But he had little else to say.

Although the townspeople were pretty sour on Marvin, many had, of course, witnessed the attack. And even some of those who hadn't seen it admitted they couldn't imagine that Marvin Zindler would make up such a story.

Overall, however, they did support their sheriff. The news of Marvin's lawsuit made the White Knight look like the Black Knight in the eyes of Fayette County residents. In fact, it produced just the opposite effect that Channel 13 had hoped for.

The folks of La Grange banded together and formed a support group. Within days after county officials were served legal papers in the dispute between Marvin and Sheriff Flournoy, a defense fund for T. J. Flournoy was started in Fayette County. After all, Racehorse Haynes didn't come cheap.[2] And of course there was big money at stake. One county judge opined, "Our county could become a disaster area if such a lawsuit were even

---

[2] In the end, Flournoy had to retain another lawyer, because Haynes was too busy with another high-profile case.

partially won."

The politicians of the county decided to promote the fund as an appreciation of Flournoy's 29 years of service. They acknowledged that a hell of a lot of appreciation would be needed to boost the sheriff's defense fund to an adequate level.

These days, it didn't take much to get the old sheriff riled up. Mentioning the Chicken Ranch or Marvin Zindler could really make him squirm. By now he was more than aware that he had stepped over the line on this one. He might have won the first skirmish, but he had already lost the war.

Not that things were going so smoothly for the complainants in this matter. At the beginning, the law firm of Baker and Botts had been contacted to represent Marvin in his lawsuit against Sheriff Flournoy. Upon hearing the soundtrack of the altercation, attorney Jim Ulmer turned to Marvin and said, "You have hell of a case, Mr. Zindler."

Yet, a few days later, Marvin and KTRK received notice that the law firm was resigning from the case. It seemed their senior partner had property in La Grange and was a "personal friend" of Sheriff Flournoy.

This wasn't good enough for Marvin's boss Walter Hawver. Hawver called the law firm and asked for an explanation of why they had withdrawn from the Zindler case.

In effect, he was told, "The law enforcement fraternity is very closely knit. This ties into the bar widely. Any of our lawyers' advice might be colored by their not wanting to get into open confrontation. It could affect referrals, witnesses, services and so on."

This was quite the about-face, and one couldn't help but wonder how far the tentacles of the Chicken Ranch really stretched — and how far, and into what quarters, Sheriff Jim Flournoy's power extended. It was enough to make Marvin wonder if he might need that bullet-proof vest after all.

Still, nothing was going to stop him. He proceeded with his suit against the sheriff and Fayette County. More frustrations were ahead, though. He was told that the Washington D.C. attorney general would not allow his federal case to go forward. Marvin was angry at the Texas officials for not pushing it. "They got scared and couldn't stand the heat," he said later. "When they needed me it was all kissy-kissy. But when I got hurt they hid. I won't forget it either."

On the other side, Flournoy's supporters went ahead with various fundraisers, selling bumper stickers and posters of the sheriff, and other souvenirs of the Chicken Ranch saga.

In the summer of 1975 they threw a big sheriff-appreciation barbecue. Tickets for the barbecue went for $10 a head, and the bash was well attended, not only by the locals, but by people from Houston, Austin, Dallas, San Antonio and other big cities. Most people seemed to have come primarily to have a good time — to drink beer, stuff their bellies with good Texas barbecue, and dance in the hot dust to a mixture of country and rock music.

But no matter; money was money. Notwithstanding the contribution of the out-of-towners' valuable greenbacks, some of the residents were offended by the outsiders' limited knowledge of the history, culture and customs of La Grange. These big-city folk didn't seem to realize there'd ever been anything else of note in Fayette County except the Chicken Ranch.

But again, money was money, and outsider cash was as good and green as anyone else's.

Sheriff Flournoy was at the barbecue, of course, shaking hands and patting backs as he moved through the crowd. He was well-dressed in a brown western-styled suit with a conspicuously large pink carnation pinned to his lapel. Someone stopped the sheriff and asked him if it was just a rumor, or was it true that Marvin had made a peace offering — a truce to end the lawsuit. At this point the sheriff did not appear to be eager to respond to that line of questioning.

Since a lot of beer was being consumed, the crowd made good use of the outhouses. One outhouse in particular drew considerable attention; it had dark black letters scrolled across its door: "MARVIN ZINDLER WAS HERE."

In a sense, Marvin Zindler *was* there, for as you moved through the crowd you could hear his name on almost everyone's lips. Many were recounting the scuffle that had led to the lawsuit. One old rancher was heard to say, "I wisht ole Marvin woulda come. We wouldn't have shot him, or nothing. But we might have tied him to the back of a pick-up and dragged him around the dust for couple of hours or so, just to tire him out a lick, you know."

When Marvin was told the story, he said, "I wouldn't go anywhere near that place. Those crazy damn farmer boys would try to kill me just so they could brag about it."

However seriously Marvin and Sheriff Jim may have taken their legal battle, it was pretty obvious that to the public, the saga of the Return to the Chicken Ranch was more of a comedy than a drama. Whenever the subject was brought up, there was always some snickering accompanying it. Remarks about Marvin's broken ribs and his scalping in the city square were a cause of mirth for some, while others took delight in Sheriff Jim's astonished amazement that he'd been busted after all by the tape he had tried so hard to destroy.

The rumor about Marvin's peace offering to the sheriff was true. Marvin had made the offer shortly before the fundraising barbecue. The terms were simple: the sheriff would turn over all monies raised for his defense of the lawsuit to the Shriners Crippled Children's Fund. (Flournoy, like Marvin, was a longtime member of the Shriners.) In return for

Flournoy's donation, Marvin would drop the lawsuit. However, the scuttlebutt was that he would push ahead with his lawsuit if the sheriff didn't accept Marvin's peace offering.

Precisely how much money was collected for the defense of Sheriff Flournoy was unknown. Besides the barbecue ticket sales, there was money from the sale of "I like Sheriff Jim" bumper stickers (one of which appeared on the bumper of Marvin's car later that week). T-shirts and numerous other gewgaws also raised cash for the defense fund. The T-shirt distributor said that he'd raised $14,000 by week's end. All told, there was probably at least $40-$50,000 in the fund after the barbecue.

Marvin said he had decided to make the offer to Flournoy because it would put the money to work for a good cause. "I don't want to bankrupt Fayette County and hurt the good people up there," he explained.

Not to mention that it would result in admirable publicity for everyone involved, and bring to a happy ending what could have been a distasteful and disastrous situation. Said Marvin, "If the sheriff is as smart as he likes people to think he is, he'd better look into it promptly."

Now, the sheriff may have been a country boy, but he was no idiot. He knew he couldn't win the lawsuit, and it would reflect badly on him because it would hurt his longtime constituents and the County of Fayette. In September, the sheriff requested that soliciting of funds for his defense be discontinued. He didn't want any more publicity, and even asked the local merchants to stop selling the Chicken Ranch T-shirts and other souvenirs. To comply with his request, the shopkeepers took the merchandise off display, but still sold them under-the-counter.

In the end, Sheriff Flournoy signed on the dotted line. Marvin may have lost the first round when he returned to La Grange and was attacked in public by the sheriff, but he won the war.

Attorneys for the sheriff and Fayette County signed civil action number 75-H621, making it known to the court that plaintiff Marvin H. Zindler had resolved the issue between himself and the defendant, T. J. Flournoy. The action stated that Marvin consented to a complete dismissal with prejudice against the defendant, and no longer desired to prosecute the defendant or the County of Fayette. The full terms of the out-of-court settlement were not revealed; that was part of the agreement. True to the agreement, Marvin would not discuss the particulars, and still won't to this day, but he did let it be known that he signed the settlement over to charity. In typical Zindler fashion, he kept nothing for himself.

With this, the feud between Marvin and Sheriff Jim was brought to a close. Of course, the Chicken Ranch story was far from over.

C·H·A·P·T·E·R 25

THE BIGGEST LITTLE
STORY IN TEXAS:
FACT, FANCY & A WHOLE LOT OF FUN

Without question, the Chicken Ranch has become a permanent part of Texas folklore. This has been due in no small part to the work of a colorful, carousing Texas-born journalist named Larry L. King — not to be confused with the suspender-clad host of CNN's *Larry King Live*. It was Larry L. who wrote the article that became the play that eventually became the movie called *The Best Little Whorehouse in Texas*.

Though a Texas native like Marvin, King has lived much of his life in New York City, with frequent trips back to Texas "to refresh his view of it." Despite his origins, King has said more than once that he's really a New Yorker, but those who know him might argue that point. Another rowdy Southern writer, Roy Blount, Jr., once wrote, "Larry L. King writes just like an angel would if it grew up in West Texas and drank."

Angelic or not, it was King's pen that helped transform the Chicken Ranch tale from a titillating news piece to a rollicking musical that has been entertaining audiences since the late 1970s. And if, in the end, King's art only vaguely imitated life — well, that's show biz, as Marvin Zindler would probably be the first to admit. For the most part, Marvin has been a terrific sport about it all, despite the ludicrous inaccuracies of the Marvin-ish character in the play and movie. (In fact, Marvin claims to have attended more than 100 openings of the play.)

But we're getting ahead of ourselves. Before there was a movie, before there was a play, there was Larry L. King's article in a 1974 issue of *Playboy* magazine. Like so many other journalists and reporters, King first got interested in the Chicken Ranch when the story broke in 1973. At the suggestion of a friend of his, King made the trip to La Grange to see what all the fuss was about. He landed interviews with several of the more influential locals, including Sheriff Jim himself. By King's account, the Flournoy interview was a risky venture for a journalist; it seems that by the time Larry got to La Grange, Sheriff Jim had pretty much had it with the media. The sheriff did grudgingly consent to an interview, in which, of course, he denied all of the allegations about the Chicken Ranch. As might be expected, his comments were laced with expletives about the situation in general and Marvin Zindler in particular.

After all was said and done, Larry L. King's take on the matter was pretty much that Marvin, et al. should have just let the Chicken Ranch be. Whatever "criminal" activities had gone on there had to have been small stuff compared to the apocalyptic goings-on elsewhere, was his opinion. His article was colorfully written, revealing, perhaps, more than the reader might have wished to know about the shenanigans of King and his buddies in those pre-AIDS days. But it did tell the tale of the Chicken Ranch, after a fashion — though Marvin says that a lot of material King wrote was "made up," and the *Playboy* article was a mixture of fact and fiction. There was one huge missing piece for sure; King never interviewed Marvin. But that didn't stop the article from being published in *Playboy*, and subsequently capturing the attention of Peter Masterson, an actor from Angleton, Texas. Masterson called King to talk about collaborating on a show about the Chicken Ranch.

That sounded like a plan to King, and once the plan had been executed, they were joined by another Texan, Carol Hall, who wrote music and lyrics to go with the story. The threesome developed *The Best Little Whorehouse in Texas* into a musical at the venerable Actors Studio, and from there, with a couple of years of hard work, frustration and headaches, it grew to its various off-Broadway and Broadway incarnations.

King and his friends signed a contract with Universal Pictures to produce an off-Broadway version of the work. After that, Universal planned to exercise its movie option as well, so all of Middle America could enjoy the story of the Chicken Ranch and Marvin Zindler — oops, make that "Melvin P. Thorpe."

Much to the delight of its creators, *Whorehouse* turned out to be one hot show. Audiences seemed to get a big kick out of the whimsical Texan-isms. Suddenly, Texas was all the rage, even in New York City. Fashion industry bible *Women's Wear Daily* credits *Whorehouse* for igniting the Texas fashion frenzy of the early 80s — the cowboy hats, boots and fringe jackets, not to mention the big Texas hair. (Eat your heart out, *Urban Cowboy*!)

The Chicken Ranch, Miss Edna and the girls, Sheriff Flournoy, Marvin Zindler, Governor Briscoe and the supporting players all showed up in the play — although, with the exception of the Chicken Ranch, all were given new names. Nobody said a word or sang a note about real persons, living or dead. Miss Edna became "Miss Mona." Sheriff T.J. Flournoy became "Ed Earl Dodd." Even La Grange became "Gilbert," Texas. And Marvin Zindler became "Melvin P. Thorpe."

King himself took a small part in some of the early productions as a La Grange — er, make that *Gilbert* — good ol' boy. All in all, *Whorehouse* exceeded reasonable expectations, and King and his co-writers were understandably pleased.

From the beginning, the show was controversial, and most of the controversy centered around the fact that the title had a *Whorehouse* in it. During the original Broadway run, three of New York City's seven TV stations refused to run commercials that had the show's title in them, making it necessary to create an alternative commercial that never once mentioned the product it was selling. The Catholic Archbishop was able to intimidate the New York City Transit Authority into removing its bus ads that bore the headline, "Have fun at the Whorehouse!" The show also became a target of religious groups, and even now faces occasional censorship. (As recently as 1999, a college outside Boston closed down a student production of the show, claiming it was "dangerous.")

Of course, controversy is good publicity. The show sure got people's attention, including Marvin's. You might have expected that he'd be grievously offended and raring to go with another lawsuit. But the truth is that Marvin can be an awfully good sport, and he was actually entertained by the stage play, as evidenced by the fact that he attended all of those openings. He has enjoyed the play all over the U.S. as well as in Canada. One memorable time was in Washington D.C., when all the senators and congressmen from Texas attended the play with him. This was the time of year for the president's State of the Union message. After President Carter's speech, Marvin attended the reception and dance at the Library of Congress with the president and the Texas legislators. No doubt about it: not only had Texas fever hit New York City, it had also reached the nation's capital.

Marvin bore no ill will towards the creators of *The Best Little Whorehouse in Texas*. "I didn't mind other people getting rich off my exploits," Marvin said. If the play made him look foolish at times, well, so what? His reasoning was that people across the country were enjoying *Whorehouse*; it put smiles on their faces and made life more fun. "True events are always whimsical," he acknowledged.

Turned out that he wouldn't be so thrilled about the movie.

Following the play's success, Universal Pictures exercised its movie option. 1982 saw the release of the film version of *The Best Little Whorehouse In Texas*, starring Burt Reynolds as Sheriff Ed Earl Dodd and Dolly Parton as Miss Mona. Like the play, the movie stirred controversy, not just because of the subject matter but because of that catchy title. When promoting or talking about the film, Dolly Parton herself usually referred to it as the *Best Little Chicken House* or the *Best Little Bleep House*.

Was Marvin as pleased with the movie as he was with the play? Not quite, and he made his displeasure known even before the movie was released. When Marvin heard that his character in the movie version was to be played by roly-poly comedian Dom DeLuise, that got his dander up. In fact, he was downright insulted.

"I'm not often offended by the play," he explained, by way of qualification. "I think they used pretty good taste in that." But the movie, well, that was a different story. After all, Marvin was accustomed to playing the hero in his broadcasts. And even though the character based on him was hardly a hero, he felt the filmmakers could have at least picked someone with a more commanding presence, somebody less clownish. Marvin, no doubt, pictured himself more as a Burt Reynolds type than a Dom DeLuise.

But, he added, "I will wait for the movie to come out before deciding whether to take this complaint to court."

Marvin's ire notwithstanding, the movie version went forward, and, yes, Dom DeLuise played the role of Marvin/Melvin. Reviews were mixed, but overall the film was praised for the strong performances. Charles Durning, who played the equivocating, side-stepping governor of Texas, received a 1982 Academy Awards® nomination for Best Supporting Actor.

And Marvin did not sue. He was, however, emphatically not happy about the movie. He said it was not like the stage play, which he thought was very good; the film version was "way off the point." It portrayed the story all wrong, he felt. He saw the movie once in its entirety, and didn't like it. But he thought he should give it another chance, so he went back — and soon decided his original opinion had been right on the money. He walked out before the show was over.

Although it cannot yet boast the 130-year history of the real and original Chicken Ranch, *The Best Little Whorehouse in Texas* has earned its share of satisfied customers over the years, in both its stage and screen incarnations. A multi-million-dollar revival of the stage play was launched in February 2001, starring Ann-Margret — in her first stage role ever — as Miss Mona. She had long been sought for this role by all three of the show's writers, Larry L. King, Peter Masterson and Carol Hall. The role of Sheriff Ed Earl Dodd went to Gary Sandy, perhaps best known for his role as Andy Travis on the 70s sitcom, *WKRP in Cincinnati*. The new production of *Whorehouse* featured new music written for Ann-Margret and lavish costumes designed by Bob Mackie. As I write this, the 2002 production is scheduled for at least 30 road trips.

Although the new production generally received good reviews, some reviewers were wondering if the show was even still relevant. After all, the world has moved on since the 1970s. What was scandalous then would scarcely raise an eyebrow now. The show's producers claimed that this latest production brought a franker, contemporary sensibility to the story. Even so, at least one Texas reviewer asked rhetorically, "Do we really need another revival of *The Best Little Whorehouse in Texas?*"

Well, the answer seems pretty clear: we may not *need* it, but a lot of folks seem to want it. Sure, the world has grown more sophisticated, and no one's going to get their broadcasting license revoked for saying "whorehouse" on the air. But some of the show's themes — love, lust, and friendship, not to mention the steadfast hypocrisy of politicians

— will probably never go out of style. Besides, the story is still entertaining, and the songs are still a lot of fun.

$$\infty \bullet \infty$$

Whatever happened to the real players in the Chicken Ranch saga, and, for that matter, to the Ranch itself? For the most part, the reality is too mundane to make for even a mediocre sequel.

Although it was closed for business permanently in the summer of '73, the legacy of the real-life Chicken Ranch went on. For one thing, customers in search of a good time continued to show up for more than two years after the closing. Either they hadn't heard the news, or hadn't taken it very seriously.

Edna Milton was reported in several locations immediately after the closing of her "boarding house." She was variously rumored to be in Austin with her sister...in Nevada, where prostitution is legal in some counties...in Houston running a new house...and in Florida, where supposedly she had vast real estate holdings. None of this was true, but according to a man in La Grange who claimed to be a good friend, she'd gotten married and moved to another small town in Texas. "She has very little money," the man added.

After the shutdown, Edna sold the Chicken Ranch — buildings, land and all — to two lawyers from Houston. In 1977 they moved a part of the building to Dallas, where they opened a bar/discotheque/restaurant called, not surprisingly, The Chicken Ranch. To add a touch of authenticity, it was deliberately left in its original shabby condition, and the original décor was painstakingly recreated. The restaurant's menu consisted mainly of chicken dishes — no big surprise there either. The surprise was that Edna Milton herself turned up as hostess.

Alas, this business was not nearly as successful as the first Chicken Ranch. Maybe it was the heating problems (which, for several reasons, had never been a problem at the old Ranch), or maybe it was the lack of customers (again, never a problem at the original location), but the Chicken Ranch restaurant closed in January of 1978. The Small Business Administration ordered a foreclosure sale, and in late June of that year, the building and furniture were auctioned off at the site of the restaurant.

This, however, was not the end of Edna's Chicken Ranch-related career. She had a silent role in the original off-Broadway production of *The Best Little Whorehouse in Texas*.

And, lo and behold, there is another Chicken Ranch brothel, but this one's legal. Opened in 1976 and named for the original, the legal Chicken Ranch is located in Pahrump, Nevada, just west of Las Vegas. Current management bills it as "The Best Little Whorehouse in the West." It contains several artifacts, such as lamps and paintings, that originally adorned the Chicken Ranch in La Grange.

Good ol' Sheriff Jim Flournoy ran for re-election in 1976 and won by a landslide. He remained sheriff of Fayette County until his resignation in 1980. By that time, he was saying that both he and his wife were sick of the Chicken Ranch and would be perfectly happy never to hear that name again. He died in October of 1982, and his funeral was attended by then-Lieutenant Governor Bill Hobby and nearly 100 law enforcement officers. Sheriff Jim was credited with solving every bank robbery and murder in the county during his 34-year term. The great irony, of course, is that the Chicken Ranch had helped in many of his criminal investigations.

As for Marvin.... well, he's one player who's still going strong, and he has moved way beyond the whorehouse story. In case you're wondering, he has never received a dime in residuals from the play or the movie, *The Best Little Whorehouse in Texas*. You can be pretty sure of one thing, though: If he had, every penny of it would have gone to charity.

There is still one "missing link" in the Chicken Ranch story. This part of the tale didn't make the stage play or the movies, didn't capture the popular imagination at all. It's one of the stories behind the story, without which, more than likely, there never would have *been* a Chicken Ranch saga at all. It has to do with one Herbert Hancock, who first put the bug in Marvin's ear about the goings-on in La Grange and Sealy.

C·H·A·P·T·E·R 26

"DEEP THROAT" SPEAKS:
THE MISSING PIECE OF THE
CHICKEN RANCH STORY

A very important segment of the Chicken Ranch saga has remained, for the most part, untold. The governor, the attorney general, the sheriffs, and, of course, Marvin, were in the forefront, and certainly in the headlines, back in the 1970s. But the man who brought the Chicken Ranch to Marvin's attention in the first place remained in the background during the time the story was unfolding, and for many years thereafter. The man who most aggressively sought Marvin's help shunned publicity, and remained an enigma. The man, who, for unknown reasons, wanted the Chicken Ranch, the Wagon Wheel and other bawdy houses across Texas closed, kept silent. Whatever his reasons, he remained a ghost, the voice only Marvin's ears could hear. He supplied Marvin with investigative reports and other needed information throughout the development of the story, but he maintained his anonymity.

This silent informant was the former Texas assistant attorney general, Herbert Hancock. In the early 1980s, at Marvin's insistence, Hancock finally agreed to an interview. He was district attorney in Nacogdoches, Texas at this time. Parts of this interview were aired, but it was severely cut to fit the time slot. The interview has never before been seen in its entirety.

Marvin began by asking, "Herb, it has been a long time since we got involved in the Chicken Ranch. Why didn't the attorney general's office and the Texas Department of Public Safety investigate the Chicken Ranch in La Grange, and the Wagon Wheel in Sealy, sooner?"

Hancock responded, "I guess primarily because of [their] long existence, and the possibility of corruption on a local basis with public officials, and the amount of money going through each of these places on a yearly basis."

"How much money was going through the Chicken Ranch each year, approximately?"

"There is an estimation based upon some car counts during that time of approximately one million to one million and a half going through each of the locations. Of course, that was a concern to investigators. Where was it going and how was it being used? There was also the possibility of corrupt public officials by just the mere magnitude of the existence of the thing."

"What about Austin? Were any state senators, legislators or even the former governor ever involved in a situation like this? Do you know?"

"Involved as participating or taking any money? I don't think so. But the fact that both of [the establishments] were able to stay in existence as long as they did would indicate someone in some location had to be in control of it, because once the pressure was put on the right spots in Austin by you and the media and then by the public, both closed down immediately. So, in that sense, it was certainly evident that a lot of people swept it under the rug and didn't pay any attention to it for some reason."

"What about Colonel Wilson Speir, head of DPS? Did he call off the investigation?"

"As far as his investigators were concerned, yes! As far as our office was concerned, no! From the standpoint of the attorney general's office, they weren't told anything other than to keep working on it but, as you know, we needed to have the assistance of the DPS as an investigative tool. They were supposedly the experts in the field."

"Do you think Colonel Speir was getting paid off? Involved in the operation at all?"

"I don't think so. We never had any proof. Probably, Colonel Speir was just pressured into a position by local law enforcement officials."

"Who did this? Do you know?"

"It is hard to say because there is no concrete evidence to this thing."

"Was it the sheriff?"

"That would be the most likely possibility!"

"What about the report the two DPS men made? Did they indicate the sheriff [was applying pressure]?"

"Yes."

"Well, let me ask you this. Was it true that the sheriff and his deputy drew a shotgun on two of these DPS investigators and ran them out of town?"

Herb Hancock was deep in thought for a minute, trying to recall what had taken place those many years ago. He slowly raised his head and looked at Marvin. "There were, if I recall my facts correctly, investigators from DPS in La Grange doing a car count on the number of cars going in and out of the Chicken Ranch and the Wagon Wheel. They were not actually investigating inside the place or anything of that nature. The sheriff confronted them and, in essence, told them that he had been running the county for a number of years and he would continue doing it as long as he was alive. The sheriff asked them to leave."

Marvin pulled out a folder from which he extracted several sheets of typed pages which had yellowed with the years. They were tattered on their edges and there were notes in the margins. Marvin continued, "Now, who wrote this report? Did you, Herb?"

"Yes."

"I have kept this report all of these years. No one has ever seen it! There is a deleted space in this report. It starts off, according to the report, with the findings of the undercover investigation from the DPS. Then there is a blank. What was in the blank, Herb?"

"Marvin, it has been more than eight years. I can remember some of the facts because at the time of the investigation we were trying to determine where the money was going. As best as I remember, it was winding up in Mexico, or it was destined for Mexico or that neighborhood. It was deleted from the report because that information was what we were trying to confirm. We were looking for specific numbers. Specific organized crime families, part of an organization. Persons and places still under investigation. That is the reason I couldn't give that information to you at the time. I do not remember their names."

This information had never been made public, nor had any detentions or arrests ever been made.

Marvin continued, "Were there narcotics involved with the money that was coming out of these houses of prostitution?"

"The money was clean when it came out of these houses, but it was money that could be used for many things. We thought narcotics could be involved."

"So, it really wasn't an innocent house of prostitution that people thought it was, where girls were just making a living?"

"I don't think that you could ever look at it as being innocent, since narcotics had been a subject of investigation. The amount of money that went through the houses went way beyond taking care of girls. The possibilities were great that public officials, local officials, were involved. There is just no way an organization like that can stay alive without some type of graft — corruption. Something to keep them in existence. For example, you know I couldn't run a house of prostitution in the county because the law enforcement agency would close it. It is a violation of Texas law. Usually law enforcement agencies won't do a particular thing unless there is a reason for doing it. You know!"

"So, the reason for not doing it would be money? Is that what you are trying to tell me?"

"What else? You know money motivates folks to do most things!"

"You are in a position to know this. Do you think [public officials] really were [involved with these establishments]?"

"I couldn't prove it. That is what prompted me to tell you about it so we could make it public — I just didn't know."

"Well, what you are saying is that you couldn't make a case. The fact is that it [graft and corruption] was there. Could you say that it was?"

"I just wouldn't go that far."

"But you did know that the money was going into Mexico presumably to buy narcotics. This you did know?"

"Yes."

"Why didn't you go through with this investigation into Mexico, where the money was being sent for narcotics?"

"Marvin, in order that I answer that question, you need to know that as an agent with the attorney general's office I did not have the ability to investigate. I was only a lawyer assigned to work with the DPS in their investigation. They were the investigative arm."

"Is that when the DPS was called off by Colonel Speir?"

"Yes. There were a lot of questions that we were not able to answer."

"Did Colonel Speir know this? Did he have the information from the DPS investigators?"

"Gosh, there is no way of knowing exactly."

"They made reports, did they not? The reports were available. I know that. Do you think that [Speir] saw this report?"

Hancock broke into a broad grin. Almost laughing, but somewhat sheepish, he answered, "I know how *I* got the report you're holding! It is a terrible thing to say at this time, but I almost had to steal it. These reports were hidden away from us (the attorney general's office) at one time."

"Why were they hidden from you?"

"I believe it was primarily because of the nature of the investigation and the magnitude of the investigation. You have to understand that these places have been in existence for many, many years. They were entrenched into the system. It was a tough battle to get information, especially when you could not go into the area without confronting local public officials who would run you out of their county. You really didn't have anyone to go to. You know, we could go down there and get a man into the place. He could certainly testify that there was a house of prostitution. It was so open. Your people, Channel 13 reporters went in and checked it out as well. I imagine that was a tough assignment." Both men were laughing now.

Marvin continued, "Do you think that there *was* organized crime — not Mafiosi, but organized crime as far as more than two people being needed to run it?"

"Certainly. The girls would come down, check in at the Chicken Ranch. They would get a physical. You know, ten to twelve girls at a time. They would be photographed and fingerprinted by the local sheriff. They would stay and then more would come in."

"So, it really was a supermarket?"

"It was a very well-run, supervised type of operation. Somebody had to be running the thing. It was not the madam herself."

"Would you consider this organized crime?"

"Certainly, in its truest form."

"Did John Hill, the attorney general at the time, your boss, ever tell you to stop the investigation?"

"Marvin, John Hill believed in doing what was right and letting the truth fall where it would. He never said anything about stopping. [He said] 'Just go ahead but make sure that you are right.'"

Next Marvin asked, "We are talking about two whorehouses. One in La Grange in Fayette County and the other, the Wagon Wheel, in Austin County. Were these two houses in any way associated with each other?"

"[No], other than the same girls from time to time working in both locations on different occasions. It appeared that some of the girls were on the same circuit. They would come through both locations occasionally.

"Just like running a restaurant. You have to change the menu in order to keep the regulars coming back, providing something new and intriguing. Change was also needed to entice new customers. Even in the whorehouse, you had a menu of your best dishes. Ones the regular customers loved and were comfortable with, but you always needed a few daily specials or a new appetizer to get the juices flowing."

"Do you feel that money for both of these houses were being used for narcotics?"

"The Chicken Ranch in La Grange, very little, if at all. The Wagon Wheel in Sealy was the one that we were able to investigate very closely as to where the money was going."

"But you said probably a little at La Grange was going to..."

Hancock interrupted before Marvin finished his statement. "That is speculation on my part at this time."

Marvin asked, "Why did you ask me to get involved in this thing? To apply the pressure? To expose the operation? You know people laughed at me when I took this on? They felt that I was meddling in some business that I had no business meddling in. Why [did you pick me]?"

"Well, I think at the time the public looked at the operation as just a whorehouse. One in Sealy and one in La Grange. There was literally no way, no legal basis, in which we could deal with the situation because of the amount of pressure that was being applied under the table and behind the scenes to overcome our investigative efforts... The truth was, pardon the expression, it was the only way that I could fight the battle. A battle that had been fought so many times behind the scenes to close it down, and had failed. To close it down wasn't possible. So, I and two or three others twisted your arm to get you involved. You were even reluctant at first."

"How come you trusted me, for God's sake?"

"Well, you and I worked a long time together and had become real good friends. That is basically the reason that I came to you. I knew you well enough to know that if you made up your mind to do something, you are so damned hard-headed that you would go ahead with it. You would take it on and stay with until Hell froze over. I knew that was what it would take in this situation.

"I am not saying that in a derogatory manner. I am saying that because you were the type of person I was looking for. The attorney general, John Hill, didn't tell me to do it. It was something that I decided on my own. I don't know what the attorney general would have done to me had he known I did it the way I did at the time."

That answered the question about why nothing had ever previously appeared about Herb Hancock's role in the closing of the Chicken Ranch. It explained in large part why Marvin was the front man, the one who got most of the wrath as well as the glory.

Marvin said to Herb, "You got lost after I got involved in this thing. I ran stories night after night. Finally, the governor closed it down. I couldn't get ahold of Herb. Herb didn't answer his phone. Herb, you were the hero. Not Marvin Zindler."

"Marvin, I told you on a number of occasions that if you took this on there would be a hell of a lot of heat generated by the public airing of this story on Channel 13."

Marvin grinned broadly, and, laughing, said, "Sure was a lot of heat. And I got all the heat."

Herb replied, "Remember the old saying, if you can't stand the heat, leave the kitchen — get the hell out. So, I got the hell out and stayed out. I stayed out of circulation because I was afraid you were going to quote me. The attorney general told me that I wouldn't be held responsible for what happened except for what they printed, and he meant you, Zindler. With that kind of attitude, I didn't want to lose my job."

"Well, I told you I would not disclose your name at all in this thing," Marvin replied. "That was the number one rule that you agreed upon before we even got started."

"I trusted you enough to know you would not disclose my name."

"Has this thing really bugged you all of these years?" Marvin asked.

"No, it hasn't. The other reason that I wanted to keep my name out of it was that I had a deep admiration for Texas Attorney General John Hill. I did not know at that time whether or not it might be detrimental to his political future. So, I stayed out of it. However, I didn't have any regrets for the approach I took. I don't think that it could have been accomplished any other way."

"Of course, John Hill was your boss at the time. Boss and Texas attorney general."

"He was, but not just my boss. I had more admiration for him than I could ever express."

"What do you think folks are going to say when they find out that Herb Hancock was the one really instrumental person in getting the two houses of prostitution closed permanently?"

"I think that it is old news."

"What about the Broadway play? The movie? Why did you decide to talk now?"

"Time between events makes it so much easier to discuss."

"This was a pretty serious situation, wasn't it?"

"Something we all laugh about now, but at the time very serious. We weren't talking only about local people, but the big boys. I am just a country boy. The governor of Texas was the biggest person on earth, as far as I was concerned. We were talking about involving the governor of Texas, the attorney general, both. And remember, I worked for one and the other I didn't know."

"Do you think that the governor and the attorney general may have been involved before I went in?"

"No!"

"But you felt other public officials in Austin could have been involved?"

"Not in the sense of taking money, but in the sense of protecting the operations at the Chicken Ranch and the Wagon Wheel. When the DPS became involved in the investigation, it put the heat on Colonel Speir. He was kind of like me. When it got too hot, he got out. You know, that kind of thing."

"Do you think prostitution would ever come back to Texas the way that it was in La Grange or Sealy?"

"I don't think that we would ever have an institution like the Chicken Ranch or the Wagon Wheel. I also don't know any part of the state where law enforcement officers wouldn't do something about it given the opportunity to do it."

"What do you think about the D.A. of Austin and Fayette County, Oliver Kitzman, where both whorehouses were operating? He didn't do anything about it, yet he was D.A. and later appointed to a judgeship."

"You are trying to get me in jail, Zindler. I won't comment on it."

"Is it usual for a D.A. to be involved in two counties?"

"Marvin, if you think there is heat from outside their county, it is nothing compared to the heat inside."

"Were you working with him at the time?"

"Unless an investigative effort is going forward and others are assisting him, the D.A. usually doesn't do a lot on his own. Kitzman would have to be crazy or insane to take this on and he is neither."

"So, he knew that you were investigating from the start?"

"I talked to him on a number of occasions during that time."

Marvin wanted to drive this point home. He well remembered his interview with District Attorney Kitzman, during which Kitzman was very ambiguous and acted as if he knew nothing about the investigation.

Marvin asked again, "So, D.A. Kitzman really did know of the investigation."

"Well, everybody knew the houses were in existence. You could sit on the road and do a car count yourself. I did a car count myself. The highway patrol would stop cars in front of the Chicken Ranch and give them tickets. It was such a busy place, the highway patrol had to regulate traffic in front of it. "So, it was wide open and well known."

"Herb, who was actually the person responsible for instigating the investigation of the Chicken Ranch and the Wagon Wheel?"

"Please understand that there had been investigations from time to time from the DPS on these two houses because they had been in existence for a long time."

"I am referring to what took place in November of 1972."

"You did, Marvin," replied Hancock.

Which, of course, was impossible, since Marvin wasn't even at Channel 13 at that time. Marvin quickly set Hancock straight on the matter: "No, you started it! You started it! Did you ask for investigators to come in as well?"

"I assisted in getting it started, but it already had gone as far as I could take responsibility. You know, ten or eleven years have passed and it doesn't make much difference now. I don't know if I can take the credit. I can tell you at the time I was deeply involved in the investigation."

"That was one of your first investigations?"

"That is correct. We are older and wiser. I don't know if I could do it again. It created a lot of hassle. But it solved a lot of problems for morale in law enforcement agencies throughout Texas. For example, police officers I work with from time to time would ask, 'If they could run a whorehouse in La Grange or Sealy, why can't we do it in Houston? Why don't our citizens have the same rights as they have?'"

Marvin said, "A lot of folks in Sealy and La Grange said that Houston, Texas has plenty of prostitutes. [Was] there a difference [between] the prostitutes in Houston [and those in] La Grange and Sealy?"

"In those days the girls who worked the streets in Houston, they did not live in a boarding house with a madam," Hancock replied. "Vice officers would pick them up and take them downtown. They would put them in jail."

"What you are saying is that there wasn't any protection for the girls in Houston and not any houses that were open and running like those in La Grange and Sealy, being protected by the sheriff."

"Protected by whomever. I don't know if the sheriff really had that much power. But there was someone who had a lot of power to keep those places open."

"Herb, did the sheriff from La Grange, Sheriff Flournoy, handle both places?"

"He certainly did help. I don't know if he did it by himself. I don't think he could do it totally by himself. I think other folks were involved."

"Do you think other officials in the county had something to do with it? Or, perhaps some people in Austin?"

"It's hard to say, because political pressure can be subtly applied to even the director of the DPS, the governor of Texas, the attorney general of Texas, particularly through the media. In these times the media will make us aware of what's happening. I think it's probably the only salvation we have. Not only here, but anywhere else."

"The media in Austin and around the state made fun of me when I began the investigation. [They called it] a crusade to close down the houses in La Grange and Sealy. Why do you think the media took that stand?"

"Mr. Zindler, you have to understand that the media is made up of people just like us attorneys. My friends basically did the same thing to me as the media did to you. That is, they made fun of [me, and asked] what's wrong with prostitutes selling their wares. [They think] that [prostitution] shouldn't be against the law.

"It's 'sex and women,' which is one of the best subjects in the world, and that's basically what it's all about. The media never did look behind the scene. They never took into consideration what one and a half million dollars could do when put into the pipeline for buying influence or buying narcotics. It's money that's not taxed."

Joseph Agris, M.D.   233

"Did anyone, including Larry King[1], come to you and talk to you about this?" Marvin asked next.

To which Hancock simply answered, "No, Marvin."

And that was the end of the interview.

So there you have it: the confession, or as close as we're going to get to a confession, from the "Deep Throat" in the Chicken Ranch story. One gets the feeling that Herb Hancock still wasn't telling everything he knew. But that's his right. Besides, maybe some things in Texas — like the Marfa lights, the lost Spanish gold in the mountains of West Texas, and the various and sundry ways in which sex and money grease the political machine in the Lone Star state — are better left a mystery.

---

[1] Marvin is, of course, referring to Larry L. King, author of the article that became *The Best Little Whorehouse in Texas*.

Marvin Zindler:

A Life In Photographs

Abraham Bernard Zindler, Sr. (Abe)
Marvin's father

Udith Meyer Zindler
Marvin's mother

Abe Zindler Sr.
1916

Marvin at about 1 year
Living at Louisiana & Pierce Street
Houston, Texas

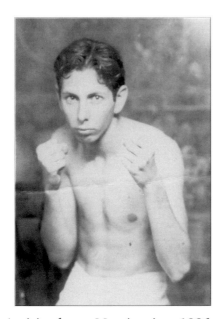

Aspiring musician Marvin, who played flute with Victor Elasandro's first band in Houston. Taken at the San Jacinto Bttleground, 1936.

Aspiring boxer Marvin, circa 1936. Taken at the Hugh Bimbo Boxing Arena on Lincoln Street, which was later changed to Buffalo Drive and, ultimately, to Montrose Boulevard, Houston.

Above: Marvin at 19 in 1940, while attending John Tarleton Agriculture College. He was in the ROTC band, a drum major who marched to a different drummer.

Right: Marvin & Gertrude celebrating with friends, circa 1945. From left: Marvin, Gertrude, Walter Volkman, Mr. & Mrs. Ronald Featherstone, Mr. & Mrs. Sam Marie, Mr. & Mrs. Harry Dawson.

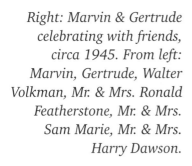

Marvin with Gertrude Kugler, the love of his life, in a photo taken at Foley's on Main Street, circa 1940

Marvin and Gertrude on their "official" wedding day April 1942

White Knight in Blue Shades

More than 50 years later: The happy couple on the cover of
Houston Lifestyle magazine, January 1996
Photo by Jennifer Binder

Auxiliary police vice squad officer Marvin, 1944, still making up his own rules — how many other police officers have you ever seen dressed like this?

Drum major Marvin again, this time at the Shriners' Convention in Atlantic City in the late 1940s

Drum major Marvin with the Shrine Band, leaving for Mexico City, 1945

White Knight in Blue Shades

A proud father shows off a picture of his daughter in the late 1940s

Marvin on the organ at the old 88 Club in the 1950s

Marvin before (left) and after his first chin job, 1954

Marvin after his first nose surgery, working in Zindler's clothing store, 1954

White Knight in Blue Shades

Top row: Marvin Jr., Helen,
Gertrude (center),
Donny, Danny & Mark
1956

Don Yarborough, Texas gubernatorial
candidate, with Marvin
at a Jaycees' event in 1956

Mid-1960s, working for the Fugitive
Division of the sheriff's department.
While bringing in a prisoner aboard
an airplane, Marvin turns his revolver
in to the pilot as a safety precaution.

Still with the sheriff's department,
Consumer Fraud Division. Even in
1972, he was looking out for the
everyday Joe (and Jane!).

By the late 1970s, Marvin was on the other side of the law ... pitching for Channel 13 in a baseball game against the Houston Police Department.

1970s: Marvin with a new friend (most likely met during one of Marvin's investigations into the cleanliness of Houston eateries)

Marvin sharing a "special" moment with talent from a local radio station

Marvin & Gertrude with then-Governor Bill Clements and Mrs. Clements at the Spindletop Ball, Beaumont 1981

Marvin, feeling relaxed while on a golf cruise with Gertrude in 1986

Marvin in his Scottish Rites hat. (In 1996 he received the Masons' highest honor of 33rd Degree.)

*Marvin cutting a rug with Doris Allis
at a Cancer League wingding, 1985*

*Marvin making friends with
one of the performers at the
Shrine Circus, mid-1980s*

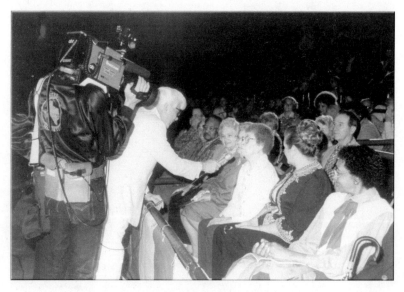

Shrine Circus Senior Citizens' Night, 1988

White Knight in Blue Shades

*Doc Joe, Gertrude, and Marvin at one of many fund-raisers
they attended together, 1991*

*1995: Doc Joe and Marvin with the late Alvin Van Black,
Channel 13's man-about-town*

Marvin and Gertrude at a New Year's Eve party at the author's home, 1992

*Marvin on what is,
for him, a bad hair day,
and what is, for everyone else,.
a rare glimpse behind those
famous blue sunglasses.*

White Knight in Blue Shades

1988: After a pre-election interview, Marvin posed with one of his heroes, President George H.W. Bush (and, no doubt, also offered Mr. Bush some free foreign policy advice).

1991: Our favorite correspondent during a visit to his preferred kind of "war" zone — the casinos at Monte Carlo

Dr. Joe and Marvin doing the town in 1998: "The Boys in White Suits"

Never let it be said that Marvin isn't sentimental: On Dr. Joe's 50th birthday, Marvin (far right) presents him with an electric clown. Dr. Joe's dog "Trucker" stands guard.

Gertrude and Marvin, each holding their new grandson, Adam, in 1994. Marvin siezes the opportunty to demonstrate the proper procedure for taking a nap.

Marvin reading Christmas stories to the kids on
Channel 13's Story Hour, 1996

White Knight in Blue Shades

At the 1999 Houston Livestock Show & Rodeo, Marvin (in hat!) tossed out the flag to start the calf scramble. Here, he's getting himself psyched up for the task, with the help of Dr. Joe (far left, no makeup) and a couple of lovely clowns.

Marvin, Harold Wiesenthal, Judge Hearn and Dr. Joe Agris on the floor of the Astrodome for the calf scramble, 1999 Livestock Show & Rodeo

*Marvin with Channel 13 news director Walt Hawver
and Channel 13 anchor Jan Carson*

Marvin, Bill Cosby, and Gertrude at the Houston Livestock Show & Rodeo

White Knight in Blue Shades

The Zindler clan, 1990

Marvin & Gertrude share a happy Valentine's Day, 1995

1995: Marvin & Gertrude enjoy the food and hospitality
at Pino's Italian Restaurant in Houston.
Pino is right there with them, making sure everything is all right.
Pino's Restaurant is a recipient of Marvin's prestigious Blue Ribbon Award.

Marvin and Pino having a good time, 1990s

Marvin getting a collagen injection from Dr. Agris, late 1980s

1996: On a medical-dental mission to China with the Agris-Zindler Children's Foundation, children's dentist Dr. Mark Urback and Dr. Agris kick up their heels.

Marvin poses with a famous poster in his office at Channel 13. He didn't think much of the movie version of **The Best Little Whorehouse in Texas**, *but he's never been one to pass up a good photo opportunity.*

Marvin Zindler - Dr. Joe Agris and his patient.

From the brochure for the Agris-Zindler Children's Foundation — Marvin and Dr. Agris with a young patient. The photo above shows her before her surgery to correct a double cleft lip.

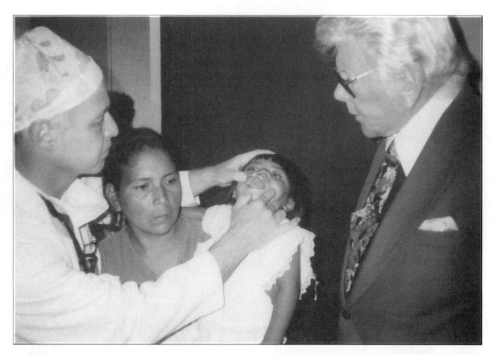

Marvin looks on as Dr. Agris examines a child with cleft palate during a medical mission to Central America, 1993

Scenes from a Russian hospital, 1995. In a true example of cultural exchange, the Russians taught the American medical team to say "slime in the ice machine" in Russian. In return, the Russians wanted an explanation of the "Rat and Roach Report." Even the kids on the children's ward picked up on it, drawing bugs and roaches for Marvin. Here a young patient shows off her artwork, and Marvin and Doc Joe pose with a six-legged "friend."

1990s: Texas Children's Hospital CEO
Dr. Ralph Feigin, Marvin and Dr. Joe
Agris with a young patient, who is
sitting in one of 25 wheelchairs Doc
Joe and Marvin donated to TCH.

1995: Marvin with former Channel
13 KTRK-TV president and general
manager Jim Masucci, and former
news director Richard Longoria

Nicaragua, 1990s: Marvin interviews
Roberto Callejas, Jr., Father Marcus,
and Roberto Callejas.

Good golf makes Marvin happy. Above he
poses with Harold Wiesenthal, Niki Devine,
PGA golf pro Don Cherry, and Bob von
Hagge, designer of golf courses worldwide.

Left: Lori Reingold, Marvin and
Bob Dows on yet another Orbis eye
care mission, this one to
Mongolia and China in 2001.
Bob just can't put that camera
down, even long enough
to pose for a photo.

*1996: A few "anonymous" friends helping the Channel 13 gang
celebrate Marvin's birthday at the studio*

*No, those aren't chef's hats, and it's not a celebrity cook-off.
The caps are part of the operating room attire in Russian hospitals; here
the gang poses in an operating room in Kungur, Russia, 1998.
From left: Dr. Joe, Lori Reingold, Dr. Ghanadi Talianski (C.E.O. of the hospital
& chief of surgery sin Kungur), Bob Dows, and Marvin,
with Gus & Jim Cezeaux in the back row.*

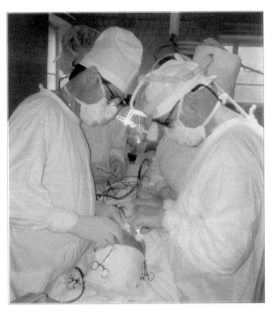

Marvin and Dr. Agris examine a young patient suffering from a cleft lip, Perm, Russia, 1998

1997: On yet another medical mission to Russia, plastic surgeons Dr. Robert Montoya and Dr. Joe Agris work on a patient.

Israel, 1999: Dr. Joe (in front) with Marvin and the gang; a stopover during a medical and teaching mission to Amman, Jordan and Damascus, Syria.

Joseph Agris, M.D.

259

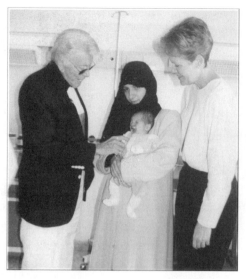

Above: Marvin and nurse Carolyn Harmon with a mother and her child, who is afflicted with a cleft lip; Amman, Jordan, 1999

Above: Russia 1997 — Bob Dows, the best cameraman in the business; and Lori Reingold, who can create a script from anything (the only question is, can the White Knight pronounce all the words correctly?)

Left: Cuba, 1999 — Some days are better than others. Here, Bob Dows learns the hard way that you never disagree with Marvin.

Right: Marvin demonstrating the proper method of exiting a Russian elevator, 1993 (the full story of this adventure is in Chapter 32).

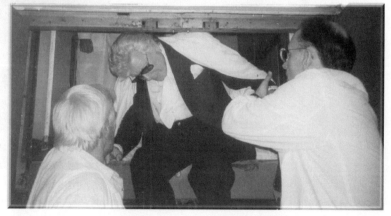

Marvin presents the Blue Ribbon Award to the kitchen at The Methodist Hospital, shortly after his second open-heart surgery, mid-1990s.

Marvin's 1995 benefit golf tournament. From left: Harold Wiesenthal, Marvin, son Donny, son-in-law Mike Rodgers, son Marvin Jr.

"Who lifted whose face?" Marvin trades playful accusations with Edda Farinola at a party, July 1997.

Another kind of "blue ribbon award": Doc Joe, Marvin and Kelli and Helen Rodgers pose with a champ at the Katy Livestock Show & Rodeo, 1997

Dung and Anh Nguyen, part of Marvin's "second family"; in 1988 he brought them out of Vietnam and reunited them with their father, Son Van Nguyen.

At a children's benefit in Nicaragua, 1997. From left: Dr. Joe, Bob Dows, Hugo Holman (C.EO., La Parenza Newspaper), Marvin, Lori Reingold & Idda Holman.

Marvin with Channel 13 anchor Melanie Lawson, December 1996

Bob Dows and Marvin shoot the breeze with former Texas Governor, now U.S. President George W. Bush, at the Rodeo Parade in downtown Houston, 1998.

Above: Three of Houston's brightest stars: Fundraiser extraordinaire Carolyn Farb, Marvin Zindler, and Star Pizza.

Above: Dr. Agris with Laura Kent and the late columnist, TV personality and magazine editor Katherine Blissard at a fundraiser in the late 1990s.

Right: One of the stars in Marvin's life, his faithful feline companion of more than 14 years, "Sweetie."

1999: Marvin, Doc Joe and Lori Reingold with Charlie Ray, American Embassy Chargé d'affaires to Vietnam.

September 2000: Lori Reingold, Marvin and Bob Dows with former Prime Minister of Israel Shimon Peres, one day before outbreak of fighting in Israel.

At the Distinguished Citizen Annual Gala, honoring Dr. John P. McGovern, M.D., Sept. 13, 2001. From left: Dr. McGovern, Mrs. McGovern, Richard E. Wainerdi.

Dr. John McGovern, center, with Dr. Charles A. LeMaistre, left, & Dr. Joseph Agris, right. Dr. McGovern was named Rotary "Man of the Year" for 2001.

Jerry Deutser, Marvin & Conrad S. Weil, Jr. at Marvin's 18th Annual Golf Invitational, August 19, 2001 (benefiting the Houston Ear Research Foundation & the Houston Eye Association Foundation).

At the 2001 Zindler Golf Tournament. From left: Doc Joe, golf pro Don Cherry, Marvin, Harold Wiesenthal, Tom Magliaro.

Schmoozing at the 98-99 Houston Livestock Show & Rodeo Corporate Night are the late Alvin Van Black, with Don Jordan, then chairman of the board of Houston Industries (HL&P), & Red Griffin, life member and then-VP of H.L.S.R.

Marvin and Henry Florsheim, ABC-13 president & general manager, accept an award for support of the Orbis eye program, 2000

Publicity shot of Marvin and the Channel 13 crew, mid-1990s.

Above: Two pros discuss the show: TV-13 news director David Stickland and Marvin in a post-show conference, 2001

Above: Crooks, cheats and n'er-do-wells don't stand a chance with these two on their tails. Marvin & TV-13 investigative reporter Wayne Dolcefino in the Channel 13 edit room, 2001.

Right: Marvin with pals Harold Wiesenthal and Libby Feingursh, April 2000

Above: A few of the folks that make 13 Eyewitness News a winner: Marvin Zindler, anchors Dave Ward & Shara Fryer, weather guru Ed Brandon, on the set, October 2001.

Left: Marvin Zindler, shortly after he went to work for "The Mouse." After Disney bought Channel 13 and Marvin signed his new contract, he and his plush pal posed for Dr. Joe Agris. Marvin picked his favorite photo from that session and turned it into the now-famous "Mickey Mouse Cards" that he hands out to his fans wherever he goes. (Noticeably absent on this card is the photo credit, and don't think Doc Joe didn't give Marvin a hard time about that one!)

Right: The White Knight in his famous blue shades; another promotional postcard for Marvin and Channel 13.

P·A·R·T

8

Marvin's REAL Best Story

The Hermann Hospital Estate Scandal

C·H·A·P·T·E·R 27

A TRUST BETRAYED

Of all the investigative stories Marvin Zindler has done over the decades, which do you think has been the most important? If you're like most people, your answer is probably, "The Chicken Ranch, of course!"

If you were to ask Marvin, though, you'd get a different answer. Without a doubt, the Chicken Ranch adventure has turned out to be his most famous, or perhaps infamous, story. But Marvin believes his most significant story was the Hermann Hospital Estate scandal, which he brought to public attention in January of 1985.

It's hard to argue with his opinion. Though the saga of the little country whorehouse was titillating, and certainly entertaining, what was going on at Hermann Hospital in the 1980s was a true scandal. Millions of dollars were at stake, and high-ranking, well-known Houstonians were involved. The Harris County district attorney's office was kept busy for more than a year, and four separate grand juries were called. One of Houston's most famous private investigators, Clyde Wilson, was involved in the case, only to be suddenly withdrawn — and then later reinstated. Even the Texas attorney general's office got involved.

When it was all over, some of the bad guys, and one bad gal, would go to jail. Others would resign their positions of public trust. Some would be allowed to return their hundreds of thousands of dollars in ill-gotten goods, and quietly slip into anonymity. And Hermann Hospital, a revered institution that had served the public for most of the century, would never be the same again.

It was, in short, a very big deal.

When Marvin went public with his information about the Hermann Hospital board of trustees' financial mismanagement, all hell broke loose. The media had a field day for years with this story. In Houston it made front-page headlines day after day, but only in

The Houston Post. Oddly enough, the *Houston Chronicle* gave it scant coverage, at least in the beginning. (We'll get into the reasons for that in just a little while. For now, suffice it to say that it's a good thing Houston had more than one daily newspaper back then.)

Marvin's entire career has been based on his uncanny intuition and his ability to sniff out hot stories. His intuition and abilities served him well on this story. He had long suspected that there was wrongdoing at Hermann, and he knew there were crooks and thieves hiding in the bedroom communities and concrete expanses of Houston. His quarry was out there; they just had to be flushed out of their hiding places. Marvin managed to do it.

Once he did, all the major media flocked to join Marvin's posse — with the notable exception of the *Houston Chronicle*. The rest of them weren't going to be left out of a hot story like this.

Like many of Marvin's big stories, this one was not without risk. He would make some powerful people powerfully unhappy, and once again he would be advised to wear a bullet-proof vest. The posse of radio commentators, television anchors and the press would be supportive, but they would only bring up the rear. They could not protect Marvin.

Not that this stopped Marvin; it didn't ever cross his mind to back out. Still believing in his own personal angel, Marvin plunged into battle, without that bullet-proof vest. As usual, his motive in pursuing this story was not to increase his ratings or draw more attention to himself. He was driven by altruism, and not a little outrage that the public trust had been so callously violated by those who managed the funds of the Hermann Hospital Estate. It was because his exposure of their misdeeds led to some badly needed changes that Marvin believes the Hermann Hospital story to be not only one of the most newsworthy, but also the most productive piece of his career. It was, he feels, "the best of the best."

In a way, the Hermann Hospital scandal of 1985 was just another sign of the times. The 1980s are not-so-fondly remembered as the "decade of greed"; there was, for example, that whole savings and loan debacle. This was also the decade in which Houston's formerly booming economy went bust, although there were those who still managed to live high on the hog through the worst of times. Living well on money one has earned legitimately is one thing, but living the good life on someone else's money — in violation of the law as well as ethical principles — is something else entirely. The latter is precisely what certain trustees and officials of Hermann Hospital, and their cronies and sweethearts, were doing. They might well have gotten away with it, had it not been for Marvin.

At the outset I want to make one thing perfectly clear (as the central figure in a scandal from a previous decade put it): this is not going to be the definitive, blow-by-blow account of the Hermann Hospital Estate scandal of '85. It might take a little searching, but you can read much more detailed accounts elsewhere.[1] This admittedly incomplete summary is mainly intended to highlight the aspects of the story that Marvin investigated and pursued.

Marvin's part in the big story started innocently enough, with a telephone call to him at home. (Come to think of it, most of Marvin's biggest adventures — and misadventures — have begun with a telephone call.) This particular phone call would be one of the most important he would ever take. It came on a January afternoon in 1985, when Marvin was taking a siesta in his favorite chair in the corner of the living room. He was half awake, half asleep, pretending to be watching a television program while hiding behind those blue glasses. Then the telephone came to life. Marvin readjusted himself in the chair just enough to reach the phone, which was on the adjacent end table.

On the other end of the line was an employee of Hermann Hospital who wanted to let Marvin know that earlier that day, a VIP had been arrested and charged with stealing an enormous amount of money from the hospital. The word was that this VIP would plead guilty to all charges, allowing him to bypass a grand jury investigation. As a result, there would not be any publicity — and without a grand jury, it would be over before anyone knew it.

It was expected that the judge to whom the VIP made his plea would be sympathetic, and the wrongdoer would be put on probation. This was a very sweet deal that would allow him to keep millions of dollars — including his profit-sharing and pension plan. There would be no further investigations into his shady dealings with Hermann Hospital. His life would go on unmarked, and his greatest fear, public acknowledgment of his misdeeds, would not be realized. And that would be the end of that story.

Of course, he hadn't counted on Marvin Zindler getting wind of it.

As Marvin listened to his caller, his blood was pumping. He sat bolt upright in his chair, attentively and anxiously listening to the story. But, as usual, that was not all Marvin was doing. His mind was racing, and he was already planning his attack. It would have to be a surprise attack, and it couldn't wait until the next morning.

Marvin's past experiences with the working of the legal system, as a deputy sheriff and as a news reporter, served him as well now as it had on countless other occasions. Never a procrastinator, Marvin was able to make the necessary decisions in an instant. Accordingly, as soon as he had hung up from his conversation with the unnamed tipster, he was on the phone with his producer Lori Reingold and cameraman Bob Dows. He told them they were all going to the district attorney's office, and they were going to go *now*. Within the hour, Marvin arrived at the D.A.'s office with microphone in hand, and Bob Dows only a few feet behind.

The D.A., John B. Holmes, wasn't in, but this didn't stop Marvin. As it happened, the assistant district attorney, Don Stricklin, was the one who was handling this sweetheart

---

[1] For example, the archives of the late lamented *Houston Post,* or the February and March 1986 issues of *Texas Monthly*, which ran a two-part article on the scandal by Harry Hurt III.

deal, and he *was* in the office. In typical Zindler fashion, Marvin knocked abruptly on Stricklin's office door and burst through, wasting no time as he confronted the assistant D.A. with what he'd heard. As he had intended, he caught Stricklin by complete surprise. Given the situation, what could the man do except admit to the deal?

So there it was; Marvin had it recorded and on film, and it would be the lead story on Channel 13's Action News that evening at 6:00. Millions of Houstonians would see it. Stricklin and Holmes both knew that once this aired, there would be an avalanche of reporters coming down to the D.A.'s office. Public opinion would be firmly against a deal in a situation like this, so bypassing the grand jury and going directly to the judge to request probation would be out of the question.

There was no way the VIP's troubles could be swept under the rug now.

Marvin broke the story on a cold dreary Monday night in January of 1985. The night must have been particularly cold and uncomfortable for the subject of his story, one William Bernard Ryan, 46, former general manager and vice president of Houston's Hermann Hospital Estate. Ryan was formally charged with theft from the Hermann Hospital, possibly hundreds of thousands of dollars; it was hinted that even millions could ultimately be involved.

Ryan's troubles had apparently started in October of the previous year, when an accounting employee found five checks that had been forged by Ryan in 1983 and 1984. The ensuing investigation revealed that the checks, drawn on the Hermann Hospital account, had been made out to fictitious individuals, and Ryan cashed the checks himself and deposited the money in his own bank account. The amount allegedly stolen on each occasion was approximately $20,000.

This alone would be a second-degree felony, which would carry with it a maximum penalty of 20 years in jail and $5,000 in fines. Ryan was not in custody at the time, but a bond had been set at $100,000.

Ryan's attorney gave the usual spiel — that his client was a fine upstanding family man, was not in jail now, and was innocent until proven guilty. "And as far as I'm concerned, Ryan is innocent," he added. (Interestingly enough, Ryan fired this attorney and replaced him with two new attorneys only a few days later.)

In his interview with Ryan, which was shown on that initial Monday night broadcast, Marvin hammered away at the accused man, showing no mercy. Ryan said, "There are many other trustees and people involved. I would like for them to come down here (to the D.A.'s office) and be humiliated like I was with the photographers and TV cameras."

Now it appeared that things were really going to get interesting. Ryan had all but said he was going to expose some of the other higher-ups in the Hermann Hospital Estate. Indeed, what came out in Marvin's interview were indications that the accusations would extend far beyond the Hermann Hospital Estate and the University of Texas Hospital system (of which Hermann had been a part since 1968).

Marvin implied that the web of improprieties would extend to two state representatives closely aligned with the Hermann Hospital, and even to a U.S. congressman. His interview with Ryan that night set the tone for the upcoming investigation, and made it clear to all those involved that, one, Ryan was not going to go it alone; and two, Marvin Zindler was not going to give up until every last one of the crooks was exposed. With this interview, Marvin opened a bigger can of worms than even he initially realized.

It was, to be sure, a cold January night, but no doubt it was Marvin's broadcast rather than the weather that sent shivers up and down the spines of many who had thought they were well insulated. Marvin was just the man to peel that insulation away.

As for William Ryan's sweetheart deal, that was completely out now, thanks in no small part to Marvin's bringing it out in the open. Don Stricklin, the assistant D.A. and also the head of the special crimes division, confirmed to the press that no deal had been made with Ryan, and the case was to be referred to a county grand jury within the next week or so. Ryan's new attorney said Ryan would cooperate with the district attorney's investigation. What else could he say?

Marvin took the viewpoint that now that Ryan had been charged with a crime, he could either "put up or shut up."

The Hermann Hospital Estate trust was set up in the 1920s with a fund established by the late Houston philanthropist George Hermann to serve poor patients. Although on one level you could look at the 1985 fiasco as a symbol of the "decade of greed," in fact this was not the first time scandal had stalked the grounds of Hermann Hospital. The original board of trustees was forced to resign when a lawsuit accused them of mismanagement of funds.

Now, decades later, it was happening again. Perhaps the problem was that there were too many close business and family ties among the board members and other Hermann officials. In 1985, the chairman of the seven-member board of trustees was Corbin J. Robertson, Jr., a Houston oilman. The board president was Jack S. Josey, also a Houston oilman as well as a rancher. Rounding out the team were John B. Coffee, yet another Houston oilman with rice and cattle interests; David Hannah, Jr., a Houston real estate developer and aerospace entrepreneur; Walter M. Mischer, Jr., another Houston real estate developer; and Edward Randall III, former C.E.O. and current chairman of the board of Rotan Mosle Financial Corporation. And last but not least was Phillip G. Warner, who was not only a non-practicing attorney, but, as it happened, the vice president and editor-in-chief of the *Houston Chronicle*.

Could Warner's presence on the board be the reason that sensational headlines appeared daily in *The Houston Post* but not the *Chronicle?* While Marvin was running his series on his Channel 13 Action News program and doubling his ratings, *The Houston Post* was on the story too, with front-page articles by Peter Brewton. Brewton had also been investigating the story from the beginning. Other television and radio reporters were clamoring for a piece of the action as well. Little appeared in the *Houston Chronicle*, however. The *Chronicle* did eventually start covering the story, but not early on, and very rarely on its front page.

In all fairness to the *Houston Chronicle*, the paper did give the story considerably more coverage in later years, particularly in the early 1990s, when scandal on the board of trustees again seemed imminent. Of course, by then the *Chronicle* no longer had an editor-in-chief on the board. As far as the 1985 scandal is concerned, however, I still think that without undercover reporters who were willing to risk everything — people such as Marvin, and Pete Brewton of the *Houston Post* — this story could easily have been squelched by the *Houston Chronicle* editor-in-chief and other board members of Hermann Hospital.

∽ • ∽

It was clear to Marvin that the story that was unfolding in the first few weeks of 1985 had all the makings of a scandal. After all, the board members were from some of the wealthiest and most renowned families in Houston. Some board members were more deeply involved than others, and there were a few who survived apparently unscathed once this year-long inquisition came to an end. In any case, there was plenty to keep Marvin and all the other investigators and reporters busy.

Following Marvin's first newscast, hundreds of phone calls began to pour in to Channel 13 and to Marvin. Many of the callers had more tips, and there were many more stories of wrongdoings in the hospital.

∽ • ∽

The evening after Marvin's first broadcast on this story, he had an unexpected caller at his home. It was after dark, and there was an icy chill in the air, but that wasn't why William F. "Bill" Smith was shaking. Smith was apparently distraught and quite anxious about making this house call.

And no wonder. Smith's and Marvin's paths had crossed on not such pleasant terms on several occasions. Not more than a year ago, Marvin had cause to suspect Smith, the former executive director of the Hermann Hospital Estate, of some inappropriate financial maneuvering. Marvin recalled telling him, "Someday I'm gonna get your ass. You are a crook." Now Bill Smith was making a house call, late at night and less than 24 hours after Marvin's news-breaking story on the Hermann Hospital Estate.

Marvin invited his visitor in and asked him to sit down. While Marvin took his time getting himself comfortable again in his favorite chair, Smith just dropped onto the couch across from Marvin. And he began to talk. At first he shared information Marvin already knew, but then things started to get interesting.

Marvin was quite familiar with Bill Smith's background. Smith had come to Hermann Hospital in 1975, at a time when Hermann was suffering from acute financial problems. The hospital was losing $7.5 million annually, and Smith, who had built a reputation as a talented executive, was hired to help reverse this trend. He was able to do it, and became well known in his own professional circles for his aggressive administrative style and for helping to develop and promote high-profile programs such as the Life Flight ambulance service. Initially the trustees of the hospital were pleased with his performance, as the hospital's books moved from the red and firmly into the black.

Unfortunately, Smith, like several of his colleagues, became involved in some improper business dealings. Late in the summer of 1984, E. Don Walker, formerly chancellor of The University of Texas, took over as president of administration of the Hermann Hospital Estate. Don Walker became suspicious of "certain irregularities" that he felt existed in the administration.

Walker and the trustees of the hospital retained the law firm of Vincent and Elkins to investigate the matter. After hearing Don Walker's suspicions, the attorneys at Vincent and Elkins hired Houston's prestigious private investigator, Clyde Wilson (who is also a good friend of Marvin's). Wilson was given carte blanche to investigate the whole situation and make recommendations. Now Smith told Marvin, "I'd heard that Clyde Wilson had been investigating the matter for several months, and that Mr. Ryan told him he had stolen in excess of two hundred thousand dollars."

One result of the investigation was that Smith quietly resigned in November 1984 to become president of the Houston Health Care Consulting Firm. Several other executives of the hospital resigned at the same time.

Again, these were things that Marvin already knew. Much of it had been in his broadcasts and on other TV and radio shows, and, of course, in articles in the *Houston Post*. (What Marvin didn't know at the time, but found out later, was that Smith hadn't exactly resigned from Hermann Hospital. He was still employed by the hospital as a "consultant," at his previous salary of more than $160,000 a year.)

Smith continued to fidget, and found it difficult at times to continue with his story. All the while, Marvin sat quietly listening, saying nothing. He knew Smith had a good reason for initiating the visit. Although at this point, Smith still hadn't told him anything he and other reporters hadn't already uncovered, Marvin knew his visitor had more to say. He was going to give Smith the opportunity, and the rope, to hang himself. He couldn't help remembering his vow, more than a year ago, to "get Smith's ass." Now he was making good on that vow, and Smith himself was helping.

The big question was, who else was Bill Smith going to incriminate? Where would the allegations stop? Marvin was patient; he sat back, smiled, and occasionally nodded his head as Smith continued.

Finally Marvin decided to take the bull by the horns and bring up another "big name." Casually he said to Smith, "I heard that Neill F. Amsler, Jr. also left his job a few months ago as executive vice-president and associate trustee of the estate."

Bill Smith nodded, and a nervous shudder seemed to pass over him. He hesitated for a minute and then began to talk about Amsler, who had been William Ryan's boss. Smith said Amsler and Ryan, as well as others, had spent quite a bit of money on several gambling trips to Las Vegas. The trips were paid for by an unnamed vendor to Hermann Hospital. Smith said this was some of the information Clyde Wilson had uncovered during his investigation.

Smith also revealed that Amsler had set up a political action committee, Friends of Hermann Hospital Estate, but did not register it properly with the Secretary of State's office. And indeed, when Marvin checked with the Secretary of State's office, there was no listing for a PAC known as Friends of Hermann Hospital Estate. Amsler had designated himself treasurer of this unregistered political action committee — an offense that was punishable with up to one year in jail and a fine of $2,000.

Much more would be revealed about Amsler's misdeeds in the weeks to come.

The two men sat there in silence. What seemed like an eternity was only a few seconds as Marvin looked hard at Bill Smith. Finally, his eyes piercing but his voice soft, Marvin said, "Where does it go from here?" He did not want to rattle his visitor, because he knew there was much more to this story. He had to give Smith time to gather his thoughts.

Smith's lips were dry and his voice a bit raspy; he was obviously finding this a very difficult meeting. During the many pauses, Marvin's mind was racing. The main thing he was trying to understand was Smith's purpose for the visit. By providing Marvin with this information, did Smith feel things would go easier on him later? Or had he simply had an attack of conscience? Why didn't Smith go to investigator Clyde Wilson, or even to the district attorney's office, with whatever information he had? Did Smith feel Marvin could present his side of the story in a better light? Surely he must have known, from Marvin's blistering comment last year, that Marvin would never hold back.

But perhaps Smith would rather have the exposure come from Marvin than from Bill Ryan, who had already stated he would implicate higher-ups. In fact by now Ryan had already implicated his supervisor, Neill Amsler, in the gambling trips to Las Vegas. Perhaps Smith felt that, despite Marvin's previous threats, his coming to Marvin meant he would not have to undergo the humiliation and be placed in the same harsh spotlight as Ryan and the others.

Smith said that the hospital trustees wanted to avoid media coverage for fear it would harm the hospital, but they now realized they would not be able to keep a lid on the story with so many people coming forward and new information leaking every day. "The only thing I'm interested in," Smith explained to Marvin, "is the media keeping it in the right perspective." Marvin flashed his famous smile, showing all those beautifully capped, sparking white teeth. Bill Smith took this as an indication of Marvin's approval to continue.

As he grew more relaxed, Smith began to reveal more. He started talking about a woman who was "a very close friend," Nancy Stack. Stack, a former Hermann Hospital employee and now an interior decorator, had moved to Dallas. It was there that she operated Brandy Rose Interiors, an ultimately unsuccessful business venture that had begun in 1983 and specialized in the interior decoration of hospitals and clinics.

It seems the main building of Hermann Hospital was in need of a facelift and redecoration. As is customary, the contract had been placed out for bids. The job would not be cheap; the administrators knew this. Most firms came back with bids for several hundred thousand dollars. The exception was Nancy Stack's bid: it was more than two-and-a-half times that amount — in excess of half a million. Yet Bill Smith awarded the contract to Stack's Dallas company.

It was known via the grapevine that Bill Smith and Stack were very good friends. Marvin, his mind still racing, knew that "good friends" was synonymous with "lovers." In any case, Smith now indicated that Clyde Wilson was looking into the awarding of the decorating contract to Nancy Stack.

Marvin knew there was more to it than Smith had thus far revealed. Wanting to encourage him to continue in the same vein, he flashed his approving smile again and made a neutral comment. He was determined not to let the subject of Nancy Stack end here, especially now that he felt he had won Bill Smith over. Very sweetly he said, "Nancy must be a very special person. Tell me more about her."

Finally Smith really began to open up. He said again that he and Nancy had a "very close, personal relationship" for several years. Then he added that she had become pregnant.

Marvin could hardly believe what he had just heard. This story now had all the elements of a soap opera as well as a scandal: intrigue, sex, mismanagement of millions of dollars, sex, possible theft...and sex.

How close Ms. Stack and Bill Smith were was shortly to be revealed to the world, in a paternity suit filed by Nancy Cecelia Stack against former Hermann official William F. Smith. The lawsuit would claim Smith was the father of her son, Nicolas Taylor Stack. It would ask for financial support from Smith to pay for her son's expensive and continued medical treatment; unfortunately, the child suffered from leukemia.

But where was this all leading? It was now obvious that Bill Smith had awarded the over-priced decorating contract to his ex-girlfriend, Nancy Stack. And one of the things Bill Smith admitted to Marvin on camera a few days later, when he went into the Channel 13 studio for a formal interview, was that Nicolas was his child. In that interview, much of what Smith and Marvin had discussed during the private home visit was made public.

Rumors abounded now. Marvin was particularly interested in two other names that had been brought to his attention: Neill Amsler, William Ryan's boss, and building manager Ray Valdez, who resigned almost at the same time Ryan did. This raised Marvin's suspicions.

Some of the hospital officials who resigned had termination clauses in their contract. Amsler claimed that he had such a contract, and he paid himself $584,000 — by withdrawing the funds from the hospital accounts without proper authorization. When Marvin made this public knowledge, the new president of the board, Walter Mischer, said the board voted to recover the money, and Amsler quickly returned it. A half million was returned to the hospital charity fund, and another sweetheart deal came to an end.

But rather than an ending, it was another beginning, for more information oozed out regarding the things Neill Amsler and Ray Valdez had been doing for years with hospital funds. Amsler and his buddies had also enjoyed some of the dozens of unauthorized trips paid for by the hospital. These included lavish dinners, hotels, and gambling in Las Vegas, supposedly paid for by a vendor to the Hermann Hospital. It seemed that kickbacks and under-the-table deals were how business was conducted on a daily basis among some of the executives, associates, and trustees of the Hermann Hospital estate.

Amsler had also borrowed more than a million dollars from the Estate, and he used some of this money to buy his home. Records had also been uncovered to show that Amsler signed a promissory note for $900,00 sto the non-profit institution.

Amsler's wife, Mollie, said news reports of allegations against her husband were inaccurate. She was right; there was much more dirt yet to be uncovered. She added that she had no knowledge of the nearly one million dollars in transactions involving her husband.

Hospital records also showed that in 1983 Amsler was paid a more than adequate salary. It was in excess of $150,000, an almost 300% increase from his 1980 salary of $62,000. Even by today's standards, that is a lot of money, and a hell of a raise.

Valdez wasn't doing too badly either. He had been at Hermann Hospital for many years, beginning as a janitor, and working his way up to building manager. As building manager, he was earning the unbelievable salary of $126,000 — in 1983 — and questionable bonuses on top of that.

Now that Marvin had opened the sluice gates and the polluted waters were pouring forth, Valdez felt that he couldn't mire them any worse when he said, "I just followed Amsler's orders to conceal expenses. Employees who failed to do so were fired. This practice was carried on for years. In retrospect, I shouldn't have done it. Everybody at the Estate did it."

Valdez considered the trips to Europe, Las Vegas and other locations to be perks, but did not report their value on his income tax forms. It seems that Amsler and Valdez were swimming in the same murky waters. But they were hardly swimming alone.

In fact, it seemed that every time Marvin baited a hook, he caught another one. In any case, Amsler and Valdez were now stuffed and mounted to the trophy plaques. How soon would it be before Marvin snagged himself another big fish?

White Knight in Blue Shades

In March 1985, the Hermann Hospital Estate filed a lawsuit to recover more than $3,000,000 in damages from William Smith, William Ryan, Neill Amsler and others. Amsler was sued for $800,000, alleging that he charged Hermann Hospital for personal trips to Europe and the Baltic Sea, furniture for his daughter's apartment, and many other improper personal purchases.

The lawsuit also alleged that Amsler wrongfully transferred ownership of a $2,000,000 life insurance policy on himself with a cash value of at least $200,000. Other allegations were that Amsler charged more than $25,000 worth of personal, non-business related expenses to his Hermann Hospital credit card, and wrongfully reimbursed himself for $9,000 worth of expenses. He also charged the hospital for two tickets to Hawaii valued at $6,400 each. This fish was slimier than most. He never took that trip to Hawaii; he converted the tickets to cash, which he used to pay for a 1982 trip to Europe for him and his wife, and a 1984 Baltic Sea cruise for himself and an associate, Floyd Wheeler.

There were also claims that Amsler used Hermann Hospital employees to do construction and maintenance work on his home and to build a fence at his ranch.

Indeed, the waters that Marvin was fishing in ran deep, and were more polluted than had originally been expected.

So many "irregularities" and conflicts of interest were being uncovered that it was hard to keep up with them all. But Marvin still doggedly followed every lead he was given. One of the big issues that concerned him was the potential conflict of interest concerning the banks where the Estate funds were deposited. "As of January," Marvin stated on one of his broadcasts, "most of the Hermann Hospital Estate's certificates of deposit, and interest-bearing bank accounts, were in banks with direct connections to hospital trustees."

During his interview with Marvin, William Smith had questioned the practice of putting the Hermann Hospital Estate's money into the banks where hospital trustees were on the board of directors. Further, Smith told Marvin that he didn't know for certain whether the Hermann Hospital Fund had received the best interest rates possible on their certificates of deposit at the bank. He revealed that the trustees didn't go out for bids when purchasing the CDs.

The largest amount of the Estate's money, $6.4 million, was in the First City National Bank, the flagship bank of the First City Bank Corporation where, as it happened, Hermann Hospital Estate's chairman, Corbin J. Roberston Jr., was on the board of directors.

Smith told Marvin he had documentation that Hermann Hospital Estate trustee Philip G. Warner was also on the board of directors at Texas Commerce Bank, and Hermann Hospital deposits of at least $1.5 million dollars were made to that bank.

In short, the relationships between hospital trustees and the banks in which Estate funds were deposited were.... well, downright incestuous.

As Marvin's investigations continued, more and more information was coming to light, and William Smith was, to put it gently, not smelling like a rose. Among the many things Smith had confided to Marvin was that large bonuses were paid to hospital executive officers. For example, Larry Bowermon, the hospital's chief financial officer, received $44,000 in bonuses, and Gary McHenry, the administrator and chief executive, received a bonus of almost $30,000. Many other hospital officials were given similarly substantial "performance bonuses." This might not have been such a big deal, but for the fact that these bonus checks were handed out only a little over a week after Bill Smith, who at that time was still executive director, had signed a letter to hospital employees explaining why 100 people were losing their jobs at the hospital.

It was the same old corporate bull that employees have been sloshing through for years. As the letter Smith signed explained it, "Any staff reduction is not the action we would like to take...but if it were not implemented, numbers would have been even larger." Smith went on to say that the decrease in patient numbers lead to staff termination. It was a familiar story: While the peons lost their jobs, the hospital managers were giving themselves large bonuses.

Marvin was on this in a flash.

In addition to these frequent excessive cash bonuses, Marvin learned some interesting things about Smith and Gulf Coast Aero, which arranged charter flights for Hermann Hospital, including those for Life Flight. Gulf Coast Aero, it turned out, also provided William Smith several favors, including a more than $10,000 Caribbean cruise in September of 1985 for Smith and his wife, as well as the generously compensated executives Bowermon and McHenry and *their* wives. It is interesting that there were no records — no pilot's logs or manifests to show the destination of the airplane trips, and no passenger lists either. The records conveniently disappeared.

In addition, Gulf Coast Aero had sent a check for $6,200 to Smith's paramour and alleged interior decorator. Yet Nancy Stack's Company, Brandy Rose Interiors, hadn't done anything in return for the money. The general opinion among those investigating was that she must have provided some "personal services." Bill Smith's girlfriend didn't get the cruise, but she got the cash.

Further investigation showed that bills for air services, decorating, furniture, even meals and liquor were regularly paid for through the Hermann Hospital accounts. Nine thousand dollars worth of furniture went to Bill Smith's significant other, and I'm not talking about his wife. Smith also approved the purchase of at least $7,500 worth of football tickets. In August of 1984, more than $25,000 was spent at the Republican National Convention for room service and banquets.

Smith later said that the allegations were "getting ridiculous," and that mud slinging was not going to solve the problems. In an attempt to turn things around, Smith's attorney, Mack Arnold, said that by focusing solely on the perks of the job, the media might miss the fact that Smith had taken Hermann Hospital out of the red. As for the perks and trips, Hermann Hospital might be a charity institution, but it was still a big business, and these kinds of things were done to impress people.

Marvin, for one, wasn't buying it. Nor was the district attorney, and nor, for that matter, was the public. Maybe a more competent spin doctor than Smith's attorney would have been able to talk some sense into those hardheads. A good PR person might have pointed out that Hermann Hospital was established to help the poor who are in need of medical care. Smith obviously felt that it was perfectly acceptable to buy $9,000 worth of furniture for his paramour, and put up tens of thousands of dollars to establish a business for her, since she was, after all, the mother of his child — a child who, unfortunately, developed significant medical problems. And wasn't that what the Hermann Hospital Foundation was for — to help poor children who had medical needs?

Smith, at Hermann Hospital's expense, was very helpful indeed to his lover and his child. At one point he advanced Nancy Stack $75,000. He also allowed her to use Hermann Hospital's name to rent office space, and, of course, lest we forget, he signed that huge contract with her for interior design work for the hospital.

A lawsuit that was later filed claimed there was a sweetheart contract between Hermann Hospital and Ms. Stack's interior decorating business. It claims that Smith used and abused his position at the hospital to support his pregnant girlfriend, and when things began to heat up, he used the money to move her to Dallas. But, again, perhaps Bill Smith was only carrying out the wishes of George Hermann in helping the poor and caring for the sick. It all depends on how you look at it.

More entanglements were revealed as Marvin and others continued their investigations. It came as no surprise to Marvin to discover that Smith and William Hicks, the onetime president of Gulf Coast Aero, had worked systematically to overcharge Hermann Hospital for charter air services. The overpayment was then diverted to Smith and his girlfriend. He used these funds to purchase expensive items, such as Rolex watches, jewelry, pleasure cruises and Colorado vacations. Smith also used the air charter arrangement to take personal trips to such places as New York, New Orleans, San Francisco and the Grand Caymans, at a cost to Hermann of at least $250,000. Yet Smith kept insisting that the funds were used for authorized, legitimate purposes.

Marvin and others, however, felt that the funds were unauthorized and were being used for illegitimate purposes. This included financing Congressman Mickey Leland's trip to Cuba in 1983, to obtain the release of a young couple being held there on drug charges.[2]

Marvin also learned that Smith served on the advisory board of a company that supplied computer software for Hermann Hospital. For his service on this board, Smith received an additional $2,250 a month. Of course, serving on several different boards

---

[2] It should be noted that Marvin personally took Mickey Leland to task on this matter, and Leland repaid $11,000.00 to the estate. He and Marvin remained good friends for the rest of Leland's life (see the chapter on Mickey Leland in the "Man on a Mission" section).

does not necessarily mean there has been a criminal violation, unless Smith had used his position to obtain hospital contracts for a company on whose board he sat. However, it seemed ethically inappropriate to accept a salary from Hermann Hospital and a salary from one of its suppliers at the same time. There seemed to be a conflict of interest at the very least.

As the investigation continued, still more was discovered about the cozy relationships between board members and banks. Marvin uncovered records that showed another $1.5 million dollars in certificates of deposits was in Republic Bank, where it just so happened that hospital trustee Edward Randall III was on the bank board.

The hospital Estate also had more than a million dollars in First City Bank Medical Center, where former hospital manager, William B. Ryan, Jr., was a trustee. By the time this was discovered, Ryan had already been indicted by the grand jury in this case. And last but not least, former v.p. Neill Amsler, who had been Ryan's boss, was also a director of the Bank of Houston, where the Hermann Hospital Estate had more than a million dollars on deposit.

But perhaps the most shocking discovery was that Hermann Hospital trustee John B. Coffee was on the board of the Central Bank of Houston, and trustee Jack Josey was its principal stockholder. Why was this a big deal? Simply because records showed that Coffee had sold millions of dollars worth of shares of Central Bank stock to the hospital.

Furthermore, many felt that the bank stock had been sold to Hermann Hospital at highly inflated values. Information leaked that investigators were looking into this sale, particularly into John B. Coffee's role in it.

Another informant came forward. Dr. Howard Seigler was a prominent Houston physician, an internist who had worked for many years at Hermann Hospital. Like Marvin, Seigler knew when to keep his eyes and ears open and his mouth shut. But, like Marvin, he also knew when to speak up. When he began to read the articles in *The Houston Post* and hear what Marvin was saying on his KTRK Action News program, he felt he might have some information that would be helpful to Marvin. Seigler was not a member of the hospital board and was not involved with the scandal in any way, but when you work many years in an institution, you see and hear things. Seigler had some information about more possible wrongdoings involving one of the banks.

The tips were flying fast and heavy now. There just seemed to be too many rumors about John Coffee's bank stock transactions, and the question of the hour was: Had Coffee sold Central Bank of Houston stock to the Hermann Hospital Estate at significantly inflated prices, at a multi-million dollar profit to himself? As usual, Marvin Zindler and

Pete Brewton of the *Post* were on the story, reporting that the Hermann Hospital Estate had purchased $3,000,000 in stock from Central Bank of Houston. The deal was initiated by John B. Coffee, who just also happened to be a director at the bank. How convenient!

Marvin also learned that an advisory director of the Central Bank was none other than former executive vice-president and associate trustee of the Hermann Hospital, Mr. Neill Amsler. Amsler sure got around.

Coffee had an explanation for everything. He said he considered Central Bank stock to be a great investment for the Hermann Hospital Estate. After all, the bank examiners had ranked it number one in the state of Texas for banks of its size. Coffee also explained that the bank didn't pay dividends on its stock, but that this didn't hurt the Estate's investment. He said that as chairman of the bank's executive committee he felt the bank was better off investing its profits rather than paying dividends. In an attempt to change the subject, Coffee pointed out that William Ryan had forged his, Coffee's, name to several checks, which Ryan had then cashed, depositing the money in his own bank account.

This was not new; Marvin had released this information about Ryan during his first broadcast on the Hermann Hospital scandal. But Coffee was up against the wall, and you couldn't blame him for taking this taking this opportunity to change the subject.

"I don't know how Ryan made it that long," Coffee said, referring to reports that Ryan had allegedly been taking money from the hospital for perhaps the past seven years. Coffee noted that several years ago a high-ranking Allied Bank officer had been sent to jail for embezzling about 17 million dollars from the Allied Bank over a 10-year period. Coffee was good, very good — always trying to direct attention to someone or something else, anywhere but towards his bank stock dealings.

But there were some people who wouldn't allow their attention to be diverted. Marvin was one, as was Pete Brewton, and private investigator Clyde Wilson.

With information from Hermann Hospital internist Howard Seigler and others, Marvin took to the airwaves with an Action News telecast, making public the stock deal in the Central Bank of Houston. This bank, he explained, was closely aligned with, if not actually controlled by, Hermann Hospital trustee John B. Coffee. Marvin pointed out that not only did the hospital purchase millions of dollars of non-dividend-paying stock, but the deal included stock personally owned by Coffee.

Coffee had admitted that as a trustee of the Hospital he voted to buy the bank's stock. Marvin pointed out this very blatant conflict of interest. But Coffee, who had already proven his expertise in throwing the blame on someone else, explained that he sold his interest in the stock to his close friend Adrian Patton, Jr., a local insurance agent, who in turn sold the stock to the Hermann Hospital Estate. The implication was that if you use a middle man, that makes it okay.

However, when Coffee was directly asked if he knew of Patton's intention to sell the stock back to the hospital, he admitted, "Yes."

There was also the matter of selling the stocks at inflated prices, and when confronted with this issue, it was clear that Coffee's repertoire of excuses had not run out. The stock's book value was approximately $20 a share, Coffee said, and yet it was sold to the hospital for closer to $40 a share. Still, as Coffee explained it, he did not think the hospital had made a bad deal at all. He explained that while stock can be sold for various prices, his stock was actually worth closer to $60 a share, because Central Bank was "solid and prosperous." This now seemed to be more than just a conflict of interest. Coffee had doubled his money overnight on the stock deal. Besides, if he felt the stock was worth $60 a share, why did he sell it for $40 a share?

Cow chips to you, sir.

Subsequent investigation by Marvin, including consultation with a stock expert, showed that the Central Bank stock sold that year only netted $17.50 a share. That's a long way from the $40 a share Coffee took from the hospital Estate. The stock expert Marvin consulted did say that stock prices varied with timing. Well, I guess the timing is right when you can get $40 a share for a stock that had par value of less than $20, and hadn't sold for higher than $17.50 in the past year. Matter of fact, it's a great deal if you can find someone stupid enough to buy it at more than twice its value.

Coffee did finally admit he owned more than 16 per cent of the bank's stock. But, he added, fellow Hermann Hospital Estate trustee Jack Josey and his family owned about 40 per cent, and the Hermann Hospital Estate now owned 28 per cent.

It was Coffeeism at its finest: divert attention to others, or, at the very least, spread the blame.

It all came down to the question of what was legal versus what was ethical. There was no problem with the hospital purchasing stock in a bank whose ownership was held primarily by hospital trustees and their families, so long as that stock was not bought from one of the Hermann Hospital Estate trustees. However, all involved in these transactions *were* hospital Trustees. Coffee got around that, of course, by using a middle man, Patton. But since he knew full well that Patton was going to sell the stock to the Hermann Hospital at an inflated price, and that he, Coffee, would be voting on that matter, the legality of his action was as much in question as the ethics.

Nevertheless Coffee continued to defend himself, saying he endorsed the estate's purchase of Central Bank stock because he thought the small bank was a "jewel." He said it had very liquid assets, as well as a conservative business approach, and was an extremely valuable piece of downtown real estate. He also explained, "We don't really self-deal at the bank. The only way the bank makes money is to make loans."

In his nightly television broadcasts, Marvin continued to hammer away at the stock deal and other allegations. A few weeks later, on February 16, 1985, *The Houston Post* ran a headline, "Hermann Trustee Pays Estate for Bank Stock." The accompanying story announced that John Coffee had paid the hospital $351,940 to buy back approximately

8,000 shares of Central Bank of Houston's stock that either he or his friend, Adrian Patton, had sold to the hospital.

E. Don Walker, the newly appointed president of the hospital, said, "The price of the stock sold back to Coffee was calculated so that the hospital's Estate fund didn't suffer any loss."

Prosecutors, however, said the move to pay back the hospital would not affect the grand jury investigation into Coffee's stock dealings. Both Coffee and Patton would have to appear before the grand jury investigating the Estate's involvement in the banks controlled by Coffee and Jack Josey.

When Marvin asked assistant district attorney Don Stricklin if Coffee's gesture could change the ongoing grand jury investigation, Stricklin replied, "It won't affect it at all... and my other comment you may not air." He continued, "It does not change the status of any potential crime if two or three years after the event and after the beginning of an investigation the questioned action is reversed by returning the money."

Meanwhile, Coffee's attorney stressed that Coffee was not admitting he was guilty of anything, but was "simply buying back the stock because there are now questions about whether it was a wise investment."

Marvin never gave up. With continued questioning, Coffee's attorney acknowledged that Coffee did "directly" sell 1,362 shares of stock to Hermann Hospital. This was in addition to the shares Coffee sold through his friend Adrian Patton. So Coffee *did* sell stock directly to the hospital while he was a hospital trustee. That's a no-no, Mister Coffee!

When Coffee was asked if he had any other stock dealings with Hermann Hospital, he admitted that in 1979 he also sold the Hermann Hospital Estate 1,000 shares — at $30 a share — in the Galena Park Fertilizer Company, of which he was the founding director. The Hospital Estate also bought additional stock in the fertilizer company at Coffee's insistence, making a total investment of more than $400,000 in the company. Coffee, however, was not offering to buy those shares back as well.

He ended by saying he still did not plan to resign from the board because of ethics or any other questions in the stock deal. After all, as he explained, "Over the years, the various business dealings which I have recommended to the hospital have resulted in many millions of dollars in benefits to the Estate." He still believed the stock was a wise investment, even though it didn't pay a dividend.

Marvin couldn't help wondering if, in the buyback, the stock price was adjusted for inflation and interest that could have been earned on the money.

As it turned out, the fertilizer deal was even smellier than it had seemed at first. It was revealed that Robert H. Park, who was then a business associate of Jack Josey, was also a founding director of the fertilizer company, and sold some Central Bank stock to the hospital as well. This went beyond a breach of ethics. This was financial incest.

In the end, all of Coffee's efforts at diverting attention away from himself were for naught. The attention brought to Coffee by Marvin's broadcasts resulted in a grand jury investigation. Much was at stake; if it could be proved that Coffee knowingly had the stock sold to the Hermann Hospital Estate at an inflated price, he could be charged with theft. And if Coffee lied to the grand jury about his part in the stock sale, he could also be charged with aggravated perjury.

Following the grand jury investigation, rumors were rampant that Coffee and other members of the Hermann Hospital board would resign. Several grand jurors who had just ended their term said the panel on which they served was shocked at the evidence of mismanagement and wrongdoing within the Hermann Hospital Estate. They felt the trustees ultimately responsible for the alleged problems should vacate their positions on the Board.

Coffee, not surprisingly, thought the comments of the grand jury were "horrible." He said, "Neither I nor any of the other six members of the Hermann Hospital Estate board of trustees will resign."

Famous last words.

The grand jury ended up indicting Coffee for perjury and theft, and a day later he resigned from the board of trustees.

∽ • ∽

Marvin's nightly broadcast on Channel 13, and *The Houston Post's* front-page headlines, had caught the attention of Texas attorney general Jim Mattox, who said that his office would investigate alleged improprieties in the administration of the Hermann Hospital Estate.

Mattox said, "When you've got people who are considered to be reputable business people on these boards, you would think they would deal with matters on a straight up-and-up basis, and I would hope that they would. But I suspect that may not be the case."

He continued, "There are suspicions of inter-dealing, and the problem of what may be out-and-out theft makes it necessary for us to take a look at it. Texas law gives my office the authority to investigate charitable estate trusts. The Hermann Hospital is a charitable estate trust." Mattox went on to say that his office was particularly interested in allegations that William Ryan had destroyed several month's worth of records when he left the hospital in October of 1984.

One purpose of the state attorney general's involvement was to help figure out how to return the Hermann Hospital to its original goal of charity care for Houston's poor, as set forth in the will of the late George Hermann. If need be, the attorney general's office would file a lawsuit to remove the remaining hospital trustees, and they would have a court appoint a special advisor to watch over the reformation of the Hermann Hospital board.

With this announcement, Charles Stricklin, director of development for the hospital, and Ray Valdez, assistant building manager, resigned. Both Stricklin and Valdez had given themselves more than substantial salaries from the hospital. Tax records in 1983 obtained by Channel 13 showed Valdez was paid almost $100,00, plus an additional $9,718. Nice work if you can get it!

∞ • ∞

The tips were still flooding in to Marvin's office. From all the phone calls and bits and pieces of information he was receiving, he had a shopping list that looked as if he hadn't been to the grocery story in a month. It seemed that all of a sudden, everybody in Houston had a story to tell, naming names and uncovering dealings that many people would be embarrassed about. Some of these dealings were merely unethical; others smacked of direct criminal intent.

At the heart of the matter was the questionable financial enrichment of many hospital officials and their friends. Perhaps people in that stratum of life considered these types of business dealings acceptable, but from the responses Marvin was getting from his nightly telecasts, most Houstonians did not. At any rate, Marvin's staff was working overtime trying to separate fact from rumors, and substantiating the allegations that were flooding his office.

Other investigators were equally busy. New auditors were working seven days a week, and in some cases on 24-hour shifts, going through the jumbled records and disorganized hospital disbursements. Daily they uncovered matters that would result in future litigation.

Marvin, who can be a master of understatement when he wants to be, said, "I had heard rumors that some of the hospital trustees were unhappy with this audit and the investigation by Clyde Wilson — understandably so!" Trustee Jack Josey countered, "Wilson has done a great job, and there will be no whitewash of any wrongdoing discovered."

Ultimately (and unfortunately for him and several others) he was right. What he didn't say was that without the champion of the people, Marvin Zindler — who stymied the initial attempt to sweep the matter under the rug — there *would* have been a whitewash.

∞ • ∞

Jack Josey had much more to say, or not say, as the case may be. On the matter of all those questionable junkets, for example — the cruises and the fishing and hunting trips — he said that each trustee had to make up his own mind about making such trips.

On the other hand, trustee Phillip G. Warner, editor-in-chief of the *Houston Chronicle* (which at this point still had little to say regarding the whole matter) had a stronger opinion. "There is nothing wrong with trustees taking judges and businessmen on hunting trips to hospital-owned ranches," he said. "The trips were taken in the ordinary course of business for the purpose of goodwill and public relations for Hermann Hospital."

Joseph Agris, M.D.   287

For Marvin and others, the question was, should a charity hospital own ranches and hunting retreats? And if so, should they be available to only a select few?

For his part, Warner seemed to be puzzled about why the Hermann Hospital Estate matter was such a big deal. In an editorial printed not in his own paper, but in *The Houston Post*, he questioned why Marvin Zindler, the Houston D.A.'s office, the state attorney general's office, several law firmss and a private detective were looking into it. Apparently Warner had not heard Jim Mattox's explanation about why the trustees were being investigated by the attorney general's office.

∾ • ∾

Strangely enough, after Jack Josey's very reassuring remarks about there being "no whitewash," he and Neill Amsler made themselves inaccessible. They could not be reached for comment when it was learned that Josey was a bank director of the Central Bank of Houston, and Amsler was an advisory to the same bank. Hermann Hospital records showed that close to 75% of the hospital's total investments in stocks and securities had been placed in Jack Josey's bank.

Marvin said, "It sounds like there has been some insider horse trading going on....It is really disheartening. I don't think anybody would ever dream of the unbelievable things people are calling in and telling me."

Josey was now under investigation by the Harris County district attorney, and the Texas attorney general, to determine his involvement in Hermann Hospital's purchase of Central Bank stock. Stock purchases from his ex-wife were also called into question.

In earlier interviews, Josey had said that he split his Central Bank stock 50/50 with his ex-wife, Elva Josey Johnson, and had nothing to do with the sale of her stock. Minutes obtained from a Hermann Hospital board meeting, however, showed that Jack Josey made the motion to ratify his wife's stock sale to Hermann Hospital. The hospital board minutes also reflected that Josey's personal attorney, and one of the hospital attorneys, were present. That was a most convenient lapse of memory on Josey's part.

Further research by Marvin showed that the hospital purchased about 30,000 shares from Josey's ex-wife for a total of $900,000. Josey was going to sign the check for the hospital, but the law firm of Vinson and Elkins suggested another trustee should sign the check. It wouldn't look good to sign a check of that magnitude to an ex-wife; people might get the wrong idea.

So John Coffee signed the check to Josey's ex-wife instead. Hospital board minutes also showed that Coffee had seconded Josey's motion for the stock purchase. Now, wasn't that convenient! Jack Josey, who previously denied he had anything to do with the sale, was still sticking to his "no comment" on the matter on Tuesday, April 2, 1985. This was the same type of stock sale that had already led to the grand jury indictment against Coffee. Would Jack Josey meet the same fate?

Another player in the rapidly unfolding drama had caught Marvin's attention early on. This one was a woman, and some say she was a scapegoat. Even Marvin felt some compassion for her when it was all over. Nevertheless, there's no way anyone could say she was blameless.

Late in January of 1985, when the tips were really beginning to flood in, Marvin and other investigators had been receiving information about kickbacks regarding the sale of property owned by the hospital. There were also allegations of outright theft. Real estate broker Susan Menke's name began to surface again and again.

Menke was 33 years old at the time. Only five years before, she had been a second-grade teacher, and now she was said to be worth millions. Needless to say, she was receiving a great deal of media attention for her rapid rise to riches in the real estate field.

Not a few people wondered how an elementary school teacher who got a real estate license when she was only 28 years old could become a multimillionaire so quickly in what was then a tight-fisted, cigar-smoking, backroom, land-dealing, good-ol'-boy system. Sexist as it may have been, many people were wondering what else she was selling. Well, it was just more fuel for the scandal.

Menke's relationship with Hermann began in 1983, when she approached the hospital about selling some land that she knew the hospital owned in Fort Bend County. She explained that she was familiar with the property in Fort Bend County. She was referred to William Ryan, and was given the impression that Ryan handled land sales for the Hermann Hospital Estate. They went out and looked at the land together.

As she explained, "He took a liking to me. He asked me to go to Las Vegas one time." But Menke denied being friends with Ryan. Friends or not, the activities she was to enter into with Ryan were to get her into a whole mess of trouble. For starters, she ended up co-brokering some land deals with him — a clear violation of the law, since he was not a real estate broker.

Like most of the wrongdoers, Susan Menke had a story.

"I felt flattered and honored that he (Ryan) asked me to co-broker a deal," she explained. "I guess I was naive, but I never questioned his integrity. And I never questioned whether he was a broker." Ryan told Marvin that he gave Menke a hospital check for about $30,000 for her brokerage fee. The check was signed by Ryan and John Coffee.

Menke said that when she started to write William Ryan a check for his share of the fee, he told her that he wanted cash to take with him on a trip. She then went to her bank and drew out $13,000 in cash and gave it to him. That should have paid for a great vacation trip!

Menke defended this, saying, "Such a deal is not unusual." Well, sure, Susan; we all know that everyone runs around with tens of thousands in cash to close deals. That's just the way that it's done in Texas, right? There have always been sweetheart deals, and sweethearts to go along with those deals...

Not too long after the first deal, Menke said that Ryan asked her to co-broker another land deal with him. This time he gave her a check for $96,000. Menke would get one-third, and Ryan would keep two-thirds. Menke wrote him back a check for $65,000. She said, "I didn't know who the buyers were, but I felt I had earned the fees."

No comment...

Marvin Zindler was on top of this aspect of the story. Investigator Clyde Wilson was on it too, of course, and he had approached Susan Menke about the real estate transactions. Wilson said, "Susan first denied accepting any money from the estate. She advised us that she didn't know what we were talking about. After we let her read Ryan's statement, she suddenly remembered it."

Continued Wilson, "She signed a full confession, then she accompanied P. M. Clinton, my chief investigator, to Tanglewood Bank and purchased a cashier's check for $48,729.45, payable to the Hermann Hospital Estate."

Susan Menke later explained that she hadn't known anything was wrong at all until Clyde Wilson approached her. She acknowledged that it is against the law to split real estate brokerage fees with someone who is not a real estate broker, but, as she had already explained, she just assumed Ryan *was* a broker, and in any case, she did give the hospital a cashier's check for her share of the original fees.

Unfortunately, this gesture did not abrogate the original intent: theft of funds. Menke's argument was that Ryan had used her to steal from the Estate.

To add to her troubles, it had also apparently slipped Menke's mind that her own real estate license was expired. Menke claimed that she accidentally allowed it to lapse. In any case, she had been selling hospital property without a license.

Referring to Marvin and the press's continued investigation and reporting of Hermann Hospital's mismanagement, Menke's attorney, Marian Rosen, said, "I think a great effort is being made to deflect the focus from some of the true culprits to people involved in very minor matters." Attorney Rosen charged that the culprits were hospital officials. "We are losing sight of the fact that all of the work she (Ms. Menke) did was to benefit the hospital."

But, darn it all, Marvin and the public still refused to see the shades of gray. They seemed to be looking at every newly revealed misdeed in terms of black and white, right and wrong, good and bad. Whether it involved a few thousand dollars or millions, it was still theft. Marvin said, "These are major cases. These are serious offenses. They can set a standard for a long time."

Based on Marvin's television reports, as well as investigations by Clyde Wilson and the district attorney's office, Menke was indicted two months later by a Harris County grand jury. She was charged with stealing more than $48,000 of hospital money by splitting two real estate commissions with Ryan. Ryan was indicted as well for his part in the two hospital land sales.

The Hermann Hospital Estate asked for $1,609,525 in damages from Susan Menke, Menke's real estate firm, and the Texas Commerce Bank National Association, which cashed the bogus checks. The lawsuit alleged that Menke performed no services in return for her fee.

Menke's attorney filed a motion in July to dismiss theft charges against Menke, but State District Judge Joseph Guarino denied the motion. Attorney Rosen said the indictment should have alleged specifically what Menke's intentions were, but the public seemed to think that had been made all too clear, and it seemed that the judge agreed.

At Menke's trial in November 1985, William Ryan testified that he had indeed used Menke to steal from the Hermann Hospital Estate Fund. He said, "Susan Menke was a means to an end…I got my mind working, and I needed some money, and I saw this as an opportunity to get some." (Under the circumstances, perhaps that was a poor choice of words.)

When Menke's defense attorney cross-examined Ryan, he testified that Menke did not do any work to justify the more than $48,000 in commissions which he had approved paying her in 1983 and 1984. Attorney Rosen presented several exhibits of maps and other information on property owned by the Hermann Hospital Estate in Fort Bend and Brazoria Counties. Rosen contended this represented information about the properties that her client developed, which would be helpful in their sale. In other words, she *had* done legitimate work for the money.

Ryan testified that one of the two hospital checks he illegally ordered written to Susan Menke was a "finder's fee" for her part in negotiations to sell the property. In fact, the land was never sold. With continued questioning, Ryan testified he had no authority to pay a finder's fee, and that, furthermore, in his nearly 15 years of working for the hospital, no other finder's fees were ever paid.

Overall, it seemed that William Ryan had been trying to soften and play down Susan Menke's involvement. He implied that this sweet, young thing was just in the wrong place at the wrong time with the wrong people, and was swept away by the intrigue.

Others disagreed. She had to enter into this with her eyes open, they said. She couldn't have just accidentally amassed millions in only five years in the real estate business.

When all was said and done, the jury convicted Susan Menke of theft of $48,729 in Hermann Hospital Estate funds.

Marvin's continued coverage of the Hermann Hospital scandal was returning hundreds of thousands of dollars to the Hospital Estate fund almost weekly. And new individuals were being sought out and indicted as well.

Marvin said that he thought the trustees had painted themselves into a corner when they denied knowledge of certain transactions, such as the Josey-Coffee Bank stock sales to the Hermann Hospital Estate. It was his opinion that they would find themselves hard-pressed in court to explain *why* they didn't know what was going on. It was strikingly obvious that they had made speculative investments and had improperly invested money in unproductive assets. They had breached their duties by participating in self-dealing. They had also expended funds for purposes unauthorized by the will that had established the Hermann Hospital Foundation. And, most disturbing of all in Marvin's view, these trustees had failed to operate a public charity hospital.

∾ • ∾

On April 18, 1985, Channel 13 announced the resignation of Jack Josey from Hermann Hospital Estate board of trustees. The following day it was a front-page headline in *The Houston Post*. Who would be the next to fall? Go get 'em, Maaaarrvin!

If the grand jury found evidence that Jack Josey and his ex-wife also had sold their bank stock to the hospital estate, Josey could be charged with a second-degree felony: misapplication of fiduciary funds. Divorce documents had been uncovered showing Josey promised his ex-wife that she could sell her stock to members of the family.

It was also interesting that Elva Josey, now Elva Johnson, used the proceeds of the stock sale to pay substantial debts owed to Josey's oil company and Josey's mother. Talk about incest!

∾ • ∾

Six months after Marvin began his investigation of the Hermann Hospital trust, a third grand jury began its probe into ex-trustee Jack S. Josey's handling of hospital funds. The count kept going up. Since Marvin's telecast in January, four people had been indicted for theft. Would Josey be number five? This grand jury, however, ended its term without taking any action, and a fourth was set for August.

Seven months after Marvin's initial reports, another cool million was recovered by the hospital. In a surprise move, Jack Josey agreed to spend at least $1,000,000 to buy back bank stock the hospital had purchased from his ex-wife when he was on the hospital board. The current trustees sent a letter to prosecutors noting the matter was legally resolved as far as they were concerned.

Jack Josey walked away without an indictment, and the hospital got another million dollars back. But Marvin was on the move again, still determined that there would be a clean sweep before it was all through.

Although Marvin never did get himself that bullet-proof vest, his safety became a matter of concern for the FBI and the Harris County sheriff's department. At one point during the investigation, Harris County Sheriff Jack Heard assigned several deputies to watch over Marvin. For his own safety, Marvin was warned not to follow his usual routine. The bodyguards stayed with him a month, and went everywhere with him, even to the golf course. They camped out in his home, and Gertrude, ever the gracious hostess, even fed them. Finally Marvin put his foot down. "If they're going to kill, me, they will kill me," he said. "No more bodyguards." I guess that's another reason for Marvin not to be president of the United States. He'd never put up with all those Secret Service nuisances hanging around him all the time.

One phenomenon resulting from the Hermann Hospital Estate mess was "the incredible shrinking board." Within the space of a few months, John Coffee was gone, Jack Josey was history, and *Chronicle* editor-in-chief Phillip Warner resigned after it was discovered that the board's bylaws prohibited lawyers from being members. The four remaining board members were Walter Mischer, Jr., Corbin Robertson, Jr., David Hannah, Jr., and Edward Randall III.

Despite the temporary decline in their numbers, there was reason to be optimistic about the future of the Hermann Hospital board of trustees. In May of 1985, Texas Attorney General Jim Mattox had dropped his lawsuit against the trustees. This would prevent a lengthy and costly court battle. The Estate wasn't getting off scot-free, of course. The terms of the agreement between Mattox and Estate officials dictated that the $4.3 million in charity care provided by Hermann Hospital in 1984 would increase to $14.3 million by 1990. Additionally, the estate would have to sell off at least $100 million in assets — chiefly real estate, buildings, and other non-income-producing investments — that were not currently dedicated to funding medical care for Houston's indigent. Proceeds from the sale were to be placed in a charitable care endowment, and in a capital and operating reserve fund to pay for new buildings and diagnostic equipment.

The board members, needless to say, were very pleased.

As for the board itself, everyone seemed to agree that it was time for a change. The four remaining trustees vowed to make the board more representative of Houston's diverse community; no longer would it be a bastion for rich and influential white males. And, indeed, the board soon welcomed its first African American, its first Hispanic, and its first woman. Marvin, who had long been doing his part to push for diversity on the board, was delighted.

Other changes were afoot too. Revisions to the board's bylaws imposed a 10-year limit on the terms of the trustees, and the longstanding restrictions against attorneys and members of the clergy were removed. Administrative safeguards were instituted to help prevent future scandals. These included stricter internal auditing and purchasing procedures for goods and services.

The new board issued a statement saying they were confident that the scandal was all but over. They were a little too optimistic, for it would take more than six months, and a fourth grand jury, before most of the final indictments and jail terms were handed down.

Still, there was reason to celebrate, Marvin felt. Not only had his exposé of the Hermann Hospital fiasco been instrumental in returning millions of dollars to the Hospital, but it also helped bring to fruition a broad-based Hermann Hospital board with new trustees who had the interest of all Houstonians at heart. Marvin felt that the new board consisted of individuals who would turn the situation around, establishing a hospital that would pay for itself and provide quality indigent care to Houstonians, as originally intended. "The new administrators," he said, "can now proceed with the business of the hospital as intended and focus on patient care."

As events of the next few years would prove, Marvin, much like the trustees themselves, was a little too optimistic on some of those counts. But if he was optimistic in some ways, he was very realistic in others. He knew that as far as the current scandal was concerned, other cow patties yet remained unturned. And he wasn't going to let loose of this investigation until every last lead was followed up and every individual involved found himself or herself in the public eye, or, better yet, behind bars.

God help the wrongdoers; Marvin and the posse were not finished.

C·H·A·P·T·E·R 28

A TRUST RESTORED?

s the first anniversary of Marvin's news-breaking series approached, the Hermann Hospital Estate scandal story seemed to be losing its luster. Public interest was waning. Part of the reason was that grand jury presentations in this very complicated case had had to be put on hold for several months, while prosecutors awaited the results of investigative audit reports. And part of the reason had to have been that the public was suffering from "scandal fatigue." Following a scandal is tiring business, and after awhile, even the most passionate followers can get pretty burned out.

In reality, the story was far from over as 1986 began. There would be more grand jury hearings, more indictments, more sentences. A number of defendants would receive prison sentences, some would receive probation, a few would get "shock probation." Some of these processes took several years.

There was no doubt the scandal had been rich fodder for the news media in 1985, and, like most scandals, it had even become a laughing matter. The Houston Press Club, at its 34th annual Gridiron Show in September of 1985, presented a skit called *The Best Little Hospital in Texas,* which relayed the story of "Generous Hospital," and included songs by the "Hermann's Hermits." The songs, parodies of 1960s hits by the pop group "Herman's Hermits," included "We're Into Something Good," a scathing mockery of greedy estate trustees, and "Can't You Hear My Heart Beat," a reference to the abject fear caused by the D.A.'s investigations.

It's true the city needed a little comic relief, but the scandal was still serious business for those involved, investigators and investigatees alike. Marvin was still on the story, of course, as was *The Houston Post,* and now the *Chronicle* as well, though for the most part the scandal still wasn't making the front page on the latter.

To Marvin, this was still a very important news story, and he uncovered yet more dirt and slime as he pursued the leads that continued to come in.

∽ • ∽

On a cold January afternoon a little over a year after Marvin's first television broadcast about the Hermann Hospital scandal, former real estate broker Susan Menke was sentenced to four years of hard time in prison. Marvin felt to some extent that she had been used, as even William Ryan had admitted at her November trial. Marvin pointed out that Menke had been cooperative and had provided information throughout the investigation and trials.

Marvin, who wanted to help Menke, did a story that was in some aspects supportive of her. He believed, as did many other people, that four years hard time was a rather severe sentence — particularly compared to others who had manipulated and stolen millions from the hospital, and were allowed to pass into anonymity.

However, Susan Menke didn't have to do hard time after all. Although she lost her initial appeal, she remained free on bond pending further appeal. In 1989 she finally served 65 days in the Harris County jail and was released on "shock probation." Shock probation was designed to give offenders a taste of two to four months in prison before being freed on probation, the idea being that the time behind bars would shock them into mending their ways.

∽ • ∽

What about some of the other key players in this scandal? Well, some did indeed slip into relative anonymity, and some went on to bigger and badder things.

Neill Amsler, Jr. pleaded "no contest" to 29 counts of theft from the estate, and received a probated sentence. He retired and moved to a ranch in Vanderpool in the Texas Hill Country — the ranch that was allegedly fenced at Hermann Hospital's expense. Under the terms of his settlement, Amsler's $2.6 million dollar life insurance policy, the premiums for which he had billed the Estate, would be made payable to Hermann Trust. This, said Amsler's attorney, would more than make up for any property he took. As for the ranch property in Vanderpool, all or part of that would also go to the Hermann Trust upon the death of Amsler and his wife Mollie.

On the other hand, Amsler's cohort, Ray Valdez, had pled "not guilty" to the charge of stealing more than $25,000 from the hospital in various ways. Valdez continued to insist that he was just a sardine amongst the killer whales, and that the gifts he accepted and trips he took were a common practice, approved by the trustees. He did admit to concealing expenses in the hospital records. When questioned by prosecutor Don Stricklin, Valdez replied that he was just following the secret procedures established by his boss, Neill Amsler. Nevertheless, Valdez received a six-year sentence. At that time, it was the stiffest sentence that had yet been handed down in the Hermann Hospital Estate matter.

Valdez's attorney said, "Valdez is being made a scapegoat for the whole scandal." Which, of course, was what everyone had just heard a few months previously, when Susan Menke received her four-year sentence.

What of Charles Stricklin, former director of development for the hospital, who resigned from his position at the same time Valdez did? Stricklin was originally charged with felony theft for purchasing an estate-owned Oldsmobile 98 at $9,000 below its value. However, he repaid the $9,000 and cooperated with investigators. He agreed to plead no contest to a reduced charge of misdemeanor theft, and was sentenced to a year's probation.

∞ • ∞

The paternity suit against William "Bill" Smith was settled in August of 1986, and nothing further was heard from Nancy Stack. Smith was indicted on a second-degree felony theft charge for allegedly taking pleasure trips to Las Vegas and New York at the expense of Hermann Hospital. No charges were brought in Smith's issuing of interior decorating contracts to his paramour. In late 1986, despite his attorney's pleas to prosecutors to look at all the good things he'd done for the hospital, Smith was convicted of stealing more than $160,000 from the hospital. In April of 1987, he was sentenced to seven years in prison, but was released on probation after serving 110 days.

Two of Smith's cruise buddies and fellow Hermann Hospital officials, Gary McHenry and Larry Bowermon, pleaded no contest to felony theft charges in May of 1986. They each received a five-year probated term.

∞ • ∞

The other big Bill, William Ryan, didn't fare too well. He pleaded guilty to charges of theft, and was sentenced to a six-year plea-bargained term. He was paroled after serving about a year and a half of his sentence, and he had his parole transferred to California, where he said he had relatives. He moved there to begin a new life.

He began a new life, all right; unfortunately, it included gambling. Actually, Ryan had been a gambler for a long time. Even private investigator Clyde Wilson had said the amount of money Ryan stole from the Hermann Hospital Estate was incredible, considering that Ryan and his family ended up without any money at all. The reason? Ryan was, among his many other vices and excesses, a gambling addict.

That addiction followed him to California; as those in the recovery community like to say, the "geographical cure" rarely works. Ryan was used to having big money, and gambling seemed to him to be the most feasible way to get it. He also apparently owed the IRS a lot of money, and claimed he couldn't get a legitimate job because they were going to attach his wages. Well, what's a fellow to do when he can't get a legitimate job, owes the IRS big time, and his gambling gig turns out not to be so lucrative? If he's William Ryan, he becomes an armed robber.

Granted, Bill Ryan wasn't just any old thug. Even the robbery investigator with the San Jose, California Police Department said that Ryan's m.o. was pretty classy, as armed robberies go. He always dressed in a three-piece suit, was always very polite, saying please and thank you, and, oh, yes, the gun was a toy, though nobody knew it until the investigating officer recovered it.

In any case, Ryan ended up in the Santa Clara County, California jail after confessing to nine holdups that, he explained, "were the only way to survive."

Marvin says, "Ryan did prison time in California, and when he completed his sentence, he returned to Houston." Dr. Howard Seigler, the Texas Medical Center internist who had been one of the informants in the Hermann case, always had a big heart and tried to help others. It was Dr. Seigler who brought Ryan back to Houston to help rehabilitate him. Perhaps the good doctor felt sorry for Ryan. Well, I guess what goes around comes around. Ryan ended up working for Dr. Seigler on his estate, serving as butler, handyman and groundskeeper. He even stayed on after Dr. Seigler died.

John B. Coffee, erstwhile stock trader, got off pretty easy, all thing considered. In 1987 he was acquitted of two perjury charges concerning his shady stock deals. His defense lawyer said that Coffee had suffered brain damage as a result of a stroke not long before his grand jury appearance, and had simply forgotten some transactions that had taken place. Well, brain damage is a nice defense if you can swing it. At any rate, a felony theft charge still remained.

Upon dismissal of the perjury charges, Coffee, who was 76 and in bankruptcy, said he felt "vindicated." It should be noted that the judge who found Coffee not guilty, State District Judge Norman Lanford, seemed to feel obliged to qualify that Coffee was not on trial "for being a liar in general or for profiteering."

As noted earlier, this is far from a complete accounting of the Hermann Hospital Estate saga. All the minutiae of what happened to whom are a matter of public record, for those who care to pursue the matter further.

In some respects the Hermann Hospital travesty was no different from dozens of other scandals. For one thing, you could hardly say that justice was completely done, despite the noble efforts of investigators, prosecutors, and, of course, Marvin. Admittedly, some of the bigger fish in this murky sea were able to dive deeper to the cleaner, clearer waters below, freeing themselves from the storm that Marvin and the press had brought to the surface. The waves of scandal rose and fell for more than a year, and the flood waters took their toll, but eventually they receded.

Isn't that the way it always is with any big news story?

Now here we are in the 21st century, and some might be asking if this old scandal is still even relevant. Marvin thinks so, and so do I.

As Marvin and others said on more than one occasion, George Hermann himself would have been outraged had he known about the appalling way in which his charitable fund has been misused over the years. Hermann, who was one of Houston's most eccentric millionaires and beloved philanthropists, would not have looked kindly on the excesses of the trustees and officials.

Born in 1843 of Swiss immigrant parents, George Hermann was, despite his generosity, a tight-fisted man who parted with a nickel only when there was no other way out. It's even said that he never married because he felt wives were just too expensive. In truth, he was terribly shy and probably socially inept. Social phobias aside, he was otherwise fearless — he fought for the Confederacy during the Civil War — and he was also a shrewd businessman. After the war, he joined a cattle drive and learned the cattle business from the bottom up. He formed a successful cattle partnership with two other men; his knowledge and their money enabled all three to become very wealthy. He also got into the lumber business, and made a fair profit from that as well.

Hermann settled in Houston, where he had fond memories of his boyhood. It was in the Bayou City that he began in earnest to amass his fortune, showing touches of genius along the way.

To solve the problem of his loggers being arrested for being drunk on the wild streets of downtown Houston, Hermann simply purchased a large downtown lot where his employees could sleep it off after a Saturday night drunk. This would avoid their being locked up and missing the next day's work. Today, that lot is known as Hermann Square, and it happens to be located right in front of City Hall. In his will, Hermann left this lot to the City of Houston. In accordance with the will, the property must remain as a "resting spot or breathing place where one can lie down and snooze, even if recovering from a night of overindulgence." According to Hermann's will, the area is a safe haven, and if you're in the downtown area and you've partied too hard, you can spend the night in Hermann Square. Under the terms of the will, you cannot be arrested for loitering or for intoxication. One wonders how many police officers and other public servants know of this…

In the 1880s, Hermann decided to travel to the big cities of the east coast. While in New York City, he was captivated by Central Park and told a friend that maybe Houston would have such a park someday. Thanks to him, it does, and it is known as Hermann Park. It covers 270 acres that Hermann owned on Fannin Street at the edge of town (and had acquired for only 50 cents an acre!).

George Hermann didn't limit his land purchases to the Houston area; he obtained properties in surrounding areas as well. It was said that Hermann traded two good mules and a wagon for 30 acres of property near Humble. Shortly thereafter, oil was discovered on his property. If his fortune hadn't been secure before, it certainly was now.

In 1914, George Hermann had problems with indigestion, and it was discovered that he had stomach cancer. There were no hospital facilities in Houston that could manage this difficult problem, so he went back east to a Baltimore hospital.

Hermann was bothered by the fact that proper medical help was not available in Houston. But that was all to change, and very soon. Before he died of his cancer on October 21, 1914, he instructed in his will that the bulk of his 2.5-million-dollar fortune be used to build a charity hospital for the people of Houston. This would become Houston's Hermann Hospital.

The hospital was to be managed by the multi-million dollar Hermann Hospital Estate Trust Fund. According to the will, the estate would be governed by a seven-member board of trustees. The board would be self-perpetuating, which, as many have said, was probably the source of much of the evil that later came.

When George Hermann died in the Baltimore hospital, his body was returned to Houston by train. The body lay in state at the home of one of his friends, and thousands of Houstonians lined up to pay their respects to this eccentric millionaire, neighbor, good friend and philanthropist.

Millions of people — indigent and wealthy alike — have reaped the benefits of the Hermann Hospital and its dedicated medical staff. Both Houstonians and visitors have enjoyed the Hermann Park and Zoo and the Museum District. All are a fitting tribute to this "tight-fisted Swiss immigrant, Houstonian, Texan and cowboy."

It was nothing less than an insult to George Hermann's legacy for the people in positions of public trust to take advantage of their position. This is just one reason Marvin got so riled up over the Hermann Hospital Estate matter.

The deeper legal and moral issues did not escape Marvin either. Beyond the insult to Hermann's legacy, the actions of the board members had made a mockery of the very concept of "trust."

The history of the trust is old, dating back to the "wardships" of ancient Rome. A wardship was a trust destined to protect the property of someone too young or otherwise not competent to make decisions. Under Roman law, the property was to be administered by a guardian or ward, and any violation of that trust was a special crime known as breach of fiduciary duty. In Roman days, a trust was considered so sacred that an unfaithful guardian was branded as "infamous," and deemed untrustworthy for any purpose whatever. Not only was all self-dealing by the guardian forbidden, but the guardian would be required to return double the money or property stolen or negligently managed.

American trust law has preserved most of this, which raises the question: Was the return of monies that Marvin secured from the trustees enough? Should the hospital trustees have been required to pay double or even triple damages? Or were their disgrace and jail terms the equivalent? Perhaps these are all moot points now, but they were questions Marvin mulled over for years.

Under the terms of the trust, a trustee must never, under any circumstances, profit or self-deal from the estate property. In the Hermann Hospital case, as Marvin points out, self-dealing seemed to be one of the smaller infractions.

Waxing philosophical, Marvin says, "Betrayal of the relationship of a charitable trust has to rank as a deep moral corruption. It corrupts the party who betrays the sacred trust, as well as the people whom he deprives of its stated good. And the intent of a good man — George Hermann, who formed the trust — is annulled. Last but not least, society itself is given scandal and bad example."

Marvin says he was flabbergasted at how little indignation there was among the local gentry once the corruption of the Hermann Hospital board came to the surface. Even today, he wonders why, but he thinks he knows the answer. "Could it be that we think the rich are different?" he asks rhetorically. "Do we place the rich in a different perspective? Do the rich sit on a higher throne?"

That we as a society are in awe of wealth is undeniable. As Susan Menke, who ended up being one of the fall guys (or gals) put it, "I was attending a meeting of these trustees in luxurious settings. I thought I was in the presence of God."

"God indeed," mutters Marvin. "The irony is that the founder of the Hermann Estate trust, although incredibly rich, was a simple man of the greatest integrity. He loved, fed and lived among the poor in life, and sought to care for them in death."

More disturbing, Marvin adds, is the ideology of a society that even today seems to believe white-collar crimes — bribery, embezzlement, trust betrayal, tax evasion — are not serious. In fact, Marvin recalls, such crimes were not seriously prosecuted until the 1960s. Why was that? To Marvin the answer is clear.

"It's because the class of people who commit these types of crime are usually the very rich, the very powerful, the 'good people,'" he says. "Good people cheat on income tax returns, good people embezzle, good officials of a hospital trust take bribes and grant favors to friends, good people administer a hospital trust fund to their advantage.

"Because these people who commit white-collar crimes are not considered dangerous to society, they get away with it for many, many years. They are the rich and the powerful who create jobs and support the fine arts and other philanthropies. As a result, what they do is not seen as a crime."

Marvin, on the other hand, feels it is white-collar crime that really devastates the moral and economic fiber of society. A charitable trust which is betrayed corrupts and hurts us all more than all the robberies and burglaries in Houston. It damages all of us to see these models, these "good people" steal and betray their office of trust. The public does not, and should not, expect that from them.

Marvin is a philosopher with a practical point of view. He still sees the world mainly in terms of right and wrong; there are no in-betweens.

As Marvin points out, scripture has it that the source of all evil is not money, but the desire for money. Though we are commanded to pray for our daily bread — for which we must have *some* money — we get into trouble when we ask for more. When we get more, most of us do not do well with it, and we lust for even more.

There are exceptions, of course, says Marvin — for instance, George Hermann. Here was a man who worked hard, and by that work and some luck came into a great deal of money in his time. Hermann continued to live simply, sharing his wealth with the lowly and the poor during his life and after his death.

Marvin's still remembers what got him the angriest back in '85-'86, as the web of the hospital board's misdeeds became more and more tangled. It was the fact that the board was indeed maintaining a hospital, "but not the hospital George Hermann intended." There was, he said, "a stench of corruption surrounding the whole enterprise."

And you know Marvin. He just couldn't stand by and do nothing.

Marvin has been involved in many provocative, interesting, and worthwhile stories in his career, but still considers the Hermann Hospital Estate scandal his most productive story. Millions of dollars of charitable funds were recovered. The hospital board of trustees was replaced with members who represented all aspects of the Houston community (well, at least for awhile). The hospital remains a viable institution and has become the teaching arm for the University of Texas Medical School. In 1997, Hermann Hospital merged with the Memorial Hospital System and is now part of the Memorial Hermann Hospital System.

Don't get me wrong. I'm not claiming, and neither is Marvin, that he single-handedly exposed the evil ways of the Hermann Hospital board of trustees back in the 1980s and made them clean up their act. Although Marvin deserves ample credit for making such a big deal about it at the very beginning, many other people were involved in bringing the story to light and the wrongdoers to justice. The original investigators, most notably Clyde Wilson, deserve much credit. It was Wilson who really helped Marvin break the story wide open. Don Walker deserves credit for insisting that the "irregularities" be investigated in the first place. And let's not forget the now-defunct *Houston Post's* Pete Brewton, a dedicated newsgatherer who, like Marvin, was willing to risk everything to get the true story. Marvin and Pete helped each other with this story almost from the beginning. It was very unusual for a TV reporter to team up with a newspaperman, but team up they did, and the resulting stories were that much better for their joint effort.

Nor is anyone pretending that this is a happily-ever-after fairy tale. A board of trustees is made up of human beings, and humans are fallible. Even though the 1980s are long gone, greed and conflict of interest didn't disappear with them. Unfortunately, despite all the troubles in 1985, despite the indictments and sentences and ruined reputations — yes, even despite the deals that were ultimately made and the reforms that came about as part of those deals — scandal threatened to rear its ugly head again at Hermann several times over the next decade. More financial improprieties came to light, and more board members were obliged to resign.

Besides that, the hospital drew criticism for turning away too many poor patients, in clear violation of the spirit of its founder, George Hermann. (Well, hospitals have to make money, don't they?) The outrage over this issue caused the hospital to forge new and better policies for the treatment of the indigent.

Furthermore, despite the nods to diversity that were made during the reforms of the mid-80s, by 1992, former Attorney General Jim Mattox and former Assistant Attorney General John Vasquez were publicly stating that they were disappointed with the makeup of the board. It was, they claimed, made up of bluebloods who were not familiar with the needs of the unemployed and the poor. Said Vasquez, "I don't believe George Hermann meant to populate the board with the elite of Houston."

But Hermann Hospital is alive and well. Over the years, and with varying degrees of success, a number of people have been hired to help clean up the image as well as the business affairs of the hospital.

People aren't perfect, and neither are hospitals; that's never going to change. In real life, most stories do not have a happy-ever-after ending, and that's probably not going to change any time soon either. One thing that has changed since the 1980s is that there is considerably more accountability for people in positions of public trust. The media as well as the public have become very sensitive to even a suggestion of wrongdoing. Improprieties still occur, but it's more difficult to get away with them for long. There are too many eyes watching — and rest assured that at least one pair of eyes is watching from behind blue sunglasses.

You could say that the 1985 Hermann Hospital Estate mess was another battle Marvin won. At the very least, he won the battle to make it public in the first place. Ultimately, however, the real winners were the people of Houston and Harris County, who could avail themselves of this excellent hospital facility. No, the war isn't over, but these days there are many more people fighting to preserve the legacy of one of Houston's most famous philanthropists, George Hermann — who, like Marvin Zindler, was also a legend in his own time.

9

Man On
A Mission

Marvin Takes On
The World

ZINDLERISM, GLOBAL STYLE

lthough Marvin Zindler is a native Texan, lives in Texas, and passionately loves Texas, he is no isolationist. Marvin has always had a keen interest in what's going on in the rest of the world, and he has been traveling the globe for several decades. Not only has he accompanied me on medical and humanitarian missions to some of the most remote and even dangerous places on the planet, but he and his crew have gone on many other newsgathering, humanitarian and search-and-rescue trips to countries all over the world. Every trip Marvin takes offers a different set of adventures, but if there is one thing that all of his journeys have in common it is this: From the moment he steps off the plane at his destination, the place and the people he has come to see fall under the spell of that one-of-a-kind phenomenon known as "Zindlerism."

Zindlerism assumes many forms. However it manifests — whether in Marvin's unique ability to maneuver through bureaucratic red tape or convoluted protocol to get his crew into countries where few Westerners have ever been, or his uncanny knack for conducting the frankest of interviews with normally reticent world leaders, or even his talent for bringing smiles to the faces of people whose harsh circumstances normally afford them little reason to smile — Zindlerism, global style, is a force to be reckoned with.

Since Marvin has been a trailblazer for just about his entire career, it comes as no surprise that he continues to forge new trails in his world travels. In October of 2000, for example, when things seemed to be getting more tense in the Middle East — again — Channel 13 sent a team out to report on the situation. Reporter Art Rascón was given the assignment of reporting on a group of Houstonians who had recently gone over there on a long-planned vacation to the Holy Land. And Marvin went to do a series of reports on politics and religion in the region. He traveled to Syria, Jordan and Israel, with one of his goals being to get Israeli and Palestinian viewpoints on current affairs. "I got answers I didn't think I'd get," he said. He always does. Remarkably, he and his team had no difficulties whatsoever entering, traveling within, or leaving any area, not even Syria, which had very rarely welcomed film crews from the West. It was Zindlerism in action, once again.

Marvin interviewed former Israeli prime minister Shimon Peres, and asked Peres if he thought Israel and Palestine would be at peace in their (Marvin's and Peres') lifetime. The former prime minister replied, "Well, looking at you and me, I think maybe so." Despite new hostilities that broke out shortly after that, Marvin said he believed that Peres still stood for peace. "They all want peace," he said.

Zindlerism may not be able to bring about peace in the Middle East, particularly in light of the events of September 11, 2001[1]; nevertheless, the accomplishments of Marvin and his intrepid team — most notably, producer Lori Reingold and cameraman Bob Dows — are nothing short of amazing. Marvin has helped bridge gaps between countless people of different cultures; his reports and series have given his television audiences an eye-opening look at the rest of the world, and Marvin himself must surely have been an eye-opening experience for the people in the countries he has visited. From a practical and humanitarian standpoint, Marvin's many missions have helped bring badly needed assistance to some of the poorest and most desperate citizens of the global village.

What I offer in this section are just a few of the many tales of Marvin's travels — and, in some cases, Marvin's and my travels. A comprehensive travelogue would fill up another entire book or two. The accounts here cover some of the adventures from the late 1980s through the late 1990s, but Marvin and I both still travel extensively, and probably will until we drop in our tracks. I hope you enjoy reading about these adventures as much as Marvin and I enjoyed having them.

---

[1] See the end of this section for some thoughts on the September 11 terrorist attack on America.

C·H·A·P·T·E·R 29

A RIGHT TO BE FREE:
VIETNAM, 1988

Son Van Nguyen was a Houston resident and an American citizen. Born in Vietnam, he had been in the United States since 1975. He had worked for a United States construction firm near Cam Rhan Bay during the Vietnamese War, but had been forced to flee Vietnam during the fall of Saigon in 1975. A devout Vietnamese Catholic fiercely opposed to Communism, Son knew that if he stayed in his native country, he would have little chance of surviving after the Communists took over.

Son Van Nguyen was also a distraught father. While in Vietnam, Son had been married with an infant daughter, and another child due at any time. When the fall of Saigon appeared inevitable, he had to make the heartrending decision to either leave his wife and baby or be killed. Because it was too dangerous for his pregnant wife to travel the road to the sea — and to freedom — she stayed behind with family. Son hoped that when the turmoil was resolved, he would be able to return or send for his wife and the children.

Son was one of the lucky refugees who made it to the sea and on to America. His wife delivered a healthy and beautiful young son, but shortly after the birth of the child, she died an unexplained death.

It was 1988 now, and Son had not seen his beloved daughter in 13 years. He had never seen his son, save for in a few photographs that had been smuggled out of Vietnam and mailed to him by friends. Over these many long years, this was the only correspondence that had reached him. The last Son had heard, the children were alive and well, living with an uncle in a small village outside Saigon, which was now called Ho Chi Minh City.

Son had family in Houston; his parents and his brother Nam had also successfully escaped Vietnam. For many years, the family had tried everything in their power to bring Son's children to the United States, but the Vietnamese government had repeatedly ignored their request to allow the children to leave. Son grew increasingly frustrated, but felt helpless to do anything.

When Son received the news that the uncle who had been caring for the children had died, he did not know whether the surviving aunts would be able to take care of them, or if they would be placed in an orphanage in Ho Chi Minh City. It became even more important for Son to try to get his children back. But so far he and his family had had no luck at all.

Then Son's brother Nam saw Marvin Zindler on television, and something told him, *Maybe this is the man to help us*. The more he thought about it, the more convinced he was that not only could Marvin help them, but he was the only one who could do so.

Nam convinced Son that going to Marvin was the best course of action. He didn't have to remind his brother that they had already asked a lot of people for help, and had only been told to do more paperwork. "That is all they do: paperwork, paperwork, paperwork," Nam complained.

So Son and Nam gathered up their many years' worth of correspondence and brought them to Marvin at the Channel 13 television studio. Son told Marvin that the youngsters had actually been approved to enter the United States in 1985, but he could not get any further answers from the Vietnamese government. The situation seemed hopeless. Son explained to Marvin that the family had all but given up hope.

The problems of the Nguyen family were hardly unique. By the 1980s, there were somewhere between 15,000 and 20,000 children and family members wishing to leave Vietnam for the United States. The U.S. government established the Vietnamese Orderly Departure Program, and later the Amerasian Homecoming Act. Marvin knew that these programs had been interrupted as the result of political maneuvering by both the Vietnamese and the United States governments. Those who wanted to leave were faced with voluminous paperwork and government red tape, and there were rumors of corruption and payoffs, particularly on the Vietnamese side.

Marvin and his staff were impressed by what the Nguyen family had done — the stacks of papers they had filled out, the records they had kept, the phone calls that had been made, and, most of all, the persistence of a father who wished to reunite his family. It was going to be a challenge, but Marvin promised Son and the Nguyen family that he would do all that he could to bring the children to Texas — "even if I have to go over to Vietnam myself."

And Marvin always keeps his promises.

To make good on his promise to the Nguyens, Marvin first went to the Houston Director of Immigration, Ron Parra. Mr. Parra updated Marvin on the immigration status of children from Vietnam. Basically he confirmed what Marvin and the Nguyens already knew, that numerous requests had been sent to the Vietnamese government, and there had not been any response to these requests.

For all practical purposes, Marvin and the Nguyens had reached a dead end. The bureaucratic route had not worked all of these years for the Nguyen family, and it was not going to work now — not even for Marvin. Marvin knew that there was no sense knocking your head against the bureaucratic wall. He has always sad, "If you can't get over the mountain, you either have to go around or tunnel through it. It may take longer, but the end result is the same."

Still, he was in a quandary. "I made a promise to Nguyen and his family that I was going to do everything possible to bring those children to Houston and reunite them with their family," he says. "I hoped that I could keep that promise. I asked myself over and over again how I could solve this problem. It became a challenge — one of the most difficult in my career."

Marvin and his staff worked very hard on this problem through many United States agencies. But they had to proceed carefully, both in Houston and Washington, D.C., because the Vietnam situation still raged in the hearts of many at home and abroad. Not only was there the problem of 20,000 children who had not been allowed to leave, but the POW and MIA questions loomed large as well. Everything was made more complicated by the fact that there was no direct diplomatic channel between the United States and Vietnam.

Even if Marvin kept his promise and got on an airplane and flew to Vietnam, he did not know if he would be allowed to land, much less to enter the country. No American aircraft had entered Vietnam air space or landed in Ho Chi Minh City since the end of the war. Marvin says, "I told the Nguyen family that there are no guarantees in this world. We can only do the best that we know how, and that is what I and my staff were doing."

Marvin had begun working on the Nguyens' case in June of 1988. Now the warm, hot, sultry months of Houston's summer were fast disappearing, the days getting shorter and marginally cooler. Marvin, who could usually cut the red tape and get to the man in charge, was having unprecedented problems with this case.

Throughout the waning days of summer he agonized over his unfulfilled promise. Hundreds of phone calls had been made, and thousands of hours spent, but at each turn, there seemed to be further bureaucratic obstruction. Marvin now understood the frustration of Son Van Nguyen and his family, and felt the weight of the fact that they had now put all of their hopes in him. By now Marvin was not only frustrated; he was mad.

He could appreciate the exasperation of all the other Vietnamese families who also wanted to bring their children and other family members to the United States. The problem had become more to him than just a matter of bringing these two children home. Marvin kept thinking about the thousands of other children still in Vietnam. He also could not forget about that one part of his promise to the Nguyens: *Even if I have to go over there myself!"* He was not unwilling to go, of course, but the logistics seemed overwhelming. Then it struck him.

Marvin said, "I thought of my good friend, Congressman Mickey Leland." He called the congressman's office and made an appointment to visit Leland and discuss the problem. If anybody could help him, Congressman Leland could.

He was right. Mickey Leland sprang into action, first contacting the United Nations in New York City. Since there was no diplomatic exchange between the United States and Vietnam, the UN could be used as a go-between. It seemed the angel on Marvin's shoulder came through again. Leland and Marvin were informed that the Vietnamese foreign minister was going to be in New York City to attend the General Assembly of the United Nations, which would be in session that month.

Congressman Leland went to New York City and met with the foreign minister, who said that he would welcome Marvin and the congressman to Vietnam.

The foreign minister said, "The chances are good that Marvin will be able to bring these two young people back to the United States if he makes such a trip." Thanh Pham, attaché to the Vietnam Mission to the United States, also welcomed the trip, and said he could make arrangements for Marvin to enter Vietnam early in September. Thanh Pham was very emphatic when he said, "Vietnam welcomes any American people, including congressmen who fly with good will. The trip will allow Mr. Zindler and the congressman to understand more about Vietnam and its government."

By now, Marvin had decided his mission would encompass more than the two children of Son Nguyen. He was haunted by the plight of the many thousands of other children, particularly the Amerasians, those who had been born to Vietnamese mothers but fathered by U.S. soldiers.

Most Vietnamese call Amerasian children "Bui Doi," or "dust children," because of the dust stirred up by the many American tanks during the Vietnam War. Amerasians suffered particularly hard times in Vietnam, because they were considered illegitimate and resembled their American fathers.

Marvin said, "Vietnam is a poor country, and having no father compounds the problem for these children. It is true any place in the world. Children always do better with their families."

Marvin's interest in Son's two children had gotten Congressman Leland fired up too. Leland decided to look further into the Vietnam situation. The U.S. State Department and others involved briefed him about what was going on over there. Said Leland, "There are also allegations that there is extreme starvation going on over there, particularly in what was North Vietnam. There are approximately one and a half million people who are suffering from malnutrition and starvation, many of whom are young children and infants."

Leland was Chairman of the House Select Committee on Hunger, so starvation was an issue with which he was passionately concerned. He and other members of his delegation intended to go to Vietnam as well, not only to help bring the two young people out, but also to make an assessment of the starvation problem. "We want to survey the situation and determine for ourselves if this is real or imaginary," he said. He would report his findings to the State Department and the United States Congress. He was looking forward to the trip.

Leland returned to Washington, D.C. after his meetings with the officials at the UN. While dining in a D.C. restaurant, he was discussing the proposed trip with members of his staff, when he met a gentleman who also had a young son in Vietnam, and had experienced the same bureaucratic frustration that the Nguyen family had gone through. He, too, had gotten no results. Leland obtained the needed information from him, and said he would try to bring this man's child out as well.

∞ ● ∞

Meanwhile, Marvin informed the Nguyen family of the proposed plans. They were overwhelmed. They could not believe that Marvin would actually try to make the trip to Vietnam.

What with the lack of any diplomatic relationship between the U.S. and Vietnam, Marvin would have to stop in Bangkok first. There would be no guarantees that Marvin and his team would be able to continue to Vietnam; they would have to get permission from the Vietnamese Embassy in Bangkok to go on to Ho Chi Minh City.

Marvin, Lori Reingold and Bob Dows departed for Bangkok on a Monday in early September 1988. Congressman Leland and several other Texas congressmen, as well as other members of the House Arms Service Committee, and other members of the House Select Committee on Hunger, departed on a separate flight to Bangkok. Marvin and Leland would meet there later in the week. Each man had his separate agenda, in addition to their mutual goal of retrieving the children.

The purpose of Marvin's trip was multi-fold, and once in Bangkok, he planned to meet with Vietnamese officials to discuss several issues. Not only was Marvin interested in bringing back 13-year-old Nguyen Thi Kim Anh and 10-year-old Nguyen Hoang Dung; he also wanted to see if he could make progress in bringing home the 20,000 others that still remained. In addition, he hoped to speak to Vietnamese heads of state about American prisoners of war and those missing in action.

Congressman Leland planned to address the drought condition in Vietnam, and look into reports that several million children were starving. Earlier in 1988, Vietnamese officials had asked the United Nations and the United States for aid, but so far, the United States had refused.

It was a long and tough trip, a journey in which the participants left with high expectations but no promises. When they finally arrived in Bangkok, Marvin and his team checked into their hotel and immediately took a taxi to the Vietnamese Embassy. They were greeted warmly, but received no indication that they were going to be given permission to go on to Vietnam. They were asked to fill out forms, and dutifully, each filled out the appropriate papers. Afterward, they were told to come back the next day at a specific time. That was encouraging.

The following morning at exactly 9:00, Marvin and the television crew were again at the Vietnamese Embassy. Once again they were greeted very courteously, and taken to a small room where they were questioned extensively regarding their trip to Vietnam. They were asked the same questions over and over again. At the conclusion, Marvin was asked to fill out more paperwork. He was starting to get a little frustrated. He had still been given no indication as to any progress regarding their request to enter Vietnam. The Vietnamese officials were invariably pleasant but very businesslike, while providing no additional information. Marvin does not have the patience for bureaucratic red tape, but uncharacteristically, he agreed to fill out more papers, and for once in his life, said nothing. It was a smart move. The paperwork completed, Marvin was told to return at 3:00 on the following afternoon.

Upon returning to the hotel, Marvin received a message requesting that he and the team report to the American Embassy. At the Embassy they were taken to a small room by members of the Embassy staff and several gentlemen that Marvin assumed to be CIA agents. Marvin, Lori and Bob were questioned for several hours. They were intensely grilled on all of the ramifications of their trip to South Vietnam. The question-and-answer session at the United States Embassy actually was much harsher and more extensive than that at the Vietnamese Embassy.

Marvin had some questions of his own. "Are there any restrictions or limitations on our travel to Vietnam?" He was told that there were not.

With that, Marvin got up to leave, but before letting the group go, members of the United States Embassy, the State Department and the CIA officials present said the meeting had been for their own welfare. And, before they could allow the group to leave, the officials felt it imperative to give Marvin and his team some advice about what they could expect — in particular, regarding the present status of MIAs and POWs. They seemed to be very nervous about Marvin's plan to pursue the topic at his meetings with the officials in Ho Chi Minh City.

Their warnings, of course, were like waving a red cape in front of a bull. If it wasn't on Marvin's agenda when he left, it sure as hell was going to be on his agenda now.

Marvin thanked the American Embassy officials and CIA agents for their concern and help, and then they left. Marvin wondered just what had been accomplished that day. To his frustration, they had not yet received permission to go to Vietnam.

At exactly 3:00 PM on the third day, Marvin and the team dutifully returned to the Vietnamese Embassy. They were taken to a small, sparsely decorated room that contained several wooden chairs placed around an old desk. The Vietnamese Embassy official asked, "When do you plan to leave for Vietnam?"

Marvin replied, "As soon as possible. As soon as you say we can enter."

Embassy official asked, "Don't you have a specific date?"

Marvin said, "Tomorrow."

"What cities are you going to go to in Vietnam?" the official inquired.

Lori replied, "Ho Chi Minh City, to meet the children of the Nguyen family."

Said the embassy official, "You will have to go to Hanoi first."

His face was expressionless as he looked straight at Marvin. "When will you return to Bangkok?"

Marvin answered, "We hope to have an audience with the Premier or Vice-Premier of Vietnam, see what changes have taken place in the city, and meet the children who will return with us to the United States. Then we will be able to leave."

Silence. The Vietnamese Embassy official slowly reviewed several pieces of paper that he had in front of him. He said nothing. He asked nothing. Then, looking up from the desk, eyes fixed on Marvin, he said, "You will leave for Hanoi, where you will meet with the Vice-Premier and other members of the Vietnamese government. You will then go on to Ho Chi Minh City." He then gave them the exact dates and times.

Marvin was thinking to himself, *You son-of-a-bitch. You knew before we got to Bangkok exactly what the schedule was, and when our travel dates would be granted. You had it all planned, but you wanted to see if we would be persistent enough to return here day after day and fill out your ridiculous paperwork and meet your demands before you would tell us!*

But Marvin knew that if he was going to be successful and keep his promise to bring Nguyen Hoang Dung and his sister Anh back, he would have to play their silly game and keep his mouth shut. Just this once. The Vietnamese Embassy official asked them to return the following morning, and he promised he would have the necessary documents so they could depart for Hanoi.

Before leaving, Marvin asked, "Do we have any restrictions as to where we may go or what we may photograph?"

"Mr. Marvin Zindler, you will be allowed to go anywhere you wish, speak with anyone you wish to talk to, and photograph freely. We welcome the trip, including the American congressmen who will be joining you."

Nothing was said about the children, but at least Marvin now knew that they would be allowed to enter Hanoi and Ho Chi Minh City. Their biggest fear was now abated. Most promising was that there would be no restrictions on their visit. Marvin had also been granted a meeting with the Vice-Premier and other members of the government. This would be the first such meeting since the end of the Vietnam war.

The team was excited now, but dared not express it outwardly at the meeting. Besides, as they were all more than aware, their mission was far from accomplished. The visas to enter Vietnam had been approved, but this in itself had been a Herculean achievement. And this was only the first step toward reuniting the children with their family.

Marvin slowly pulled his chair back, stood up, nodded approvingly, and flashed a big smile as he reached across the desk and shook hands with the Embassy officials. Lori thanked them and reconfirmed the time that they should return the following day to obtain their visas.

This ended Marvin's frustration. He was used to picking up the telephone and getting what he wanted, and though it hadn't happened as quickly as he was accustomed, it seemed he was finally making some progress. His meeting with the CIA had proved fruitful, he had to admit. Some of the things they had told Marvin about remaining calm, polite and quiet had already paid off.

Marvin had also been advised not to pursue his objectives during his meetings with the lower-level officials, but rather to wait until he met with the Vice-Premier before making his requests. Once again, he was going to have to exercise patience and discretion.

As they left the Embassy, Marvin turned to Lori and said, "We are one step closer to keeping my promise to bring these kids back home. You work so long for something . . . we knew that there would be no guarantees on this trip, but I always knew that I could do it with the help of my angel."

With visas in hand, the next logistical problem was how to get from Bangkok to Hanoi. Congressman Leland solved this by arriving in Air Force III. Marvin, Lori and Bob would be traveling with the congressmen on Air Force III to Hanoi the next day. For this portion of the trip, ABC Television would reimburse the United States government for their air travel aboard Air Force III. It was interesting that this segment of the trip would cost Channel 13 more than the entire rest of the journey, but there was no other way in or out for Marvin, his producer and his cameraman.

It had been a full day, and Marvin had an audience with the Vice-Premier the next day, so all of them returned to the hotel and bid each other an early goodnight.

Finally they were in Hanoi, and the meeting was about to begin. Marvin and the television crew were taken to a large room, simple in its elegance. There was dark wood paneling, well-tailored but not ornate. The carpet, however, was a plush red. The Vice-Premier of Vietnam was already sitting with Congressman Leland. Behind the Vice-Premier, at a small desk, was a young man who seemed to be a scribe. He began taking down everything that was discussed.

The other U.S. congressmen who had accompanied Leland were seated in a semicircle facing the Vice-Premier. Marvin was seated directly in front of the Vice-Premier. Several high-ranking members of the Vietnamese government were also present.

Bob Dows positioned the tripod-mounted video camera very close to Marvin's left shoulder, so that he could focus on both Marvin and the Vice-Premier. Bob's Vietnamese counterpart positioned his cameras next to Bob.

Like all state meetings, there was a certain degree of rigidity and formality, but to Marvin's surprise, this quickly disappeared. After the usual formal introductions, the Vice-Premier began, "You know, we have committed many mistakes, big mistakes. We were big dreamers." He paused, looked over the group, and continued, "We dreamt of a society where people could work and enjoy happiness, and happiness would be brought to them by the government and by the Communist Party. But happiness must be [brought] by the people [themselves]. So, the Society of Vietnam looks like a charity house. The people now expect the government to distribute happiness to the people. People are waiting to receive happiness."

The Vice-Premier slowly raised both arms over his head, and with his hands, began making a circular motion as he continued, "A very — how to say — a great Utopia. A very, very beautiful dream, but a bad reality."

His honesty and sincerity surprised everyone. He lowered his arms slowly and deliberately, stretching out his hands, palms down, toward Marvin. "There is no such paradise in this world." His palms came to rest in his lap. He shifted in his seat, turning to his right, looking very intensely at Congressman Mickey Leland. Again he raised his right hand slowly upward, pointing toward the heavens as he said, "Paradise comes only after you are dead."

Now, with index finger extended and fist clenched, the Vice-Premier continued, "Before, we hated capitalism so deeply because of exploitation." Both his hands were open now, cupping the air as if holding a very delicate object. He continued, "We were dominated first by the French, later by the Japanese, and so on for more than 100 years. Now we must learn from capitalism."

Marvin never thought he would hear this — and he had it all on tape: not just a revolution of thought, but an exclusive story as well!

The Premier showed the first sign of relaxing as a big broad smile appeared. His eyes seemed to widen and sparkle. He stood, raising his right hand, and waving it in the air toward Marvin. "We must learn from capitalism — but not everything!" In a jovial manner, he continued, "Exploitation, no! Advertising, no!" Laughing now, he shouted, "War! No war! No war! But we must learn. I have received books from the United States...on how the West grew rich, for instance. I am studying these."

This was the first "official" interview that anyone had been granted, much less allowed to film, since the end of the Vietnam War. The statements the Vice-Premier had just made to Marvin gave a new insight and a new direction to Vietnam's future. It clearly demonstrated that the leaders of Vietnam realized the difficult social and economic situation their country was in. Even though they had not turned to the west publicly, they were studying American economics and development. They had gone to great lengths obtaining books from wealthy Texas businessman (and future U.S. presidential candidate) Ross Perot, and others, to learn the best means of achieving change.

Marvin didn't wish to lose the honesty and good will of the moment. He had done his homework, and was prepared to do more than just ask for the release of the children. He seized this opportunity to ask about the POWs and MIAs. "One of the wounds of the Vietnam War is our Missing in Action and the Prisoners of War issue," he said. "Approximately 1,760 Americans — which includes over 150 Texans — are listed as missing in Vietnam. The lingering question remains: Are there any prisoners of war left?"

It took a lot of guts for Marvin to ask this question. Hanoi had previously called a halt to discussions on MIAs and POWs in angry response to a United States' policy statement that ruled out diplomatic relations with Vietnam until Vietnamese troops were withdrawn from Cambodia. However, although the American Embassy in took a dim view of his decision to bring up the subject — and had made it abundantly clear that it was an area they hoped he would *not* pursue — the CIA hadn't specifically forbidden it.

As usual, Marvin's instincts proved to be right. In the next few minutes, he accomplished more in his personal conversation with the Vice-Premier of Vietnam than all of the negotiations that had taken place in the previous 10 years.

The Vice-Premier responded by saying, "We will have a joint investigation and excavation everywhere the Americans desire."

The United States congressmen and other guests could not believe what they were hearing. They weren't prepared for Marvin's direct approach, much less the Vice-Premier's direct response to Marvin's questions.

Marvin, wanting to clarify this promise, responded, "Everywhere the American team wants to go, you are going to let them go?"

The Vice-Premier leaned forward, resting his elbows on his knee, and looked Marvin straight in the eye. "Your American teams can go everywhere — you can go too. For example, if on the American side, you have 100 spots to investigate, you send a team to each spot to investigate, and if they say they would like to have an investigation, we will accept. It will take 60 days for 100 spots. You must at least have how many teams?" He paused, thoughtfully. "To be practical?"

He sat back in his chair, very relaxed, as if engaged in a conversation with an old friend, and then continued, "For excavation, it is not on the road, mostly in the jungle. You need to bring the team, to bring the equipment, you know."

Marvin again wanted to reinforce this commitment and clarify any stipulations that might be imposed. Now he leaned forward too, closing the distance between himself and the Vice-Premier. Everyone in the room had their eyes on Marvin and the Vice-Premier. You could almost hear them breathing.

Marvin asked, "Are you going to give 60 days or 90 days? Or are you going to give the American investigation teams whatever time they need?"

The Vice-Premier suddenly flung his arms out wide and said, "Yeah, yeah, yeah. If they would like to have a fast excavation or whatever they need, they can do it. There are no living Americans in Vietnam. I understand the wounds of war are still with the American people. That is a pity. The moral wounds of war. We must — how do you say — close this chapter. Why continue to maintain these wounds of war? It is no good for the people of Vietnam and the U.S. — America."

The room again grew completely quiet. All that could be heard was the scratching of the scribe's pen as he attempted to take down the conversation. Congressman Leland didn't say a word. He sat expressionless, with his chin gently resting upon his folded hand. The others in the room were steadfast in their focus on the Vice-Premier and Marvin, who had clearly become the center of attention.

The Vice-Premier continued, "So for the wounds of war, for the MIAs, we do our best."

Marvin got the clarification and the promise that he sought. It was not lightly given, for it was recorded by Bob Dows' camera, for all the world to hear and see. What started with a simple request to unite a family had gotten Marvin the interview of a lifetime, an interview the world had never expected to receive in 1988. For his part, Marvin claimed that he was not a war correspondent and definitely not a diplomat, only a man who sought to right wrongs. On that day, however, he was the consummate chronicler of the agonies of a war long over, and had achieved a diplomatic success that was the envy of the most sophisticated political negotiators.

Marvin was confident that the Vice-Premier was telling the truth when he said that there were no more Americans in Vietnam. He was also confident that joint American and Vietnamese investigations and excavations of crash sites and battlefields would begin immediately, finally answering questions about American MIAs for their loved ones at home, and for the 156 still missing in action from Marvin's home state of Texas.

Having gained these concessions, Marvin next voiced his hope of retrieving the two children from Ho Chi Minh City, of having them return to Houston with him. Marvin explained that he was there to fulfill a promise he had made to the children's father. There was also the child of the father to whom Congressman Leland had made his promise in that Washington, D.C. restaurant. But these three children were only the very tip of a large iceberg. Marvin wanted to know how soon the Vice-Premier would be willing to release the other 20,000 children, and allow them to come to the United States.

Again, all that could be heard in the room was the scratching of the pen as the scribe took down Marvin's remarks. Would Marvin be successful in retrieving ten-year-old Nguyen Hoang Dung and his sister, Nguyen Thi Kim Anh? Would he be successful in negotiating the release of the third child, and the thousands of other children that still remained behind? In what had so far been a very direct, yet cordial meeting, would the Vice-Premier continue to honor Marvin's requests?

Marvin sat patiently, if intently, waiting. He was, as usual, dressed all in white, and was the only one wearing a tie in this heat — but not a drop of sweat appeared on his brow. He flashed his famous Zindler television smile, the corners of his mouth on the left side turned up ever so slightly. And he waited.

The Vice-Premier again leaned forward, and with a wild, very animated gesture, he threw both hands out and said, "I have told my American friends. They can take all the children." He maintained eye contact with Marvin, and slid forward to the very edge of his seat. With both hands outstretched and palms gently cupped, she raised his voice and repeated, "Yes, you can take all of them."

He lowered his left hand to his knee, and with his right hand still outstretched, he raised it toward Marvin and said again, even more forcefully, but with a broad smile on his face, "Take all of them."

Marvin's smile turned to laughter. The Vice-Premier began to chuckle, as well. For the first time since the meeting began, the scribe stopped writing, as the entire group burst into joyous laughter. Everybody seemed very relaxed, as if a great weight had been lifted.

The Vice-Premier gently slid back in his seat. He shifted his weight so that he was leaning on the arm rest to his left, giving his full attention and directing himself to Marvin. "I know how it is — for me, for my father — and I understand the suffering of these children." He slowly placed his right hand over his heart and continued, "Children who are fatherless everywhere...must suffer [for what their parents] did." He then sat back into the chair, placing both hands on the armrest in a very relaxed manner.

Marvin replied, "We really appreciate this meeting, and what you have said and done here regarding the thousands of other children who have been separated from their families."

So it had finally happened. The next day, Marvin would fly to the air force base at Ho Chi Minh City to meet the children. Starting that day, September 9, 1988, and continuing through September 12, the Texas Congressional Delegation would hold talks and make arrangements for the release of the other children. They would also hold discussions that would lead to American teams excavating crash sites and battlefields to help answer the MIA question. *Thank you, Mr. Zindler.*

On the flight from Hanoi to Ho Chi Minh City, Marvin recalled his meetings at the U.S. Embassy in Bangkok, where he had been told that the children's names had been placed on a "special priority list" several years earlier. The Vietnamese, however, had never agreed to release the children or provide them with exit visas until now. Marvin asked the State Department officials and the Director of the U.S. Orderly Departure Program what the problem was. The State Department's spokesperson said, "We put these children on our priority list three years ago, but were not allowed to see them until last week."

"What was the problem?" Marvin wanted to know.

"Well, there are many pieces to the problem. One is that the Vietnamese government controls all aspects of the program until people are allowed to depart from Vietnam, so my office is only able to issue letters of introduction and deal with special cases on a special priority list — also a special humanitarian list. But the Vietnamese have to ultimately respond to that and allow access to these people. Some people are allowed to see us right away, while others are held for years and years, and repeated requests for them often go unanswered."

Marvin got right to the point. "I have heard stories that people had to buy their way out of Vietnam with gold. I have heard a lot of stories, and I believe most of them to be true, that people leaving Vietnam have to pay somebody some amount of money to get through the system — graft." He paused a moment, then continued, "Whether it is at the local level, perhaps not even an official, but from our interviews with refugees, most people had to make some payment to somebody to get them through the Vietnamese system and out to freedom."

In one brief afternoon, Marvin would change all that.

Air Force III touched down in Ho Chi Minh City. It was the first United States government airplane — and the first United States delegation — to land there since the Communists had taken over 13 years earlier. Marvin and his ABC television team were driven from the airport through Ho Chi Minh City, past the former United States Embassy building, which had since been converted by the Vietnamese government into an oil research center. Its high white wall glistened under the rays of the hot afternoon sun. Theirs was the only automobile on the road, which was clogged with tricycles and an occasional motor scooter. Many of these conveyances were loaded with large baskets filled with laundry, foodstuffs, and household supplies.

They traveled through Ho Chi Minh City's downtown section, and past the Saigon River, where several people were bathing themselves in the shallow waters along its edge. Marvin could see a number of fishing boats paddling out to sea. They soon arrived at the government house, where they were to have tea and meet the officials of Ho Chi Minh City — a customary and obligatory ceremony for guests. Unknown to Marvin, the three children that they had come for had been driven from their rural home in the Mekong Delta to the government house in Ho Chi Minh City. They were only a few feet away from Marvin, behind a screen, awaiting their presentation.

The children suddenly appeared as if out of nowhere: Dung and his sister Anh, as well as the third child, whom Congressman Leland was going to take back to Washington, D.C. They were clean, their hair was neatly cut, and they were dressed in new clothing. It was obvious they were nervous, but they had smiles on their faces. Marvin looked at Dung and Anh, the children he had come for — the children their father had feared he would never see again. The promise that he had made so many months before was now becoming a reality.

Marvin shook the children's hands, and all three responded warmly. Lori presented each of the children with T-shirts and letters from their fathers telling them not to be afraid. The letters explained that they would be going on an airplane with Mr. Zindler and his friends to join their fathers in America.

And so their mission was accomplished. In a matter of minutes, the team was out of there, before anyone could change their minds. Relatives and friends had come to say goodbye; they wanted to come to America, as well. One uncle told Marvin that he had seven children. He introduced the children to Marvin, and said there was also an unmarried aunt, whom the family was working hard to send to Houston in the future. Marvin wished he could have taken them all along right then, but is simply wasn't possible.

But now there was more hope for the future, for those who wanted the opportunity to be free.

Marvin's car sped through Ho Chi Minh City's streets to the airport, where Air Force III awaited them. As they walked across the tarmac to board the aircraft, a young lady jumped from the back of a motor scooter that had suddenly appeared on the roadway.

What was happening? Marvin prayed there would not be any trouble, now that they were so close to leaving. The young lady ran up, bearing a small carry-on bag that she said contained gifts for the children's family in Houston. It also contained a fish, so that the children could have food on the trip home. The fish would also be an offering to the family at home, if there was any left by the time they go there. Marvin didn't need to unwrap the package to know that there was, indeed, a fish inside. As a matter of fact, with one whiff, everyone in the car could accurately describe the package's contents!

For security reasons, there was some hesitation, and a short argument resulted, but it was quickly resolved. The bag, fish and all, was accepted. Marvin eagerly boarded Air Force III for the first segment of their long journey to America.

Lori eventually decided that the fish had to go. Its pungent odor was beginning to permeate everything and everybody, and she knew that United States Customs would never let it through. The children were understandably upset at this, as they were worried that they would not have any food for the rest of the journey. They were also planning to present what might be left of the fish to their parents. The children found it difficult to understand that there would be more than enough food on the plane, and that, once they arrived in the States, the luxury of a supermarket — an entity beyond their imagination — was awaiting.

The first stop would be Bangkok, where they would stay overnight in a local hotel. Marvin will never forget how Dung sat in the hotel bathroom for hours, slowly turning on the hot and then the cold water faucets, shutting them off and turning them on again. The children were amazed. It was the first time they had seen hot and cold running water.

Later that evening, one of the boys went to use the toilet. He seemed to be in the bathroom for an inordinate amount of time, so Marvin went to investigate. Marvin saw the child standing on the toilet seat trying to figure out how to use the device. It only took Marvin a few minutes to solve this simple problem, but it made him wonder how quickly the children would adapt to the society that they were about to be thrust into. After all, they were from a small jungle village in the Delta, with no amenities that could compare to what they would encounter in a metropolitan American city.

The next day, Marvin had his answer. The entire Houston branch of the Nguyen family was there to greet them, as were many of their neighbors, friends and business associates. They were all on hand for the arrival of Marvin and Son's children at Houston's Intercontinental Airport, for a reunion they had thought would never come.

These children, Marvin thought, were going to be just fine.

Marvin was right. The children have been well nurtured by their family, and have remained in close contact with Marvin over the years. They join the Zindlers at many family functions, and Marvin considers them his second family. On a sad day shortly after Thanksgiving in 1997, Anh and Dung, along with their parents and grandmother, joined Marvin and many others at the memorial service for Gertrude Zindler.

In the years since their move to Houston, Anh finished college; she lives and works in Houston. Dung also attended the University of Houston. Both are American citizens, saying "Thank you" by working hard and giving back to their new country.

Marvin's efforts in 1988 resulted in the United States Department of State negotiating a program whereby 2,000 Vietnamese children would be released to their families in this country each month. Marvin opened the doors for further American teams to investigate crash sites and many other areas throughout Vietnam. This proved to be enormously helpful to investigations into the MIA and POW questions that had loomed so large in the American consciousness.

On several counts, Marvin had accomplished what most people had thought to be impossible. When asked how he did it, Marvin just smiles and gives the credit to that angel on his shoulder. Between you and me, I have the feeling that even his angel must be amazed.

C·H·A·P·T·E·R 30

INTO AFRICA: THE SEARCH FOR MICKEY LELAND
(ETHIOPIA, 1989)

Houston Congressman Mickey Leland was a good friend of Marvin's, and over the years, the two worked together on a number of community activities. Both were interested in children, at home and abroad, particularly in programs to improve their health and nutrition. Marvin was impressed with what Leland was doing to alleviate starvation in third-world countries, and felt Leland was very sincere and committed to these efforts. The friendship between Marvin and Leland lasted many years, and even survived Leland's minor involvement in the Hermann Hospital Estate Scandal.

Sadly, that friendship would come to an end in August of 1989.

During the 1980s, Mickey Leland made several trips to Ethiopia to investigate the medical and nutritional health of the country's children, as well as the nutrition and health of the population in general. He also wanted to ensure that United States donations of food and other life-sustaining necessities were actually reaching the people who needed them.

In August of 1989, Leland went to Ethiopia again as head of a nine-member delegation. As Chairman of the House Select Committee on Hunger, Leland felt it was his duty to see firsthand that supplies were reaching those who needed them, and not disappearing into the black market.

On Monday, August 7, 1989, Marvin received information that the plane carrying his good friend and 16 other people had not been heard from when expected. The aircraft was considered downed, but no other information was available. Leland, his delegation and seven Ethiopians had left the capital of Ethiopia, Addis Ababa, earlier on Monday.

They were going to tour a refugee camp in the southwest part of the country, near the Sudanese border.

The Ethiopian capital had a curfew, and when Leland's twin-engine plane did not land at the refugee camp, and did not return to the capital before the curfew, it was declared missing.

According to a member of the U.S. Embassy staff in Addis Ababa, the grasslands of the Sudanese area adjacent to Ethiopia was the logical place to search, because it would be easy for an aircraft to land there even though there was no landing field. The twin-engine Otter aircraft carried enough fuel for circling in the area, the Embassy official explained, and could then make its way into Sudan to land on the grassy planes. This scenario gave hope that Congressman Leland and his staff were still alive.

This was not the first time that Mickey Leland had been "lost." He had been missing in Africa in 1972. Of those circumstances Leland later explained, "I got lost in Africa. I mean, nobody knew where I was. My mother thought I was dead. My grandmother had just given up. But the fact is that I got totally absorbed in Africa."

On the 1972 trip, Leland had been alone. He was meeting people who were having a very deep influence on him and simply got so absorbed that he forgot to make any outside contacts. It didn't occur to him at that time that anyone would be worried.

Even knowing Leland's capacity for getting totally wrapped up in a project, many people were worried now — including his close friend, Marvin Zindler. The situation was obviously serious.

Communication between the U.S. and Ethiopia was limited because of the lack of technical equipment in Ethiopia. Video technology was not available at all there. In addition, Ethiopia and the U.S. did not have full diplomatic relations. Because of these factors, it was going to be a true challenge for journalists and others to get accurate information on what was happening. To make matters worse, Ethiopia had rigid rules; there were strict requirements on who got in and who didn't. To further muddy the waters, the United States Embassy in Addis Ababa and officials in Washington were giving out conflicting information on whether the Ethiopian government had waived visas for journalists wishing to go to Ethiopia.

Meanwhile, Houston news crews and television stations were getting ready for a long and costly watch in one of the most inaccessible areas of the world. They hoped that their funding and equipment would help in locating Leland and his entourage.

The first problem was getting visas for the news crews. Reporters were leaving en masse for Washington, D.C. to acquire their visas. All three Houston network affiliates coordinated efforts with national and international network news operations; the networks would be a big help in setting up the necessary satellite communications.

Marvin was devastated by the news about his friend's disappearance. On Tuesday, August 8, he contacted his regular production team, producer Lori Reingold and cameraman Bob Dows. Marvin told them to go home and pack.

Richard Longoria, Channel 13's news director at that time, approved of the trip. He knew Marvin had many very good reasons for wanting to go to Ethiopia. And he felt confident that if anyone could get information on what had happened to Leland, it was Marvin. Longoria said, "Zindler knows how to get things done. He is gutsy, energetic, and when he sets his mind to something, especially to help a friend, nothing will stop him."

While Lori Reingold and other members of Marvin's production crew were hastily packing, Bob was making a last-minute check of the video equipment, as well as the special equipment that would be needed for satellite transmission, telex, etc. Of course, none of this equipment was available in Ethiopia. Meanwhile Marvin's wife, Gertrude, was assisting him at home. As usual, his fingers were nimbly running over the buttons of the telephone, making travel arrangements. There were no direct flights to Ethiopia; they would have to make a connecting flight in Germany. It was at this time that Marvin first met Sue Mecklenburg with the Houston office of Lufthansa Airlines. She was very helpful during this emergency situation, and on many of the trips Marvin and I took together in years to come.

Marvin asked, "When is your next connecting flight for Ethiopia?"

Sue replied, "4:45 PM. Can you make it, Mr. Zindler?"

"We'll be there. Book three seats, please."

"How else can we help you?" Sue asked.

Marvin said, "We are traveling light, but we will need special attention for our delicate video and transmission equipment."

"I'll have someone meet you who can take care of that for you," said Sue. "Do you have your visas and other papers, Mr. Zindler?"

Marvin said, "No."

That might be a problem. Sue explained to him, "We can get you to Frankfurt, where you'll have to change planes for your flight to Ethiopia, but when you land in the capital of Addis Ababa without the proper papers, they can either hold you in a detention room or jail, or put you back on the plane!"

Marvin said, "I told you we have no papers."

"Then you will have to sign a release at the airport for yourself, Lori and Bob," Sue replied. "If you are detained by the Ethiopian security police, Lufthansa Airlines has no responsibility. And if the Ethiopian secret police put you back on the aircraft and send you back to Frankfurt, you will have to release the airline from any expense regarding your travel. I am sorry, Mr. Zindler, but this is completely out of our hands, and you will have to travel at your own risk."

Marvin said, "Got-damn it, Sue, that's my friend out there, and we are going to find him. We will be on that flight, and let me worry about the rest."

This is the gutsy and feisty Marvin that we all know and love! Richard Longoria was right; if anybody could get information on the missing congressman, Marvin could. He was on that 4:45 Lufthansa flight with his production team. Knowing that going to Washington, D.C., for clearance and visas would only evolve into a logistical nightmare, what with all of the other television and news teams congregating there for the same purpose, Marvin had decided to avoid the red tape. He felt he could handle each situation as it came up.

"Obviously, the desire to get more information and get the information as quickly as possible was utmost in my thoughts," he later said. "Each hour for us was taking on a new dimension." He felt there was no time to waste.

And so, while other news reporters and television station crews were crowding into Washington to get visas, Marvin was already over the Atlantic heading for Ethiopia. This was always what set Marvin apart from everyone else. He was flying by the seat of his pants, but it wasn't the first time, and it wouldn't be the last.

Marvin was still confident that his friend was alive, and he, Marvin, was going to bring the communication equipment that was going to help find him. This is how Marvin approached all of his stories, and his life — with a very positive, upbeat attitude. "If you are going to get something done, you have to go to the top or do it yourself."

One thing in Leland's favor was that the plane he was in, the twin Otter, is a short-takeoff, short-landing aircraft with two engines mounted on the wing above the fuselage. That design puts the engines high and away from the ground, which is one reason it is the type of plane used in many relief operations. It does very well in rough terrain, and is able to land in a small clearing or field. It has even been used successfully in rescue operations, including those in earthquake zones. The twin Otter is used all around the world for carrying cargo and passengers. It is very popular as a "bush" plane and gets five gold stars as a tough utility plane.

Marvin had been on many trips to remote areas of the world, but traveling to Western Ethiopia would be the most dangerous he'd been on thus far. The flight to Ethiopia would encompass a variety of landscapes, and difficult weather conditions.

Ethiopia is made up of a series of high tablelands, some several thousand feet. Even in the dry season, a heavy cloud cover is ever-present, hiding the peaks of even the lowest ranges of the mountains. There are days when all you can do is just sit around because you can't see anything but fog. Finally, when you are able to take off, you pass over grassy flatlands, dense jungles, and more mountains, where the cloud cover and fog are often so thick there is zero visibility.

The other danger in flying across Ethiopia was that there was a very active military, and an unstable military situation. If the fog, cloud cover and mountain ranges didn't get you, bullets might. And very often, if friendly fire didn't get you, the rebels would. Leland himself had not been at such a disadvantage on this count, since he had an agreement with the government and the rebels to give him safe passage. He had that much credibility in the area. But those who would be flying into Ethiopia to look for him would not have this advantage.

Marvin assessed the situation. Fortunately, there was no action taking place in the area where Leland and his group were planning to fly. That was one less worry.

∾ • ∾

Later on, when talking about the Mickey Leland episode, Lori Reingold said, "Marvin had his ups and downs, even though he presented a very outwardly optimistic appearance, citing reasons to believe his friend and the missing party were safe." Bob Dows chimed in (and he was not the first to say this), "Marvin can be very persistent in these types of matters." During their long flight, Lori said, there were more ups than downs. Marvin was determined that he was going to get the needed information from local and government channels.

On the flight into Ethiopia, Marvin was at times solemn, and at other times talkative, reflecting on the many occasions that and his and Leland's paths had crossed over the years. Like Marvin, Mickey Leland had used his position — in Leland's case, a decade in Congress — to champion the causes of this nation's minorities and needy. Leland juggled his agenda between local, national and international problems. He did a great deal for minorities in the Houston community, and later became involved in national and international issues as well.

Marvin spoke of how Leland had risen from the street of Houston's impoverished Fifth Ward, making extra money flipping hamburgers at a neighborhood burger joint. Leland worked hard, receiving a Bachelor's of Pharmacy degree from Texas Southern University in 1970. He taught pharmacy there, and worked as a pharmacist for a couple of years. But he always had an interest in politics and felt that was the way he could best help those around him. He was elected to the Texas Legislature in 1972.

Marvin affectionately recalled when Mickey was first elected to the Legislature. "He was a young turk with wild hair and an uncanny ability to irritate the establishment," Marvin chuckled. "He was perhaps even militant about the white-black relationships of those times. But he has gotten much more practical, and has matured into one of the best public officials in Texas, and in the country."

Adjusting himself in the limited space afforded by his airline seat, Marvin continued, "I can see Mickey's graying goatee, and those eyes that always flashed of mischief. His principles haven't changed an inch. He just traded the outward marks of militancy for a more muted style as a congressman. But Mickey remains a feisty advocate of liberal programs." What Marvin liked most was Mickey's attitude that if he felt he was right and he could help somebody, he would be the one leading the charge.

Just like Marvin himself.

Marvin continued to reminisce. "Leland worried some supporters, and angered those who opposed him, when he visited Cuba and spoke warmly of its leader, Fidel Castro, early in his congressional tenure." This resulted in some interesting political and philosophical discussions between Marvin and the new congressman, as Marvin is, to put it mildly, not an admirer of Castro's policies.

It was, perhaps, serendipity that Leland later visited Cuba to bring back two Houstonians who had been imprisoned when their aircraft had mechanical trouble, and they had to land in Cuba. They were detained on drug charges, and Leland helped engineer their release.

Marvin, telling about this now, opened his eyes, sat bold upright, and in an animated voice said, "That is when he and I got into it. Leland used two aircraft — one paid for by Houston's Hermann Hospital Estate, and another in which funds were sought from Channel 13 and *Houston Magazine* to carry reporters." Marvin recalled interviewing Leland about accepting more than $11,000 for the trip from the Hermann Hospital Estate, as well as funds from KTRK-Channel 13.

Marvin flashed a big smile then, and almost chuckled as he said, "Mickey paid it all back, perhaps from his own pocket. We met at a fundraiser, shook hands, and that was the end of it. We have worked on many worthwhile projects together for the impoverished, hungry, and medical needy of Houston. Presently, I was in the midst of it with Mickey to save the Fifth Ward."

It was a long trip, and Marvin dozed restlessly for a few hours. When he awoke, he wanted to talk about his friend again. He spoke of how they were working together on the Allen Parkway project, and how much Leland had helped the impoverished residents of Houston. Marvin went on to say that Leland had a very sincere dedication to the Houston community, and was active in trying to resolve differences between African-Americans and Jews. Leland supervised an ongoing 10-year program through which African-American youths from Houston would spend six weeks in Israel to learn more about the Jewish culture.

"He is always trying to help others," Marvin said.

If prayer could have turned things around, this story would have had a happy ending. As they were landing in Ethiopia, Marvin said a prayer for his friend and the other members of Leland's party. Back in the States, meanwhile, the Reverend Jesse Jackson, also an old friend of Leland's, went by the congressman's office and led his staff in a prayer for Leland's safe return. Thousands of fervent prayers were being said the world over.

Would these prayers be answered? To those looking for hopeful signs, the weather in Ethiopia at least provided a bit of encouragement. Wednesday, when Marvin landed, the weather improved for the first time in several days.

Marvin was the first Houstonian to arrive, and he brought with him the first of the television and press corps. He was also the first of Leland's friends to get there. With Marvin and his crew was the video and satellite equipment needed to transmit the necessary information. In a few minutes, they would be disembarking, and some of Marvin's anxieties returned. Would he and his team be allowed to enter Ethiopia without the proper documentation? Would they be arrested or sequestered as so many others had before? Would they be returned to the aircraft under guard, and forced to leave?

As they prepared to disembark, Lori Reingold removed extra batteries, tapes and communication equipment from the overhead bin. Bob Dows lovingly ran his hand over the top of his video camera, which he never allowed to leave his side. If anything happened to it, they would have no visual documentation of their trip. Marvin, adrenaline pumping, mind racing, stood tall, adjusted his blue glasses, and descended from the aircraft.

All eyes were on Marvin, who strutted with confidence, shoulders back, wearing an immaculately pressed suit and brightly colored tie — in a country that didn't know what ties were, and where, given the stifling heat, few, if any, ever wore a jacket.

They passed through customs without any difficulty. After presenting their passports, which were stamped in the usual manner, they were questioned regarding their visas and other necessary papers — which, of course, they did not have.

The authorities were polite, but stern, and ushered them to a secluded room within the terminal. It was sparse, containing nothing more than several chairs in which they could sit. Their passports and press cards were confiscated, and they were locked in and told to wait. They were informed that the secret police would be contacted after the local authorities reviewed their passports. They remained secluded for a little more than two hours, at which time several men in military uniforms entered the room. Each time, their hearts dropped. They felt sure that at the very least they were going to be detained. Worse yet, they could be placed on the next available airplane and deported.

It was Wednesday, August 9, 1989, only two days since the first reports had reached the United States about Mickey Leland's disappearance. Unbeknownst to Marvin, the United States Government had mobilized an impressive fleet of aircraft that day, including a U-2 spy plane to look for Leland and his party. In an interview Wednesday, President George H.W. Bush said, "This matter is of great concern to us. The Ethiopian authorities are going to get all the cooperation we can give them."

At the Ethiopian capital, Addis Ababa, more equipment arrived. A C-141 Star Lifter had been dispatched by the Defense Department from West Germany, with a 21-person medical treatment and evacuation team. Also scheduled to arrive were 27 other experts in search and recovery, and weather and communications. En route was another C-141 Star Lifter with search and rescue crews, and two HC-130 aircraft with special operations / search equipment and personnel, as well as air-to-air refueling capability for helicopters. On its way too was a C-5, largest of the U.S. aircraft, with heavy-lifting ability for oversized cargo. There were also four MH-60 helicopters, which were actually modified Black Hawks that could fly at a very low ceiling and set down easily in small jungle clearings. These helicopters were equipped with night-vision equipment.

If state-of-the-art technology could have turned the situation around, this story would have had a happy ending.

∞ ● ∞

Meanwhile, Marvin and his production crew were still in custody.

Then, unexpectedly, the door to the room in which they were confined opened, startling them. Several military types entered; one gentleman stepped forward and introduced himself as the head of National Security. He said, "Mr. Zindler, we know who you are. We know why you are here. Welcome. I have a car and driver for you and your team. We will take you wherever you need to go."

Marvin said a soft prayer and thanked the guardian angel on his shoulder. I don't know if it is Marvin's imposing appearance, regal manners, or just dumb luck, but I have seen it happen again and again. In this case, it might also have been the great esteem in which Mickey Leland was held in that part of the world. Of course, Marvin insists it was that angel on his shoulder.

Marvin obtained permission to attach his video and voice equipment to the Ethiopian satellite communications link, and he quickly sent the first reports back to Houston and the world. On Friday, August 11, 1989, four days since Congressman Mickey Leland's plane was reported missing, Marvin reported that continued bad weather and failure to locate signs of the missing aircraft near the apparent source of two radio signals had prompted searchers to refocus their efforts on the original flight path of the aircraft, rather than the radio signals.

The United States Embassy spokesman in Addis Ababa told Marvin that rescue workers on foot and in planes had unsuccessfully scoured rugged highlands north and southeast of Ethiopia's capital, where the distress signals were first detected by satellites. So far their efforts had been fruitless. "They have pretty well exhausted those areas," the spokesman said, "and now they are going back and concentrating their efforts along the original route."

Marvin reported, "I am here to find my friend, but I'm less optimistic now, only because they are now telling me they had two false alarms that they originally told us were good signals."

This undermined Marvin's confidence, since there had been nothing new to report for four full days. Trying to be philosophical about it, he said, "It is understandable that in this terrain something substantial may take time, even with the new highly technical equipment which has just been flown in for this search."

By mid-afternoon that Friday, heavy clouds, rain and low visibility forced suspension of the aerial search.

Later that afternoon, Marvin met with U.S. Congressman Gary Ackerman, Democrat, New York, who had been with Leland on his previous trip to Ethiopia. Ackerman arrived on the second C-130 transport and sauntered off the plane in fatigues. With him was

United States Representative Allen Wheat of Missouri and House Sergeant-at-Arms Jack Russ.

Marvin reported, "As dawn broke here today (10:15 P.M., Thursday, Houston time), reconnaissance aircraft were again en route to the search area. There are now paramedics aboard the aircraft that have the ability to parachute into any landing or crash site. Ethiopian helicopter crews are also participating in the search. They are flying aircraft that can land in small jungle clearings as well." You could hear the sense of frustration in Marvin's voice.

It was Ethiopia's rainy season, and the search had been slow because of bad weather almost from the start. That interlude of relatively good weather that occurred when Marvin had landed did not last. Roads were virtually impassable at this time of the year, so hope lay with the air reconnaissance missions. Marvin compared an aircraft hidden under this dense jungle foliage to an aircraft hidden by a winter avalanche and not discovered until the spring thaw. It was not a very reassuring thought.

On Saturday, August 12, another close friend of Leland's, Houston City Councilman Ben Reyes, landed in Ethiopia. Reyes told Marvin he had been worried from the start, and didn't buy those "you know Mickey" reassurances. True, Leland was never one to keep to a schedule just for the sake of a schedule — but Reyes had a feeling this was an altogether different situation from that time Leland had been "lost in Africa" before. Marvin stood with Reyes as the evening's chilling wind was blowing in and darkness approached. They watched until every helicopter and search plane had landed, painfully aware that as Saturday came to a close there was still no news of their friend. There was little for Reyes and Marvin to do except wait, and reminisce.

Marvin recalled a particular night in the summer of 1970, a night marked by one of many protests in which Leland took part while he was a student leader. It was during the turbulent days of the civil rights movement, and this was a particularly stormy confrontation between black militants and police. "Leland was taken to jail," said Marvin. "He was bloody and his shirt was torn off, and they were carrying him in." But, as Marvin acknowledged again, "He has changed a lot since those early militant years."

Marvin recalled Leland confiding in him that he was going to "try to work within the system to change things." At the time, he was planning to run for a seat in the Texas House of Representatives, in a newly-drawn Harris County district. Leland won the election, then went on to shake up the traditional power brokers when he walked on the House floor wearing an African-print shirt, high-heeled boots, and an Afro hairstyle. That, too, changed in time, and Leland quickly befriended the powerful, using his considerable charm and unwavering sincerity to gain their support for his causes.

The reminiscing took Marvin's and Reyes' minds off of their anxiety for awhile, but never for long. There was still no sign of Leland's plane, and no real news.

Finally there was news, but it was not what they wanted to hear.

On Sunday, August 13, 1989, in a choked voice, and with some difficulty, Marvin reported, "Authorities located the wreckage of Mickey Leland's twin-engine Otter aircraft. It had crashed, nose first, into a steep mountainside with all indication that it had burst into flames with impact. There was scattered wreckage and all aboard are believed to have died instantly." The plane was discovered just 35 miles northeast of the refugee camp where it had been headed. Marvin was the first to report the sad news. The recovered bodies were flown to a nearby town, and then by a C-130 Cargo aircraft to the Ethiopian capital. From there, the deceased would be transported to an air base near Madrid, Spain, and then on to the United States.

Marvin said, "In the final analysis, the local townspeople were right. They reported on Tuesday they heard an airplane circling, apparently trying to find a landing spot, near their expected destination." The wreckage had been found in the general area of the villagers' accounts.

At the time of the crash, Leland's wife, Allison, was pregnant. He also had a three-year-old son.

At home, Mickey Leland's death was mourned on a hot and sunny Houston day with gestures ranging from simple tributes to emotional outpourings. Even at the Houston Astros' baseball game, a crowd of 27,000 sat in silence to honor Congressman Leland before the start of the game. From the streets of Houston's impoverished Fifth Ward, where Leland grew up, to Capitol Hill and the Presidential Retreat at Camp David, tributes poured in for the 44-year-old congressman who had embraced the fight against world hunger as one of his most passionate personal missions.

Marvin said, "He died trying to help others live."

But the legacy of Mickey Leland lives on. He is remembered as a hero, not only to the thousands of people he helped, but to many who have followed in his footsteps, fighting the good fight for the hungry and needy in Africa and the whole world over.

C·H·A·P·T·E·R 31

A LINE IN THE SAND:
MARVIN IN THE PERSIAN GULF (1990)

It was a typical Houston summer. Temperatures were in the high 90s and occasionally broke the 100 mark, but it didn't compare to the 115 to 130 degrees the Middle East was experiencing.

On July 17, 1990, Marvin was in the newsroom when he noticed a priority international release just coming off the wire services. According to the release, Saddam Hussein, the president of Iraq, had angrily and publicly threatened Kuwait and the United Arab Emirates with war. Saddam accused them of shoving a "poison dagger" into Iraq's back by exceeding oil production quotas set by OPEC, thereby driving down the price of oil. Their greed, Saddam said, had prompted them to conspire with American and Israeli imperialists to sabotage Iraq. They had stopped acting like Arab brothers.

This didn't seem to carry any particular importance at the time, as the quarrel over OPEC quotas was old hat. Saddam's problem was that he owed 80 billion dollars in war debts from the Iraq/Iran War, and wanted to jack up oil prices so he could pay the debts more easily. The other Arab Gulf leaders had repeatedly refused to go along, and now, no one was paying particular attention to his babbling. He had run Iraq as a military state for 11 years, and had yet to turn on his Arab neighbors.

Marvin and Dave Ward, who was now standing at his side, were looking at the wire service release together. Both being experienced newsmen, they immediately realized that Saddam had overstepped himself on this occasion. Blunt threats were almost unheard of in the Arab world. Marvin and Dave Ward looked at each other and said, almost in unison, "They are going to go to war."

The United Arab Emirates were the first to ask for help. Kuwaiti armed forces were put on full alert, but the Amir, Sheikh Jabir Al-Ahmad Al-Sabah, overruled his generals, and ordered the troops back to their garrisons. Based on experience, the Amir assumed that Saddam could be placated with money, as he had been in the past when Kuwait had contributed billions of dollars to the war against Iran. But now, Saddam was claiming that Kuwait had stolen $2.5 billion worth of oil from the oil fields that both Kuwait and Iran shared.

American diplomats felt confident that Saddam would not attack. The conventional wisdom among the international diplomatic community and the U.S. State Department was, "No Arab nation will ever attack another Arab brother. Saddam is merely saber-rattling to gain leverage over Kuwait and OPEC in the oil-pricing debate."

As Marvin turned away from studying the release about Saddam's threats, the first reports of unusual Iraqi troop movements north of Kuwait City were coming over the wires. Between Marvin's intuition and Dave Ward's experience as a newscaster, they were right more times than the Washington, D.C. diplomatic community. But thsere were enough local stories and other problems to concern themselves with. Marvin was receiving hundreds of letters a day from children who needed medical care, the families of elderly who were being mistreated in nursing homes, and others who were suffering because their air conditioning wasn't working in the middle of the sweltering Houston summer. There was also the "Rat and Roach Report" — Marvin's famous review of area restaurants' cleanliness, or lack thereof — and it needed to be completed for the coming Friday.

A little over two weeks later, however, on August 2, 1990, Marvin and Dave's hunch proved all too true. The Iraqis had crossed the border and entered Kuwait. It was 4:00 A.M. Kuwait time, and one brave soul climbed out onto the U.S. Embassy roof in Kuwait City, where he could link directly with Tampa, Florida via a satellite radio. In a very calm but anxious tone, he said, "The Iraqis are in downtown Kuwait City."

The Embassy was located only a quarter mile from the main Kuwaiti palace, a key objective for the Iraqis. Unnoticed, the maverick broadcaster remained on the Embassy roof throughout the morning, providing a running commentary on the battle for the palace and for Kuwait City. From his strategic location, he spotted men in civilian clothes signaling to Iraqi helicopters where to land. The Iraqis had thoroughly prepared, going so far as to plant Iraqi agents in Kuwait City to act as ground controllers for the incoming helicopters and other forces. So much for the notion that "an Arab would never attack a brother Arab."

The Iraqi forces crossed the Kuwait border, their armor moving forward, with special-forces units and helicopters spearheading the attack. There was no mistaking that they had a battle plan. Was this what the international diplomatic community was referring to the previous week, when they were trivializing Hussein's threats as being "saber-rattling?" In three days, the worst-case scenario materialized. Iraq had captured all of Kuwait and was poised on the Kuwait-Saudi border.

Among the world's standing armies, Saddam's ranked in size behind only those of China and the Soviet Union. The Iraqi military machine consisted of 900,000 men, including eight elite Republican Guard battalions. Saddam's arsenal included some of the best weapons the world's international arms dealers had to offer. The greatest fear arose from Saddam's threats to use chemical weapons. His forces were now in a strategic pause, busy re-arming and re-equipping, before continuing any other offensive operations. They had their best units on the border, ready to attack Saudi Arabia. When — and if — they planned to move forward was anyone's guess.

Then, on August 9, 1990, Saddam ordered the borders of Iraq and Kuwait closed, entrapping more than 13,000 westerners and other foreigners, changing the entire nature of the crisis.

The taking of American hostages would be a cause for war. What the American public did not know was that, if Saddam started using U.S. Embassy employees and other Americans stationed in the area as hostages, the only way the United States could retaliate — lacking any real forces in the area — would be with a nuclear strike on Baghdad. There was little else to offer.

Would it go that far?

Meanwhile, Saddam kept pouring forces into Kuwait. It was estimated that more than 130,000 soldiers, 1,200 tanks, and 800 artillery pieces were digging in, with more arriving every day. All this was accomplished in less than two weeks.

It was mid-August, and Houston was sweltering in the heat and humidity. Marvin and I were scurrying around town in the Channel 13 van. With Bob Dows at the wheel, we were on the 610 Loop on our way to visit a child in need of medical care. Kuwait seemed so remote at the time; nevertheless, we found ourselves discussing the present international situation as we drove.

Lori Reingold said, "I don't see us going to war over Kuwait."

I responded, "Saddam is not rational. With his forces amassing on the Kuwaiti border, he's not likely to stop there." Marvin said he hoped America's show of force in Saudi Arabia would cause Saddam to back down, so that some kind of a compromise could be reached.

That same day, President Bush held a news conference and delivered a fiery speech calling for "the immediate, complete and unconditional withdrawal of all Iraqi forces from Kuwait." He labeled Saddam Hussein a liar and went on to compare him to Adolf Hitler. Bush spoke of sending U.S. forces "not simply...to protect resources or real estate, but to protect the freedom of nations." He ended his speech by saying, "There is no substitute for American leadership, and American leadership cannot be effective in the absence of American strength."

From the tone of this speech, we all felt that President Bush was not bent on compromise. We were going to war. Marvin had been right. He said, "President Bush and the United States have now drawn a line in the sand." Would Saddam cross it?

The operation would be dubbed, "Desert Shield," which would reflect the United States' resolve to defend the Arab peninsula. As yet, however, nothing had been discussed about going on the offensive. Meanwhile, Pentagon sources were telling ABC television and other journalists that the United States' defenses would be impregnable by the end of the first week. Marvin and Dave Ward did not believe that for a minute. If Saddam had not halted at the Kuwait-Saudi border to reorganize and re-supply his troops, as well as to contemplate the United States' and the world's reaction, he could have overrun the Saudi oil region in just one week. Dhahran knew it too!

The few American soldiers stationed in Saudi Arabia were paratroopers from the 82nd Airborne Division. The paratroopers had nicknamed themselves, "The Iraqi Speed Bumps," knowing full well that, indeed, they would not be much more than speed bumps to a concentrated Iraqi offensive. Iraq's massive armor divisions could roll over them in a few days. The United States paratroopers could only produce a temporary delaying action, and continue to pull back and hope that they either would be reinforced, or that the U.S. would send helicopters to get them out of there. Marvin said it would have been reminiscent of the United States' retreat of Pusan early in the Korean War — a very disturbing thought.

Saddam's forces held their position at the border. In fact they almost doubled in number and began to dig in along the Saudi border.

Meanwhile, the U.S. established a naval blockade. More personnel and equipment would be arriving in Saudi Arabia by ship every day. President Bush had activated some 200,000 reservists; the men and women, along with millions of pounds of weapons, ammunition and other supplies, were arriving in giant C5A aircraft that were winging their way across the Atlantic in convoys, one behind the other. It was thus that the nickname, "Aluminum Bridge to the Middle East" was derived. It was the biggest airlift ever to have been implemented. Ultimately, more than 300,000 persons, and millions of tons of equipment, would be airlifted in a very short period of time. And, before it was all over, so would our fearless knight-in-white, Mr. Marvin "I'm-no-war-correspondent" Zindler and his intrepid team.

August was drawing to a close, and Saddam announced that he would use westerners as human shields to keep the United States from bombing Iraq. It was painfully obvious to Marvin that, at this point, the United States couldn't do much about American hostages in Iraq or Kuwait.

Meanwhile, more and more military personnel and reservists were leaving the United States every day, heading out for who knew what perils in the deserts of the Middle East. Marvin and Dave Ward were becoming keenly aware that Texas was sending its young men and women, as well.

Even as Marvin kept reiterating, "I am not a war correspondent," he also knew that, with summer drawing to an end and Thanksgiving, Hanukkah and Christmas quickly approaching, the Texas contingent, as well as other members of the armed forces, would be missing their families. Their families would be worried, wondering if their sons, daughters, husbands and wives were alive and well. Many of these young men and women had never been outside Texas, much less the United States. Marvin began to contemplate a trip to Saudi Arabia.

A cultural crisis loomed large for the American troops and for the Saudis as well, triggered by the sudden flood of tens of thousands of Americans into the small kingdom. Actions and attitudes that would go unnoticed in the United States — and in many other parts of the world — appalled local Saudi merchants and city dwellers in Dhahran. Merchants were shocked when off-duty women soldiers went browsing in their shops, wearing military garb with their assault rifles flung over their shoulders. These troops were in a war zone, and as such, were instructed to keep their weapons with them at all times. While they were following orders and their own common sense, their actions were offensive, even blasphemous, to the Arabs.

But it did not stop there. There were angry complaints that some of the American women were actually disrobing in public. In truth, some of the American soldiers — including the women — were unloading boxes of medical supplies, and, in the more than 100-degree temperature, would remove their fatigue jackets and work in T-shirts, exposing their arms.

This was worse than scandalous to the Saudis. Since Saudi women never showed their arms or legs in public, the Saudis were appalled at the Americans' "obscene" display.

The T-shirts themselves were offensive to the Saudis. Some depicted palm trees, camels and a tank in the desert. When a member of Saudi royalty was asked what was offensive about the T-shirts, he replied, "We don't like the image of a tank in our desert."

"But there are tanks all over your desert."

He responded, "Yes, but we don't want this advertised to our people."

The Saudis were apparently also offended about another T-shirt that had a map of Saudi Arabia and several cities marked on it. The Saudi royal explained, "The location of our cities is classified." When it was pointed out to him that every atlas has maps of Saudi Arabia showing the exact location of these cities, he said, "We don't allow maps inside Saudi Arabia."

Well, now, that could have posed a big problem. Very accurate satellite-generated maps had been issued to all United States and European troops, since without the maps, the troops could not function in the desert. No one wanted to touch off a cultural or religious backlash in Dhahran or any of the other Saudi Arabian cities, but everywhere the U.S. soldiers turned, they found that something else they'd done, quite without malice, offended these people whom they had come to help.

Yet another cultural clash was coming, and everybody knew it. The holidays were approaching, and the troops expected to observe Christmas and Hanukkah. And what of the very high-profile — and indisputably Jewish — Marvin Zindler? The Kingdom of Saudi Arabia was the guardian of Islam's holiest cities: Mecca and Medina. Already Baghdad radio was beaming messages into Saudi Arabia that Americans were going to defile their shrines and their women. The Iraqis were using the American and European partners' military presence to prey on the fears of the less sophisticated Saudi citizens. The Saudis' insistence on religious purity notwithstanding, they had to recognize that our troops could not be denied the right to practice their own religions. But the troops would have to do so discreetly.

Granted, there were some non-Islamic people who didn't know the meaning of the word "discreet," and whose actions were nothing short of arrogant. There was, for example, the fundamentalist Christian group in North Carolina, who called themselves Samaritan's Purse. They had the bright idea of sending unsolicited copies of the New Testament — in Arabic! — to the troops. Attached to each Christian Bible was a little note in English that read, "Enclosed is a copy of the New Testament in the Arabic language. You may want to get a Saudi friend to help you read it." That was just the beginning of the problem.

This incident was followed shortly thereafter by reports that a Jewish rabbi had entered the country and was saying, "For the first time in history, the ram's horn will be blown on Islamic soil." Jews blow the ram's horn as part of their observance of the Jewish New Year, the holiday of Rosh Hashanah. And so it went. There was a religious as well as a military presence. The Saudis were not pleased with this, but, after all, they had wanted — and had actually requested — military help.

Now that Hanukkah and Christmas were coming ever closer, King Fahd was being besieged by religious activists in his country. During these Judaeo-Christmas holidays, talent shows such as those brought by Bob Hope and other entertainers had historically entertained the troops, the origin of such shows going back to World War II. The Saudi King was very adamant in demanding a guarantee from the United States and its allies that no female entertainers would be brought in. The Saudis wanted assurance — of all things — that the Dallas Cowboys Cheerleaders and other female entertainers would not be coming to the Saudi kingdom. The King said, "There will be no talent shows. There will be no girlie shows for the holidays."

The allied troops had to learn that Saudi law was the law of the land. Just as we require foreigners to obey our laws while in the United States, the Saudis had every right to require us to obey their laws. This included doing without the female entourage that accompanied Bob Hope and others.

However, they did not object to Bob Hope himself....nor, thank goodness, to Marvin Zindler.

At one point, more than 1,500 members of the press had managed to obtain the proper visas needed to enter Saudi Arabia. The media had enjoyed unprecedented access to Saudi Arabia, and reasonable access to any of the armed forces' units, since the beginning of the crisis. A little-known fact was that, at one point, the Saudis had decided to ask all news reporters to leave. The allied and United States central commands finally interceded successfully on behalf of the news corespondents, as they felt that the American people — and the world at large — needed to know what was taking place. It was felt that the American public and the rest of the world would have to weigh what they heard, and keep the news in perspective. The largest contingency of reports was from the United States and Great Britain, but many of these stations televised worldwide.

A negotiated settlement in the war no longer seemed possible. Marvin said, "Strategically speaking, anything short of an Iraqi defeat is a losing proposition." By now, most of the world saw it the same way. It seemed inevitable that what was originally a defensive operation, designed to deter and defend, would become an offensive force. More than 200,000 Americans were now baking in the desert sun, and more troops were arriving every day.

As Christmas approached, the Saudis reemphasized their ban on females performing for the troops, but their demands went even further. Soldiers were asked to turn off their radio transmitters. When a Saudi prince was asked what the problem was, he said, "It is the broadcasting of your Christmas carols."

General Norman Schwarzkopf said he could solve that. Schwarzkopf explained that Christmas carols come in two forms: one form is instrumental and the other is vocal. Schwarzkopf would allow his troops to broadcast the music without the words. The Saudis also wanted reassurance that religious observances, Jewish and Christian, would stay as discreet as possible. The Saudi leadership was emphatic that there would be no display of religious symbols, no outdoor nativity scenes, and, of course, that the ban on female entertainers would extend all through the holidays, as well.

Even that did not satisfy all of the religious zealots in Saudi Arabia. Some of these Muslim fanatics were also insisting that the Saudi government ban Christmas cards from coming into the Kingdom unless they were allowed to censor them. But when the Muslims realized that should their demands be met, they would have to deal with the hundreds of tons of letters and packages that poured in every day, they soon gave up.

Regardless of all these restrictions, Marvin Zindler and others decided to visit the troops in December. It would be good for their morale, and it would be a chance for them to to let their loved ones back home know they were safe. Bob Hope announced that he would be there by December 24. Unlike shows of the past, Hope would be forced to leave the actresses and dancing girls out of his performances. Unfortunately, some of his equipment also failed to arrive. The show went on, however, even if it wasn't very long.

Even though Marvin continued to say, to me as well as anyone else who would listen, that he was not a war correspondent, he was not going to miss this opportunity. He was going to be there and lend his support. He especially wanted to give a Texas-sized "Howdy" to the American soldiers. He knew that the best Christmas present he could give the troops and their families back in Texas was the chance to see their loved ones. Marvin was going to bring the story home for the holidays.

But....the State Department said no visa for Mr. Zindler. The American Embassy said no visa for Mr. Zindler. There were enough correspondents there already, they said, and some had gotten hurt. As a result, the military did not want to be responsible for any more television reporters, especially a white-hairpiece-wearing, blue-sunglassed Texan who did not know the meaning of the word "NO."

Now, Texas did not win its independence and become a country all by itself without fortitude, ambition and guts, and if you've read this far you know that Marvin had them all, in spades. When everything else failed, the Kuwaiti government came through, issuing the needed travel papers for Marvin as well as his faithful sidekicks, Bob the cameraman and Lori the producer.

The camera equipment was packed, and extra videotapes and batteries secured faster than a cow could swish a Texas fly from its backside. Gold coins were purchased and hidden away in money belts in case of emergency, since it was the only form of currency that would be acceptable in the Middle East should an emergency arise. It would also be a means of acquiring access to transmission cables and satellite hookups to send the news back home. Marvin donned his best and whitest hairpiece, packed a couple of extra pairs of blue-tinted glasses, and of course, his white suits. Inside Marvin's vest pocket was a list of all Texas-based military units that had been sent to Operation Desert Shield.

Marvin and his news team left Houston for Dhahran. After 36 hours of travel, they stepped out of the airplane into a blast of desert heat. The temperature at the military airport was 115 degrees in the shade, and it was only midmorning.

Marvin and the team disembarked without any problem, passed through immigration, and cleared customs with all their equipment intact. Not even a pair of blue glasses got broken. The military offered Marvin an appropriate outfit for the temperature and desert conditions: a khaki uniform and combat boots designed to negotiate the soft sand. Marvin, true to his image, insisted on wearing his white suit and white loafers.

A few days later, the folks at home would see the immaculately dressed Marvin walking through the desert, trudging in the sand, sinking up to his knees at times, and making every effort to do it as gracefully as possible as he extended a hand to the Texas contingents. Though Marvin always says he carries an angel on his shoulder, others have said Marvin is using up his nine lives rather fast. With SCUDs bursting overhead and sniper fire in the street, Marvin "I-ain't-no-got-damned-war-correspondent" was there, shaking hands and filming on-the-spot events for the folks in television land back home.

Along with other reporters, Marvin, Lori and Bob would be staying in the five-star Meridian Hotel, one of the high-rise luxury hotels adjacent to the airport. It was later learned that United States military intelligence had been receiving reports that the hotels had been designated by the Iraqis as primary targets, since they were next to the airport. Needless to say, the Saudi and Allied military commands were not particularly pleased to have so many reporters sheltered in hotels that had been designated as primary targets.

To make matters worse, Marvin made a potentially dangerous *faux pas* just shortly after his arrival. He was doing a stand-up shoot in the busy hotel lobby, and things were not going well. In an attempt to break the tension, Marvin turned to his cameraman, and in a loud voice said, "Here is to you, 'Rabbi' Dows." This could be heard throughout the lobby. His crew wanted to kill him. This was not the place where 'Rabbi' could be said, even in jest.

Fortunately, the blunder did not set off an incident, and the next morning, Marvin and his team began the grueling task of videotaping three stories a day. They were still working out of the Meridian Hotel. They weren't any too happy about being in a "primary target" either, but where else could they go at that point? At any rate, like it or not, Marvin was now a war correspondent like all the rest.

Marvin was able to commandeer ground transportation, and he and his crew were driven out to the military airfield, where the stateside flights were coming into Dhahran. Marvin was looking, in particular, for flights from Texas.

By this time, many of the troops had been there for months. They were missing their families. Marvin's arrival was cause for overwhelming emotion, not just because he was a celebrity, but also because it was exciting just to see someone from home who was not wearing military fatigues. The young men and women felt that Marvin was a link between them and the loved ones they had left at home.

The heat emanating from the tarmac exceeded 130 degrees. Marvin stepped out of the car, shoulders back, head high, wearing an immaculately pressed white suit. His white hairpiece was glistening in the sunlight, and of course, he was wearing his blue shades. He briskly strutted to the area where soldiers were exiting a flight from Houston. Bob Dows was right on his heels, with the customary 50-pound camera on his shoulder and another 35 pounds of equipment strapped to his waist. In this heat, Bob was sweating profusely; Lori was mopping his brow so he could see through the lens of the camera. And Marvin? Why, Marvin looked as if he had just stepped out of his air-conditioned room. You would have thought the King of Saudi Arabia himself had come to greet the incoming Texans. A cheer went up when they saw him. There was handshaking and backslapping all around. Some simply said, "Howdy, Marvin," and flashed him a big smile.

Others paused a moment longer to say they were so pleased to see a familiar face. Several took this moment to communicate to their loved ones. "Hi, Mom and Dad. I'm okay." "I love you, Darling." One soldier said, "My thoughts will be with you and the kids

White Knight in Blue Shades

for Christmas."

At that, a young fellow standing behind Marvin shouted, "You are wrong. Now that the 'Texas boys' are here, we are going to clean this mess up and bring y'all home for Christmas!"

A loud cheer went up.

Marvin continued to shake hands and chat with the soldiers, pausing occasionally when one whipped out a small pocket camera and requested a picture with him. They respected Marvin, but they were at ease with him, too. One young fellow grabbed his hand tightly and with a chuckle said, "I know there ain't gonna be any slime in the ice machines while you are around, Mr. Zindler."

Marvin replied, "Ain't seen no ice machines, son." He paused for a minute, then continued, "I don't think they have much water on this desert, and what water they do have, no one has been able to freeze for millions of years."

Everyone began to chuckle.

Someone shouted, "I bet it's even too hot for the roaches." More laughter. Marvin and the troops were in very good spirits. Marvin stayed until the very last soldier had disembarked, shaking more hands than a politician. The troops all seemed a bit more comfortable and a lot less apprehensive after visiting with Marvin, but I've gotten used to seeing that. He has that effect on people wherever he goes. Marvin was a big hit with military units from Texas, of course, but he made appearances at other military camps throughout Saudi Arabia, where he was received with almost the same degree of excitement.

You couldn't very well come to Saudi Arabia and not show the folks back home some camels, so Marvin and his news team started driving in search of camels. Once you left the military air base and headed out across the desert, all that could be seen in any direction was sand. You couldn't tell where you were — a very eerie, unsettling feeling. Marvin was wondering, "How will our troops respond to this? There are no landmarks. No houses. No trees. Just hundreds of miles of sand in all directions. You would go around in circles if you didn't have a compass and a map. You could be lost out here and no one would ever know it." Marvin's musings were interrupted when, out of nowhere, a single camel appeared on the side of the road. They stopped some distance from the animal so as not to frighten it.

Bob, who was sitting in front holding the large professional video camera across his lap, slowly opened the door of the car, stepped out, and stood motionless for a few seconds. Then he slowly raised the camera to his shoulder. A blast of 130-degree midday heat reflected off the sandy desert floor. The camel started to move off. Bob walked out into the desert, following the camel, trying to get its picture. He hoped that it would stop and turn, so that he could get a picture from the front rather than just the rear. He was so intent on getting his picture of this camel to show the folks back home, that he didn't realize he had walked almost a half mile into the dunes. When he stopped walking, the camel turned and looked back at him, and he got his picture. Suddenly, Bob realized he could not see the road from where he stood. If it weren't for his and the camel's footprints in the sand, he would have no points of reference to guide his return to the car.

Bob was sweating profusely. You would think that he had just taken a swim, as his clothes were soaked through. Meanwhile, Marvin and Lori had remained in the car with the air conditioner on.

That 50-pound camera felt as if it weighed a ton, and the return trip seemed much harder and longer than when Bob started. Only a few moments before, he had been pursuing the camel, trying to get that perfect shot. His mind had been fixed on the task. Now, all he could think about was finding the road, getting something to drink, and stepping into the air-conditioned car. As he backtracked over several more dunes, he finally saw the road in the distance. As he approached it, he thought he was seeing a mirage. He continued in the direction of the car, numbed by the heat and the weight of the camera, and mesmerized by what he was watching. Then, he began laughing at himself. It was not a mirage.

Bob had just chased half a mile across the desert to get a picture of a single camel, and while he was gone, an entire herd of camels had surrounded Marvin's car. They were curious animals, poking their heads through the windows and checking out the vehicle. As Bob got closer, he could hardly lift the video camera to his shoulders again. It seemed like a Herculean task, but he did it. He began photographing the camels as they milled around the car, seemingly fascinated with Marvin and Lori.

As Bob continued to film, he noticed a dust cloud in the distance. He was so caught up with the filming and the antics of Marvin and the camels that he paid little attention until the dust cloud was almost upon them. They had been told that sandstorms could come up suddenly in the desert, and that occasionally there were dust funnels as well. Everyone was getting a bit anxious, as this seemed to be an ominous sign. The camels stopped milling around Marvin's car and began turning away, their ears turned upwards. This did not look good! By the time Bob crossed the last few sand dunes to the car, the group was surrounded by military Hummers with 50-caliber machine guns drawn down upon them. Marvin was repeating his mantra to himself (and not for the last time): "I ain't no war correspondent."

Then suddenly, a deep authoritative voice was heard. "Who the hell are you and what the hell are you doing out here?"

Marvin answered, "MARVIN ZINDLER from KTRK Channel 13 television news, in Houston, Texas. We are taking pictures of camels in the desert." Everyone immediately burst out laughing. The camels remained clustered between Marvin's car and the Hummers. The soldiers who were standing by the machine guns reached down into the cab of the Hummer and came up with a small box. Immediately, the camels moved to the side of the Hummer. Bob again mounted the video camera on his shoulder and began filming the friendly military forces and the camels. As he zoomed in for a close-up, Bob began to chuckle. Marvin and Lori could not figure out what was going on. The soldiers were feeding the camels Oreo cookies, and the camels were loving it. One of the soldiers said, "We never travel without our Oreo cookies. Every place in the world that the military has sent us, kids and adults alike have enjoyed Oreos." But camels?!

Marvin remarked, "They are not one of my favorite animals, but I can see that they have good taste, too."

Several of the Hummers took the lead, while others fell in behind Marvin's car, and the entourage escorted King Zindler and his team back to the military base.

And so it went: three major stories a day, and long, hot, arduous days they were. But Marvin knew how much the young men and women stationed in Saudi Arabia appreciated this, and how the families back home were looking forward to seeing their loved ones on television and knowing they were well.

The United States space program and the number of shuttle flights had rapidly expanded over the years. Space travel had taken on an international flavor. There had even been a Saudi astronaut aboard one of the shuttle flights. In Dhahran's downtown business section, a monument to the astronaut — and to the Saudis' participation in the space program — had been erected. The next day, Marvin and his crew set out to film it. No sooner had Marvin stepped from the car and walked toward the monument than horns began honking. People were shouting, "Hi, Marvin!" "How are you doing, Marvin?" "Glad to see you, Marvin!" No matter where Marvin went in Saudi Arabia, this kind of reception was repeated.

Later that day, Marvin and his team took the road out of town, again crossing the desert as a line of United States military Amtraks and tanks passed them by. They stopped the car and Marvin got out. Lori shouted, "Are there any tank soldiers from Houston in there?"

There was a few moments' pause, then someone began opening one of the hatches of a nearby tank. A head appeared, and then the shoulders. The soldier began waving at Marvin and yelled at the top of his voice, "Slime in the ice machine!" Then, apparently embarrassed, he quickly slid back into the hatch and slammed it closed.

The next day, the Joint Information Bureau (JIB), which is run by the military and authorized to work with the many journalists from around the world, offered to fly Marvin and his team into the desert, where they had set up a new airfield in only a few weeks. This was where the C5A cargo carriers were coming in, caravan style, from the United States, across the "Aluminum Bridge to the East."

The JIB would fly you in, let you take your video, help you obtain your interviews, and then fly you out. Marvin really appreciated this wonderful opportunity for himself and his team to see and film the entire operation firsthand. The JIB was so helpful that the next day Marvin, Lori and Bob returned to see what other help they offered "war correspondents." They eagerly joined another military guided tour that inadvertently ended up in the same place they had gone the day before.

This proved to be very interesting, as the same aircraft were sitting in the exact same places they had been the day before. The same men — soldiers? PR people? — that Marvin, Lori and Bob had been allowed to interview the day before were stationed in exactly the same places, and performing the exact same tasks that they had been performing the day before. The cargo that had been placed on and along the airfield was in the same spot. Nothing had moved. Nothing had changed. Everything had been laid out perfectly. It provided the press an opportunity to get a picture of the bag cargo carriers, the equipment and the men in battle uniform with the desert in the background, the sun coming over their shoulders.

The JIB had done its job very well indeed. It had been a setup, staged just for the press's benefit. The JIB had arranged for the press to get only those pictures it wanted them to take, in as efficient a manner as possible. They would fly the news correspondents to this Hollywood-like military set in the desert, let them get their video and still pictures, and allow them to interview men and women in combat garb — men and women who were actually trained public relations people who had been stationed on the set. After that the Army would fly the correspondents to Dhahran or Riyadh, no wiser. The only mistake was that they had taken Marvin, Lori and Bob on the same tour twice.

After that, Marvin and company did not seek any further help from the JIB, and spent their time with the men and women from the Texas contingency and other "real" combatants. Marvin was there to bring the real story home to their families for Christmas, not to participate in a propaganda program.

Marvin, now a full-fledged war correspondent whether he liked it or not, quickly realized that this massive buildup — which had initially been presented to the press as a means to deter and defend — was obviously the preparation for a future offensive action. Marvin said that he got a sinking feeling in the pit of his stomach, what with Iraq showing no sign of responding to the United Nation's embargo, and hundreds of thousands of young Americans now stationed in the Saudi desert. By this time, the United States and their allied forces had put in place twice as many soldiers and three times as much armor as had originally been designated for Desert Shield. Marvin suspected that Washington was about to confront the question of what to do next, but he knew that these men and women would not be coming home for Christmas. Hopefully, they would all return safely at some future date.

Marvin reported that the Defense Department's tally on the air lift and sea lift expenses to date were almost 1.9 billion dollars. Japan, who would not commit troops, pledged one billion dollars to safeguard Saudi Arabia. King Fahd had promised to pay transportation costs, housing and other expenses within his kingdom, but not *to* it. And more forces continued to arrive every day. In speeches broadcast over Baghdad radio, Saddam Hussein called King Fahd and Egyptian President Mubarak traitors to the Arab cause. Marvin knew in his heart that no one would be leaving before the Iraqi threat had been eliminated, and he also knew that fighting could begin any day. The window of opportunity to go on the attack shrunk as the Muslim holidays approached. In a few months, in March, when the Muslim holy month of Ramadan arrived, everything would stop.

In the next few days, the desert had grown a little cooler, and somewhat more bearable, with the temperature only hitting 100 degrees. As Marvin traveled to isolated front-line camps with names like All-American and Victory, he discovered there was little to take the soldiers' minds off the heat, sand, flies, and the big question, which was, as yet, unanswered. A constant in every conversation was whether they would be going to war, and if so, when they would be going — or would they be going home for Christmas? Marvin said, "No one was telling them what to expect."

So when rumors spread that a rotation plan was in the works, a lot of young men and women were hoping that they would be home in time for the holidays, but Marvin doubted it very much. He said, "I don't blame them for hoping, but all they have to do is look around. We are going to fight, and it's gonna be soon."

While this buildup was taking place, the Iraqis had put more than half a million troops along the Saudi border. Rumors were rampant that the Iraqis might use chemical weapons. The big question was, would the United States and its allies use unconventional weapons if the Iraqis brought chemical warfare to the battlefield? Then, on December 6, Marvin learned that Saddam would immediately free all of its foreign hostages; Saddam called this a humanitarian gesture to promote peace, and added that Iraq had built up its defenses to the point where "human shields" were no longer necessary. This was now being called the "Saddam line," made up of approximately 4,300 tanks, more than 3,000 pieces of artillery, and more than half a million men. Iraqi soldiers, who had spent several months digging in, creating tank traps, laying mine fields, and building trenches and forts, were in position. The "Saddam line" extended along the entire southern border of Kuwait, and 40 miles further along the southern border with Iraq, a total of more than 175 miles in all.

The Kuwaiti royal family, with the Crown Prince of Kuwait, had set up headquarters in exile in Saudi Arabia. While Marvin was there, he availed himself of the opportunity to interview the Crown Prince, as well as the King of Saudi Arabia. The prince sent one of his luxury aircraft to take Marvin and his team, as well as other reporters, to his headquarters for the evening. The Saudi aircraft was absolutely exquisite. Anything one could want was on board. It was an evening, and an interview, to remember.

Back at the hotel, Marvin, Lori and Bob were standing at the information center. There was a strict rule that there would be no interviews in hotels. Lori reminded Marvin, "We are not going to do any interviews; we're just going to stand in the main lobby area."

Wrong! Within minutes, members of the armed forces flocked around Marvin...but of course, they were not doing any interviews, just greeting folks from back home. It was through these contacts that Marvin and the team were able to hook up with some flyboys, and they made arrangements to travel with them to Riyadh, where Marvin planned to meet with contingencies from other Texas air bases.

Though the Gulf Arabs are not usually aggressive people, every leader Marvin had spoken with wanted to attack and destroy the Iraqis who were occupying Kuwait. Marvin also found most Kuwaitis to be quite arrogant about their wealth. Their arrogance is a trait that is frowned upon in the Arab world, but Saddam had now attacked an Arab brother. The attack had been unprovoked, and his army now sat poised on the Saudi Arabian border, threatening this country as well. Marvin said, "None of them could live with that."

Marvin heard such comments as, "America should lead, and we are ready to follow."

Others told Marvin, "Our war with Iraq has already begun."

From locals as well as our soldiers, Marvin heard, "Saddam has got to be destroyed."

"We can't let him get away with this," Marvin said. "As far as the Gulf is concerned, a negotiated settlement would be a disaster."

Lori, Bob and Marvin returned to their hotel, and went to bed that night looking forward to making the trip to Riyadh and visiting with the Texas Air Force contingency the next day. The next morning, however, Marvin learned that all flights were canceled. There were rumors that Saddam would fire SCUD missiles toward Israel from western Iraq. It was feared that Israel would then feel forced to enter into the war. Dozens of Israeli jets took off from their bases. Fortunately, the Israeli jets remained within Israeli air space. General Colin Powell reported that he had persuaded Tel Aviv — at least for now — to call back its jets. Meanwhile, Patriot missile batteries stationed around the Dhahran Air Base were made ready to intercept the SCUDS. The Patriots, originally designed as anti-aircraft weapons, had only recently been modified to intercept incoming missiles. Since the Patriot missiles had never been battle-tested, everyone was very anxious and uneasy with the situation.

It was painfully obvious that Marvin and his team would not be allowed to fly to Riyadh under these new circumstances. But Marvin figured that he had his stories, and that it was time to let folks at home see their sons and daughters were fine, and were just as worried about their families at home as those at home were about them. In the grand scheme of things, perhaps Marvin's angel was telling him that it was time to get the hell out of there.

There were still more than 1,300 reporters in the war zone. At any one time, as many as 180 war correspondents — in groups of two or three — were scattered across 175 miles of the front line.

This time, Marvin really meant it when he said he was no war correspondent. He took his angel's advice, and told his team it was time to go home — NOW! Marvin, Bob and Lori packed their equipment, and carefully hand-carried their precious videotapes aboard their flight. They returned safely to Houston for Marvin's special Christmas programs.

For the men and women left behind in the desert, however, it was not yet time for homecomings. As Marvin and others had predicted, Desert Shield did, indeed, evolve into Desert Storm. The clouds that hung over the desert were not all sandstorms any longer. They were black with the smoke of burning. And the winds that had once whistled across the dunes were drowned out by the thunderous echoes of war.

Which, as we all know, is not Marvin's beat.

C·H·A·P·T·E·R 32

To Russia With Love
(1993)

Marvin had been wanting to go to Russia for a long time. His thoughts began to turn frequently to that vast mysterious land in 1979, but at that time, the world was in turmoil, and the Cold War was still in full force. In December of 1979, Russian forces numbering 130,000 invaded Afghanistan, and installed their own premier. The Afghan prime minister died in the invasion.

In the late 1970s, Marvin was also considering a medical mission to Central America, particularly Nicaragua, whose population is always in need of medical help. Unfortunately, the Sandinista forces had taken control of Nicaragua, and a guerilla war was going on. Those who had formerly been in power became known as the Contras, and were now fighting against the Sandinistas. Central America was in turmoil too. Even so, Marvin (and I) did eventually get to go to Nicaragua, more than once... but that's another story.[1]

Despite the widespread upheavals in the late 1970s and early '80s, Marvin was optimistic. He felt that Communism throughout the world was coming to an end. Thanks to communications such as radio, television and the press, those oppressed under Communist systems were coming to know that there was a better way.

Marvin liked to say, "People will always dream of capitalism, prosperity, and freedom of choice. If Communism is so good, then why do they need a wall in Berlin? It surely isn't to keep people from coming over to the Communist side!"

Meanwhile, Marvin watched and waited. He kept a sharp eye on world affairs, making predictions that were often contrary to the prognostications of other world watchers. In the late 1980s and early 1990s, as the struggle for freedom intensified and democracy

---

[1] See the chapter entitled, "The Power of a Photograph," in this section.

began breaking out all over the countries behind the Iron Curtain, it became apparent that Marvin's predictions were coming true.

At the same time that massive pro-democracy demonstrations were making news in China, ethnic conflicts and independent movements began to shake the Soviet Union as well. As Marvin had predicted, that empire began to crumble. Czechoslovakia became a free nation, and dissident playwright Vaclav Havel became its first democratically elected president in 1989.

Freedom and the desire to participate in the capitalistic system resulted in massive pro-democracy demonstrations in East Germany too, and, in late 1989, as Marvin had also predicted, the hard-line East German government crumbled, and soon after, so did the Berlin Wall.

"They all want to be free," Marvin reiterated.

A new light shone upon the solidarity movement in Germany, and upon Europe as a whole. A series of major democratic and economic reforms followed. By December, the Polish Peoples Republic had become a free nation. There were reverberations throughout the Communist countries, with the notable exception of Castro's Cuba.

The USSR continued to disintegrate as ethnic and separatist pressures increased. Mikhail Gorbachev's program of political and social reform faltered, and the Soviet economic system began to disintegrate as well. Marvin was still spouting, "It's hell to be poor!" — and this was illustrated graphically in world events, every day.

In May of 1990, Boris Yeltsin became President of the Russian Federation, riding the widespread feeling of discontent to a position of power. The Soviet economy was in a shambles. Soviet arms and political commitments to regional allies were discontinued; under the Communist system they could not afford it. As a result, Soviet forces began their withdrawal from Eastern Europe. Without the USSR, the Warsaw Pact effectively dissolved. Marvin was right again.

Ironically, Mikhail Gorbachev was awarded the Nobel Peace Prize for guiding the progress toward what Marvin had said was going to happen anyway: the collapse of the USSR and the return of the Soviet satellite nations to self-rule and democracy.

The world was changing rapidly, and all the while the media, particularly television, brought world attention to these massive changes and the worldwide struggles for freedom and democracy. Marvin was pleased to have what amounted to a front-row seat to these events.

As Marvin had predicted, the Cold War continued to recede. The ensuing weapons reduction left Russia with — according to them — a 60% retaliation capability. The Russians claimed that many of the remaining missiles were sitting in their silos in the Ural Mountains. Especially given the misinformation the Russians had provided during the Chernobyl crisis, Marvin wanted to know the real truth. He wanted to see for himself. Now there was even more of a reason to make that long planned-for visit to Russia.

Furthermore, with the reopening of Russia, the end of Communism, and the rebirth of religious freedom and Russian capitalism, the American public was looking to the press for more information on this "new Russia."

In short, it was high time for Marvin to visit Mother Russia.

I guess it was time for me to visit Russia as well. Medicine outside of the cities of Moscow and St. Petersburg was equivalent to American medicine in the 1940s and 1950s. Medical supplies were few and far between, and antibiotics and pain medicine were difficult, if not impossible, to come by.

Furthermore, with all the fighting from within Russia, as well as throughout its satellite nations, not to mention the Serbian genocidal "ethnic cleansing," civilian casualties were astronomical — especially among children. I, along with a medical team from the world-renowned Texas Medical Center, was asked to join an American team of plastic and reconstructive, orthopaedic, and vascular surgeons to work on these children in the alleged safety of the United Nations protected zone. Accordingly, a medical mission trip, with Marvin along, was planned for 1993.

We had been assured that, with proper visas and travel papers, we would have unlimited access. It took all of a year for Marvin and me, with the help of ABC-Television and the Russian consulate's office, to acquire the proper documentation and arrange for medical and lecture facilities and scheduling, as well as customs clearances for medical, photographic and television equipment. We knew that we had to dot all our I's and cross all our T's if we wanted this trip to come off at all.

But there were snags along the way. To begin with, there was Marvin. You know Marvin; he's never been one to back out of an adventure, and he had been wanting to go to Russia for years. For some reason, though, he was being unusually cautious now. He kept warning me, "Snipers will shoot at medical personnel, international peacekeepers and television correspondents. No one is safe." Finally he told me, "The angel on my shoulder feels I should remain at home."

Nevertheless, I received several phone calls encouraging me to go. I decided not to listen to Marvin's angel this time — after all, it was his angel, not mine — and I busied myself with the task of readying equipment and supplies. But then there were more snags. In the end, family commitments and obligations at home made it impossible for me to travel at the originally scheduled time, and I was forced to reschedule the trip.

Several days after my would-be departure date, the International Television News Station broadcast news of the bombing of the children's hospital in the United Nations-protected "safe" zone, where we had all been scheduled to work. Local doctors and medical personnel were the first to leave the facility. The American medical contingency and other foreign-aid groups remained with the casualties in the bombed-out structure, attempting with what supplies they had to care for the children. Finally, under United Nations protection and in armored vehicles, the American doctors were brought through the lines. Serbian aggression was again condemned by the United Nations, but words were unable to stop rockets and snipers' bullets.

Marvin, as usual, had been right; there was no protection, even for doctors or news reporters. (Well, I guess I have to give some credit to that angel too.)

Of course, we had no intention of giving up the idea of going to Russia, since the invitation still stood, so we proceeded with our plans. We were invited to the central and eastern cities of Perm, a major military and university center with approximately 1.2 million inhabitants, and Kungur, a smaller city at the base of the Ural Mountains, with 50,000 people living in the region. These cities are several thousand miles from Moscow — 22 hours on the Trans-Siberian railroad, and then several more hours by jeep or bus into the Ural Mountains. It was here that the need for medical care was truly critical, and, as it happened, where the missile silos that Marvin wanted to see were hidden.

We hoped against hope for the United States and the United Nations to step in and stop the atrocities and bring the terrible "civil wars" to a quick and successful end. Marvin's producer Lori and I continued sending letters and faxes to the appropriate Russian authorities. Safety for our group was still a prime concern. There was no way to enter central or eastern Russia without passing through Moscow, which was under strict, if ineffective, military control at this time. I knew that angel on Marvin's shoulder was going to have to work overtime.

Marvin seemed more optimistic this time around. He, of course, was not going to Russia to chronicle the unrest. As he had stated so many times before on our journeys through troubled lands, he reiterated, "I am not a war correspondent." Marvin's plan was to give his audience a look at the New Russia. This trip was going to be *TO RUSSIA WITH LOVE.*"

As far as the other doctors, the medical assistants and I were concerned, this was also a trip "To Russia With Love." What we had planned was a medical, teaching and humanitarian mission to the cities of Perm and Kungur. We had received warm letters of invitation and were assured that the people of both cities looked forward to the arrival of the American medical team and, of course, Marvin. Since there were no hotels or restaurants, we would be guests in private homes. It would give us all the opportunity to talk to the people, and to see a part of Russia that Americans had never seen before.

In fact, the cities of Perm and Kungur had been virtually isolated for over 70 years. No foreigners had passed through their gates, much less an American. The presence of a number of military bases, as well as factories producing jet engines, technical equipment and rockets — not to mention the installation of intercontinental ballistic missiles (ICBMs) in the Ural Mountains — had resulted in the closing of these cities to Russians and foreigners alike.

The Russian consulate had provided our visas. The clincher was that Marvin agreed to allow the Russian television station to film every step of the trip. In turn, Marvin would be allowed to film freely. The letters Marvin had received not only guaranteed our safety, but gave Marvin the freedom to travel and videotape whatever he wanted. To Marvin's surprise, this included the underground ICBM installations, which had been reported as having been destroyed after the famous arms reduction agreement. However, that agreement had only covered some 40 percent of the ICBMs. As it turned out, the Russian officials were happy to show both the deactivated missile silos and those still armed....

....But I'm getting ahead of myself.

Marvin's producer Lori had sent many faxes and letters to Russia, but communication and language were a problem. There were also many uncertainties. We had to be prepared for anything, and almost anything could go wrong.

There were many logistical and technical problems. For example, the electrical current in the United States was 110 volts, but in Russia it was 220. We were also told that there were severe current surges or fluctuations in the areas we'd be visiting. Current electric converters and surge protectors would be needed for all the medical and television equipment. Bob Dows and Lori Reingold worked late nights and all of one weekend packing the delicate electrical equipment, cameras, extra batteries, battery chargers, converters and lighting systems that would be needed to film the medical expedition. Marvin was there on Friday to offer encouragement, advice and much-needed technical support. Considering that Marvin doesn't know the difference between a battery charger and a converter, it was rather comical, but it made the task of preparing less monotonous. Of course, while Lori and Bob returned over the weekend to complete the packing, Marvin was hard at work on the golf course.

I had worked late nights and through the entire weekend as well. Because we didn't know what to expect, or what would be available in Perm or Kungur, we had to pack medical equipment, instruments, operating room supplies and medications to cover any conceivable situation. The medical supplies needed to be wrapped carefully to protect them from breakage. Every possible problem or emergency that could arise had to be planned for. The instruments were pre-sterilized, then wrapped in bubble-wrap and placed into waterproof bags. These were then packed into special crates for shipping. It was a slow process.

Dr. Gus Cezeaux, the anesthesiologist who would be accompanying me, worked through the evening, checking and re-checking his list to be sure that everything was included. Once the operating room equipment, converters, surge protectors and instruments were packed, Dr. Cezeaux had to do the same for the anesthesia equipment and monitoring units. We did know there would be no monitoring units in Kungur or Perm.

Medications were needed, particularly drugs to prevent infection and alleviate pain, as well as antihistamines, decongestants, cardiac drugs and vitamins. Many of these had been donated by American pharmaceutical companies over the past six months. The remainder, I purchased myself.

Then there were the children to consider — children who did not have any toys, who had never held a soft, cuddly stuffed animal. There would be little girls who had never owned a doll, little boys who had never thrown a baseball or Frisbee. The Agris-Zindler Children's Foundation, The Woodlands Merchant Association, and a number of very generous individuals donated many of these items, as well as much-needed children's clothing. All this had to be boxed for shipment to Russia, as well.

Finally, at about 2 A.M. the day of our departure, everything was packed, and the checklists completed. Everyone was tired, especially Marvin, who had been through an exhausting weekend of golf. There was a feeling of exhilaration, yet there lingered a haunting, nagging feeling that something might have been forgotten, an important and very necessary item or medication left out.

Later that day, my good friend and traveling companion, Mr. José Dixon, volunteered his services and his van to take the cases of medical equipment, medication and toys to the airport. Often overlooked is the time, personal sacrifice and effort that all the team members contribute to making a medical mission of this magnitude safe and successful. It was done with a deep sense of conviction and caring, and truly was a trip *TO RUSSIA WITH LOVE.*

Mr. Dixon, Gus Cezeaux and I loaded the van at The Methodist Hospital in the Texas Medical Center. Helping us was Jim Cezeaux, Gus's son, who was to go along as our interpreter. Jim had studied Russian for four years, and was not only fluent in that language but also in several of the dialects spoken in the areas we'd be visiting. He had also studied Russian history, social policies, politics and geography, so he was well-versed in Mother Russia as well as in the mother tongue.

With the van packed, we began the 45-minute ride to Houston Intercontinental Airport. Upon our arrival at the airport Bob Dows already had his camera rolling, and was capturing the hectic scene as the group began unloading the many crates of equipment and personal luggage.

As has been our usual experience, the airport baggage handlers and airline personnel were most courteous. (Yes, really.) They applied *Special Handling* tags on the boxes of medical equipment to indicate their fragile contents. Fortunately, all travel papers and visas were in order, and it went smoothly and quickly, thanks to everyone's contribution to the effort.

Everything was proceeding smoothly, when it hit me: Where was Marvin? Team members were busy marking and tagging the baggage and crates, but Marvin was nowhere to be found. Lori and Bob were clearing their passports, processing their tickets, and securing the television equipment, but where was Marvin? I was at the airline counter with teams, passports and visas. Still, no Marvin. Lori repeatedly glanced over her shoulder toward the lobby area, but Marvin was nowhere to be seen. Time was short, and everyone was working furiously to get all the equipment and supplies tagged and onto the conveyor belt.

Most of us (with one notable exception) had been up virtually all night packing, and had had little sleep. We were tired. We were all looking forward to finally boarding the aircraft and getting the opportunity to push back and relax. But where was Marvin? Finally, just as we were gathering up our carry-on luggage and preparing to go through the security check, we heard a commotion in the main lobby of the terminal.

Someone in the terminal was shouting, "That's Marrrvinnn Zindler!" We turned in the direction of the commotion. It was as if the Pied Piper had just arrived; admirers, young and old, had spied Marvin and rushed to greet him. Some were clamoring for autographs, some just wanted to shake his hand. His London Fog raincoat was draped over his shoulders like a cape, and the fluorescent lighting of the terminal cast a sheen over his white hairpiece and reflected off those blue sunshades. Marvin was smiling cheerfully, shaking hands and stopping every few feet to sign an autograph. The knight in white shining armor had arrived, and now the trip could finally begin.

I couldn't help but wonder, *What would they think of Marvin in rural Russia?*

After all the flurry and commotion, thank goodness, the flight for Russia left on time and was uneventful. It gave the team a chance to catch up on some much-needed sleep and to visit with each other and with Marvin, who took great joy in telling us about the wonderful golf game he had played over the weekend. When we landed in Moscow, he seemed refreshed but anxious to stretch his legs.

The Moscow Airport was an experience in itself. The facility was very old, the lighting was inadequate at best, and, inconveniently enough, all the signs were in Russian, which only our interpreter could read. As we disembarked, we were herded like cattle, first through immigration and then on to where the passports and visas would be stamped before we would be allowed to enter the country.

The ABC Television affiliate in Moscow had sent several people to meet Marvin and the group. They "greased the wheels" to get the television equipment through customs smoothly, quickly and intact.

I did not fare quite so well with my medical equipment and supplies. Though I had documentation to clear them, the customs officials were not going to accept this. They opened several of the boxes, more for show than actual inspection. They only did a quick and rather cursory review of what was brought.

Finally, with the last of the customs papers stamped, everyone helped pick up the boxes of supplies. One of the team members asked what to do with several boxes that were now opened. I have learned never to travel any place without several rolls of yellow duct tape, which I now removed from my carry-on luggage. Within minutes, the boxes were again securely bound and ready to be removed from the customs area.

Any type of wagons, dollies or porter services are minimal to nonexistent in most foreign countries, and this was true at the Moscow Airport as well. The only way the medical crates and personal luggage could be moved out of the terminal was for everyone to lend a helping hand. First, all the crates of medical supplies and personal luggage were gathered in one corner of the terminal, where Marvin and a few members of the team could keep a watchful eye to ensure that items would not suddenly disappear. Meanwhile, other members of the team carried as many items as they could manage out of the terminal to a van.

We were met in Moscow by members of the Hudson Corporation, a division of McDermott, an American company working out of Moscow. They had been kind enough to provide a van, and they offered to help the group during our overnight stay and our transfer from Moscow to Perm. Even their CEO came to greet us. After numerous trips, all of the supplies were moved from the customs area and loaded aboard the Hudson Corporation van. It was only to be an overnight stay. Rather than taking the 22-hour ride on the Trans-Siberian Railroad, we were going to fly. We were to leave with the medical team early the next morning, bound for the small local airport, where we would board Aeroflot, the Russian airline, for Perm.

We took only our personal luggage to the hotel. It was felt that transferring the equipment up to and back from the hotel, and then back to the airport, would be too cumbersome. There was also some question about the safety of storing the equipment at the hotel. The Hudson Corporation volunteered to keep the van in their secure compound in Moscow, and then meet us in the morning to take us to the airport. This was a pleasant and welcome surprise; it sure made things much easier for everyone.

By now everybody was excited; the adrenaline was pumping. You could see it in their faces and hear it in their voices. As we boarded a van for the Cosmos Hotel, Bob Dows sat with his video camera in the front seat, while I sat by the window with my cameras. Marvin and Lori were directly across the aisle. The rest of the team, typical of tourists, had their cameras out as well.

It was a sunny, clear crisp day. We opened the windows of the van as we left the airport and headed into central Moscow. The driver described the sights along the way.

Private cars, we learned, were a luxury in Moscow, and most people traveled by public transportation, electric trolleys being the major mode. Trolleys had been prominent in most American cities from the 1930s through the 1950s, when the bus and private automobiles replaced them. But in Moscow, the clock had been turned back. The swish of the trolleys over the rails, the clang of the bell when they started and stopped, and the crackling of the sparks from the overhead electric wires filled the air. The driver traversed this maze smoothly and comfortably.

I was kneeling on my seat, my head on my arms as I leaned out the window with a video camera mounted on my shoulder. So intensely was I was concentrating on photographing a very beautiful monument dedicated to the Russian cosmonauts that I was oblivious to a trolley that was approaching the van from behind. There would be only inches between the van and the approaching trolley, surely not enough room for my head and video camera. Everyone in the van gasped as I quickly slid back into my seat, video camera still running, at almost the same moment that the trolley slithered past. Marvin said, "I can't wait to see that on video tape. It ought to be quite exciting."

The Hotel Cosmos is quite old, but is considered five-star by Russian standards. By American standards, however, it is reminiscent of a $30.00-a-night motel, with bathrooms befitting what one would expect to find in a rundown mobile home. On the hotel grounds, there were hawkers selling all kinds of souvenirs and wares. At the front of the hotel were armed guards who admitted only foreigners with passports. Once again, there was no one to help with any baggage. Remember, Russia had only been opened to the outside world for less than two years, and had not yet begun to comprehend — much less implement — the notion of being service-oriented.

The lobby of the hotel was large, musty and dark, with only a few seats available. In the corner was a small booth where money could be exchanged, and next to that was a small souvenir shop. There was a long counter area, but only two clerks. Here, we presented our passports and travel documents and were given room assignments. Marvin had been warned not to trust the elevators in Russia, but he wasn't about to climb stairs all the way to the sixth floor. After exiting the elevator and walking down a small corridor, we were surprised to see a steel floor-to-ceiling gated area with an iron door in the center. It almost looked like a cell block in a prison. Behind the door, a full-bodied lady sat at a desk. She took her time unlocking the door. Again she required us to show our passports and room assignment cards. Only then were keys issued to our respective rooms. She put the room assignment cards into a slot behind her desk, from which she withdrew the keys.

The rooms were sparse. Each room had two single beds. Our footfalls as we walked across the carpet stirred up little clouds of dust. The bed, nightstand and furniture were dotted with cigarette burn marks, and the smell of stale smoke hung in the air, emanating from the stained bed covers and draperies. As you can imagine, non-smoking rooms were not an option. Thank goodness the windows could be opened, albeit with a 1950s-style hand crank. Even if it became cooler later in the evening, I was going to leave the windows open, so that the night air might do battle with the residue of stale smoke.

There was a small dresser with a mirror at the far corner, but no other amenities in the room. On the sixth floor, each room had its own bath, a small but adequate facility with hot and cold running water, an antiquated porcelain sink and a bathtub. Scarred white tiles ran halfway up the walls.

It was a beautiful day with a crisp breeze. A few hours of daylight remained, and we wanted to enjoy every minute of it, because once we reached the cities of Perm and Kungur, we would be working 12 to 14 hours a day. When we left our rooms, we went through the security process in reverse. We returned our heavy, oversized keys to the Amazon lady on the sixth floor, and she gave us our room passes and locked the gate behind us. Talk about security in a military state!

Marvin exchanged some dollars for rubles and we all went for a walk. There was a very nice tree-lined park across from the hotel, and we were told that only a few blocks away was Moscow's fairground.

Lining the road was a succession of small one-room structures, painted yellow and containing glass fronts. These were referred to as kiosks, and in each storefront, there was a small slit with a sliding panel in the glass. From these tiny one-room stores you could purchase almost anything. One kiosk was filled with shoes, the next contained videocassettes and disks. Others had packaged goods and clothing. This was the beginning of private enterprise in Moscow.

What was interesting was that you couldn't touch or try on anything. You would point to what you wanted, and the proprietor would put it up against the window so you could get a better look. If you then wished to purchase it, the price was agreed to, the items paid for, and then — and only then — were the items passed through the small slit. It seemed very strange when compared to the open markets and department stores that Americans are accustomed to, where you can browse, examine, touch and try on goods before they're purchased. Theoretically, Russia is free and open to capitalism, but fear, suspicion and mistrust still carried over from the old system.

As we strolled down the street, absorbed in idle chatter and our private musings about the "new" Russia, we were frozen in our tracks by the staccato rat-tat-tat of machine gun fire very nearby, virtually around the corner from where we stood. The shots were followed by the squeal of tires against the pavement as vehicles screeched to a halt. Naturally, this sequence of events got everyone's attention.

People were running; some were fleeing the sound, others were rushing toward it. What followed was a sound all-too-familiar to the news crew — that unmistakable noise of two vehicles colliding. After a few seconds of quiet, shouts could be heard.

It always makes good sense, when you hear gunfire, to be going in the opposite direction, but curiosity — and the very real possibility of the need for medical help — drew us toward the situation. Bob Dows, with his video camera on his shoulder, was already in the lead, with Marvin just behind him. When Marvin turned the corner, he could see tire tracks extending the length of the block. The street was empty except for a few onlookers who were standing well back, gawking at what had taken place. The loud, almost ear-piercing wail of emergency vehicles and police sirens could be heard approaching. Marvin and Bob ran past a young couple who were clutching each other, obviously too frightened to move.

A brand new Mercedes sedan had careened off the road onto the sidewalk and struck the building. It looked as if it had bounced 15 feet along a concrete wall and flipped. Now it was lying on its side across the sidewalk. Fresh blood was splattered on the windshield and dripping from the car onto the pavement. No one could be seen inside the vehicle. There were no cries for help.

We stood at a safe distance to the far side of the street, as police and emergency personnel cordoned off the street and slowly approached the vehicle. Marvin was facing the driver's side of the Mercedes sedan. There were two rows of machine gun bullet holes, running from the front of the vehicle to the back. Marvin doubted that anyone inside the car could have survived the fusillade, much less the impact of crashing into the concrete wall at such high speed. Bob, consummate news cameraman that he was, captured it all on film for the viewers back home.

Marvin would later learn that this was not an isolated event. The largest number of Mercedes sold in Russia at that time were to the "new rich," which some had termed The Russian Mafia. The opening of Russia could be compared to the flapper-and-gangster era of the 1920s to 1930s in the United States. In Moscow and other Russian cities, a thriving, illegal underground market had developed in the wake of Russia's new-found freedom.

There were those who tried to exploit the return to a capitalistic system, bringing rise to the cottage industries of loan sharking, protection money, prostitution, gambling, alcohol, black market cigarettes, and all other vices from which huge profits could be harvested. The scene before us was no accident. Someone had trespassed, or overstepped their boundary. Perhaps one of the Mafia Dons, or whatever they called them in Russia, had attempted to take over a bigger territory, or it may have been the result of a personal vendetta. Regardless, we couldn't help but think what a waste it was of a beautiful automobile, to say nothing of the lives lost.

The police went about their business in a very regimented, orderly manner. They quickly closed off the street and ushered the bystanders away. Marvin and Bob took the cue and left also, satisfied that they had their video pictures. This was to be the first of several instances where Marvin and his television crew were able to document the activity of the Russian Mafia. With the return to capitalism, everyone in Russia wanted to be an entrepreneur, and the fever was quickly expanding throughout Moscow and into smaller towns and villages.

Several of the kiosks we passed were blackened, their glass shattered, and the inside completely burned out. But there was nothing in these shops that could reasonably be expected to result in a fire or to produce the kind of destruction that we had seen. The ABC affiliate host in Moscow was able to explain this to Marvin. They told him that you could not open a kiosk or any business in Moscow without paying protection money. Some shopkeepers had attempted to forego this ransom, and others may have been late with their payments. The Mafia knew that if they were going to keep the kiosk owners in line, they would occasionally need to make an example of what happens when their "customers" didn't pay up.

Marvin was told that the Mafia's favorite tactic was to throw a hand grenade through the small window in the front of the kiosk. The construction and size of the kiosks were such that the blast would be pretty much self-contained within the kiosk's metal walls. The offending owner was eliminated, and his merchandise inside the kiosk destroyed, but adjacent businesses and passers-by on the street rarely incurred injury. It was sort of a criminal version of a "surgical strike."

Marvin commented, "I would find this very persuasive if I was a businessman in

Moscow."

Russians, it was clear, were playing by a different set of rules these days, and the main rule by which they seemed to be playing was, "Anything Goes." The downfall of the strong Soviet military gave rise to corruption, crime, chaos, and confusion, as well as overwhelming opportunities. Greedy opportunists and the Russian Mafia were in a deadly serious business. They employed bomb blasts, kidnappings, and murder with the same aplomb that an American business might use a stock merger. Marvin said at the time that he believed that organized crime activity in Russia was going to get a lot worse before anybody put a damper on it and got it under control. So far he's been proven right.

When Marvin asked the affiliate host where the police were, he was told, "They don't seem to come around unless a catastrophic event occurs. The police take the usual reports and nothing further seems to happen."

"Is that because the officials themselves are corrupt?" Marvin inquired.

"Yes, that is why. They can — and do — buy their way into a ministry or whatever for amazingly small amounts of money. Realize that the average Moscow policeman only makes five dollars a day. The Mafia easily supplements not only the local policemen's incomes, but they pay bribes all the way to the top. When the agency that is supposed to protect you is working for the agency that is suppressing you, there's not much you can do. But this is changing — slowly, but in a positive direction. As the economy improves and wages increase, this kind of thing will not be tolerated."

Marvin asked him, "In a country where handguns are prohibited, and machine guns and hand grenades are limited to the armed forces, how does the Mafia get such fire power?" The only answer he got was a shrug of the shoulders.

Being a good newsman, Marvin wasn't satisfied with the non-answer. Using his interpreter, Marvin sought answers where he has always sought them. He went to the man and woman on the street, to small business owners, larger businesses, and even American firms doing business in Moscow. The story from everyone was the same. Funds were in short supply. Many people were without jobs, and those who were working sometimes didn't get paid for weeks or even months. In order to live, people were selling their personal possessions, even precious family heirlooms. Those who had been in the military and had since been discharged were now selling everything; not only their medals, but also their automatic weapons, grenades, and even state-of-the-art night scopes were for sale. You didn't have to go to some obscure black market to get this stuff either. All you had to do was go to the central square any day of the week, or better yet on the weekend, and these items would be openly displayed.

We wanted to see this for ourselves, so we ventured out to the square. Even with the descriptions we had been given, we were stunned by what we found. A great-grandmother, who had not gotten her social security check for six months, was selling some family heirlooms, china and silver. A middle-aged gentleman who had not received a paycheck for three months was selling his television set, video tapes and some records. Next to him were two older ladies who had made a quilt and were offering it and some crocheting for sale. It was like a gigantic garage sale; sadly, many of the items were family keepsakes. It broke our hearts, knowing how painful it must have been for these people to sell off their treasures, but the harsh truth was that, in order to eat, they had to relinquish them. A few items were luxuries, purchased in better times, but most were basic housewares items and clothing. As we walked through the market, the people called to us, imploring us to look at what they had for sale.

At one table we passed, Marvin began to get the answer to his question about where all those firearms were coming from. The table was piled with military gear; some grenades were in a box under the table, and a beautiful night-vision rifle scope lay across and end of the table. Such a scope would cost $2,500 to $3,500 in the United States, but the asking price here was only $300. I was curious, so I examined the scope and began to bargain. Within a few minutes, the gentleman was willing to sell it for only $100 cash.

Everywhere we saw evidence of the fear that the Russians had for their currency and the economy. The U.S. dollar was the only stable currency in Russia, and was jealously hoarded. There were more United States one-hundred dollar bills in Russia than in any other country in the world. The ruble had significantly depreciated, to the point where one U.S. dollar was worth about 600 rubles. If you cashed a $100 bill, you got back 570,000 rubles. You needed a sack to carry them in, and if you didn't think about their relative value (or lack of it), you felt like a billionaire. Not only were there 100-, 500-, and 1,000-ruble notes, but because of the inflation, there were 50,000-, 100,000-, and 500,000-ruble notes as well. Even in Moscow, however, you rarely saw such large notes, and in the market, if you had anything bigger than a fifty, you probably couldn't get change for it.

An elderly lady was sitting beside several boxes on which she was displaying some crocheted hankies. She looked up at Marvin as he walked by. Her face was marked with the many wrinkles of hard, tough years, but her eyes were big and bright as she smiled at Marvin. With his interpreter at his side, Marvin extended greetings to her and asked her name. As he complimented her on the intricacies of her needlework and its beauty, she stopped crocheting and began to smile. You could see in her eyes that she was nervous and fidgety at these inquiries. The presence of so many strangers — to say nothing of a television camera — was very unusual. It was perhaps the first TV camera she had ever seen.

Marvin asked her, "How did you get to the market?"

The lady replied, "I walked."

Marvin gave her a big, broad smile and asked, "How far from the market do you live?"

The *babushka* replied, "About three kilometers." She still seemed a little nervous. She wouldn't look directly at Marvin, though she wasn't as fidgety as she had been at first.

Marvin continued, "You have many things to carry. Do you not have a car?"

"Only businessmen, merchants and the very wealthy can afford to have an automobile."

"You have public transportation. Why don't you take the trolley?"

"It's very expensive! It costs five rubles."

She was now looking up with a big smile at Marvin, her previous apprehension washed away. Marvin, however, seemed lost in contemplation. He was trying to divide five rubles by 5,700 to make a dollar. The rest of us were doing the same mental calculation. Almost simultaneously, we realized that there is no coin in the American monetary system small enough to represent this very, very small amount. Yet, she felt that five rubles was very expensive. Marvin wondered what she would have thought of his hotel room, which cost half a million rubles a day. That was more than she had seen in her lifetime.

I asked, "How long does it take you to crochet one of those beautiful handkerchiefs?"

She replied, "About a week, depending on the detail."

Marvin and I took a quick glance at each other, and knew that this pleasant old lady was not going home without some rubles in her pocket that night. And there was not going to be any bargaining over price either. The price she asked for the handkerchiefs was more than reasonable, only a few dollars each. To her, that would mean a lot. Marvin and I selected several items. She was now chatting rapidly with the interpreter. Her nervousness had long since disappeared. She raised her head toward Marvin and said, "American? American?"

Marvin looked down, nodded and said softly, "Yes."

Americans were not often seen in these small local markets. Beyond St. Petersburg and Moscow, an American was a rarity. After all, Russia had been closed for over seven decades. If an American or any foreigner other than those from the communist bloc countries visited, their movements were severely restricted. Foreigners were required to travel with a Russian guide from the Russian state-controlled In-tourist Service. Visitors were limited to tourist attractions, some churches, museums and restaurants in central Moscow and St. Petersburg. The rest of Russia was basically off limits, unknown, a mystery. The impression those in charge wanted to portray was that of a successful, dynamic, cosmopolitan, educated and thriving metropolis.

While Moscow and St. Petersburg might have lived up to this impression, the rest of the country did not. Once outside these two major cities, Russia qualified as a third-world country. Fifty percent of the people used outside toilet facilities. Many homes did not have electrical power, and therefore no refrigeration. Thus, the local market was — and still is — the center of all activity. Many hours have to be spent shopping each day for fresh meats and vegetables, if and when they are available. In rural Russia, many of the homes still have wood-burning stoves for heating and cooking.

This image is certainly not what most Americans have been led to believe for the past two decades. Cosmonauts, spaceships, space stations and high-tech intercontinental ballistic missiles appear across American television screens and in American magazines and newspapers. The Russians have the technology, but it is limited in both application and scope to a very small, elite group.

The Russian middle class is growing, but slowly. A nurse makes about $100 a month, that is, approximately four dollars a day. A surgeon will make $400 to $500 a month, which is only $10 to $15 a day. Schoolteachers earn about the same. The impression that the Russian news media has fed the American public for so many decades is fast dissipating.

Marvin and I completed our purchase of the handkerchiefs, and the old woman appeared overjoyed at her good fortune. She grabbed Marvin under the arm and gave him a big hug. She then turned and gave me a hug, as well. She thanked everybody and wished Marvin well. As we left, several of the vendors gathered around her in boisterous conversation. It wasn't long before the entire market knew that "wealthy Americans" were there. They couldn't have gotten the word out faster if they had owned cellular telephones.

The sun was setting now, a glowing red fireball in the sky. It was beautiful but toxic, for these fantastic colors were produced by the terrible Moscow pollution. The wood-burning stoves, the diesel trucks and diesel boilers, the uncontrolled and unrestricted emissions from coal-run power plants, and the large industry in and around Moscow were all spewing pollutants into the air. We could smell them when we took a deep breath. We felt he could taste them in the air.

Bob had been carrying the 50-pound camera, along with extra batteries and tapes, for the whole time we were wandering about, and was understandably tired. Out of compassion for him (as well as our need to sit back somewhere and absorb all we had encountered), we agreed that it was time to start back to the hotel and dinner. We arranged to meet in front of the restaurant.

I arrived at the restaurant first, along with anesthesiologist Dr. Gus Cezeaux and interpreter Jim Cezeaux. There was a small anteroom with a bar, and the three of us found a table near the door and awaited Marvin and the rest of the group. There was no problem finding a table, since there were only two other people in the bar area.

These happened to be two very attractive and scantily clad young ladies. Several other young women, who looked to be in their early twenties, sat on a bench just in front of the restaurant. They seemed to be making a particular point of parading themselves in front of the table where we were sitting. They were tall; most of them at were at least five-foot-six and a couple were six feet tall. They were all dressed in tight-fitting, revealing, and, I must say, very attractive outfits.

Needless to say, these beautiful young ladies became the topic of conversation. I proclaimed that my interest in them was only from a cosmetic, esthetic, plastic-surgery point of view. Jim and Gus just laughed.

As we continued to watch (with purely professional curiosity, of course), the women strutted their stuff. They crisscrossed the small room so many times it was dizzying. Each of us proclaimed a favorite. Jim liked a raven-haired young lady who was about five feet, eight inches tall. She had a gorgeous figure, with beautiful legs that she exposed through a long slit in a body-tight knit. Her black three-inch-high spikes exaggerated her height and sensuality as she walked. She clutched a small black purse in her hand, and occasionally waved or chatted with other ladies as she sauntered through the room.

Several other members of the medical team joined us at our table. Then Marvin, Bob and Lori arrived, and the activity began to escalate. Lori was the only woman at our table. As the young ladies began to turn, smile and occasionally wink at the gentlemen, Lori began to laugh. At first the group was naive about what was taking place, but soon it became very obvious. The young ladies were again the topic of conversation, and each of the men was commenting on his favorite and her attributes.

Just then, a particularly striking lady entered the room. I turned to Marvin with a big smile and said I thought many of the young ladies were quite attractive, but I had just found my heart's desire. Marvin nudged Lori, and she turned to see the new arrival.

This young lady must have been about 25 years old. She stood at least six feet or taller. She was dressed all in white, with a peasant-type white blouse which exposed a very ample bosom, almost to the nipple. Perhaps the word "blouse" is inappropriate, since this appeared to be the only item of clothing she was wearing. It was more like a chemise or nightgown with two thin spaghetti straps gently caressing her shoulders. As she entered the room, she paused for a moment, one knee slightly flexed, her head turning slowly as she took in everything. The almost transparent chemise ended just below her crotch, exposing very long and shapely legs.

Everyone at the table was suddenly very quiet, but only for a few seconds. We were all looking at each other wide-eyed, and it's my guess that everyone had the same thought at the same time: *Was there any more to that outfit, or was that really all she was wearing?* She walked slowly, gracefully from the dining room entrance toward the bar, passing in front of our group. The chemise was made of a very light material, which gently moved to and fro with each step. It couldn't have been better if we had paid $100 for a front row seat at *Les Folies Bergère* in Paris.

My goddess had large, almond shaped eyes. She paused, turning toward our table with the most penetrating glance, which I imagined to be directed at me. Then a big broad smile passed her lips. (Have I mentioned she was beautiful? I say this purely as a cosmetic surgeon whose job it is to notice these things.) She wore black open-toed shoes with about a two-inch heel. They were laced with a wide black velvet ribbon that crisscrossed over the ankle and continued in this fashion almost to the knee, where they were tied in a large bow.

By now Marvin and the entire group were all staring, but this did not seem to bother her. She just smiled back.

I said, "That one's my favorite."

Marvin leaned across the table and said, "If she gets those thighs around you, you're going to stop breathing and we're going to be out a plastic surgeon on this trip." Everyone began to laugh.

I'm not sure if she heard what he had said, and wasn't even sure if she understood English. But she did understand laughter, and, with the entire group laughing (except for me), she seemed uneasy. She moved from the bar area to the back of the room, and Jim, glancing over my shoulder, saw that she was taking a seat with the raven-haired young lady that he found so attractive.

I suggested that Marvin interview the young ladies, and Jim immediately volunteered to be Marvin's interpreter. Several members of the group said they felt they could handle the interview for Marvin, if Bob would just run up to his room and get the camera.

Marvin quickly responded, "This is prime-time television — a family show." He didn't feel that an interview with these young ladies would classify as newsworthy. In fact, we did get to converse with several of the women after dinner, and it was most interesting, as you'll see in a moment.

Now, though, it was time for dinner, and Marvin proceeded to the dining room, with the rest of us following. The dining room was painted and furnished in red, but the decor had nothing to do with the young ladies who were parading about the halls outside. Rather, it was a remnant of the Stalin / Communist era. The hammer-and-sickle was still displayed above doorways and atop buildings throughout the city. Since the collapse of the Soviet Union, pictures of Stalin were not as omnipresent any more, but red Russian flags and the hammer-and-sickle were everywhere. Even though the USSR was a thing of the past, our dining room had all the trappings of the 1950s.

We were seated at a large round table. The conversation was brisk and covered all aspects of politics, history and our desires and expectations on this trip. As we left the restaurant, we had to pass through the bar again. There were many more beautiful young ladies sitting and walking through this area than there were customers. Jim's raven-haired beauty and my fair-haired Zena were sitting at the table by the exit. They smiled as Jim approached, and then one of the young ladies — it turned out that they did speak a little English — asked if we were English.

Jim said, "No, Americans."

Like most others we'd met that day, they were surprised. I whispered to Jim to use little if any Russian at first, so they would perhaps feel more at liberty to speak candidly among themselves.

I sure had some questions for them. I wanted to know who they met at this hotel, which seemed virtually empty except for our medical team. They replied that most of the businessmen that came to the hotel were from Scandinavia, Germany, the Russian satellite countries, and occasionally from Cuba. They had never met an American before.

The next question seemed almost stupid, but I wanted it answered, nonetheless. I asked, "What type of work do you do?" To my amazement — and that of the others standing there — they said they were students. We all stood there with our mouths hanging open. Nothing was said for a few seconds.

Finally I asked, "What are you doing here?"

The two girls almost replied simultaneously, "We're working."

White Knight in Blue Shades

The young ladies could see we were puzzled. They had a short, whispered conversation amongst themselves. Then tried to explain to us in English what they were doing, but they did not have the vocabulary to express it.

I gave Jim a nudge, and we looked at each other with big grins on our faces; then, in fluent Russian, Jim introduced the group. He explained to the young ladies the purpose of our trip.

If you'd thought they were surprised when they were told that the group was from the United States, when they heard Jim's impeccable Russian, they were not only surprised, but startled. You could see it in their faces.

It quickly became apparent that these were not your ordinary ladies of the evening. They were beautiful, well-dressed, polite and quite educated. They were now holding an intellectual conversation with Jim. He told Marvin and me that most of the other young ladies in the room were also college and postgraduate-level students. So what were they doing "working" here?

With the collapse of the Soviet Union in 1992, their education stipends had ended. There were no funds for their apartments in Moscow, and if they were going to continue with their education and live in the style to which they were accustomed, they were going to have to work. Unfortunately, too many people were out of work, and conventional jobs were impossible to find at any level. Those working in government and city positions had not received their paychecks for six months.

And a person had to make a living...

The conversation progressed to other social and economic changes. The young ladies were very open in describing what had taken place over the past several years in the medical, educational and political arenas, and they were more than willing to discuss the everyday hardships that had befallen most city dwellers.

The conversation was fascinating, but it was late, and time to take our leave. As Marvin and I went through the hotel lobby to get our keys, we again had to show our passports before we could enter the area where the elevators were located. From there, members of the group got off on their respective floors. Again we had to show our passports and room passes, which were exchanged for keys. The heavy iron doors were then locked behind us as we moved down the hall to our rooms. We were told to keep our rooms locked, and not to open our doors if anybody knocked.

That all seemed pretty strange. You couldn't get into the hotel or past the guards without a foreign passport. You couldn't get from the desk to the elevators without your passport and your room pass. You couldn't enter a floor until you showed your room pass, whereupon a cell-like iron door had to be opened by an attendant. You then had to give your room pass to the floor attendant to get your key. What more could you ask for in terms of security?

We all met for an early breakfast the next morning, and were seated at uncomfortable, long, heavy wooden tables, scarred by many years of use. The room was poorly lit, and adorned with virtually no amenities. The chairs had hard wooden seats and uncomfortable, upright wooden backs. There was an inverted cup and saucer at each table, and a white porcelain dinner-sized plate that had also seen many years of wear.

A waiter who looked more like a sergeant in the army came to our table. He was dressed in typically drab grey-green. He stood almost as if he was at attention and never smiled as he methodically turned each of the cups over, asking if we wanted coffee or tea. He said nothing else — no greeting, no small talk, no friendly gestures at all. He left and presently returned with some cold meats, which Marvin said were the worst looking deli-style he had ever seen. The waiter placed two thin slices of breakfast meat on each plate — not one, not three, but two. This was followed by one slice of black bread and then a single latke, a fried potato pancake. We looked at each other to see who was willing to try what first. Most were only willing to risk coffee or tea and the black bread. The waiter stood to the back of the room in rigid military fashion. He did not approach the table again, and didn't ask if anyone wanted more.

The black bread was actually quite good, and some of us wanted refills of coffee and tea. We tried to get the waiter's attention, and though he was looking directly at us, he didn't move. Finally, Jim the interpreter walked over and asked the waiter if he would bring more tea, coffee and bread. His answer was *nyet, nyet, nyet.*

It seems that breakfast — if you could call this a breakfast — was included with the room, and serving sizes were quite specific, and not negotiable. You got one of each, period.

Marvin said, "Communism may have ended, but if the Russians expect to develop a tourist trade, they've got a lot to learn."

Marvin even offered to pay for more tea, coffee and bread, but the waiter did not know how to respond. It was just not done. There was no way to pay for the food in the dining hall. There was no way to charge it to your room, and they didn't accept credit cards (only a few very elite restaurants in Russia could do so); furthermore, the use of a personal check was unheard of. In fact, most Russians had never even seen a credit card or a checkbook. Needless to say, breakfast was over!

Since there was no baggage service, we had to go through the routine again of showing our passports and room cards in order to pick up our carry-on luggage and return to the lobby. Once we were there, we were to meet the van, which would take us to the local airport. Some of the members of the team were nervous about the morning's flight on Aeroflot. Others — such as Marvin and myself — were more fatalistic. Marvin tried to reassure everyone, saying, "My angel will be watching over all of us during this flight."

We had good reason to be nervous, I suppose. Each year, a listing is published which ranks airlines from the very best to the very worst. For each of the previous ten years, Aeroflot had been on the bottom of the list. Also listed were the airlines that had the greatest number of crashes or mechanical failures. Aeroflot had the distinction of being at the top of that list. To make things even scarier, the month before we had arrived, an Aeroflot plane had gone down. Two months before that, another Aeroflot aircraft had crashed, and about six months earlier, several Aeroflot planes had experienced mechanical problems and difficult landings.

Most people have the misconception that Aeroflot is a single airline. It used to be, when it was controlled by the Russian government. When the Soviet Union dissolved, Aeroflot was sold off into many smaller companies, all bearing the Aeroflot name. Even though each company carried the same name, the individual companies were responsible for their assigned region and for the maintenance of their own aircraft. As such, there were no standards, and maintenance was haphazard, at best. Many of the planes were old and had been used long beyond their life expectancies.

Improvement of air service within Russia simply was not a priority at that time. Most Russians did not make enough money to be able to afford to fly. You had to be very rich, or work for a major company, to even have a car, and the same held true for airline travel. While flights emanating from Moscow and St. Petersburg were common, many of these were on other major international carriers, based in — and regulated by — Europe and the United States, and catering to businessmen and tourists from those countries. Flights within Russia were infrequent, emanating from smaller private airports which only catered to intra-Russian flights. There certainly weren't many people interested in flying to the Ural Mountains or Siberia, except perhaps for engineers and executives with some of the oil and mining companies that were developing these regions. So flights were frequently empty.

When Aeroflot was a single government-controlled airline, it was subsidized. Now that it had been divided into multiple small independents, the subsidies had evaporated. With few paying passengers and no subsidy, the airlines' income was minimal or nonexistent. Maintenance and safety as we know it in the United States wasn't a problem — it simply didn't exist! And so, even though Marvin was quite confident, the anxiety some of the members had about boarding Aeroflot was understandable.

To catch our Aeroflot flight, we were driven to a small airport about one hour outside of Moscow. Again, it was dimly lit. There was only a single window to check in, and the attendant insisted on weighing each piece of luggage, even though we had official papers from the government for transport of the medical equipment. The clerk insisted that the group's luggage was overweight, and that there would be an additional baggage fee. However, anything we could carry on would not be weighed. Neither the size of the suitcase nor its weight mattered, and it didn't matter if it wouldn't fit in the rack above the seats. All that mattered was that it would fit in the aisle or on an empty seat, and that you were willing to carry it on and off the aircraft.

I had several collapsible dollies, and selected some of the larger, heavier pieces of luggage to avoid additional charges. Marvin insisted that his personal luggage be carried aboard as well. God forbid he should lose a suitcase with his extra blue glasses, hairpieces and white suits.

After the pieces of luggage to be carried aboard were selected, the rest were weighed. The clerk at the check-in window became friendlier as the medical team went through this process. Jim Cezeaux explained the purpose of our trip to her. She finally flashed Marvin a smile, rounded off the total number of kilograms, and cut Marvin a deal on the extra weight. She was almost embarrassed, but said she would have to charge something. Marvin, I and several other members of the team each contributed several crisp new ten-dollar bills. This seemed to please her very much. I doubt if the money ever got back to Aeroflot. She took the cash with a big smile, and offered Marvin a handshake and a thank you.

Bob and Jim started loading the dollies with the larger suitcases. The clerk was now leaning through the small window of her booth, and she began motioning them to bring the carry-on luggage to her as well. They were very happy to do so. Not Marvin, though. He still insisted that his two large, very heavy personal bags would have to go aboard the aircraft. The transaction took about an hour, and it was almost flight time, but the clerk did not seem to be in any hurry.

Bob decided he could not trust the video camera to the cargo hull. If anything happened to the camera, the trip would be for naught from a news perspective. Lori Reingold had a backpack with extra batteries and the video tapes, and would not let these out of her sight during the entire trip, either. There were several cases containing delicate medical equipment, and I was also afraid that the medical equipment might be damaged if stored with the cargo. I decided that these cases would be carried aboard as well.

There were only two other gentlemen in the terminal. They were dressed in business suits, each with an attaché. They stood together in one corner taking all of this in. Unless there were more people waiting outside, our small group and the two businessmen would be the only ones flying.

This was not the kind of airline terminal most Westerners are accustomed to seeing, with elevators, escalators and an air-conditioned boarding ramp that reaches out to attach to the parked aircraft. This was just a one-story building, sitting out on the middle of the tarmac and two small runways. All of us would have to help carry the equipment — and Marvin's suitcases — more than a hundred yards onto the tarmac, then up a steep flight of stairs to board the aircraft. I took one of Marvin's suitcases (have I mentioned they were large and heavy?), and Jim Cezeaux took the other. Several members of the team assisted by carrying the more delicate medical instruments. Lori strapped on the backpack with the video equipment, and Bob Dows hoisted that heavy camera to his shoulder. The meticulously dressed Marvin, followed by this motley crew, headed across the tarmac to board the plane. With his suit and tie, hair combed to perfection, and of course his blue shades, Marvin marched across the tarmac, looking for all the world like one of the Communist leaders or the Czar himself, followed by his train of porters.

Thankfully, Marvin's angel came through for us. Our plane was one of the newer aircraft owned by Aeroflot, perhaps 10 years old. It was still, shall we say, rustic by Western standards, as was the general attitude of the plane's crew. There were no seat assignments, but that didn't really matter, since there were about 180 seats available. And there were only sixteen of us, plus the two businessmen. As expected, Marvin's two pieces of luggage would not fit under the seat, nor in the small overhead racks, so they were taken to the rear of the plane and left sitting in the aisle.

Contrary to what one would expect, there were no complaints from the pilot or flight attendants. If you needed to use the restroom in the rear of the plane, you would just have to step over them — the suitcases, that is, not the pilot or flight attendants. Most of the delicate medical equipment was in small boxes, which, like the remainder of the personal luggage, would fit in the racks or on adjacent seats. There were no complaints about leaving boxes or packages on the seats, either.

Just as Marvin selected his aisle seat, the engines revved up. A light went on over-head, telling the passengers to fasten their seat belts, but nobody walked down the aisle to see if you did. Some of the passengers simply ignored the signs. None of the flight crew questioned whether the seats were upright or the tray tables were locked in place, and there were no announcements. The aircraft started just started taxiing, followed by a rather abrupt lift-off. The door to the pilot's cabin was half open, and swung gently back and forth as the aircraft gained altitude.

Many of us had chosen window seats so that we could see as much of the terrain as possible. We would be crossing Russia, going into (or, hopefully, over) the Ural Mountains, about 1,600 miles northeast of Moscow, to the city of Perm.

After the aircraft leveled off, a small, battered metal cart was rolled down the aisle, arrayed with several colorful plastic soup bowls that looked like the plastic dinnerware you would purchase for a two- or three-year-old child. The bowls were bright red, orange, yellow and blue. I wondered if Aeroflot did their shopping in the local five-and-dime store. The bowls were filled with red bubblegum-flavored soda pop, and were offered to each of the passengers. We were told that if we preferred a hot beverage, a bowl of hot tea would follow. There were no other amenities, but we could get a refill so long as the supply lasted.

About a half-hour into the flight, the cart reappeared. On it were two bags of pea-nuts, a single chocolate bar, a plastic bag with some hard candies, and some assorted crackers. At first, we assumed that these were complimentary, but quickly learned that they were for sale. One of the nurses was contemplating purchasing the chocolate, but upon examining the package, she thought better of it, and returned it to the cart. The wagon moved on. A few minutes later, when the flight attendant returned from the rear of the plane with the cart, the nurse had changed her mind and decided to purchase the chocolate after all, but it was gone. One of the businessmen had already acquired it. The nurse asked the flight attendant for another package, and was informed that there was only one package of chocolate, two packages of the hard candies and two packages of peanuts. Once they had been purchased, that was all there was. Even here, supplies were very limited.

One of the medical technicians decided to take a nap, and pushed the button to recline his seat. The back of the seat promptly fell out, and he reclined rather more suddenly than he had intended. The flight attendant, hearing the noise, reappeared. She was obviously quite accustomed to seeing such malfunctions, and very calmly indicated that he should change his seat. In a few minutes, she came back with a roll of duct tape and secured the back of the seat. In what I envisioned as a Russian version of the kind of pantomime demonstrations we Westerners are accustomed to seeing at the beginning of every flight, she also showed us that you could deliver a good kick to the backs of the seats and tilt them forward. You could then pick up your feet and rest them on the seat in front of you. Try that on any American or European airline!

After a few bowls of red pop, Marvin and several of the team needed to use the toilet facilities. There were two toilets in the rear of the plane, but only one was working. It was not very clean, and surely didn't compare to American or European standards. There was no seat on the commode, and there was a small sink that dribbled some cold water, but there was no soap to be found. There was one very soiled towel hanging from a hook, obviously meant to be used by all, and there was no toilet paper. Of course, just to get to the restroom, you had to jump over Marvin's suitcases and the other boxes, which were still sitting in the center of the aisle.

The flight remained smooth, and our spirits were high in anticipation of the new adventures that lay before us. It was Marvin's birthday, and an impromptu happy birthday sing-a-long took place. Some of us, knowing it was Marvin's birthday, had brought along some small gifts. Others dug into their carry-ons, where they had stashed chocolate and other candies. Marvin was definitely surprised, maybe even a little embarrassed, and was grinning from ear to ear (and even blushing a little, if you can believe it) by the time we finished singing "Happy Birthday."

Lori Reingold, whose birthday was three days after Marvin's, was even more surprised when we decided to make it a joint celebration. Marvin whispered to me that he wondered what the two businessmen sitting at the rear of the plane must think of the crazy Americans.

There were only two flight attendants aboard. After they served the passengers we did not see them for the rest of the trip, save for their comings and goings from the galley to the pilot's compartment. Toward the end of the flight, the captain came back and greeted Marvin. He was friendly, shook hands with everybody, and then took his turn climbing over Marvin's suitcases on his way to the toilet.

As we approached Perm, the sky became darker and the cloud cover heavier. Large raindrops were beginning to strike the aircraft, and there was almost no visibility. The plane began to descend, reduced its air speed, and lowered its flaps. The noise was deafening, and a bit unsettling, but the plane eventually came in for an uneventful landing.

There was only a small one-story building, which we assumed was the terminal, and a metal shed to its far side. While we waited for the stairs to be brought up to the plane, a machine that looked like a medium-sized farm tractor was slowly coming toward the aircraft. Hitched to it was a battered wooden wagon. Marvin said he hoped this was for our luggage, and not the passengers. The portable staircase was pushed across the tarmac by four men, and positioned alongside the plane. It was secured with a loud clunk, followed by a loud swish when the front door was swung open. The two businessmen had already climbed over Marvin's luggage, and were waiting up front to disembark.

Bob Dows, who had been cradling the video camera the entire trip, hoisted it to his shoulder and descended the stairs. Several members of the group who were carrying the more delicate medical equipment followed him shortly.

Marvin was dragging one of his suitcases behind him with some difficulty. Unfortunately, it seemed the carpet in this aircraft was neither glued nor otherwise fixed to the underlying metal floor. As Marvin dragged the suitcase down the aisle, the sections of carpet began to lift and fold, making it difficult for the small wheels of the suitcase to roll over them. The carpet now lay in crumpled sections across the floor, piling up behind Marvin as he dragged both carpet and baggage along. What a sight!

American and European aircraft typically have lights in the aisles, and, in case of an emergency, these lights are used to guide you to an exit. Naturally, our plane had no such "amenity." Several of the team members re-boarded, picked up Marvin's suitcases, which were now in a pile of crumpled carpet, and took them down the ramp.

What had begun as a light, cool drizzle was increasing in severity as we disembarked. There were no covered walkways, and only Bob and I had any rain gear handy. There were eight people waiting beyond the gated area, several of whom had umbrellas; they were allowed onto the tarmac to escort members of the group to the small terminal building.

As we peered through the terminal window, we could see four men removing the baggage, one item at a time, from the underbelly of the aircraft, and placing the luggage into the open wagon. The tractor brought the wagon to the tin shed adjacent to the building in which we were waiting. We had to go outside again to claim our luggage; to our immense relief, everything had arrived in satisfactory condition.

The doctors from Perm had come to meet us with a school bus and a small van. They had brought bunches of beautiful red gladiolas for the ladies. There were warm handshakes and hugs; it was as if it were a family reunion, with no one paying any attention to the fact that it was raining. Everyone went to the shed and grabbed whatever they could carry, and helped load the bus. The equipment was stored on the seats and along the aisle in the back of the bus. Some of us chose to ride in the bus, while Marvin, Lori, Bob and one of the interpreters went in the van.

It was a two-hour drive from Perm into the Ural Mountains to the city of Kungur. Driving through Perm, we could see that it was a heavily industrialized city. There were many coal-powered electric plants, each spewing heavy gray-black smoke from its tall stacks. The stench of the smoke hung oppressively in the air.

Perm was, for all practical purposes, a forbidden city. Most Americans — indeed, most Russians — do not even know it exists, much less where it is located, even though it has a population of more than three million people. Maps were routinely falsified in Russia, so that the topography and location of Perm and Kungur were uncertain for decades. If you were born there, you lived and died there. You were required to have two passports; one was an international passport, difficult to get unless one was politically connected, held a high military rank, or held a high-level position in industry. These international passports were usually issued from Moscow, never from Perm. The other version was the red passport, which allowed the holder to travel within different regions of the USSR. In the U.S., it would be like a resident of Houston, Texas needing a regional passport to go to San Antonio. However, except for high-ranking military personnel and high-ranking members of the communist party, no one was issued a regional passport, either. For the average citizen, Perm was their home, their entire world. Perm was where they went to school, worked, married, raised a family, lived and died. They would have no contact with the outside world.

Perm was a military stronghold whose factories produced military goods — everything from uniforms and boots to jet engines for military aircraft, and rockets for intercontinental ballistic missiles. Being closed to other Russians as well as to all outsiders, Perm had developed its own infrastructure, including a large university dedicated to the sciences and medicine. There were also hospitals — general, pediatric and women's, and even a cardiac center. In order to support this large industrial center, a massive supply of electric power was needed. It seemed that every few miles, we saw another of the large electric power installations.

Between the industrial areas were white apartment buildings, six to eight stories high, all built by the government in the same style. They lined the streets as far as one could see, and there were no amenities, street signs or numbers on the buildings. Marvin said, "I can't imagine how you could tell one from the other. With alcoholism being a major problem in Russia, I can just see a guy coming home drunk one evening, looking down miles of these apartment complexes in total bewilderment as to where he was, where he would go, and which one was his." Private homes as we know them in the United States were rare. Electricity and water were provided free, and rents were minimal. However, this was all beginning to change.

As the bus made its way through Perm, all of us were slowly grasping the magnitude of this mission. It was like entering a time warp and stepping back into the 1940s. An entire society, three million people, had been restricted, not only in their movement, but in the news they received from the outside world. It was, in so many ways, as if time had stood still. A trolley ride was less than a nickel, a loaf of bread a dime, and a sack of potatoes, a quarter. There were no billboards along the roadside. Perm had a few movie theaters and several restaurants, but in Kungur there were neither hotels, theaters, nor restaurants. Most people walked to work, to the market and to school. There was no taxi service, just the electric streetcars and a few aging buses. Only the privileged few had an automobile. The military, of course, had their trucks and jeeps. The cars that were seen were more than 30 years old, and typical of American cars of the 1950s. They came in one color: black.

A couple of decades ago, "earth colors" were all the rage in the United States. In Russia, earth colors such as grey, black and the dark military greens had been the only colors available for many decades. There were few bright colors to be seen. You sure couldn't lose Marvin in this crowd. He always stands out, but here, his immaculate white or bright-colored suits, white hair, and blue glasses set him dramatically apart from the populace. In fact, even a tie was almost unheard of, and a sports jacket or suit was rarely seen.

The city of Perm has rightly been called a study in ambiguity. On the same street in Perm, less than a hundred yards apart, is the birthplace of Russia's great ballet master, Sergei Diaghilev, as well as the place where the last Czar's brother, Prince Mikhail Romanov, was seized and executed without trial. These two events, commemorated to this day in Perm, remain a vivid reminder of how Russia's capacity for creative genius and its appalling brutality are able to coexist side by side in the lost city.

The Perm region was the gateway to the Gulag System, a series of prison camps that was the KGB's arm of repression. During the Stalin years, thousands of Russia's top intellectuals, musicians and artists passed through Perm on their way to and from the Gulag prison camps in the Ural Mountains. Those fortunate enough to survive the forced labor and the subzero winters in the camps were not allowed to return home to Moscow, Leningrad or any other major city once released. In the eyes of the Soviet authorities and the KGB, their crimes made them forever enemies of the state, to be kept far from the urban centers, where it was feared they could again do the most harm.

Thus, exiled, many of Russia's finest minds settled in the city of Perm. An unintended and unexpected result was that the city blossomed from a provincial backwater country town into one of Russia's foremost cultural, medical and academic centers, and was renowned for its theaters, art, scientific institutes and medical facilities. In a triumph of the human spirit, Perm showed that even Stalinist repression could not extinguish the flames of intellectual, artistic or scientific genius.

Stalin and other members of the proletariat soon recognized Perm's rising intellectual significance, and figured out a way to exploit it to their own purposes. Stalin turned the city into a center for rocketry, space and other defense-related enterprises. During the Cold War, Perm thrived economically and grew. The population within the city swelled to more than one million, and the surrounding region to an additional two million. Finally, with the break-up of the Soviet Union in 1992, both the Gulag prison camps and the secret defense industries began winding down.

Sadly, however, there is still no happy ending for the city of Perm. With the collapse of the Soviet Union, the Perm Aeroengine factory, the city's largest employer, and the nation's most important producer of rocket and aircraft engines, was facing bankruptcy. Marvin was told that Aeroengine's largest customer, the state airline Aeroflot, "cannot pay its bills, and cannot borrow money." The factory's work force had been reduced by 30%. It was expected that more pink slips were coming. This factory and many other industries in the Perm region were losing the battle for survival.

Traveling through Perm, we could already see the results. For the first time in decades, young people, who had no prospects for employment, were leaving the city for the surrounding farms, willing to put up with outdoor plumbing, so long as there was work and food. The seeds of a social explosion had clearly been planted; it was very obvious to all of us. Marvin felt that the neo-Stalinists — and their friends in the KGB — had begun to sense public disillusionment with the uncertainty of reform, and were actually longing to return to the stability of the past. To Marvin, that was a frightening thought.

Still, like much of Yeltsin's new, more democratic, capitalistic Russia, the small towns and villages to which we were going were doing quite well. They could sell what they grew as they wished, either locally or in the larger cities. The money that they obtained from these sales was theirs, to be put back into their farms and homes, or used for some of the amenities that they had been denied for so many years.

The evidence of this new way of living was turning up in all sorts of places. Fresh coats of green and white paint had spruced up the walls of the homes in Kungur. Churches reopened their doors, and the icons so long hidden within their walls or buried in grave sites were again adorning the sanctuaries. Western items were making their way into the economy, and here and there, individuals were seen wearing brighter clothing. Those blacks, greys and browns were slowly being replaced with blues, yellows, bright greens and reds.

Of course, even though bread lines and borscht had been traded in for blue jeans and burgers, all wasn't well in the new Russia. The Russians had been under more than 70 years of oppression. They were just coming out of the Dark Ages, and were left confused, poor, and, by twentieth-century standards, ignorant. Their plight, Marvin noted, was alarmingly similar to that of the United States during the Great Depression.

As the school bus reached the outskirts of Perm, the city seemed to end abruptly. There were military checkpoints along the road, and although these were stilled manned, few vehicles were required to stop. Stopping and checking vehicles seemed to be done in a random manner. Only a few years ago, no one was allowed through these checkpoints except for the military personnel, foodstuffs and military products shipments. We were the first foreigners to set foot in this restricted city in over 70 years. The only outside contact the people of Perm and Kungur had had were with some of the engineers and workers from Communist East Germany and the Eastern Communist bloc countries that had participated in the building of the Trans-Siberian rail line. That an American could be allowed to enter Perm and continue on to Kungur was difficult for many local Russians to grasp, especially the older generation, who had never been allowed to leave the Perm region. In fact, it seemed almost ludicrous that the first foreigners to set foot in Perm were Americans, particularly someone such as Marvin Zindler.

The bus slowly climbed along a one-lane road into the Ural Mountains, passing through beautiful, densely wooded forests, interspersed with open fields where dairy herds grazed languidly. There were small towns and scattered farms. The military and industrial center, with its spewing smokestacks and diesel fumes, was left far behind. As we traveled further into the Urals toward the town of Kungur, the air grew clear and crisp.

Most of the homes in the region were made of wood, and many were rustic-looking log cabins, some more than 300 years old. In the winter, when temperatures dropped to 40 below zero, few people ventured outside, save for necessity.

Home-crafts, in particular wood carving, were very popular. Each of these wood-framed homes was adorned around the windows and doors with the most intricate wood-carvings I'd ever seen. Each carving was unique.

As the bus wound its way into the mountains, it seemed as if we had passed through yet another time warp, this time all the way back to the nineteenth century. Alongside each log cabin, firewood was stacked as high as the roof, in anticipation of the coming winter. We learned that the wood stove in the center of each of these homes was used for keeping the inhabitants warm as well as for cooking. There was no indoor plumbing, the toilet facilities being 20 to 30 yards from the home. The old adage about an outhouse being 20 yards too close in the summer and 20 yards too far away in the winter must certainly have applied here. Most of the homes did not have electricity. We were all quite humbled as we began to realize the level of privilege that even the poorest Americans take for granted.

My great-great grandparents had been farmers in Belehar, a region of White Russia, and I imagined that this was probably how they had lived. It amazed me how little had changed in the past hundred years in these areas.

We were also to be the first foreigners to enter Kungur, which, like Perm, was neither a tourist nor industrial center. There was no reason for foreigners to visit this area of Russia at all. With the Perm Region closed, even to other Russians, closely-knit clan-like family units had developed within the cities of Perm and Kungur. Since not even relatives or friends were allowed to travel from other parts of Russia into this region, it was left in total isolation.

Kungur is a city about the size of Bellaire, Texas, where Marvin grew up. Aside from being comparable in size, the two places have little in common. For the next 10 days, Marvin would be living with the family of an English teacher in Kungur. She had never met any-one outside of her schooling who spoke English; Marvin's Texas twang and slang were quite a surprise to her, to say the least. A small four-room apartment on Lenin Street was home to her family of six, and they were lucky to have it. There was hot water — a luxury here — and an indoor bathroom. The bathroom was small, about the size of a restroom on an airliner, with just enough room to turn around in. Even though it was tiny by American standards, when winter came it was quite the luxury.

Marvin got up at four every morning, since it took him several hours to prepare. With only one bathroom for a family of six — and now, Marvin — everybody was going to have to be on a tight schedule and take their turn.

Marvin was honored with his own room, with a Murphy-style bed that pulled out from the wall. It would have been more than adequate, except for the fact that it was not level, but slanted from the wall to the floor. Marvin says he spent several restless nights hanging on, but finally gave up and slept on the floor.

Errant beds aside, the food was wholesome, and the apartment warm. Marvin said, on more than one occasion, "I never knew they could cook potatoes (which is the staple of the Russian diet) in so many different ways."

On our first morning in Kungur, the medical team and I were at the hospital by sunup. We had come halfway around the world to help these children, and it was time to get busy. Mothers and their children started to line up at the hospital in the dark, cold, early morning hours. A few sat on a wooden bench, but most were standing along the poorly lit, damp hospital hallway. The paint was peeling from the walls, there was one small light bulb hanging from an unshielded fixture, and many necessities were scarce in Kungur's Children's Hospital.

It was here that we saw, graphically and firsthand, the harsh realities of the end of an empire, an empire so accurately described as lingering in the Dark Ages. We hastily maneuvered some desks and chairs into a corner room just off of the main hallway, so that we could utilize the light from the two large windows. We had come to help the children, but we found, as always, that we had come as much to learn as to do and teach.

These were some of the patients we had come to help:

Sergei was 21 months old. He had a cleft on the left side of his lip, which extended into his palate. It pleased us greatly to know that he would grow up to be a good-looking young man, thanks to the operation that I, and the rest of the surgical team, would perform the next day.

Yakov was nine months old, also with a cleft of the lip.

Little Lenya was four years old, and had a severe burn.

Little Ula was five years old. She had a cleft palate, a hole in the roof of her mouth that made it difficult for anyone to understand her.

Maxim was five and a half, and also had a cleft palate.

Tanya had a cleft lip, which had been repaired, but her palate had not, and she too had difficulty communicating.

And those were just a few of the many children who desperately needed our help.

We didn't waste any time, and got right down to business, working closely with our Russian counterparts.

$$\infty \bullet \infty$$

Marvin, who soon joined us at the clinic, watched and spoke with the mothers and children throughout the day. Each child was examined, a medical history taken, and photographs and a permanent record prepared. The instant developing cameras we had brought were a curiosity and a source of fascination to the Russian doctors and patients alike. Most had never had a photograph taken of them, much less the kind that developed before their eyes.

The room was becoming dark, the sun was setting, and a chill was in the air as the last patients were seen and photographed. I very quickly saw that what I had heard about the state of the medicine in this area was accurate. Medicine here was indeed from another era. They were practicing on a level of 1940 — or maybe even earlier — in terms of sterilization and cleanliness. There were chronic shortages, and they lacked most medications easily available in the United States and Europe. There were almost no antibiotics, and the few they did have were severely rationed.

Marvin was surprised that there was almost no pain medication, and that even after surgery, pain medication was rarely given. They had no disposable items, most notably, syringes or needles. Glass syringes and stainless needles were boiled and reused each day. Surgical gloves were washed, dried, powdered and re-used until a visible tear occurred.

In fact, as I was soon to learn, each surgeon was allowed only one pair of gloves for the entire day. When the surgeon completed an operation, he did not remove and discard his gloves, but went to the scrub sink and washed the blood off of them, then soaked his hands — with the gloves still on — in an antiseptic solution for three minutes. The solution was quite similar to what Dr. Lister (of Listerine™ fame) used more than a hundred years ago. After soaking, the surgeon would proceed to the next surgical case, wearing the same gloves. Doctors and nurses repeated this throughout the day, until the last case was completed. This practice has not been followed in the United States since the 1930s.

(You should have seen the Russian medical team's faces the next day when, as we American doctors completed the first surgical cases, we removed and discarded our surgical gloves. The Russian doctors looked on in amazement, and the Russian nurses gathered around the interpreter, all speaking at once, in raised voices. I explained it was customary to wear a new sterile pair of surgical gloves for each case, and that I had brought a case of sterile gloves, enough for the entire week. This concept was totally foreign to the Russians.)

The anesthesiologist, Dr. Gus Cezeaux, seemed to be dumfounded about what he was learning. "The way anesthesia is given in Russia is different than what we do at The Medical Center in Houston," he said. "It is not what I am used to. The Russian doctors work very hard for their patients, making do with what they have, but they are desperately in need of equipment and supplies."

With the medical clinic completed, Dr. Cezeaux and I wanted to store the donated medical equipment and supplies that we had brought in an area close to the operating rooms, which were upstairs. We also wanted to see the operating suites, as we wanted to eliminate as many surprises as possible prior to the next morning's surgery.

Dr. Ghanadi Talianski led Marvin and the medical team along the poorly lit first floor corridor, past the emergency room. They stopped for a few minutes, and we were introduced to the Russian doctor in charge of the emergency room. Marvin could see a patient being brought in on a military-style stretcher, which was really nothing more than two sturdy poles wrapped with a burlap cover. Two attendants were carrying him to a hard, unpadded wooden table that rested in the center of the room, which was otherwise devoid of any other equipment.

Marvin exclaimed in wonder, "This is the emergency facility!"

We moved further down the hallway, passing several small administrative offices, to a small lobby-like area where there was a very tiny elevator. Little did we know that we were just about to step into another "interesting" experience.

The little elevator could not accommodate more than three people, so Dr. Talianski held the door for Lori and two female surgeons who had been working closely with my medical team and me. Dr. Talianski then took the rest of us to the back of the corridor, where there was a very ample freight elevator.

Typical of freight elevators, this one had two doors divided in the middle, one of which opened upward, and the other downward. The metal doors were heavy, and with my help, we were finally able to slide them apart. The copper-plated metal gate was then retracted. Marvin, Bob, I with the medical team, and a half dozen of the Russian doctors and nurses entered. Using a pull rope, we closed the two heavy freight elevator doors. Then the folding brass metal gate was slid across the opening, making contact. A loud click was followed by the whine of the cables, and with a sudden jerk the elevator started to move slowly upward. It continued its ascent for several floors, and then abruptly stopped.

This did not seem to bother our Russian host, who slid the brass gate up and back several times, trying to make contact and restart the elevator. Each time, the elevator would make a lurching motion. The whine of the cables and equipment was clearly audible — and somewhat scary. The elevator remained frozen between two floors. Of course, there was no telephone in the elevator. There was a small button, almost invisible, near the ceiling in the right hand corner. One of the Russian doctors pressed it, and an ear-shattering whistle blast echoed throughout the elevator shaft. The doctor pressed it several more times.

Two of the Russian nurses who were with us were clutching the railing in the back of the freight elevator; they seemed very nervous. A Russian doctor closest to the front of the door began to bang on it in hopes that someone would hear, but it was the end of the day, and the hospital was virtually empty. Our only hope was that Lori and the other two Russian doctors, who had preceded our group in the smaller elevator, would start to wonder where we were. Perhaps they would hear the banging.

The space in the elevator was snug, but not uncomfortable, and Bob Dows, as usual, began filming. This broke the tension somewhat, and everyone started to laugh. Someone pressed the emergency button again; still no response. The Russian doctor continued to knock on the elevator door.

After a few minutes, the noise did draw the attention of Lori and the other Russian doctors. It didn't take much Russian to understand what was being said. Our Russian friends were understandably embarrassed about this glitch. However, everyone, including Marvin, was tired, hungry, and more interested in getting out of the elevator than worrying about protocol and embarrassment.

One of the ladies took the stairs down to the main apartment to see if she could find someone in maintenance who knew what to do. Meanwhile, Lori and the remaining Russian doctor went to the floor below and tried to lift the heavy outer door. Others tried to assist them from within the elevator. Suddenly the metal doors came apart. The cab of the freight elevator was still suspended between floors, though, and there was a drop of at least five feet to the hallway. With the elevator stuck between floors, there was only a three-foot opening that you could crawl through to get to the hallway below. Those trapped in the elevator would have to sit or lie down on the elevator floor and roll out through the opening, hoping to land on their feet while not falling back into the empty elevator shaft, which would mean a four-story drop to certain death. The least that could possibly happen was a few bruises; the worst, no one wanted to think about. Some did not like the idea of hanging their arms or feet over the edge of the elevator. Should the elevator begin to move in either direction, it would be catastrophic. We also wondered if the elevator would begin to slip as the load lightened. We really did not know what we could expect from this antiquated piece of equipment. A sudden lurch, and a leg or an arm — or a life — could be lost.

Everyone pondered these questions, laughing nervously as we awaited help from the maintenance department, which did not seem to be coming. Meanwhile, Bob was laughing and filming the predicament. Finally, one of the Russian doctors laid down on the elevator floor and rolled through the opening, landing on his feet. Lori and the Russian doctors grabbed him to keep him from falling backward into the elevator shaft. Since the elevator remained stable, he encouraged others to follow suit, which several did. That still left Marvin, several of the nurses and myself in the elevator. One of the nurses stepped forward. She wrapped her skirt around her legs, and with my help, rolled through the opening and into the arms of the Russian doctors who had already made the jump.

The elevator, though considerably lighter, still remained fixed between the floors. So far, everyone seemed to be able to make the jump without any difficulty. I was the next to leap through the opening, and landed successfully on my feet. One nurse remained, clutching the hand railing along the elevator's back wall. You could see the fear in her face, and the tears were streaming down her cheeks. She wasn't scared; she was terrified. Calming voices in both English and Russian went out to her. Marvin and the doctor who remained in the elevator put their arms around her. She slowly released her grip and moved forward to the edge, where Marvin literally threw her through the opening into the arms of the doctors on the floor below. She began to cry and laugh simultaneously, and everyone began to clap.

Now only two people remained in the freight elevator. Marvin was wearing his white suit, his raincoat draped over his shoulders like a cape. Everybody was looking up through the three-foot opening to see what was going to happen next. Marvin sat down at the edge of the elevator and extended his spindly legs over the side. He leaned forward and pushed off to clear the opening. Dr. Talianski and I grabbed him as he came forward. Marvin landed upright, but was unbalanced, and began to fall backward toward the open elevator shaft. Talianski and I had a good grip on his arms, and steadied him. An audible gasp could be heard from those standing in the hallway. Seconds later, everybody was shouting and clapping. Marvin had a big smile and was laughing too. Naturally, Bob had gotten it all on film. I remember thinking, "Just wait until the folks back home see this one."

The last of the doctors easily cleared the opening. Everyone knew that they would be talking about this for a long time to come. This was to be just one of the many exciting experiences during Marvin's first Russian adventure.

We continued down the hallway, and Dr. Talianski asked if anyone would like to use the small public elevator. It was no surprise that there were no volunteers. Dr. Talianski pointed the way to the staircase, and finally we made our way to the upper floors, where the operating rooms were located. Even Marvin helped carry the equipment. Dr. Talianski unlocked the room adjacent to the operating suites, so we could safely store the medical equipment. Then everyone returned to the main hallway and peered through two large, glass windows across from the main operating room so they could better determine what facilities and equipment were available.

Everyone was tired and hungry. We took the staircase down to the first level, where we were greeted by members of the families who would be taking us back to their homes for the night.

The next day, the first day of the surgeries began bright and early. It was a sunny, cool, comfortable morning, and the team gathered at the hospital. The children were already there, awaiting our arrival. The surgical nurses were busy setting up the operating suites. The Russian physicians were anxious to interact and exchange medical information with their American colleagues. This was a long awaited meeting, as such an exchange had not taken place with Americans for years beyond the Russians' memory.

White Knight in Blue Shades

As the American and Russian doctors began working their miracles with the children's faces, Marvin went into the streets of Kungur to see what Russia was really like. He took in the sights and talked to the people, gathering more material for his planned series.

Other than the outdoor market, there was only one grocery store in all of Kungur. There was some food on the shelves, but not a great variety, unless you liked three meals a day of cabbage and potatoes. Irena, a schoolteacher making five dollars a day, said that the prices, for what little there was, were expensive.

Marvin asked her, "What about chicken and meat?"

"Meat is expensive for our people, but chicken is the most expensive when available in our grocery stores. It costs 400,000 rubles. It is too expensive for us."

That would be about five dollars in U.S. currency for an entire chicken. It was very similar to what chickens in a Houston grocery store might cost, but expensive to Russian folk, nonetheless, representing an entire day's wages. When you compare this to a bus ride that cost only 100 rubles — less than a penny — you get a better picture of how prohibitively expensive it is. When Marvin commented on the comparison, the school-teacher said that 100 rubles was too much also. "Most people will walk or take their bicycle before spending that."

In order to survive, town folks had to have small vegetable gardens of their own. Here they raised the staple, potatoes, as well as fruits and vegetables of their choice. Without this, they could not survive the brutal Russian winters.

Marvin left the grocery store, where clerks and shoppers alike were stunned to see him and his television crew. During the filming, the clerks had stood rigid and silent, but as soon as Marvin turned to leave, all of them burst out chattering at once, and questions followed him to the door.

Marvin and his entourage crossed the street and walked about a block away to a new market. Marvin approached a video salesman who was, at first, reluctant to speak with him. The salesman thought that Marvin was from the Russian State Police, and until the interpreter explained what Marvin and the group were doing, the salesman was not going to express any opinions. The video salesman was shocked to find out that Marvin was an American.

As Marvin traveled through the city, some of the residents were afraid to talk with him, while others could not wait to meet him. Almost everyone was in disbelief when they found out he was an American. On occasion he was mistaken for a German.

After talking to the video salesman awhile, Marvin and the crew returned to the jeep and continued up a bumpy road through the dark Russian woods — the woods that held a deadly secret.

∾ ● ∾

The team had had to get special transit papers to visit this area. It was a well-guarded secret that even those who lived in this region were never allowed to see, and feared even to discuss. The deadly secret these mountains held were intercontinental ballistic missile silos, many more than 100 feet deep. Some of the silos had been dismantled — their entrances detonated as part of the American-Soviet Arms Agreement — but not all.

This was the first time a westerner was ever allowed to see these installations; chalk up another Zindler "first." Even the CIA would have liked to have this opportunity, yet in a few short weeks, Marvin would be showing the installations to the American public and to the world.

Marvin spoke with a Russian colonel about the missiles; it was an absolutely unforgettable interview. Marvin has been known to put people on the spot before, and he really did it this time. When he asked the Russian colonel where the ICBMs were pointed, the man was hesitant to answer. But with typical Zindler persistence, Marvin again asked, "Where are these missiles going?"

Still no answer.

With voice raised and finger pointed, in that classic tell-me-or-you'll-be-sorry gesture of his, Marvin again asked the military officer, "Where the hell are these missiles going?"

The Russian colonel, raising his arm and pointing his finger into the air, bellowed out, "Ammerrrica!!"

Marvin could understand the colonel's predicament, and his embarrassment at having to proclaim in front of the Channel 13 cameras that there were still missiles on the launch pads, and that they were still pointing toward the United States.

As Marvin said in his report later, "The truth of the matter is that the ICBMs are still there. They are still functional, and there is an unstable Russian government....A government still in possession of a nuclear arsenal large enough to destroy much or all of humanity."

∽ • ∽

On the way back to town, Marvin stopped at Kungur's ceramic factory, thinking to pick up a few souvenirs and spread a bit of that unimaginable American wealth. To his disappointment, he discovered that the factory did not have boxes in which to package their goods, as they were wholly unprepared for anything resembling a tourist who might wish to take their goods halfway around the world. Two years earlier, the State-run factory had become private, but nothing had changed in that time. The pictures of Lenin still hanging on the factory walls, made a clear statement that this place had deep roots in Russia's past.

Telling me about this later, Marvin shook his head, saying, "It's the next generation we came to help."

Marvin's next stop was a turn-of-the-century merchant's house that was now an orphanage where some of our little patients lived. We had of course brought gifts for the children, probably the only toys the youngsters would get that year, because there was no money. Marvin left some of these toys with the orphanage director, along with a check that amounted to about two million rubles, probably the first check she had ever seen.

The small local bank said they could cash the check, and the director assured Marvin that the money would be put to good use for the children.

It really pleased Marvin to see that folks were getting back to religion in Russia. Deep in the Russian woods he visited a tiny farming community of another era, a village where tradition had survived the country's many upheavals. It was the home of Dr. Talianski's great-grandfather, who was a rabbi. Dr. Talianski, the only Jewish doctor in an area where there was only one other Jewish family, described what it was like: "You fight for your existence in Russia all the time to get your education, to be a doctor, to be better than others. All Jewish people fight for life too."

The closest Jewish synagogue to Kungur was two hours away in Perm. Though a city of 3,000,000, Perm was home to only 5,000 Jews. The synagogue, probably one of the older ones, had been closed since the Russian Revolution. In fact, the Communist Party had put one of their offices in the synagogue. But it had been reopened three years prior to our arrival.

Other places of worship were also reopening after seven decades of Communism and Soviet atheism. Religious repression had ended, and one of the blessings of a world turned upside-down was that religion in Russia was thriving. Marvin stopped at a beautiful Russian Orthodox Church, which under Communism was first used as a children's cinema, then a fire station, and later, a prison. The people were now rebuilding it, restoring it to its former glory and purpose. While some things were slow to change in Russia, the reemergence of the churches was happening at a rapid pace. People were returning to the church and turning to God. One of the Russian doctors mused, "Maybe it is because of our troubles."

Not far from the church was the local shoe factory, one of the few nonmilitary private attempts at capitalism in the area. When the Russian government stopped subsidizing the factory, it went bankrupt, as did the bank that repossessed it. It was a struggle, but the shoe factory, after three years, was getting on its feet. A fertilizer company had purchased and reopened the shoe factory.

The factory was reminiscent of sweat shops in 1930s America; more than a hundred women labored 12 hours a day over sewing machines, earning only $60 to $80 a month. They provided boots to the military in lieu of paying taxes. Other boots were sold to oil field workers in Siberia. I wondered what the IRS would think of an arrangement like that!

Finally Marvin and the crew made their way back across town, returning to the century-old city hospital to rejoin the Houston doctors. It was late in the day when Marvin arrived at the hospital. As he entered, he found that everyone was very excited, for the hospital

The trip was a real eye-opener, and not just for the Cuban patients that Marvin and the American doctors were able to help.

Marvin sees Cuba not as a communist threat, but a nation in turmoil and in need of humanitarian help. When he arrived in Cuba, he found a devastated country, so desperately in need of food and medicine that he felt United Nations involvement was needed to take care of the Cuban populace. The biggest problem was — and is — that Castro's political power must be separated from these humanitarian efforts, a task Marvin feels can and must be accomplished.

Due to the embargo, Americans cannot travel directly from mainland United States to Cuba. To circumvent this obstacle, Marvin and the group flew to Mexico City, where Aeromexico Airlines was kind enough to take the group from Mexico City to the small airport in Havana. There a group of Cuban physicians awaited them, and took them by car to a small hotel. Marvin and the physicians were aghast at what they saw. Havana, once a city of grandeur, has been devastated by the political regime in power, as well as the longstanding embargo.

Marvin says, "What do most Americans know of their small island neighbor? When asked, some remember the Bay of Pigs, some remember the missile crisis, but most think only of Fidel Castro."

Indeed, there are still many who remember seeing Castro on television in the 1960s, when he said, "What [would you have us] do? You leave us without petroleum. Khrushchev gives us petroleum... Khrushchev buys our sugar. Here (in the U.S.) your leaders speak about aggression to Cuba. Khrushchev speaks about helping defend Cuba. Khrushchev is a friend. Russia is our friend." Given the prevailing atmosphere during those Cold War years, it isn't surprising that most Americans viewed Castro — and, by extension, Cuba itself — as a genuine threat.

Much has happened since Castro gave that interview. The Soviet Union is gone, the missile crisis has passed, and there is no one to purchase Castro's sugar at inflated prices. What remains of the communist bloc is so poor that it is unable to supply food, arms or equipment. Thus, the little island has been slowly and effectively strangled.

It wasn't always like this. Cuba was once the richest and most prosperous of Spain's colonies. Its strategic location made it a target for acquisition by the British, the Portuguese, even the Americans. The United States, which tried without success on several occasions to purchase Cuba, was deeply involved in the economic and political affairs of this island nation for a long time. Through U.S. investment, Cuba became the richest of the Caribbean islands. In addition, since the island had no snakes or large predators (save

The small local bank said they could cash the check, and the director assured Marvin that the money would be put to good use for the children.

It really pleased Marvin to see that folks were getting back to religion in Russia. Deep in the Russian woods he visited a tiny farming community of another era, a village where tradition had survived the country's many upheavals. It was the home of Dr. Talianski's great-grandfather, who was a rabbi. Dr. Talianski, the only Jewish doctor in an area where there was only one other Jewish family, described what it was like: "You fight for your existence in Russia all the time to get your education, to be a doctor, to be better than others. All Jewish people fight for life too."

The closest Jewish synagogue to Kungur was two hours away in Perm. Though a city of 3,000,000, Perm was home to only 5,000 Jews. The synagogue, probably one of the older ones, had been closed since the Russian Revolution. In fact, the Communist Party had put one of their offices in the synagogue. But it had been reopened three years prior to our arrival.

Other places of worship were also reopening after seven decades of Communism and Soviet atheism. Religious repression had ended, and one of the blessings of a world turned upside-down was that religion in Russia was thriving. Marvin stopped at a beautiful Russian Orthodox Church, which under Communism was first used as a children's cinema, then a fire station, and later, a prison. The people were now rebuilding it, restoring it to its former glory and purpose. While some things were slow to change in Russia, the reemergence of the churches was happening at a rapid pace. People were returning to the church and turning to God. One of the Russian doctors mused, "Maybe it is because of our troubles."

Not far from the church was the local shoe factory, one of the few nonmilitary private attempts at capitalism in the area. When the Russian government stopped subsidizing the factory, it went bankrupt, as did the bank that repossessed it. It was a struggle, but the shoe factory, after three years, was getting on its feet. A fertilizer company had purchased and reopened the shoe factory.

The factory was reminiscent of sweat shops in 1930s America; more than a hundred women labored 12 hours a day over sewing machines, earning only $60 to $80 a month. They provided boots to the military in lieu of paying taxes. Other boots were sold to oil field workers in Siberia. I wondered what the IRS would think of an arrangement like that!

Finally Marvin and the crew made their way back across town, returning to the century-old city hospital to rejoin the Houston doctors. It was late in the day when Marvin arrived at the hospital. As he entered, he found that everyone was very excited, for the hospital had a special visitor. Russian President Boris Yeltsin had sent a representative to meet with Marvin and the American doctors. It was a great honor.

The representative said, "I came from Moscow to meet with the American doctors, who were bold enough to come to such a place like Perm from Houston, Texas. It's like traveling from Earth to Mars."

"They're brave guys," Marvin agreed, and then asked him, "What does the future hold for medical care in Russia?"

"The main problem for us in Russia now is the lack of financing of health care."

Marvin continued, "You know about what is happening in the United States with a President who wants national health care for everybody?"

"Yes. Your President Clinton is not very knowledgeable about this subject, and should study this question in detail. Medical care cannot change overnight. Look what has happened to us with a national health care system."

When Marvin met with the Russian doctors after a long day in surgery, they said something that they had not been allowed to say for the last several decades, surprising even Marvin. "We're 50 years behind in medicine. Can you help us? Pride in medicine — it is impossible in Russia now. Many of our people live below the poverty level, and can't pay the high price for private care. We are so pleased to have the American doctors here helping and teaching us."

Marvin asked them, "What do you see for the future of Mother Russia?"

"Change comes with great difficulty," one of the doctors said. "During the years of Soviet power, people did not have to think. The government was responsible for their life. Everything is changed now." The doctor continued, "Energetic people are starting to earn a living now. Others are used to the old ways. They cannot cope. They cannot survive and don't like it."

Another added, "Many would like to be dependent on the government because of their economic situation. Sometimes they work weeks, even months, and there is no money to pay them. They feel that before this newfound freedom, a paycheck was guaranteed. The State-run businesses and organizations had the ability to pay, but not anymore. Most factories have half the people they employed during the Soviet State-controlled economy."

Added another, "When they cannot pay, they now give workers some of the products so they can sell them to friends, neighbors, or in the open street market, just so they can eat."

And another said, "Doctors and nurses have no tangible products to sell. It is very difficult for us now."

Our little patients were apprehensive at first, but eventually figured that it was okay for them to play. Soon, they were running all over the hospital, and playing with the toys that Marvin and I had brought for them. Although there was little pain medication to go around, the toys seemed to take their minds off their pain. One thing that has remained strong is the Russian spirit, and nowhere is this more apparent than in the children.

Marvin knew that it was these youngsters who would carry Russia's newfound freedom into the next century. One of our patients told Marvin, "It never even crossed my mind that I would ever be operated on by an American. Thank you, thank you. I am happy I had a chance to be their patient. We need their help. I want the American doctors to return to Russia — soon."

For the next week, the Houston medical team worked 14 hours a day. We were determined that all of the children would receive medical and surgical care before we had to leave. Marvin and the television crew followed our progress.

Before we left Russia, Marvin had the opportunity to interview the mayor of Kungur. I include a portion of that interview here.

Marvin asked, "Will Communism ever return?"

"I am sure, never, never. There is no way back. There is no returning."

"When did you become a Communist?"

"In 1947 I joined the Communist Party. In 1975, I read Solzhenitsyn and began to have doubts. Now, you can see, I am anticommunist." This frankness surprised even Marvin.

The Russian generosity was overwhelming. The gift of friendship that we received from Kungur's mayor, his staff and the people who housed us made us all feel more than welcome. The daily struggle these people faced as they came out from under seven decades of strict Soviet Communist control was beyond anything that we could have imagined. They faced the difficult task of changing from a controlled economy to a free-market enterprise — and they faced it with resolve, bravery and a hope that was far beyond what their plight could justify.

All of us — Marvin as well as the other Houston doctors and myself — had come here to learn as well as to teach, and learn we had. What we hadn't expected was that we would learn more about the human spirit than about politics or economics. And each of us knew that we would return to Russia.

Upon returning to Houston, Marvin, Lori and Bob put together a five-part series called, *TO RUSSIA WITH LOVE,* set to the haunting balalaika music of the *Dr. Zhivago* theme. The series aired on Houston's Channel 13, and, as Marvin had intended, *TO RUSSIA WITH LOVE* introduced Americans to a Russia they had never seen or heard of before. This was not the stereotype that had been fostered in the minds of the American public for the past several decades, with the glory of armies passing through Red Square in front of Stalin's tomb for review. This was not the Russia that launched a Sputnik. This was the heartland of Russia, little more than a third-world country, struggling to maintain its mystique as well as its power base.

As we had expected, Marvin, the crew and I did return to Russia. We made a yearly trip there through the rest of the 1990s, and I'm sure we'll be going back. Naturally, each trip we took inspired another week-long news series, done in that inimitable Zindler style.

Not only had Marvin realized his longtime dream of traveling to Russia, not only had he opened the eyes of many Americans to the "new" Russia, but *TO RUSSIA WITH LOVE* won Marvin and his crew an Emmy Award for Best News Series in 1995.

Not bad for a guy that everyone had once predicted "would never last on television."

C·H·A·P·T·E·R **33**

A COUNTRY EMBARGOED:
CUBA (1998)

here is a small island nation less than 100 miles off the coast of Florida, which for decades has been looked upon as a threat to American freedom — but is it? Very few Americans have been allowed to visit Cuba since the early 1960s. Cuba is officially a forbidden destination for most United States citizens, off limits to all save journalists, educators conducting research, and people who have relatives there. Those who are permitted to go are limited to the bare minimum of spending during their visit. As I write this, the U.S. State Department has maintained a trade embargo for over 40 years, prohibiting all forms of trade with Castro's Cuba. Initiated by the United States, and supported by many other nations (though, notably, not our good neighbor to the north, Canada), this embargo has severely tapped this tiny nation.

In 1998, Marvin Zindler secured permission to go to Cuba, joining doctors from Houston's Eye Institute and the Lions Eye Bank, including Dr. Amuel Farge, President of the Pan American Association of Eye Banks, Dr. Marshall "Bose" Hamill, Dr. Kirk Wilhelmus, and Dr. Alice Matoba.

The purpose of the trip was to assist Cuban doctors who performed badly needed ophthalmological procedures, including corneal transplants, on patients in Havana. Due to the embargo and all of the attending rules and regulations, the Americans could not actually perform operations. But they could exchange information with their Cuban counterparts. And, indeed, it was a teaching and learning mission for both sides.

Marvin had his own mission, too, beyond reporting on the doings of the medical team; it was his plan to take to the streets of Havana and talk to the people. If he could not open the world up to Cuba, he could at least do his part to show Americans the surprising and sometimes dismaying realities of this once and future paradise.

The trip was a real eye-opener, and not just for the Cuban patients that Marvin and the American doctors were able to help.

Marvin sees Cuba not as a communist threat, but a nation in turmoil and in need of humanitarian help. When he arrived in Cuba, he found a devastated country, so desperately in need of food and medicine that he felt United Nations involvement was needed to take care of the Cuban populace. The biggest problem was — and is — that Castro's political power must be separated from these humanitarian efforts, a task Marvin feels can and must be accomplished.

Due to the embargo, Americans cannot travel directly from mainland United States to Cuba. To circumvent this obstacle, Marvin and the group flew to Mexico City, where Aeromexico Airlines was kind enough to take the group from Mexico City to the small airport in Havana. There a group of Cuban physicians awaited them, and took them by car to a small hotel. Marvin and the physicians were aghast at what they saw. Havana, once a city of grandeur, has been devastated by the political regime in power, as well as the longstanding embargo.

Marvin says, "What do most Americans know of their small island neighbor? When asked, some remember the Bay of Pigs, some remember the missile crisis, but most think only of Fidel Castro."

Indeed, there are still many who remember seeing Castro on television in the 1960s, when he said, "What [would you have us] do? You leave us without petroleum. Khrushchev gives us petroleum... Khrushchev buys our sugar. Here (in the U.S.) your leaders speak about aggression to Cuba. Khrushchev speaks about helping defend Cuba. Khrushchev is a friend. Russia is our friend." Given the prevailing atmosphere during those Cold War years, it isn't surprising that most Americans viewed Castro — and, by extension, Cuba itself — as a genuine threat.

Much has happened since Castro gave that interview. The Soviet Union is gone, the missile crisis has passed, and there is no one to purchase Castro's sugar at inflated prices. What remains of the communist bloc is so poor that it is unable to supply food, arms or equipment. Thus, the little island has been slowly and effectively strangled.

It wasn't always like this. Cuba was once the richest and most prosperous of Spain's colonies. Its strategic location made it a target for acquisition by the British, the Portuguese, even the Americans. The United States, which tried without success on several occasions to purchase Cuba, was deeply involved in the economic and political affairs of this island nation for a long time. Through U.S. investment, Cuba became the richest of the Caribbean islands. In addition, since the island had no snakes or large predators (save

White Knight in Blue Shades

for a few big reptiles), it was perceived — rightfully so — as a traveler's paradise.

But Cuba's fortunes were to change in the mid-twentieth century.

In 1925, when Marvin was just a toddler, the Cuban Communist Party was formed. Founded by the island's disenchanted, the party at first had only a minimal direct influence. Very soon, however, Marxist concepts appeared in Cuban writings. The Cuban people were dazzled by the apparent simplicity and clarity of Marxist theories, and felt that all Cuban problems could be explained through class struggle and, of course, Yankee imperialism. How quickly they forgot that it was "Yankee know-how" and "Yankee dollars" that had made Cuba the richest island in the Caribbean.

In 1933, Fulgencio Batista y Zaldívar, a sergeant in the Cuban army, led a successful coup, and for the next seven years he ruled Cuba through figurehead presidents. He was officially elected president himself in 1940. Though he retired in 1944 and moved to Florida, a military coup in 1952 returned him to power. Although Batista was the dominant figure in Cuban national affairs for a quarter of a century, that was all to change in January of 1959.

A new leader, young and bearded, had been trying for years to overthrow the Batista regime. Exiled to Mexico in 1955, he was now back in Cuba, and for the past two years had led a guerilla war in eastern Cuba. He began directing the influence of his forces to the western provinces, quickly assuming the leadership of the urban communities. Eventually, his resistance fighters marched into Havana, and the Batista regime was history. Audacious and effective in his military campaign and political skills, persuasive and commanding as a public speaker, Fidel Ruz Castro had become the leader of the future Cuba.

The old rules no longer applied. The rebel army became the defender of the new revolutionary state, sweeping aside the parties that had structured political life in Cuba for decades. Castro declared that only the Communist Party (Partido Socialista Popular, or PSP) would be acceptable. For the next four decades, Castro upheld a revolutionary faith and implemented a new order.

In 1959, when Castro and the Communists took power, the value of United States investments in Cuban sugar, mining, utilities, banking and manufacturing exceeded that of every other Latin American country except Venezuela. The United States also accepted about two-thirds of Cuban exports and supplied about three-quarters of its imports. This foreign trade accounted for much of Cuba's national income.

But, as Marvin says, "You wouldn't know it today." Indeed, what Marvin and the medical team saw when they visited Cuba was a country that seemed uncharacteristically out of control. The embargo imposed on the island for the second half of the twentieth century had resulted in absolute collapse.

The embargo came about because of events in 1960. That was the year the Cuban Council of Ministers, under Fidel Castro, authorized expropriation of all American-owned property in Cuba. This was followed by the expropriation of all large U.S.- owned industrial and agrarian enterprises, and the confiscation of all American banks by the Cuban government. The United States government, under President Eisenhower, retaliated by prohibiting exports to Cuba.

The swift and dramatic changes in U.S.-Cuban relations that took place under the Castro regime paralleled Castro's reorganization of Cuba's internal political and economic affairs. The consequence was a massive immigration to the United States by educated and well-to-do Cubans. Washington favored this immigration by establishing social programs for the new arrivals. The aim of these government-sponsored programs was to discredit Castro and his new government.

Most early Cuban immigrants came from the economic and social elite; the adult males were typically professionals, managers and executives. These were followed by more white-collar workers. This group of new Cuban immigrants would experience relative economic and social success in the United States over the next 30 years. Politically, they constituted a strong anti-Communist force, which of course was welcomed by the U.S. government. Castro, on the other hand, was left with semi-skilled and unskilled workers. (He retaliated in the early 1980s by sending some of his less desirable citizens to our shores.)

Nearly 40 years after that first exodus of Cubans, Marvin and the doctors were experiencing first-hand the resulting economic and social devastation. As Marvin noted, "The Cuban population has declined. Hunger and disease are rampant, and the economy has collapsed. Ninety percent of the island's cattle are gone. The tobacco industry has virtually ceased. Communications have broken down."

In contrast, Cuban-Soviet relations had improved markedly during this period, and remained friendly until the collapse of the Soviet Union. In 1960, Prime Minister Nikita Khrushchev declared that Soviet missiles were prepared to defend Cuba "in a figurative sense." The first formal military agreement between Russia and Cuba was signed within weeks, wherein the Soviet Union pledged to "use all means at its disposal to prevent an armed American intervention against Cuba." In return, in December of 1961, Fidel Castro proclaimed, "I am a Marxist-Leninist and I will be so until death." This, of course, only heightened United States government hostility toward Havana.

The Castro government socialized most industries. This hadn't worked elsewhere in the world, and it did not work in Cuba either. Cuba was utterly unprepared; it lacked technical personnel, because they all fled to the United States or were in Cuban prisons. The Cuban economy collapsed. The Cuban government froze prices, and rationing was imposed for most consumer products. The ration card has become a fixture in Cuban life ever since.

"But even ration cards have no value if there are no products to purchase," Marvin points out.

When price freezing and rationing failed, the Cuban government changed the currency overnight; those who did not have their funds in stateside banks could not exchange old for new pesos. Their savings were worthless, and the Cuban economy fell further.

Castro saw money only as a unit of accounting, and he declared money would not be used to assess profitability. Material incentives, wage differentials, bonuses, and overtime payments were all phased out. The new central government would allocate resources and set prices.

Castro ended financial accounting as the world knows it, and auditing of accounts was also discontinued. Statistics were kept only in physical quantities — for example, the number of pairs of shoes produced, not their value. Those who worked overtime would be expected to do so voluntarily and receive no extra pay, because money was seen as a source of capitalistic corruption.

Eventually, however, Castro himself would recognize, and announce in a dramatic speech, that the Cuban economy lay in ruins. But Castro needed a scapegoat, so he launched an attack on the bureaucracy that he said was crippling the economy.

Marvin and the doctors were seeing firsthand the degree to which Castro's "moral incentives" had failed to stimulate production and productivity. The economy's poor performance, and the resulting inability of the average Cuban citizen to provide for a family, caused a gradual decline in all aspects of Cuban life.

The evidence was everywhere. For example, Marvin learned that abortion had become legal and easy. "The abortion rate has been rising steadily," he said. "I could hardly believe it when I was told that two out of five pregnancies were ended by abortion. Only Bulgaria, Japan, and the Soviet Union have higher abortion rates." Indeed, abortion has probably become the main method of birth control in Communist Cuba.

On the other hand — to give credit where it is due — Castro's government did show some impressive achievements, most notably, in education. The government has accomplished near-universal attendance at primary schools. Under the Castro regime, there was a sharp reduction of illiteracy, and not only in children. The educational program was expanded to include an extensive adult education system.

The universities, however, have had a more dubious history. They were organized on the broad industrial model, to train professional personnel in a hierarchical system. They de-emphasized liberal arts, and did not allow active intellectual criticism or political, social or economic problem-solving.

"It was very obvious to us," says Marvin, "that the central figure in Cuba's revolutionary politics is still Fidel Castro. His leadership remains charismatic."

Though hardly a religious man, Castro feels he was "elected" by a supernatural authority or, more accurately, some "historical force." Castro once said in a speech, "History, as a god, elects the revolutionary leader to act with and for his followers." He felt a that as a "man-god," an elite, he must lead the people and awaken them to their historic responsibilities. To remain in power, he had to convince the citizens to share in that conviction, and for the most part he has been successful. His rule has been made possible by his charismatic performances — not to mention the support from the Soviet Union and eastern-bloc nations. But in the early 1990s the Union of the Soviet Socialist Republic collapsed, leaving Castro without aid.

∽ ● ∽

The Cuba to which Marvin traveled was, as he noted, "a country running on empty — empty grocery store shelves, empty gas tanks, empty pocket books."

So strong and all-encompassing was the United States' trade embargo that Marvin and the American doctors had not been allowed to bring medicines, medical supplies, or the corneas for transplants that would restore the sight of patients in Havana. But don't ever count Marvin out. "Where there's a will, there's a way," he always says, and he almost always finds a way.

In this case, the way was through South America. Marvin, with the help of the Pan American Eye Association, simply had the corneas shipped in from the eye bank in Bógota, Colombia. The director of the Bógota Eye Bank, Anna Maria Condana, was able to bring in the corneas, since Colombia was under no restrictions. The cornea transplants and other ophthalmological procedures would make it possible for many Cubans to see again.

Marvin thinks the embargo on food and medicine should be lifted, and wonders if United Nations involvement might be necessary. "Most importantly," he declares, "Fidel Castro should step aside and let the Cuban people, a people that all but stopped living over 40 years ago, go back to living — and seeing — once again."

∽ ● ∽

The morning after they arrived in Havana, Marvin and the doctors were taken to the hospital, which was housed in the former National Bank of Cuba. The bank, like all banks and other properties, had been acquired by Castro's government many years ago. "The opulent bank lobby speaks of a different Cuba, the Cuba of the past," Marvin noted. "Now this bank lobby is the waiting room for hospital patients."

The American medical team joined their Cuban associates to screen patients, discuss medical problems, and plan for the surgery. While Marvin looked on, Bob Dows got it all on video. No one had been allowed to film in Cuba for years, but, as usual, Zindlerism made it all possible.

Marvin couldn't get the plight of the Cuban people off his mind. He and his team left the hospital and set out to discover exactly what an embargo of this severity and length of time does to a country. He found the answers when he went to the people in the streets of Havana.

"Havana is a city that is really beautiful from a distance," he says. "Now, viewed up close, Havana and its people look worn out. Unfortunately, Fidel Castro looks the other way while his people go without food and medicine."

Marvin noticed that even as Havana's beautiful buildings were deteriorating and crumbling through neglect and lack of money to repair them, their former elegance shone through the peeling paint and cracked plaster. There were abandoned vehicles and barren streets, and tenements and multi-apartment dwellings where beautiful private homes once stood.

Marvin and his television crew were allowed to travel freely throughout the city, and were not restricted in any way, nor were they followed. They were allowed to do their story as they saw fit. They stopped their car along what must have been a beautiful thoroughfare in central Havana at one time; yet on that day, theirs was virtually the only vehicle there.

Marvin saw an open storefront where an elderly gentleman was sitting quietly in a rocking chair. With the help of his interpreter, Marvin asked this 69-year-old grandfather, "Is the food problem the worst it has been in many years?"

"Yes, the worst — a major problem in Cuba."

Marvin and the team walked further down the street and introduced themselves to Juan and Miguel, who were sitting on the steps in front of a restaurant, once privately owned but since confiscated by the Cuban government. Marvin peered through the door and saw that no one was inside, and nothing was cooking.

Marvin remarked on how clean, and even shiny, the stove looked. It would have gotten a blue ribbon on his Friday night restaurant report. Not a rat or roach to be found, and no slime in the ice machine. This would have been a good thing, save for the fact that the cleanliness was the result of disuse, rather than conscientiousness. There was no food to cook and no money to buy it with, so the once elegant restaurant sat idle.

A 29-year-old man named Juan told Marvin, "There are shortages of all food products."

Glancing across the street, Marvin saw youngsters playing in groups, as they do everywhere. He strolled across the street and, with a big smile, reminisced as he saw one group of children playing marbles and another mumbledy-peg — two games that he himself had enjoyed years ago, and that are commonly played by children throughout the world.

Marvin and his television crew continued walking along the narrow street until it suddenly opened onto a large plaza across from a cathedral. Several teenage boys were playing baseball. They had no equipment; an old broom handle served as a bat.

Marvin asked one of the youths, "What would you like to be when you grow up?"

The young man replied, "A big-league baseball player in the United States." Suddenly he handed Marvin the bat, and the boys all begin to giggle. Without hesitating,

Marvin stepped up to the chalk mark. Lori Reingold cheered him on. "You can do it, Marvin! Show them what you've got."

Bob Dows, with video camera at the ready, zoomed in as Marvin took the stance. The young pitcher wound up; it was a fast ball, right down the middle. Marvin swung, and you could hear that distinctive crack as the ball met the hard wood. It was obvious that Marvin made solid contact with the ball, smashing a line drive clean across the plaza, at least a hundred yards. The outfielder was on the run, but there was no way he was going to be able to snag it. The young people and the bystanders began to clap and cheer.

I don't think anyone figured Marvin had it in him, but Marvin is strong and in good shape. He can drive a golf ball very well, and he is on the golf course several days a week. It is his good golf swing that did him well at the plate that day.

Everyone came up and shook the old gringo's hand. As they bid the youngsters goodbye, Marvin and the television crew turned down a side street near the old cathedral. On every corner, Lori, who spoke some Spanish, noticed that the same sign hung in one empty storefront window after another. Their translator and driver explained that the old storefront was used as the headquarters for The Block Committee. The sign indicated this storefront was one of 80,000 Block Committees for "the defense of the Revolution."

In actuality, the Block Committees are Castro's grass-roots eyes and ears, whose purpose is to report anyone who is dissatisfied with the Castro regime. The Block Committee members are the informers and the caretakers of a neighborhood, and another one of Castro's means of control. It is amazing that the committee persons always seemed to have just a little more than anyone else on their block. Rank has its privileges, even under communism.

As Marvin and his team walked the back streets of Havana, Marvin commented, "It looks as if time stopped in the 1960s, just after Castro took control." There were few cars, and most were big tail-finned American cars of the past, held together with bailing wire and welds. Auto parts were difficult to get, as were automobiles themselves. Most of the cars were abandoned or parked on the side of the road because in the 1990s — again, as a result of the collapse of the USSR and communist regimes in Europe — fuel was more than just scarce; it was almost impossible to come by.

The team's interpreter explained to them that East Germany's incorporation into a unified Germany had led to a particularly drastic reduction of Cuban trade from 1989 to 1991. "Today there is no trade with Germany any more," he said. "The Soviet Union reduced both its economic subsidies and the transfer of weapons free of charge to Cuba. Both of these subsidies have been canceled by the Russian federation and by other successor states of the former Soviet Union."

Marvin asked, "What happened to the cost of these necessities when the Russian supply line stopped?"

The driver replied, "Some trade continued with the eastern bloc countries, although generally at the higher international market prices, and at levels well above those of 1989. This made it impossible for the Cuban people to purchase even those few commodities that were offered in trade."

Further down the street there was a grocery store, typical of those of any small Cuban town of the 1990s. Marvin saw that the shelves were empty — well, almost. He noticed that there were six eggs, two on a shelf and four on the front counter. "Can you get milk?" Marvin asked the proprietress, Mrs. Castro[1], who was sitting in the corner.

Mrs. Castro replied, "The priority for milk is for children and old people. I cannot get milk."

"How many eggs can you purchase?"

Mrs. Castro said, "Cubans are rationed four eggs every 15 days, and rice is rationed at five pounds per person per month."

"What about sugar, beans and other staples?"

Mrs. Castro, who seemed very comfortable talking with Marvin, replied, "Beans and sugar are also rationed."

As Marvin left the grocery store, a middle-aged gentleman was walking toward the group. Marvin asked the man, "If the United States ended its embargo, would it put food on the shelves?"

The man answered nervously, "I prefer to remain silent," and continued to go on his way.

Marvin just shook his head, mumbling, "I think that says it all."

Marvin and the group continued walking toward the seawall and the beach. The sun was going down as they walked through the district. There were more people on the street now, and many were riding bikes. The bicycle had become the major means of transportation since gasoline had become all but unavailable. Most of the bicycles had been made in Communist China.

Tenements lined Havana's once rich and plush seawall district. Century-old, once elaborate Spanish homes along the seawall were now divided into apartments. They were run down and badly in need of repairs, but without supplies or money to buy the supplies, they would continue to erode.

In Cuba, housing shortages are a major problem. This too has been aggravated since the 1990s, partly as a result of the end of the Cold War and the collapse of the Soviet Union. In addition, beginning in 1990, Cuban troops were withdrawn from Ethiopia, Somalia and Nicaragua, as well as Angola. The almost simultaneous return of tens of thousands of Cuban soldiers to their homeland in the early 1990s put a strain on housing.

Not only was there was no housing for these young men, there was no place for them in Cuban society. There were no jobs, and the heightened economic austerity caused a

---

[1] No relation to Fidel Castro.

sharp decline in living standards. Most goods and services were even more severely rationed than before.

At the same time, political repression against dissident groups became tougher. The number of "prisoners of conscience" rose, and the role of the Block Committee as Castro's eyes and ears took on even greater importance. Instances of corruption surfaced throughout the government, signaling to Cubans that even their government had become disloyal.

"Under these circumstances, only one thing seems clear," Marvin says. "Living standards will continue to fall for most citizens, no matter who governs their country and under what kind of regime."

Under these severe conditions, the ordinary citizenry has recently spoken out with sharp criticism of many government services. There also has been a loss of prestige by the Communist Party; to many, it is no longer an institution *of* the people; now it is an institution *against* the people.

As Marvin and his team walked through the tenements, they met a young woman named Theresa. Theresa told them, "There are no jobs. The American embargo makes life very difficult. Food is scarce."

She motioned for them to follow her into a small two-room apartment that had been allocated to her and her family. Pointing to a series of crude wooden cages that lined one wall, Theresa said, "I have to raise chickens in order to have enough food and some eggs. It is only for my family."

Walking further along, Marvin and his team saw that each single room was home to an entire family. They were introduced to Allyssa Calbraha, who greeted Marvin warmly. Allyssa said she was a teacher for the mentally retarded, and department director of the local school. She was more than happy to share her observations about the everyday struggles of Cubans.

"There is no food. No medicine. You have to raise your own chickens or go without. Due to bad diets and decreased resistance to infection, thousands of children go blind. There recently has been an outbreak of polyneuritis due to lack of vitamins in the diet. Well, it is back to green medicine."

Marvin asked her, "What is *green* medicine, please?"

She replied, "Herbs, green leaves, trees and plants that produce natural products." She continued, "Because of food shortages, children and older folks suffer the most. People go blind, but what can you do when there is no food, no medicine, and a very limited access to the basic necessities of life? In a Communist-controlled country, the state owns everything, pays slave wages, and Castro's peso is not worth the paper that it is printed on."

Later Marvin said, "It is a big problem. These people have no food, no medicine." He acknowledged that most Cubans who had fled their little island thought he was abdicating his responsibility, perhaps even betraying the ideals of democracy and freedom, by suggesting that the United States do away with the trade embargo against Cuba. To these people, Marvin says, *"No!* My concern is only with food and medicine, particularly for the children. Unfortunately, as long as Fidel Castro is in power, the country will continue to decay and the people will continue to suffer."

Marvin and the team were now on their way back to the hospital to observe the Houston doctors and the eye operations. Upon arrival at the hospital, Marvin, Lori and Bob were escorted to the operating room. The Houston doctors, of course, were observing.

Marvin said, "The doctors were allowed to observe, confer, exchange information — but under the embargo, they could not operate, because operating would be providing a service. They could assist, teach, help, discuss...but not actually operate. These were limitations which had to be carefully followed, since any break in this could lead to Fidel Castro claiming the embargo was over."

No matter how difficult it was, the Houston doctors, their medical personnel and Marvin and his team had to abide by these strict criteria if they were going to be allowed to help these people and return safely with the story — and without causing an international incident.

The operating room at the Eye Hospital was impressive, to say the least. Amidst all of this poverty was a facility that amazed even Marvin. None had ever been built to this magnitude, not even in the Texas Medical Center, and possibly not any place in the United States. A stainless steel conveyor belt or track moved through several rooms; attached to this conveyor belt were operating tables. The belt moved very slowly, passing through various "stations."

This was an amazing piece of engineering, designed in Russia. It worked very well and was incredibly efficient. It was one of the many things that the Soviet Union had provided for Fidel Castro, but since 1990, medical supplies were not available to Castro and his people anymore. Surprisingly, and fortunately, this fantastic piece of equipment was still operational. For many in the group, seeing it in action was a first-time experience.

Patients were placed on an operating table, and the conveyor belt took them from station to station. A single step in the operation was performed at each station as the patient moved slowly along the conveyor system. At the first station, the patient would receive a local anesthetic and eye drops, at the next station, a sedative or additional anesthetic. When the conveyor belt moved the patient to the third station, an ophthalmologist would initiate the first step in the surgical procedure. The first doctor's entire job was to make the initial incision, nothing more. The doctor would release the operating table from the conveyor belt for a few minutes, do the specific tasks he was assigned in this multiple-staged operation, and then let the patient continue along the next station. At the next station, another eye doctor would do the next stage in the procedure. The patient would continue from station to station until the last station was reached, where bandages were applied, the straps removed and the patient taken to a recovery area.

The conveyor belt would continue. A new patient would be placed on the empty operating table as it moved again through the same series of stations. At some of the stations, there would be more than one person caring for the patient, often a team of doctors and several nurses. Still, each one was responsible for a specialized portion of the operation. None of the doctors ever undertook an operation from beginning to end.

This was, needless to say, a unique concept, designed to treat as many people as quickly as possible with the maximum of safety. This conveyor technique for eye surgery had proven to be very effective throughout Russia and the Communist bloc.

Meanwhile, the Houston doctors were working with their Cuban counterparts one-on-one, restoring sight with the corneal transplants that were sent from Colombia. Corneal transplants are not operations that can be done with a conveyor belt technique.

Marvin was introduced to Sylvia, who seemed quite anxious, but was looking forward to the opportunity to see again. It was getting late, and the medical team and Marvin would return the next day to see the results of the corneal transplants.

It was bright and sunny the next day when Marvin and the doctors returned to the hospital. Marvin was pleased, almost giddy. "Sylvia and others like her who have not been able to see for years will now have the opportunity to do so," he said.

And that, after all, was what the Houston eye doctors and Marvin had come for. As Marvin walked down the hall to the recovery area, he was introduced to Oscar Santos Ramos. Oscar had received a corneal transplant several days ago, and the doctors were about to remove his bandages. Marvin still grins when he remembers this. "Guess who was the first person Oscar saw after being blind for more than ten years?" he says.

Yes, it was Maaaaaarvin — white suit, blue glasses, white hairpiece and all, holding a microphone in Oscar's face. "What color are my glasses?" asked Marvin.

To which, an elated Oscar cried out, "*Azul* — blue."

"What color is my hair?"

"*Blanco* — white."

Laughing like a child on Christmas morning, Marvin declared, "I must be a hell of a sight for sore eyes." Even now, thinking about this, I find myself wondering, *What would I think if I had been blind for ten years and the first time the bandages came off, I saw Houston's shining White Knight, complete with blue glasses, white hair and impeccably tailored suit?*

In the next room was Sylvia. Marvin approached her and said softy, "Hello, Sylvia. You were scared going into the operating room."

Sylvia replied, "*Si*."

"Can you see now?"

Said Sylvia, "I can see very well. I am so happy." She had a big smile on her face, and her cheeks were flushed as she reached out and grabbed the hands of Marvin and her doctor.

∞ • ∞

Marvin later said, "Oscar Santos and Sylvia are just two of the many people that I met on this trip that I will never forget — and I don't think Oscar will ever forget me either."

And then he turned more serious. "Cuba is still one of the most beautiful islands in the Caribbean, but only from afar. But Castro will soon be gone. I see free elections in the near future, and a country reborn. Where there are now empty harbors, there will one day be cruise ships.

"But right now the Cuban people are suffering, suffering, suffering. Most of all, it is a shame that so many people are suffering for a political idea, an ideology that no longer has any application anywhere in the world."

It is in those few statements that one gains a glimpse of the Marvin Zindler I know. Beyond the outlandish showmanship, and beyond the pit bull who fights a very public battle for the ordinary person, there is the private visionary who dares to dream on a scale much broader than the one into which he insinuates himself. Where his acts are for the benefit of individual people, his hopes encompass the entire society in which the individual lives, and beyond. For this reason — and many others — I am gladdened to be able to claim him as my friend.

C·H·A·P·T·E·R 34

THE POWER OF A PHOTOGRAPH
(NICARAGUA, CHINA, RUSSIA, 1990s)

It has often been said that a picture is worth a thousand words. Marvin learned this lesson well in his "Night Hawk" years, when he roamed the streets of Houston with his ever-present, sometimes obtrusive, camera. Early on, he discovered the power of a photograph to inform, amuse, inspire, enrage, and, yes, titillate. Over the years, as Marvin and I have traveled the globe together, we have discovered that a photograph holds far more extraordinary powers too. Many indigenous peoples believed, and some still do believe, that having one's photo made will steal one's soul. To the contrary, Marvin and I have found that photography can serve to illuminate the soul — not only the soul of the person being photographed, but the soul of the photographer as well.

Maybe one reason Marvin and I are such good friends is that we have so many things in common, and certainly one of these things is our love affair with photography. Like Marvin, I'm never without a camera. There's always a camera (along with film and batteries) in the glove box, another in the trunk of the car, and often a mini-camera in my inside pocket or in a hip pocket. And, like Marvin, I've never been embarrassed to use it.

While Marvin's interest has been geared more to newsgathering, I have, for many years, been keenly interested in photography as an art and as a means of medical documentation. And, for both Marvin and me, photography is also a way of keeping a journal of our lives. I have a collection of more than 40,000 photographs, most of them taken since the late 1970s. Many are photos of Marvin and his children and grandchildren; in fact, I've taken most of the photos that exist of Marvin and his family in the past couple of decades. And there are hundreds of pictures of international dignitaries Marvin and I have met, and world events we've witnessed, during our travels together. Some will make you laugh. Others will make you cry. Most of the photos are candid; they offer behind-the-scenes insight, and, consistent with the old adage, they often reveal far more than even the most eloquently written travel essay.

But the photos that have always meant the most to Marvin and me are the ones that were taken during medical missions around the world. The children have always been the closest to my heart and to Marvin's, too.

It was 1991. The Contra-Sandinista conflict was coming to a close; Nicaragua was still an armed camp, but military confrontations had decreased markedly. A new president had just been elected: Violeta Chamorro, the country's first woman president. During the course of the ten-year-long Civil War, which was finally coming to an end, the country's medical system had been destroyed. Medical equipment, supplies and medications were almost nonexistent. The children and the elderly suffered the most.

I made my first medical mission to Nicaragua with Marvin and a Channel 13 crew that year. The focus of the trip was Nicaragua's forgotten children, those who, as Marvin says, were "the poorer than poor: those who have nothing."

We flew to Managua, Nicaragua's capital, and then traveled overland with a military escort to the city of Chinandega. The next morning Marvin and the medical team went to the old hospital where we were told that we would see 30 to 40 children. To our surprise, there were hundreds waiting. The children and their families had been arriving for days, many having walked miles to get there. They had camped out in the hospital courtyard and along the clinic buildings. They arrived with only the tattered clothing they wore.

At the clinic, I photographed each child, alone and with his or her family. The photos would provide identification, documentation, and a means of planning additional surgical procedures, if needed. Many of the children were hesitant to have their photos taken, for varied reasons. Some were simply embarrassed. They had disfiguring deformities — cleft lips, unsightly birthmarks, burns. Others were frightened, having never seen a camera. Many of the pre-teens and teenagers with cleft lips wore bandanas to cover their affliction. Other than close family members, no one had ever seen their faces. These children were kept at home, secluded from public view, and many had never attended school, so their interaction with children other than their siblings had been very limited.

Each family in turn was brought to the cell-like exam room. There was no ventilation in the room, and temperatures exceeded 100 degrees. We on the medical team were drenched in our own perspiration. A single unshielded light bulb hung from a frayed, exposed wire in the ceiling. A discolored, thin, tattered operating room sheet was taped to the wall as a background for the photographs, and a shaky old cane chair for the patients sat in front of this backdrop. On the other side of the room was an antique steel examining table, too heavy to be moved out of the way. There was no other equipment or supplies, save for what we had brought with us.

A Nicaraguan nurse stationed at the door admitted one family at a time. We began the clinic at seven in the morning, and finished at eleven that night — and still they kept arriving.

Juan was one of our first patients. He was a handsome young man of about eight years old, and was big for his age. He kept close to his mother's side, as though he were an appendage. When she moved, he moved. Juan wore a towel-like bandana, which covered his lower face. It was a dirty, multi-colored piece of cloth, badly frayed along its edges, and looked as if it had been torn from an old dishcloth. The bandana was folded into a triangle, covering all but his eyes. Juan would not speak to us; his mother told us his name. With the help of my nurse/interpreter, I obtained a medical history, and began to develop a rapport with Juan and his mother.

When it was time for the examination, Juan refused to remove the bandana. When I attempted to remove it to examine Juan, he began to cry. I have worked with children for 30 years, and have two of my own, so I knew what to do: I resorted to bribery. Along with medical equipment, I had brought crayons, coloring books, baseballs, small puzzles and lollipops. I first offered Juan crayons and a coloring book, and his hand shot out and snatched them up in an instant. His big eyes sparkled. Marvin wondered if there was a big smile behind that bandana, as well. I again attempted to remove the bandana, but Juan drew back into his mother's lap. His eyes never left mine, and he said nothing. He didn't have to. We all understood.

I asked everyone except for Marvin, Juan and his mother — including all the nurses and other personnel — to leave the examination room. Next, I offered the boy a lollipop. Very timidly, as if in slow motion, Juan slid from his mother's lap and took several steps toward me. Juan took two more steps forward, hesitated, looked over his shoulder at Mom, who put her hand on his back and gave him a gentle, reassuring push. He took several more steps toward Marvin and me, still clutching the box of crayons and coloring book as tightly as one would hold a priceless treasure. We figured that they were probably the only coloring book and crayons he had ever had. Juan wanted a big lollipop that Marvin was holding out for him; he had turned away from me and his eyes were locked on that lollipop. He was now standing directly in front of Marvin and me. We were face to face, and our eyes met again.

In my best Spanish, I asked Juan, "Why are you here?"

Juan looked over his shoulder again to his mother for reassurance, then, turning back to me, he blurted out, "To fix my mouth."

"Juan, do you go to school?"

"No," he replied.

"Do you play baseball or other games with the children?"

"I just stay at home," he answered.

"If I promise to fix your lip tomorrow, so that it will look like the other children, will you remove the bandana?"

There were tears in his eyes. He was trying to be so very brave. Juan reached up and pulled the bandana down. It slid over his face and hung limply around his neck.

The examination proceeded uneventfully. Juan had a large cleft lip and a cleft palate that had gone untreated since birth. With the Contra-Sandinista War, there had been no money, and limited access to medical treatment; what doctors there were never attended to anything but the acute problems that war brings. Juan — like all the other children who were brought to us that day — were the forgotten ones. After the examination, I repeated my promise to fix Juan's lip, so that it would look just like the other children. Juan shook Marvin's and my hands, and even Marvin had a tear in the corner of his eye.

At this point, I showed Juan my camera. Juan said, "I have never had my picture taken." In fact, no one in his family had ever had a photograph taken of them — and, for that matter, virtually none of the children and families who were in the clinic that day had ever had a photo taken.

"Juan, would you like to be the first to have a photograph of yourself?" Marvin asked him.

Marvin explained that I would take some pictures, one now and another when Juan's lip was repaired. Slowly, a beautiful wide smile crept across Juan's face. His eyes were huge with excitement; he had forgotten all about the bandana and his facial deformity. He beamed at us, and said, "Si."

That was when it occurred to me that the best way to make friends and ease the anxieties of both patient and family was to give them an instant photo. It was easy enough to make two photos — one for the patient and the family, and one for the medical file.

Juan was the first to have his photo made, standing quietly in front of the makeshift background while we shot it. He was amazed as the photo was ejected from the slit in the front of the instant camera. When Marvin handed Juan the undeveloped photo, the boy ran and sat on his mother's lap. Bob Dows captured it all on video. We were absolutely mesmerized by the expressions on the faces of Juan and his mother; their bewilderment was very apparent as they looked at the small blank cardboard square that Marvin had placed in their hands. We watched as they turned the undeveloped photo over and over in their hands, puzzled.

Jeannie, my nurse, told Juan, "Hold it by the edge, and keep watching the center of the paper." Marvin, who was extraordinarily patient with Juan as he is with all children, positioned the boy's fingers along the edge. Juan looked up at Marvin, wondering what was supposed to happen.

The room was dark, so the instant photo developed slowly. Juan and his mother sat looking patiently at what appeared to them to be just a blank piece of paper. All of a sudden, Juan's eyes grew larger and a big smile appeared. His mother had an expression of disbelief.

Juan exclaimed, "It's me. Look, mama, it's me."

The expressions on their faces, and the excitement in Juan's voice, were gratifying to us. Juan suddenly jumped off his mother's lap and ran to the door with the photo in hand. He began shouting to his siblings, who were waiting in the courtyard next to the clinic building with the other children and their families. Juan stood there very excited, waving his new prized possession.

The other patients and their families in the hot, crowded courtyard were also amazed. At first, they too were in disbelief of Juan's explanation of the photograph. Juan, in his excitement, had forgotten his cursed affliction, and bounded through the clinic door without his bandana on. He was suddenly the center of attention. He stood there, showing everyone his photograph, which became even more brilliant in the sunlight. Soon, a crowd gathered around him. Marvin and I stood in the doorway and watched this heartwarming sequence unfold. It was a very powerful and emotional experience for Marvin, me and the rest of the medical team.

After the excitement in the courtyard was over, I called Juan back to the exam room. All of us — patient, mother, Marvin and everyone on the medical team — were laughing and crying at the same time from the joy of the situation. It was overwhelming. And Juan still had not made any indication that he wanted to replace the bandana. He returned to the examining room, where I was discussing the surgical and postoperative care with his mother.

Only minutes before, Juan had been very reluctant to remove the bandana and have his picture taken. Now, he gladly stood in front of the makeshift photographic screen for more photos. My good friend and assistant, Mr. Barrett Phillips, and I completed a standardized series of preoperative 35mm slides, as is customary for all our patients at The Methodist Hospital in Houston. Juan followed Mr. Phillips' instructions explicitly, then suddenly stopped and stared at the group. The boy stood motionless, and stared for what seemed like minutes, but was actually only seconds.

I asked him, "Juan, what's wrong?"

He replied, "Where are my pictures? They did not come out of the mouth of the camera!"

A logical question, considering the circumstances. Nurse Jeannie explained to Juan that there were different kinds of photographs — the instant kind, which I had taken first and which Juan was now holding in his hand, and the 35mm slides which had just been taken. She explained that these would have to be sent to a special laboratory in Houston to be developed. At first, Juan seemed disappointed that he was not going to get to see these photos. But Marvin told him that when we returned, I would have the other photos with me.

I told Juan, "The instant photograph is a present." I also explained to him that I would take another rapid photo after the surgery.

"You'll look very handsome in it," I told him. "You must wait a few days after the surgery before we take the final photograph."

As promised, Juan's operation was scheduled for the next day. He and his mother left the examining room without the bandana. Juan would never wear it again. I kept this tattered piece of cloth as a reminder, a memento of a very important lesson I learned that day: THE POWER OF A PHOTOGRAPH...TO MAKE A FRIEND...TO CHANGE A LIFE.

Most of these children had never seen an instant photo. And so I became not only their surgeon, but a magician and entertainer as well. After the experience with Juan, the use of the instant photos became standard practice on this and all subsequent trips.

The use of the instant photos became more and more important, for practical as well as sentimental reasons. I used them to document the preoperative surgical problem and, later, to compare and study the postoperative results. The instant photos also provided a reference file from which the slides and other color prints could be identified as to patient and family when we returned to Houston.

The latter was particularly important because many of the children would require two or more operations. In Nicaragua, as in many other third-world countries, there were no street addresses as we know them. To locate a family, you needed a "descriptive" address. For example, "Mr. Juan Garcia Lopez, city of Chinandega, across from the vegetable market, one block north of the pharmacy, and adjacent to the bakery." This would be a typical mailing address for a family. Furthermore, there were few telephones, and these were usually found in businesses or the homes of a few well-to-do individuals. Even these were often not working. And so the instant photos aided in locating the children and their families on future trips. Hence another "power of a photograph": to make possible recognition, identification and future medical care.

Marvin and I returned to Chinandega, Nicaragua in 1994, along with Marvin's crew, and the surgical teams from The Methodist and St. Luke's Hospitals. This time it was not a photograph, but the photographic equipment that Bob Dows and I had brought, that was to exercise a special power — in this case, the power to save a mother and her yet-to-be-born child.

We were at the San Vicente Hospital in Chinandega. The hospital and its equipment were turn-of-the-century, and the doctors and nurses were overworked, but very dedicated, doing the best they could with what little they had.

It was not uncommon for the electrical power to cease without warning. Electrical failure, intentional and unintentional, was a carry-over from the Contra-Sandinista Civil War. In some areas of Nicaragua, the locals could almost predict when they would be without electrical power, usually between 3:00 and 6:00 PM. Some days, it occurred as early as 1:30 PM. On other days, they had electric power until 4:00 or 5:00 in the afternoon, but then it would go off and not come back on until late in the evening. Occasionally, there was a sudden, unexpected, and prolonged loss of electrical power, which extended well into the evening, rendering further surgery impossible. Perhaps the rebel forces had blown up a transmission tower or a transformer. In recent years, however, except during severe and prolonged rainstorms, electric power had usually been uninterrupted throughout the day.

On our earlier trips, we brought large battery-powered lights. But as the military situation stabilized in Central America, we began carrying only small portable flashlights in our belts. All team members were required to carry our mini-flashlights in our belt packs, or tied to the drawstrings of our operating scrub suits. It can be a bit unnerving, to say the least, when you are operating and the electrical power goes off, unless you are prepared for such a circumstance.

Unlike The Methodist Hospital and other modern medical facilities in the Texas Medical Center, which have backup generators that go on automatically in just a few seconds, the hospitals in most third-world countries do not have this luxury. The few that do have backup generators often lack the diesel fuel to run them. On other occasions, the generators were so badly in need of repair and lacking the proper parts that they did not work, anyway. Thank God this is gradually changing.

During Marvin's and my early medical missions in Central America, it was not uncommon that the electric power would fail while I was in the middle of an operation. As you probably know, operating rooms have no windows, and when the lights went out, we could not see our hands in front of your faces. And that was the least of our problems. All equipment would stop too. The respirator would stop, forcing us to maintain the patient's breathing by hand (a task that is easily and quickly accomplished if you are experienced and know the equipment). Without electric power, there was no suction available to remove secretions or blood, since the suction pumps were electrically driven. The surgeon would also have more difficulty stopping the bleeding, because the electric cautery unit would also not function.

Many of the countries that Marvin and I visited had no monitoring equipment such as EKG, pulse and blood pressure machines, so our medical team would bring these highly sophisticated devices with us. All the monitoring equipment for pulse, respiration, blood pressure and other vital signs are electrically driven. Our personal equipment that we bring on all our medical mission trips has several hours of battery power as a backup. Some countries to which we traveled had recently acquired similar equipment but, to our surprise, they never had any batteries. So, when the electricity failed, the monitoring equipment failed, as well — and all for the lack of an inexpensive battery.

When the power stops, everything must be quickly converted to manual, and the medical team needs to be prepared to work without power. Each situation must be evaluated in mere seconds, and acted upon immediately. This requires an extraordinary individual capacity to work under very stressful circumstances. It also requires that a team be experienced and competent, and that they work well together. The medical team must know what to do instinctively. Some members thrive on these adrenaline rushes, while others prefer not to.

In 1994, we were in Chinandega during the rainy season. The mornings were always clear, sunny and bright, but in the late afternoon, the air would become very still; not even a leaf would flutter. The humidity would become all but intolerable. Suddenly the sun would disappear and the sky would quickly darken, as the wind gradually increased and the temperature dropped. Everyone would comment on how much cooler and more comfortable it was, and how quickly it had all happened. Lightning would flash across the heavens in a myriad of patterns; it would shoot from the heavens in recurrent rapid flashes, illuminating the sky and the surrounding area for miles. Marvin always enjoyed the lightning in these Central American storms. Then torrents of rain would come down — large drops the size of marbles, falling with such force that you could only see a few feet in front of you. Driven by sudden gusts of wind, the rain formed sheets of water which were highlighted by the perpetual lightning flashes. It was the best light show Marvin and I had ever seen.

It was on such an afternoon that I was in the operating room. The surgical procedure was over, and I was just placing the last of the skin sutures when the electricity went out. The operating room was black; we couldn't see a thing. I took a deep breath. My mind was racing. Thank God the operation had been completed. What if this had happened just a few minutes earlier?

Our only concern at this point was to switch to manual and set the monitoring equipment on battery power. This was not a problem, as we had already begun to wake the patient up. All that was needed was to maintain the oxygen level at this point. The only concern, and a small concern at that, was that the anesthesiologist would not have a suction machine available, since it was electrically driven. But he could deal with this.

We had several small flashlights readily available, but even with these lights, my nurse assistant standing in the back of the room was almost invisible in the darkness.

Then it happened — a commotion in the hallway between the operating rooms. Since our patient had now awakened and was doing well, I carefully opened the door of the operating room. The hallway was black. I saw two shadowy silhouettes frantically groping the walls and working their way to the adjacent operating room. Their conversation was excited, anxious and rapid.

It seems that just before the electrical failure, a pregnant woman had been rushed into the adjacent operating room for an emergency Caesarian section. All was in readiness; then, just as the surgeon made his first incision into the woman's abdomen, the lights went out. The surgeon could not control the bleeding because he could not see anything. The electric cautery equipment used to stop bleeding was not working because of the power failure. In the pitch-black operating room, the surgeon could not find it anyway. The infant was undelivered, and still in trouble. Without sufficient light, they could lose both mother and child.

All of these possibilities were going through my mind in just a few seconds while I was standing in the hallway in total darkness. As if running on automatic, I began shouting out orders to my team members, assuring others and questioning the anesthesiologist about the patient's stability.

If you have ever watched the television program M*A*S*H, you might be able to better envision the seemingly chaotic yet very much controlled activities that were taking place in this operating room. In some ways it must have been a very frightening scene, and it certainly was a noisy one. You could hear the sharp crack of lightning and pounding of rain amidst the din of the shouting.

If the mother and infant were to survive, the medical team would need a bright light, not just a few small flashlights. What was needed was a light that could illuminate the entire operating field and allow the surgeon to proceed with the delivery of the baby, and then control the bleeding. Otherwise, there was a very real possibility that both the mother and child might die.

Then Marvin's angel must have come through again, because at that moment I remembered the camera equipment we had brought along. It was all organized and kept together in one specially made large case. Even though it weighed more than 60 pounds, I had been carrying it to and from the hospital every day. Although it was not visible in the darkness, I knew exactly where the case with the camera equipment was: on the floor, against the rear wall of the operating room. I remembered the camera case contained a set of 50,000-candlepower video lights, as well as several recently-charged heavy duty batteries.

The lights could be operated independently from the video equipment. All that was needed was to attach the batteries to the video light source and, presto, the room would be aglow. Each battery at full power would give 20 minutes of light. There were half a dozen fully charged batteries, more than enough to do the job.

As I stood in the hallway contemplating my next move, I realized I could not see a thing. It was like being in a darkroom. With my palms pressed against the outside wall of the operating room, I worked my way along. I bent over, trying to avoid the operating table and other equipment, when suddenly I struck my head on the heavy metal instrument stand. For a few seconds, I became entangled in a myriad of wires and connectors that crisscrossed the floor of the operating room like the tentacles of an octopus. I untangled myself and worked my way carefully around the only table in the room, and then I stumbled again. My head hurt but it was not bleeding; in any case, I had no time to think about that now. It was the camera equipment I was seeking. But it wasn't in its usual spot. Someone, in an attempt to be helpful, no doubt, had moved the case of camera equipment from its usual location along the central portion of the back wall and to the corner of the operating room — where I had just stumbled over it.

Well, at least I'd found it. Fortunately, because I packed and repacked this case on a daily basis, I knew where each item was located. I couldn't see anything, but I knew that the right and left compartments contained the batteries, and the light would be in the central compartment. All I needed to do was to connect the two. It took me only seconds, and, like magic, the room was aglow.

As I left the operating room, I cast a beam of light over my little patient and the anesthesiologist. The patient was still doing well; the anesthesiologist gave me a thumbs-up sign. Everything was fine in this room.

All this took only seconds, but it seemed like hours in the darkness. As I left my operating room, I called for my operating room technician, Mr. Barrett Phillips, to join me. The two of us rushed across the hall to the operating room where the C-section was being performed. As the video lights lit up the room, we could see that the surgeon had put a large sterile gauze pad into the open abdominal wound, and was applying pressure to control the bleeding. It was a good move, but without a light, he could not complete the Caesarian section.

I glanced at the anesthesiologist, who immediately indicated the mother was stable and that she had control of the situation from the anesthesia aspect. But they had to get the baby out!

Barrett Phillips is six feet tall, and was able to hold the video light in a central location well above the operating table. This would illuminate the entire field and the instrument tray. I gave Mr. Phillips the light and extra batteries so I could assist the surgeon in completing the Caesarian section, delivering the baby and stopping the bleeding.

There were no bassinets in this hospital; a nurse came in with a wooden box. The nurses lined the box with some sterile operating room towels, and the surgeon placed the baby — a little boy — in it. The child still was not crying. With a small hand syringe that we had brought with us, the nurses suctioned the newborn's nose and mouth — and at last, thankfully, a loud cry rang out. It seemed to blot out the rain and thunder. I wanted to clap and jump up and down, and I'm sure everyone else in the room did too, but our hands were all busy assisting the surgeon.

A nurse came in with a kerosene lamp and set it on the small table next to the baby. The kerosene lamp looked as if it had come out of an old western museum or had been hanging on the side of a Conestoga wagon that carried settlers across the United States in the nineteenth century. It glowed brightly, and a sooty smoke came from around the top. But it provided the light that the nurses needed to care for the baby, who was now doing well.

Meanwhile, the video light was becoming dimmer and dimmer, and Mr. Phillips' hand was beginning to shake. In fact, he was already using his left hand to support his right elbow against the weight of the video light and its batteries. He clearly needed some relief. The surgeon was already suturing the skin and did not need my help anymore, so I removed my gloves and took the heavy light from my assistant. The room went dark except for the glow of the kerosene lamp in the far corner, where the nurses continued to work with the baby. I switched batteries, and again the video lamps glowed brightly, illuminating the entire room. In a few more minutes, the surgeon had completed his task. The mother was stable, and the baby boy was still doing well.

The obstetrician placed his arms around my shoulders and thanked us as we all walked over to look at the new arrival. The tiny boy was again crying, his skin was pink and he was responding well. Those bright video lights, along with some quick thinking and the willingness of everyone to pull together, had made it possible.

And maybe, just maybe, Marvin's angel had something to do with this one too.

As you can well imagine, the loss of electrical power during a surgical case is in itself a serious problem. Other ramifications, often overlooked, are the scared and frightened family who, waiting for their loved one, find themselves suddenly sitting in the dark. It happened many times when Marvin and I were in these remote hospitals in Central America. The family would be fully aware that their child was being operated on when the electric power failed. Can you possibly imagine their anxieties, fears and shock when this happened?

Marvin has seen their faces, and has helped to comfort them. Knowing the family members' anxieties in these circumstances, as soon as the operation was over, I would go to the waiting area and reassure them. When Marvin and I approached them, we would typically find the family sitting close together, huddled in prayer. After all, when the power failed in the operating room, it failed throughout the hospital. You didn't have to tell the family there was a problem; they knew it the same time the doctors did. The only difference was that it was their child or loved one on the operating room table. We could see in their eyes and faces that they wanted desperately for us to tell them that everything was all right. With God's help, Marvin and I have always been able to be the carrier of good news. And quite often, we have been able to capture the reaction to that good news with our ever-present cameras.

Again and again Marvin and I have experienced the power of photographs to help make friends and remove fear and superstition. The old superstition that a photo steals one's inner spirit or in some other way violates one's inner being is really quite widespread; we found evidence of it all over the world, from the jungles of Central America to the far reaches of the Ural Mountains of Russia and across China. To some, the camera — and especially the photograph — was taboo.

Oddly enough, this was not true of the rapid photo, and that was a puzzle at first to Marvin and me, and to my medical team. Eventually, however, I began to realize that maybe it wasn't so much the photograph, but the photographer. At first many of the subjects were apprehensive, even scared of a stranger, and of the camera itself. Some may have felt the camera was an intrusion upon their privacy. Somehow the instant photograph changed all this. Seeing one's likeness appear, in a matter of minutes, on a small square of paper held in one's own hands, seemed to hold a wonderful magic that overcame fear and superstition. In fact, in some circumstances, the over-enthusiastic responses to the rapid photos actually frightened Marvin and me.

I remember a medical mission in the far reaches of China, where the people had never seen an American, let alone an instant camera.[1] I went to the market alone one

---

[1] I was accompanied by a crew from Houston's PBS station, KUHT, Channel 8. Channel 8 produced a half-hour feature about this trip, and they have aired it several times.

White Knight in Blue Shades

afternoon and, as always, had all my cameras with me. Every time I tried to take a photograph, the subjects turned away or covered their faces. Some even hid as I approached. I surmised that it was not just the camera that bothered them, but the cameraman as well. Even with my telephoto lens, I was not having much luck.

I walked to the center of the vegetable market, where there was an old lady with very striking facial features. She sat on a three-legged wooden stool behind a well-used wooden cart that was filled with vegetables. I wanted to take her photo. She wasn't sure what to make of it or of me. I showed her my camera, and, using some sign language and what few words I knew, thought I had made her understand what was to happen. To this day, though, I'm still not sure. At any rate, I could see by her facial expressions and her body language that she was very anxious and suspicious of this stranger, but curious, as well.

Other people in the market were shouting advice, and some seemed to be teasing her. While this distraction was going on, I took her photo. The flash startled her. I was worried about the response, not just from her, but from her friends as well. There was none. She just sat there, bewildered.

I slowly approached her, and indicated that the instant photo was a gift. She looked at the blank, black piece of paper, then at me, with a look that clearly told me she thought I was crazy. Perhaps not wanting to insult me, she accepted the photograph. As I had seen people do many times before, she began turning it over and over again, examining it closely and periodically looking up at me. Seeing nothing, she stretched out her arm to return it. Just then, her image began to appear. I repositioned the photo in her hands, so she could better see what was happening. As the outline of her face began to appear in the instant photo, I made a circle around it with my fingertip. She did not say a word. She was mesmerized; I could see her eyes focus on the photo as it was developing. As her image appeared, she let out a scream. It startled me enough that I jumped back. She began to laugh, and she turned to the other vendors in the market, waving the photograph with excitement, exclaiming over what she had just witnessed.

In seconds, I was trapped. Hundreds of vendors and shoppers crowded in on the two of us. At once, everyone wanted to see "the magic photo." I suddenly felt claustrophobic, perhaps even a little panic-stricken. A lady next to my subject was pointing at herself, as were other vendors in the vicinity. Everyone was shouting at once and gesturing with their hands. They wanted a photograph. Only moments ago, they had hidden from my camera. Now, everyone wanted their picture taken. The crowd pressed in on me until I could hardly move. It was frightening.

I looked around for a way out, and began moving along the line of wooden carts and food stands, taking instant photos and handling them out. This made it possible for me to work my way to the edge of the crowd. Then, I ducked under a cart and, in a crouched position, continued working my way under the carts to the edge of the market. I then climbed on some wooden boxes that were stacked at the rear of the market and watched the excitement. It was unbelievable.

Now I felt more secure, so I grabbed my 35mm camera and started photographing the scene. No one was paying any attention to me anymore. Smaller groups gathered around each person to whom I had given an instant photo, as the proud owners showed off their prizes.

All the while, I kept taking pictures. With all the excitement, I could not change the film fast enough. When everyone's curiosity was satisfied, the crowd began to disperse. Vendors returned to their vegetable stands, and shoppers proceeded to purchase their needed produce. Again I began walking through the market. The atmosphere had completely changed. I was greeted with smiles, and the vendors waved from behind their vegetable-laden carts.

The old lady who was given the first of the photographs got up from her stool and stopped me. She asked if she could pay me for the picture.

I said, "No, it is a gift."

She put a hand on my chest, indicating she wanted me to stay put. She returned to her cart and wrapped some fruit in an old newspaper and insisted that I take it. She then gave me a big hug and a kiss on the cheek. This exchange was repeated by many who received photos in the market.

Of course, everyone wanted an instant photograph. Some wanted a picture of just themselves, while others brought friends together and wanted a photograph of the entire group. I took and gave away photos until I ran out of film. With each picture I took, I was offered something in exchange — bread, vegetables, fruit, dried meats, or whatever they had.

Later, I learned that not only had these folks never seen an instant photo, most had never had a photograph taken of themselves, though they were all middle-aged or older.

When I walked through the market the next day, I was greeted warmly. Some people proudly held up their photos that I had taken the day before. Others had their photos displayed on the post or wall next to their produce stand. The atmosphere had completely changed. The POWER OF A PHOTOGRAPH is not to be underestimated. It changed suspicion and fear into warmth and friendship. It went even further than that; the rapid photos became a means of barter. This occurred not only in China but in many other places as well.

Marvin was not on this trip with me, but we later discussed what had happened to me at that market in China. He laughed sympathetically, because the same thing has happened to him on many occasions. We both find the universality of the phenomenon remarkable.

On one of our many trips to Russia, Marvin and I took a train from Moscow, approximately 1,500 miles north by northeast. We crossed Russia into the foothills of the Ural Mountains (for more about our adventures in this area, see the chapter, "To Russia With

Love"). The train stopped at many small towns and villages along the way. Stops were brief, only five to ten minutes at the most. Many local women and a few men, mostly in their 60s and 70s, came to the platform carrying handmade baskets containing cured meat, cakes, breads and other farm produce. I took rapid photos from the window of my train compartment and, if the train stopped for a long enough time, Marvin and I would take photos from the small platform that connected the cars to each other. We were often joined by Lori Reingold and Bob Dows, who, as usual, had the big Channel 13 television camera.

In one small Russian town along the route, a grandmother came to the train to sell her produce. She walked up to Marvin and me, carrying a basket of freshly baked bread and rolls which she was offering to sell to the passengers. Marvin purchased some bread, while I took her photo and gave it to her. At first, she stood there examining the undeveloped photograph, wondering what to expect. As her image began to appear, she started jumping up and down and twirling about on the platform, just a few feet from the train. Other vendors who were clustered around selling their produce to the passengers suddenly stopped hawking their goods, ran from the train and encircled her. The chatter, gestures and facial expressions were a joy to see.

There was so much commotion on the platform that the conductor allowed Marvin, Bob and me to leave the train for a few minutes and take additional photographs. All too soon, the whistle blew, and slowly the train began to move. I was still taking photographs. I turned, ran, and jumped aboard. Before we left, several of the vendors ran to Marvin's coach window and insisted that Marvin and I take some of the bread, fruit and dried meat they were offering for sale. It was a pleasure to see their smiles, hear their laughter, and be a part of this short but joyous interlude. The conductor later told Marvin that they were very impressed that I had given them the photographs as gifts, asking nothing in return.

Marvin and I have been visiting small villages in remote parts of the world for many years now. Whenever we return to a place we've visited before, we are always greeted as friends. Occasionally, a proud mother will see Marvin and me taking a walk down the narrow street in the cool of an evening, and will invite us in for a cold drink. Invariably, she will point to the photographs we had taken of her and her children years ago, the only ones she has ever had. The memories those photographs invoke will always remain.

As may be evident to anyone who knows about his long career in the media, Marvin Zindler has always known the "power of a photograph." He always understood what could be accomplished with a still camera, a movie camera, and later a video camera. Whether it be in the ability to bridge a cultural chasm, to ease tensions between strangers and make of them dear friends, or just to remind us of the places we've gone, the things we've experienced, or the changes we've been able to make in the lives of others, the camera has served as catalyst, bridge, and chronicler.

And what might seem to someone else as little more than a dusty pile of unidentified photos will always be, to both Marvin and myself, both journal and testament to our lives, and to the lives that we have touched and been touched by.

THE TEAM TAKES A TURN...
A FEW WORDS FROM LORI & BOB

I have had the unique opportunity to travel to a number of foreign countries because of my job as a television producer. More than that, I have had the pleasure of traveling with a group of dedicated people who came to help... to teach... to change lives for the better. We have been to countries that were closed to westerners for decades — among them, Ethiopia, Bulgaria, Vietnam, Mongolia. We were among the first Americans to visit inner Russia following 70 years of Soviet control. We made four trips to the Urals near Siberia. We were on three missions to Cuba, which was closed to most Americans for decades. We were in Israel, Jordan and Syria.

Each time, we went to document Houston doctors helping, training, improving lives. And each time, we brought our viewers to these "off-limit" countries, bringing an understanding that people are the same the world over. Looking back on our visits, it seems as though we were ambassadors for our country. We made friends with former foes, and our friendships have lasted. No matter where we went, the people we met wanted the same thing: the best for their families, and to go about their daily life in peace.

– Lori Reingold, Marvin's producer

∽ • ∽

One of the joys of my life is being able to travel. Another great joy is being part of a great team. When a person can do both at the same time, great is raised to "great to the highest power."

Having grown up during the Cold War, many of us were told that "the Russians will bury us." As producer Lori Reingold wrote, "This did not happen, and we came to Russia to help the grandchildren of the very men who had threatened us."

Joseph Agris, M.D.

When I got off the plane in Perm, Russia, for the first time, I expected to see supermen. In August, the rain and wind were cold, and there were no supermen or women, just the warmest group of people one could hope to meet. We have traveled to Perm and Kungur, Russia, four times, but I will never forget the faces, the flowers, and the hugs on that first trip. These things took away that cold chill, and made us feel at home.

The team has traveled to Russia, China, Bulgaria, Jordan, Mexico, Vietnam, Central and South America, the Middle East, Cuba and Mongolia — and wherever we have gone, we have helped the people. But the doctors and nurses are the real stars. They give up their practices for as much as three weeks, provide all medical care free of charge, and also provide hospital supplies for operations and patient care.

Another important team member is KTRK-TV Channel 13, a Disney-owned and operated station. They have paid for us to travel and bring back stories so people at home can see for themselves what it means for a team of doctors, nurses, field producers and reporters to reach across the world and help.

I am one television cameraman who has had the profound good luck to be able to travel and make friends in places where, most of the time, you can't even drink the water.

– Bob Dows, Marvin's cameraman

THE WORLD GOES ON, THE MISSIONS CONTINUE...

LIFE AFTER SEPTEMBER 11

When the Cold War ended, with the "good guys" having won, it seemed like a happy ending to a long, dark story. As the terrible events of September 11, 2001 must surely have proven, however, there are no happy endings. While virtually no one longs for the return of the decades-long struggle between democracy and communism, there is no doubt that the September 11 attack has left those in the free world shaken and wondering about the nature of the "new" enemy. We don't have communism to kick around anymore, but now there is terrorism, and in many ways it is so much more devious than our "old" enemy.

Though not even Marvin, prognosticator extraordinaire, could have predicted the details of the September 11 attacks on New York and Washington D.C., he had been saying for many years that the U.S. should be more prepared for possible terrorist actions. We saw the warnings with the 1993 attack on the World Trade Center, but there were many other signs before and after that.

Since the September 11 attacks, many Americans have been saying the world will never be the same again. But that is not really true. For many years, Marvin and I, along with Lori Reingold and Bob Dows, have journeyed to places where terrorism, or the threat of terrorism, is an everyday occurrence. It is something the people in those countries live with and take for granted. American life was, for a long time, blessedly free of such threats. As a result, most Americans have been relatively isolated from the terrible struggles faced by much of the rest of the world. Now the world has come crashing in through our front door, forcing us to view events in a whole new way. The world is not different because of the September 11 attacks; only our awareness of it has changed. In any case, most people, Marvin included, agree that it is past time for us to awaken from our complacency and take a more active part in preventing future atrocities.

We cannot accomplish this with the sword alone. As I write this, the U.S. is gathering its allies and has begun striking back against this enemy that will not show its face. Our leaders have repeatedly said they are prepared to fight an all-out war on terrorism, no matter how long it takes. Marvin and I both believe we should support our country, but we also believe that if we view a "war on terrorism" as the only answer, it will indeed be the same old world, only worse. If we become little more than counter-terrorists, then the terrorists will have won.

In the end (corny and 1960s though it may sound), compassion and understanding among the different peoples of the world are the forces that will prevent future terrorism. As Lori and Bob indicate in their comments in this section, people everywhere really are the same, at the most profound level. They want the same basic things in life, and, given half a chance, most folks are more than willing to reach out to make a stranger feel welcome. September 11 did not change that. Marvin still believes that most people — yes, even in the Middle East and Central Asia — want peace. This belief comes from years of observation of, and interviews with, everyone from world leaders to the man and woman in the street. Marvin and I think that if all of us can learn to focus more on our basic similarities, we will have come a long way towards making terrorism obsolete. That may sound idealistic, but it is an ideal worth working for.

I guess you could say that promoting compassion and understanding has always been the underlying purpose of Marvin's travels, and mine as well. On our many missions we have played the role not just of reporter or healer, respectively, but each of us has, in our own way, been a goodwill ambassador as well. Few would argue that the world still needs good will, now more than ever. That is one reason Marvin plans to continue his travels, and so do I.

The mission of the Agris-Zindler Children's Foundation remains the same (see the section at the end of this book). My medical missions will continue, and, with God's help and the assistance of Marvin's ever-present angel, Marvin and Lori and Bob will be right by my side, documenting it all. And we will continue to make new friends, while sharing our experiences with other Americans so they might better understand the human side of world events. Marvin may continue to protest that he's no war correspondent, but that won't keep him from traveling to the world's hot spots whenever he can, just so he can find out what's really going on and tell the folks back home about it.

Terrorism be damned, the world goes on, and so will we. The best we can do is continue to try not to be in the wrong place at the wrong time. If that means Marvin's angel will have to put in even more overtime, so be it. We haven't heard one word of complaint from that angel yet.

Marvin's Mailbag

A Sampler

MARVIN'S MAILBAG:
A SAMPLER

Marvin Zindler receives hundreds of letters daily. Some are angry missives from people who just want to let off some steam, but most are desperate pleas from folks who feel they have nowhere else to turn. Perhaps they have been ill-treated by local businesses, agencies or utility companies. Maybe they just need assistance negotiating bureaucratic red tape. Or perhaps they are simply bewildered by, or fed up with, "the system" — the rules, regulations and procedures that are supposed to help us, but so often do not. In many cases these folks have pursued every possible avenue to solve their problem, with no results. They see Marvin as their last hope for getting something done.

Some of the letters are touching, some are funny, some are just plain off-the-wall. A few are completely incomprehensible. Naturally, Marvin also gets more than his share of cheers and jeers — praise from people who love him, curses from people who don't. He welcomes them all. Marvin employs a full staff to help him handle his mail, because it really matters to him that everyone who writes to him gets a response (and, whenever humanly possible, a solution to their problem).

In this section you'll find a small sampling of Marvin's mailbag. The letters are in no particular order, by subject matter or anything else, and are presented pretty much as written; they haven't been edited except for spelling. There's also a brief summary of the action taken, where applicable. (With exceptions as noted, all letters received a response, whether or not they required action.) Of course, writers' names have been omitted.

∞ • ∞

Rumors of My Death Have Been Greatly Exaggerated...

Dear Mr. Marvin Zindler:
I am a 75 years retired veteran, and I will be 76 on the 28th of March.

The IRS returned my income tax I filed, and stated I was deceased. *I am not dead.*

I received my Social Security number in 1941, and used the same SS# all of my life.

So, I filed my taxes again, and I haven't heard from the IRS yet. If the IRS keeps stating I am deceased, I will lose my benefits, and I am on a limited fixed income.

I called the IRS and I keep getting a recording.

I am writing to you because I believe that you can get some answers for me. I need your help.

Thank you very much.

Signed,
(A man)

Action taken: IRS contacted; appropriate names and telephone numbers forwarded to the writer.

∞ • ∞

"They're B-a-a-a-a-a-ck! The TV People!"

Dear Mr. Marvin Zindler:
I have a trouble with AirWaves. The T.V. Studio people can communicate with me. My head hurts. I need to talk to you about the T.V. Studio people communicating with me. It causes parts of my body to bother me. It affects my brain. I haven't been back to a doctor for a year. So, I need help getting back to a M.D. I will be waiting for an answer from you, Mr. Zindler, very soon.

Your friend,
(A man)

Action taken: Referred to Harris County Medical Society; telephone number and other referral sources.

White Knight in Blue Shades

Hey, We TOLD You the Cost of Natural Gas Was Going to Increase

Dear Mr. Zindler:
I would like for you to help me with a problem with the gas company. There seems to be a misunderstanding with my bill. My gas bill was $181.00 for last month. During the coldest month, December, it never gets over $48.00. I called the gas company about the problem. They said that they would send someone out to read the meter. I received a letter that the meter was not reading properly. We never have bills over $50.00. I need your help.

Thank you,
(A man)

Action taken: Letter answered, gas company sources contacted.

Landscapers or Wreckers? You Decide

Dear Mr. Zindler:
I am writing with hopes that you can help solve my problem. My car was parked outside my apartment building. Some time during the day a landscaping crew was working. The left front side window and the left front headlight assembly were shattered by rocks. Upon seeing the damage done to my car I took pictures, and notified the apartment management. I was given the name of the landscaping company. I immediately contacted the landscaping company to explain the damages, and ask for restitution. I was told that the message would be given to the owner and he would call me back.

I have placed numerous calls, left numerous messages, none of which have been returned. I faxed a letter as well. I sent the photographs and an estimate of the repairs needed for my car. I still have not heard from the landscaping company. I have reported them to the Better Business Bureau. I had hoped that this would resolve in a friendly manner. Obviously the owner of the landscaping company sees it differently.

Thanking you in advance for your time and attention to this matter.

Sincerely,
(A woman)

Action taken: Letter sent, company contacted.

I Paid, But It Doesn't Work...

Dear Mr. Zindler:
I am writing you about my car getting fixed. I paid the mechanic $798.00 to fix my car. He put another used motor in it, and the electrical got a shortage in the motor. He finally finished hooking it all up again, so it could pass emission inspection. I drove it home that same night, and all the transmission fluid leaked out. Now the mechanic don't want to fix it. Please, need action on this.

Thank you,
(A young man)

Action taken: Letter sent to all concerned, and, I'm sure, a lesson learned.

∾ • ∾

Expanding Dollar, Shrinking Product

Dear Mr. Zindler:
I would like to complain about the price of a chocolate bar. It has gone up more than 100%. The bars have gotten thinner and smaller. Maybe only half as large. Actually that is more than a 200% increase since you are paying more and getting less. I would like for you to look into this as soon as possible.

Yours truly,
(A boy)

Reply sent (but, alas, even Marvin can't do anything about the high cost of chocolate).

Taken For a Ride

Dear Mr. Zindler:

I purchased a vehicle from XYZ Auto Sales. On Wednesday I took my car back to XYZ Auto Sales because it was running hot. He called me a few days later and told me that my motor had burned up so I asked him would he fix the motor or give me another car or my $700.00 back. He told me no! So, I just wanted to ask you what should I do?

Signed,
(A woman)

Action taken: Letter sent, company contacted.

Frustration, Frustration, Frustration... Yes, It's the IRS Again

Dear Mr. Zindler:

I certainly never thought that I would be writing you, but I have a problem with the IRS. I was audited last year. I went to the audit where I stayed for five hours.

They asked me to come back. I said I would contact my accountant, but the IRS officer said that was not necessary. I thought it was, and I did.

My accountant said, no problem, he would fix it up. He went out *twice*. Then my accountant transferred to a different office. The accounting company said no problem. They would fix it.

In short, they are taxing me for more money than I earned that year. I am sorry that I had a bad year. When you are in business for yourself, that happens. Can you help me?

Signed,
(A man)

Action taken: Letter sent; IRS contacted; case closed.

Cheated Out of a Bonus?

Dear Mr. Zindler:

I am a hospital employee. I serve as a surgical orderly. I have worked the same job for six years and two months. I resigned recently. Before my resignation *all* employees were assured a year-end bonus. All of the employees that I work with received the bonus except me. Even some friends of mine who were laid off.

First of all, I was entitled to a bonus. I had a good evaluation. Now that I have resigned they are saying that I am not entitled to my bonus. I have talked to everyone. I have worked very hard for more than six years. I am entitled to the bonus.

I called again, and they told me that I am not eligible. I feel that I have been cheated. I need your help dearly. I do appreciate and thank you for taking the time out to read this letter.

Sincerely,
(A woman)
P.S. Enclosed are copies of my excellent evaluations. And the bonus notice.

Action taken: Letter sent; supervisor and hospital contacted.

∽ • ∽

Not Guilty, Not Me!

Dear Mr. Zindler:

I am forwarding this letter to you in hopes that I might find help in you. I am currently incarcerated. It was a mistake in the lineup. I have been in prison six years.

Now Immigration and Naturalization wants to deport me.

I have tried many non-profit organizations and they all turn me down. Mr. Zindler, I watch your news on how you help other people. My family lives in Houston, but they cannot help me. Mr. Zindler, any help that you can provide will be greatly appreciated.

Sincerely,
(A man)

Reply sent.

Nowhere Else to Turn

Dear Mr. Zindler:

...I am hoping that you can help me... My son is confined to a wheelchair. He sleeps on a special bed. The controller on the bed which raises it up and down does not work. He needs to have it elevated to breathe properly and for poor circulation in his legs.

I called the company. They are no longer in business. I have moved to Houston recently since the death of my husband. I do not know where to turn for help.

I feel as though you will be able to help me with this problem.

Thanking you in advance for any advice or help that you may be able to give.

Sincerely,
(A woman)

Action taken: Writer was sent a letter containing social service information, and companies that deal with this problem were contacted.

"You Saved His Life"

Dear Marvin:

Thank you for saving my husband's life. Your willingness and unselfishness to go public with your series on prostate cancer was very admirable. One of the best series you ever had. A real public service. Men are such babies. They never want to go for an examination.

Your story on prostate cancer helped me convince my husband to have the examination and the test. It was found early. He was cured. You saved his life, and probably many, many others with your program. God bless you!

Signed,
(A woman)

Thank you letter sent.

Busted in the Workplace

Dear Mr. Zindler:
I work for a large multi-national company. This is my first job. I have been working here only a few months. I am trying very hard to follow the dress code and their rules, but because of my rather generous endowment, my neck line seems to be too low for them. The less well-endowed girls who work in the same office wear low-cut and tighter clothes than I do, but I am a 44-DD.

The large breasts are very uncomfortable. I am also tired of being stared at, and now discriminated against for my rather generous bust line.

I do not care to wear a sack-type dress to work. I would like to have plastic surgery. Please help me in my dilemma.

Sincerely,
(A young woman)

Action taken: Marvin contacted me; surgery performed; no fees charged.

You Can't Please All of the People All of the Time

Marvin Zindler:
You can go to hell!
(No name)

Marvin chose not to respond to this one, and, it should be noted, he did not go to hell, preferring Houston in the summertime.

Am I Legally Married?

Dear Marvin:
I am one of your regular listeners. You do so much good for so many people.

I never thought that I would be writing to you, but I need your advice. I got married by a preacher in a small country town. We thought it was so romantic. I never went to City Hall. I never took the license. I want to know if I am married. Maybe I am only a common-law wife. If I am not married, I do not wish to get married. He has gotten so impossible to be with. I don't get along with him now. Please give me a holler as soon as you get this letter, with your advice.

Love you, Marvin,
(A woman)

Action taken: A letter was sent to the appropriate license bureau and county clerk's office.

Slime in the School Cafeteria?

Dear Marvin:
I go to (name of school deleted). I don't think our school cafeteria is very clean. I want to know if it is clean before I eat lunch here again. This is my school address. I also drew a picture of my school so you will know where the cafeteria and lunchroom is. Marvin, don't tell my mom, and don't tell my teacher or anybody where you got this.

Signed,
(Student, age 10)

Action taken: Marvin checked the health reports on the school, and visited the cafeteria. The student's anonymity was protected.

Same Medical Tests, Different Fees?

Dear Marvin:

Recently my mother and I went to the doctor for our yearly physical. We had the exact same tests performed. My mother is 79 years old. I am 59 years old.

Should someone on Medicare receive a different charge than a person who has regular insurance? I called and asked the business manager at the clinic where we had our tests the same question. His reply was, "No, you should receive the same charge for the same test."

They did not know my mother and I were going to the same doctor for our physicals, and having the same tests done at the same time.

I received my bill shortly after my mom received hers. My bill was $1,129.00. My mother's bill was $322.03. As you can see, they charged my private insurance company four times the amount they charged my mother for the examination and the same tests.

I went to the business office and confronted them with the bills. I showed them the difference between my mother's bill and mine. They immediately sent me a revised bill for the $322.00, the same as for my mother's. A month later I got a third bill from their billing department to send to my secondary insurance company for $1,458.00. The secondary insurance company was billed even more. Why the difference?

My concern is how many times have they done this sort of billing before??!! I would never have known the difference had I gone to the doctor alone. Since I went with my mother and we had the same tests I could make a comparison. How many other times has this happened? Is this why our insurance costs are so high? It is not the doctors; it is the hospitals, clinics, HMOs, and the new for-profit medicine. You need to investigate this.

Sincerely,
(A woman with a cause)

Action taken: Marvin did a TV program uncovering these deceptive practices.

Lost in Storage

Dear Marvin:

I am writing this letter in concern for my sister-in-law's furniture that got put in storage by her landlord. She is on Section 8 housing, and the house that she was living in didn't pass inspection. Her case worker told her that she could stay there until she found another place to stay. Her landlord didn't like the idea and put her furniture in storage.

The storage company wants to charge her $20-$30 per day. You should only have to pay that for a full month's storage. Now she has lost all of her furniture and can't afford to buy new furniture. I know that you are supposed to keep letters to you short, so I will stop here.

Thank you,
(A lady on behalf of her sister-in-law)

Action taken: Letter sent; appropriate social service contacts made.

∾ • ∾

Expensive Air

Marvin Zindler:

I have to save my allowance to go to the movies and buy snack food. I work very hard for extra money and my allowance. Then you buy a small bag of potato chips. When you feel the bag they are just sealed-up bags of air, but you think you are feeling a full bag of chips. When you open them there are only four, maybe six chips, inside. That is not fair. I pay good money, and get only air. I think you ought to set them straight. Please investigate this problem.

Sincerely,
(A young girl)

A letter and autographed photo were sent to this young lady, who very eloquently spoke for most of us when she wrote, "I pay good money, and get only air."

"Fleeced"

Dear Mr. Zindler:
We commend you for the excellence in assisting the needy as well as the "fleeced."

Your sense of humor is truly appreciated, and we enjoy watching your programs.

We know that you like to investigate the contractors who do shoddy work, and your televised programs have exposed a lot of the so-called "bad guys." The owners of our townhouse community (mostly senior citizens on fixed incomes) have a dilemma, and I would like to share it with you.

We signed a contract with a pool company to repair and refurbish the pool at the far end of our townhouses. The contractor did drain the pool. The pool popped out of the ground, taking the decking and the walks with it.

The pool company said they finished their work, and they were not responsible. The pool company has avoided our phone calls, and refuses to discuss it with us.

We have had three pool companies tell us that the repairs are incomplete and the company that we hired is negligent and responsible for what happened. They estimate the costs for installation of a new pool at $20-$23,000.00.

We would like to have our pool back. Please help.

Action taken: The company was contacted, and the "bad guys" exposed.

Polished, But Good!

Action 13, Mr. Marvin Zindler:
I purchased a product by mail with the promise of a "lifetime guarantee." It is supposedly a paint restorer for the paint of cars, but instead the product has ruined the paint on both of my cars. I have contacted the company for help in this matter by certified letter and received no response. Even a professional detail shop was unable to remove the product with the removal kit that the company sent them. Since then, I have heard that this has been a common problem with this product. The appearance and value of both my cars has been diminished. I ask that you please assist me in resolving this matter. Your help is greatly appreciated.

Sincerely,
(A man)

Action taken: Marvin pursued the matter, but, unfortunately, like so many of these fly-by-night businesses, this one was no longer in operation.

Plastic and Reconstruction Surgeon Needed

Mr. Marvin Zindler
Dear Sir:
I am in the 10th grade. I go to high school in Houston, Texas. The reason I am writing you is that I have a major problem. I am only 16 years old and I wear a size 48-DD. When I go to school I have to sit with my breasts on the desk. I have problems getting in and out of the desk at school. Of course, people have their words, but I just try not to think about it. I also have rashes under my breasts from time to time. I also have back and neck pain. My back hurts so much at times that I have to miss school. My mom tried everything. She took me to the HMO doctor, and to her doctor at her job. We were told the insurance company did not cover the cost of this operation.

I love to play volleyball, but the weight of my breasts prevents me from playing the game. It also prevents me from most other sports.

I know that you can get things done, and as you say yourself, "It is hell to be poor." So, please help me get some much needed positive results.

Yours truly
(A 10th grader)

A letter was sent to the young lady explaining that, contrary to what she and her mother had been told by the HMO doctors, breast reduction for medical reasons is an insurance-covered procedure. Many companies, and particularly HMOs, try to discourage this procedure, even when it is deemed medically necessary.

All I Want for Christmas is an Operation

Dear Marvin:

My teacher is helping me write this letter. I have a lump in my face. The knot in my face keeps getting bigger. My mom took me to a doctor who said that he could take it out, but there would be a big scar on my face. I don't want a big scar on my face.

Also, when he told my mother how much it would cost we could not afford to pay for the operation.

It is getting bigger, and the other children tease me at school. Christmas is coming and I don't want to go back to school after Christmas. You know lots of people. Please help me get my operation.

Thank you,
(A young lady)

I successfully removed the tumor from the young lady's face, for no charge, thanks to the generosity of the Methodist Healthcare System.

A joyous Christmas was had by all, and the young lady returned to school. Marvin did a special Christmas show about this case; see the account in Chapter 12 of this book, "A Day in the Life."

This is truly one of the most gratifying cases Marvin and I have been involved in. This young lady, along with her school mates, family, friends and neighbors, has since held a bake sale, and with the help of the local Girl Scout troop, contributed nearly $500.00 to the Agris-Zindler Children's Foundation.

Thank you, from both Marvin and me!

- Doctor Joe

When I Said I Wanted to Stay Home and Get Plastered, This Is Not What I Meant...

Dear Mr. Zindler:

I accepted a free inspection of my heating and air conditioning unit. While in the process of inspecting the heating unit in the attic, [the technician] fell through the ceiling into my kitchen.

He was all right, but there was plaster everywhere and a big hole in my ceiling. He apologized and said it was his fault, but the company wouldn't pay for damages. We have called on several occasions, and even forwarded a letter of the circumstances, but we haven't received any word from the company he works for. Please help us get the ceiling fixed.

Sincerely,
Covered in Plaster
Action taken: Letter sent; company contacted and ceiling repaired. Another happy ending!

Give 'Em Hell, Cowboy!

Dear Marvin:

I like your new hairdo. I also like the new collarless shirts that you have recently begun wearing. Where can I get some of those shirts?

You are the world's best-dressed cowboy, and you are doing just great. I never miss one of your programs. Go get 'em, Marvin. Get both barrels blasting. I have been a fan of yours for a long time. Too many years to put it in writing. You have become a legend in your own time. God bless you and your friend, Doctor Joe Agris.

I say a prayer for you both, and your staff every evening. Give 'em hell.

Sincerely,
A cowboy

The writer was sent a nice thank you note, as well as information on where he could purchase those famous Stubbs Davis shirts worn by "the best-dressed cowboy."

Senior Citizen Wants to Become American Citizen

Dear Mr. Zindler:

I am an 86-year-old man. I came to the United States as a refugee, and received my permanent visa.

I have always wanted to become an American citizen because I love this country, and I also want to be able to vote. Due to this ambition I recently applied and presented the necessary documents required.

It has been a long time since I have applied, and they did not return my documents nor give me an appointment for my examination. I have inquired several different times about becoming a citizen. I have no answer from the I.N.S. As I told you before, I have inquired numerous times, and was recently told by the I.N.S. that they now do not know what happened to my application, and my accompanying documents. I filed all the correct papers, copies enclosed. I feel that there is some bureaucratic incompetency in the handling of my papers.

Please, I would appreciate if you would investigate this problem. You are the only person that I trust to do something. I want to become a citizen. Since I am a very old person an immediate response would be appreciated.

Respectfully,
Old man

Action taken: Letter sent to writer; I.N.S. contacted, papers located, citizenship granted.

Roaches and More

Dear Mr. Zindler:

I am a student at (name of school deleted). I cannot begin to tell you the horrible conditions that I and several other students have witnessed. One reported seeing roaches on the salad bar, and a roach fell on her while she was waiting in line at the grill. There is always something spilled on the floor, and I am sure there is slime in the ice machine.

The prices are even worse. A pack of Gummi® Bears, which would cost $.50 at a store anywhere else, will run $1.50 here. They forget we are students, and we don't have money coming out our ears.

Please help.

Sincerely,
(A student)

Action taken: Letter sent; complaint investigated.

Dog Nappers

Dear Marvin:

Recently our pet Rottweiler was picked up by Animal Control from our home. A neighbor witnessed the entire thing. She saw our two dogs sitting quietly on our front porch. They left the mixed-breed dog and took only the thoroughbred. I have the name of the city employees who took her. I immediately went to Animal Control, and attempted to pick her up. I was told to return on Saturday. When I did, I was told that she was not in her cage, and was missing. Apparently stolen.

Since then I have gotten the usual bureaucratic runaround. I have been referred to City Hall. City Hall referred me to the police department. The police department said that if there was no forced entry at the kennel, then how could she be stolen? I returned to the police department and was told by Officer (name omitted) very bluntly that my missing dog was not one of their priorities, but I am being given the runaround. I then called the supervisor of the Animal Control Department. He refused to give me his name. He claimed that he had not been informed about it.

The dog was more than a pet. She was part of the family. The children continue to search the street, hoping that they will find her. I lie awake at night wondering if she is hungry, scared, or neglected.

I honestly think that this was planned, and that one of the city workers at the Animal Control Unit took her. I have called everybody. I can get no answers. Please help us. If anyone can get to the bottom of this, you can.

Sincerely,
(A mother)

Action taken: Letter sent; authorities contacted; alleged dognappers under investigation.

Teacher Seeks Help for Student

Dearest Marvin:

I know that you get many letters asking for help, but we are desperate. I teach at a junior high in Texas. There is a young man in my class who has a skin condition. This student is extremely bright, but because of this skin condition is developing a behavioral problem. He is raised by a grandmother who works, and they are not on any social services, but have little or no money. Marvin, please, please, please help us. You do a wonderful service for mankind.

Sincerely,
(A teacher)

Action taken: Letter answered, and Marvin referred the case to me. I was able to help the young man.

They Assured Me That It Was a Good, Dependable Car...

Dear Mr. Zindler:

I have a big problem. Three months ago, I purchased a car from (name of dealer deleted). Now (after the sale), I understood that they sold the car, "As Is." BUT THEY ASSURED ME THAT I HAD A GOOD, DEPENDABLE CAR. The first month I replaced the heater. The second month I had to get a new oil pan and gasket kit. I also found a leak in my transmission. The third month my engine went out on me.

I had the car towed to three different mechanic shops. They all said my oil pump plus many other things were wrong, and caused the engine to quit. I was told the motor was in bad shape, and it was just a matter of time before it goes out.

Now the motor will cost me $250.00 to repair or replace. This used car lot is not a "fly by night" operation where one would expect these problems. This is a long-time established business. They have many locations throughout the Houston area. I tried to work something out with them, but they would not cooperate. Because of this unexpected financial problem, my wedding plans are demolished. I still have a $276.00 car note and need $250.00 to fix the car. Can you help me resolve this situation?

Thank you,
Taken for a ride

Action taken: Letter sent to all parties.

Too Big for the Lot

Dear Mr. Marvin Zindler:

I went to purchase a mobile home to put in my mother's backyard. The mobile home that I selected was too large to fit the property. A salesman came to the property and took the measurements. He told me the property was too small to place the mobile home on.

I asked for my deposit to be returned back to me. The mobile home company refused to refund my $1,095.00. They told me I still had to purchase the home, and put it somewhere else. I told them I did not want to live anywhere else. I told them I did not need to buy a mobile home if it did not fit on my mother's property.

They said [I had already been approved] by three banks, and when I asked the names of the banks, they refused to tell me. I asked for a copy of the documents that I signed, and I was refused them also.

When I checked with the banks I received credit denials from all the financial companies. So, I have no approvals. I again requested my $1,095.00 back. The company refuses to give me my money. Please help.

Signed,
(A woman)

Action taken: Letter answered. Mobile home company contacted.

Take it Off/Put it On, Take it Off/Put it On

Dear Marvin:

I have wrote you before. I have been having problems with the telephone company, about my phone bill. They are always charging me something I don't know about, and then when you write them, they take it off, and then they wait and put it back. After a few months it is back. I just cannot pay them all that money. Please help me. I am on disability, and this isn't much, but it is a lot for me.

Thank you,
(A woman)

Action taken: Letters sent to all parties; social services contacted.

Taken to the Cleaners

Dear Mr. Zindler:
My complaint is against (name of dry cleaner deleted). They cleaned a lady's long-sleeved blouse for me. They returned the garment to me with a crisp burn on the lower right-hand sleeve. They refused to take the responsibility for the damage (so what else is new?). I called every day for more than 30 days, but to no avail. They just give dozens of reasons why they are not liable for the damage. The list of reasons goes on and on. They have also become extremely rude in their communication with me. They have expressed no integrity and absolutely no diplomacy.

Mr. Zindler, I would be most appreciative if you would investigate this serious matter for me.

Thanks,
(A woman)

Action taken: Letter answered; dry cleaning establishment contacted.

Thirty-Pound Tumor

Dear Mr. Zindler:
I am writing in request for your help for a woman who is in great need of surgery. She is only middle-aged and has her whole life in front of her, but she needs surgery because of a 30-pound tumor in her stomach. It will kill her. She has a doctor who said that he will do the surgery for nothing, but we cannot find a hospital that will take her in, and she has no insurance and no job. We can raise some money for her because she is well liked by many people in this area, but we do not think that it will be enough to pay for the entire hospital bill.

Your help is desperately needed for this wonderful lady. Please see if you can help.

Signed,
(A woman)

Action taken: Letter answered; doctor and hospital contacted.

Testing, Testing, Testing...

Mr. Zindler:
My daughter would like to have her six-year-old tested to find out if he has a learning disability. She is on a fixed income. Do you know of a place that she could take him? And maybe payment plans could be worked out.

Signed,
(A lady)

Action taken: Letter answered; referral sources provided.

Have Ambience, Will Work

Dear Mr. Zindler:
Please, I need your help! I have been out of a job for several months and I am seeking employment. I have registered with two personnel agencies, and have filed my applications, but so far nothing has happened. I have seen you on TV and you have helped many people, hopefully you can be helpful to me.

Now I badly need a job. My money is almost gone. I really want to work and provide for myself. I enjoy people and feel I have a lot to offer. I would love the chance to work hard for some company. Sharing my ambience I am bringing good will to the company.

I would greatly appreciate anything you could do for me! Looking forward to hearing from you soon.

All my best,
(A man)   Resume attached

Action taken: Contacts made via employment agencies.

I Want to Pay My Taxes, But...

Dear Mr. Zindler:

I need help. I AM CONFUSED. I want to get back in the tax system, but I am told that it is illegal. I am told that it is unfair, I am told everything. I just need to be told the truth for once, by someone I can believe, and I thought nobody better than you, Mr. Zindler.

Ever since 1985, my wages in the past have been taken, and then nothing was took. That is just one example. See, I probably made the biggest mistake in my life. See, I haven't even filed taxes, for the last four years. I know that I probably have to pay some taxes. I don't mind at all. What I do mind, is that what they say I owe, if I start paying now, I would have died at least twice before I could at least pay them (the IRS) off.

Thanks a whole lot.

(Signed with initials only)

Action taken: Meeting with IRS and help in tax preparation.

Wonder Pill: Fact or Fiction?

Dear Marvin Zindler:

You are my last hope, and I am in need of help. I am a hardworking student trying to start a good career. I got a job at a weight-loss clinic. I first went for an interview. I was given a job description, and what I would do with the patients, the doctor, and what great benefits this weight loss company had to offer. I thought that this would be a great opportunity, so I resigned my previous steady job for this one. I was told there would be two doctors. The lady that interviewed me, her husband was a doctor and would fill in on the weekends. After beginning this new job, I learned the husband "doctor" was not a doctor but a truck driver, and there were no benefits. In addition, they did not take out taxes from the employees.

This upset me so much I naturally made documentation for myself in case I would need them. They told patients and employees things that were fraudulent. For example, the business card stated we had the "Weight Loss Wonder Pill." People would call in asking questions about the "wonder pill." I did not know what to say since there is no wonder pill.

The clinic manager went through my personal belongings while I was at lunch.

When I returned she called me into the office and showed me notes that I had made. She accused me of trying to sabotage the clinic, and terminated me. She gave me my check and took out for medical which we never received.

I believe the manager was trying to cover up for what has been done wrong. Also, this manager is currently calling my past employees trying to dig information out on me. I know she has no right to do that. I need your help, and you need to stop this clinic from ripping off innocent people.

Sincerely,
(A woman)

Action taken: Letter answered; letter sent to appropriate bureaus.

Murder, She Wrote

Mr. Zindler:
I am seeking help pertaining to my case because I have been wrongly accused of first-degree murder. With all due respect, if you will allow me to brief you on my case. If any more information is needed you may obtain it, and I would highly appreciate it if you would look into my case for me. I cannot afford a lawyer, and during my incarceration I have accomplished more wisdom and knowledge of the law through the law library here. Therefore, I am more than aware of the many loopholes in my case. If nothing else, it is more so to have justice done in Texas.

Sincerely,
(A woman prisoner)

Action taken: Letter forwarded to legal agency.

The Same Old Bait-and-Switch...

Dear Sir:

In 1997 I signed a lease for a new vehicle. The assistant manager informed me that the contract was binding and had no applicable grace period. It had a fixed monthly payment, and option to buy out. The next day I was called at my home by the salesperson to return to the company for more paperwork.

I called the dealership and was informed by the general manager that he had a better contract. It was not to my advantage. It was a higher rate. He said that was due to the fact that the dealership would lose $3,000.00 if the new contract was not signed. I declined to enter into a new contract. He told me that he would have to take the truck back if I did not accept the new higher rate contract. He tore up the original contract, and insisted on taking the keys to the vehicle. The contract that, just a few days ago, he insisted was legal and binding with fixed rates.

Mr. Zindler, you need to investigate (car dealership name omitted) and their sales representatives, (names omitted).

Surely you are aware of the fact that "bait-and-switch" tactics utilized by unscrupulous businesses are illegal, and further that such practices can incur heavy penalties. Also, tearing up a contract by a salesperson and trying to enter me into another contract, one with higher interest rates, warrants the attention of the state attorney general's office.

Not only was this blatantly illegal, but these actions constitute fraud. I would like you to investigate these practices, and to rectify this unfortunate situation.

Sincerely,
(A man)
Action taken: Letter sent to all parties; "bait-and-switch" tactics investigated.

This Gentlemen's Club Was No Gentleman!

Dear Marvin:
I used to work in one of those "gentleman's clubs" (name omitted) at the front desk answering phones, and taking cover charges. Employees signed in and out, and at the end of the shift a manager would write the number of hours worked beside the employee's name. My checks were not what I had calculated them to be (they were smaller), and when I reviewed the records, they came up short (records enclosed).

For example, the manager wrote in eight hours when I actually worked 10. When I asked about it, they told me to fill out a reimbursement form (I did). I was told the check for the remaining amount of what I was due would be with the next regular paycheck. It was not!! Needless to say, every time I brought it up I was given a different response. The check was always "in the mail." I was cheated out of a lot of overtime hours. A friend suggested that I write you. I am tired of people taking advantage of me and others, and getting away with it. I am not the only employee they do this to.

Thank you,
(A young lady)

Action taken: Letters sent; complaint investigated.

Dead or Alive?

Mr. Zindler:
Would you please help me find out if my son is still alive? I cannot get correct information from the warden. I cannot get information from people in the prison. Here are copies of letters other inmates wrote me because they are afraid for my son's life. Please let me know what you can find out.

Thank you,
(A worried parent)

Action taken: Letter answered; authorities contacted.

Money Order, Money Gone

Mr. Marvin Zindler:
My husband bought a $245.00 money order at the Post Office. He put the money order inside an envelope with a letter. He took the receipt from the clerk, but did not fill out the money order. He returned the envelope to the clerk who took the letter. Needless to say, the letter and money order never reached its destination.

I know the money order will not be refunded to me because it was not filled out. I do have the receipt to this money order.

I have put a trace on the letter, and on the money order. However, I do feel this Post Office needs to be looked into. Your help will be greatly appreciated.

(A postal patron)

Unfortunately, there was nothing Marvin could do except point out that this was a $245.00 lesson — the lesson being that because a money order is just like cash, certain precautions need to be taken immediately. The purchaser should fill out the money order on the spot, and should keep the receipt in a safe place.

One House, Two Owners!

Dear Mr. Zindler:
I had the opportunity to buy a house. The house I wanted to purchase required a $1,000.00 deposit. I submitted the funds for the house. I was informed by the agent that the house was mine. I was very excited and went to the house only to find that someone else was moving into it. I was in disbelief! I went out to find the agent who took my money and sold me the house. I am still looking for him. I also want for him to give back my money that I worked so hard for. I am asking that you help me recover my money. I am enclosing proof of purchase of the house, and the $1,000.00 deposit.

Thank you,
(An honest, hard-working lady)

Action taken: Letter sent; matter investigated.

Rocket Launcher, Satellites and More

Mr. Zindler:
I have promised a close friend of mine that I would try to find a way to resolve a major problem that has been part of his life for over 40 years. He created a way to assist in launching rockets and satellites abroad. His invention was used without any regard to his identity. He tried to prove that he was the one that created this beneficial device, but his requests were overlooked by the proper authorities. There was a news report that dealt with this on June 17, 1958. Enclosed are also copies of letters from top authorities which neglected to properly investigate the matters at hand.

Sincerely,
(A friend)

Frankly, I'm not sure if Marvin was able to help this person or not. But it would make an interesting book, don't you think?

Sponsor Me?

Dear Marvin:

I am active in the band. I am one of the few that have been selected to travel about the U.S. playing in the marching band. We travel for two months to many different cities while learning how to be a better musician.

One of my friends told me that you twirled the baton, and were very good. They said you were the drum major in a marching band. The reason for this letter is to ask you for your assistance ($500.00). With this help I will be able to tour two months this summer. Any amount you can contribute will be greatly appreciated.

Sincerely,
(Teenager)

Action taken: Reply sent. Sponsorship requests arrive almost on a daily basis, and significantly increase just prior to summer vacation. Marvin was able to get several people to contribute to the sponsorship of the teenager who wrote the letter above.

What Was That Question Again?

To Mr. Zindler:

I understand that one is held accountable to be knowledgeable of the law. The law interpreted as having been ratified by a lawmaking body of duly elected individuals.

If you understand any valid law under a license, the form not generally available for application, until after the fact, a court secretive precaution to deprive senior citizens of funds. Please explain the validity to me. There is need for the county to make full restitution to all those caught up in this fiasco with accumulated interest.

Sincerely yours,
(Senior citizen)

Action taken: Some things are just not answerable, or even definable... Marvin tries his best, but maybe this one should have gone to Marilyn vos Savant at Parade *Magazine.*

Whose Child? Which Father?

Dear Marvin Zindler:

I am writing to let you know that my fiancé has fathered a child two years ago. Recently we ran into the baby's mother. She confronted him, and said, "I am going to make you suffer." He replied with, "Go ahead and do what you have to do." A month later he was subpoenaed on his job...

A few weeks later he went to be questioned at the D.P.S. office. He volunteered to have a parental test taken. He never received any information concerning the result of the test.

He continues to pay welfare and child support as a result of this subpoena.

My concern is obtaining legal services to take care of this matter. If you could refer us to legal representation, please.

The infant and mother would not take the test. We do not think the child is his even though the mother is giving the child his last name. Please help.

Sincerely,
(A young woman)

Action taken: Information on legal services forwarded.

Marvin Can't Do Anything Right

Mr. White Wig:

I would like to add another plague to those we all know. Cow chips should rain upon you. Cow chips on your white boots, cow chips on your white suit, cow chips on your white wig.

Signed,
A Businessman

*Must be a disgruntled businessman, at that. Perhaps he was caught on Marvin's Friday night "Rat, Roach and Slime in the Ice Machine" report. Besides, Mr. Businessman — and listen up good, because Marvin is really starting to lose his patience — **it's not a wig, it's a hairpiece.***

Marvin Can Do No Wrong

Dear Marvin, Sir:
You have created an impressive record down through the years in helping disadvantaged people. You are a treasured resource that residents of Houston prevail upon constantly when we believe that we have been imposed upon by the Establishment. Your help has proven to be invaluable to the poor, and we are grateful. God bless you.

Sincerely,
(A woman)

The lady was sent a nice thank you note by Marvin.
By the way, I agree with her completely.

- Doctor Joe

"People
Helping People"

About the Agris-Zindler Children's Foundation

FOR DOC JOE'S & MARVIN'S KIDS...

ABOUT THE AGRIS-ZINDLER CHILDREN'S FOUNDATION

The way a society treats children is a measure not only of its social responsibility and qualities of compassion but also of its commitment to enhancing the human condition for future generations. If today we can guarantee the dignity, equality and basic human rights of children, as the Convention on the Rights of the Child seeks to ensure, the men and women of tomorrow will be able to bring this planet closer to the goal of peace, progress and justice for which we are all striving.

- Javier Perez de Cuellar
Secretary-General of the United Nations

Every two minutes a child is born with a birth defect. Cleft palates, disfiguring birthmarks and other defects are "silent catastrophes" that can ravage any child. Even if the condition does not threaten a child's health and is "merely" cosmetic, it can be psychologically and emotionally devastating. These children need special attention, yet a heartbreaking number of them fall between the cracks of the system.

THE AGRIS-ZINDLER CHILDREN'S FOUNDATION, a non-profit 501(c)(3) organization founded in 1981 by JOSEPH AGRIS, M.D., and MARVIN ZINDLER, exists to help these forgotten children. With your help, we have been able to deliver badly needed care to children in some of the poorest areas on the planet, including Central America, the Middle East, the former Soviet bloc, China and many other places. We have also helped many children and their families in the United States.

The Agris-Zindler Children's Foundation is dedicated to identifying the problems, bringing about solutions, and mobilizing resources for the implementation of needed care and support services. This encompasses medical care, surgery, medications and prostheses, as well as family support. And, while these clinical applications are certainly needed, research leading to cure or prevention is also paramount.

We owe to children the best that we can give. Every child has a right to necessary medical care. But not all children are born equal. The world is full of desperately poor children whose families can scarcely afford food and shelter, say nothing of medical care. However, though medical care is often costly, it is an affordable cost... if we all give something.

Give a child a chance,
by giving your tax-deductible gift to the
Agris-Zindler Children's Foundation today.

Send your check or money order, made payable to **THE CHILDREN'S FUND**, to:

The Agris-Zindler Children's Foundation
6560 Fannin Street, Suite 1730, Scurlock Tower
Houston, Texas 77030

Please include your name, address and daytime phone number. We also accept Visa, MasterCard or American Express. Please call (713) 797-1700 to give credit card information, to obtain information about matching funds for employers, or to find out how you can volunteer of your time and services to help "Doc Joe and Marvin's kids."

And remember... all profits from the sale of *White Knight in Blue Shades*, the authorized biography of Marvin Zindler, will be donated to the Agris-Zindler Children's Foundation.

"The kids" thank you!

JOSEPH AGRIS, M.D., D.D.S., F.A.C.S.

It's said that if you want something done, and done right, ask a busy person. That would be our "Doc Joe," whose deep passion for his work, and love for his fellow man, make it almost impossible for him to say "no" when someone needs his expertise. Besides being one of Houston's premier cosmetic, plastic and reconstructive surgeons, with a busy practice in the world-famous Texas Medical Center, Doc Joe is a philanthro-

pist, especially when it comes to
education issues. To address
Marvin Zindler formed The
Foundation to deliver
kids all over the world.
well- read in the arts
a world traveler and
awesome black-and-
won wide acclaim.
work on a book that
of the best of these
spent over four years
material and photos
bringing the same
that goes into all of his
book not only as a tribute
Marvin Zindler — a man who
can, legend — but also as a way

children's health problems and
these concerns, Doc Joe and
Agris-Zindler Children's
needed medical care to
A true Renaissance man,
and sciences, Doc Joe is
a photographer whose
white collection has
(He is currently at
will showcase some
photos.) Doc Joe
researching the
for this biography,
passion to this project
endeavors. He wrote this
to his long-time friend,
is truly a Texas, and Ameri-
to help fund his and Marvin's

favorite charity, which is, of course, the Agris-Zindler Children's Foundation. (For more information on this organization, please see the preceding section of this book.) When he's not off on a medical mission to some remote corner of the world, Doc Joe is in Houston, Texas, tending to his practice and planning the next project or mission. The photo on this page was taken on one of his many medical missions to Central America.

∽ • ∽

O·R·D·E·R MORE

WHITE KNIGHT IN BLUE SHADES
The Authorized Biography of Marvin Zindler
By Joseph Agris, M.D.

Name_____

Address _____

City, State, Zip _____

Please send me:

_____ copy / copies of the hardcover Collector's Edition at US **$50.00*** per copy. TOTAL:_____

_____ copy / copies of the quality softcover edition at US **$20.00*** per copy. TOTAL: $_____
* Add US **$3.00** per copy for shipping & handling (US **$7.50** outside Continental US)

Enclosed is my __ check __ money order in the amount of $_____
(Please make payable to The Children's Fund)

Please charge the above amount to my __ Visa __ MasterCard __ American Express

Account number _____

Expiration date _____

Name as it appears on card_____

Mail this order form with your payment to:
THE AGRIS-ZINDLER CHILDREN'S FOUNDATION
6560 Fannin Street, Suite 1730
Scurlock Tower
Houston, Texas 77030

Purchase a copy for a friend...It's a wonderful gift, for your friend and for
"Doc Joe's & Marvin's Kids." All proceeds from the sale of this book will be donated to

THE AGRIS-ZINDLER CHILDREN'S FOUNDATION.